Those who dream by night in the dusty recesses
of their minds wake in the day to find that all was
vanity; but the dreamers of the day are
dangerous men, for they may act their dream
with open eyes, and make it possible.

T. E. LAWRENCE

CHASING THE LONG RAINBOW

Hal Roth

BOOKS BY HAL ROTH

Pathway in the Sky
Two on a Big Ocean
After 50,000 Miles
Two Against Cape Horn
Always A Distant Anchorage
Chasing the Long Rainbow
Chasing the Wind

Chasing
the Long Rainbow

. . . .

The Drama of a Singlehanded Sailing Race
Around the World

by $H A L\ R O T H$

MAPS BY DALE SWENSSON

SEAWORTHY PUBLICATIONS, INC.
Port Washington, Wisconsin

Printed in the United States of America.

Book design by Jacques Chazaud.

Library of Congress Cataloging in Publication Data

Roth, Hal, 1927 –
Chasing the long rainbow : the drama of a singlehanded sailing race
around the world   / by Hal Roth ;   maps by Dale Swensson.
p.   cm.
Originally published : New York : Norton, c1990.
Includes bibliographical references (p.   ).

ISBN 0-9639566-6-3 (pbk.)

1. BOC Challenge Race.   2. Roth, Hal, 1927-   . 3. Sailors-
-United States—Biography.   I. Title.
[GV832.R65   1990]
797.1'4'—dc21

97-14641
CIP

Seaworthy Publications, Inc., 17125-C W. Bluemound Rd. #200, Brookfield, WI 53005

This book is for
Jacques de Roux.
Born 1937.
Lost at sea
near Green Cape,
Australia,
December 1986.
He was my friend.

Contents

Maps

Photographs

Illustrations

Metric Equivalents

NOTE: Every country in the world (including Canada and Mexico) except the United States uses the metric system for weights and measurements. Since this book is about a world voyage, it's impossible not to use the metric system in a few places. Handy equivalents are:

LENGTH:
1 inch = 25.4 millimeters or 2.54 centimeters
1 foot = 304.8 millimeters or 30.48 centimeters or .3048 meters
1 yard = .914 meter
1 meter = 3.28 feet
1 meter = 100 centimeter or 1,000 millimeters
1 nautical mile = 6,076 feet or 1,852 meters

VOLUME:
1 quart = .946 liter
1 gallon = 3.785 liters
1 liter = 1.057 quarts or .264 gallons

AREA:
1 square foot = 929 square centimeters or .0929 square meters
1 square yard = .836 square meter
1 square meter = 1.196 square yards or 10.76 square feet

WEIGHT:

1 ounce (avoirdupois) = 28.35 grams

1 pound = 453.59 grams or .453 kilograms

100 grams = 3.527 ounces

1 kilogram = 2.2 pounds

1 long ton = 2,240 pounds or 1.016 metric tons or 1,018 kilograms.

1 metric ton = 2,204.7 pounds

1 gallon of fresh water (3.785 liters) weighs 8.33 pounds or 3.77 kilograms
(and occupies 231 cubic inches)

1 gallon of salt water (3.785 liters) weighs 8.556 pounds or 3.875 kilograms

1 liter of fresh water weighs 1 kilo or 2.2 pounds

1 liter of salt water weighs 1.02 kilos or 2.26 pounds

CHASING THE LONG RAINBOW

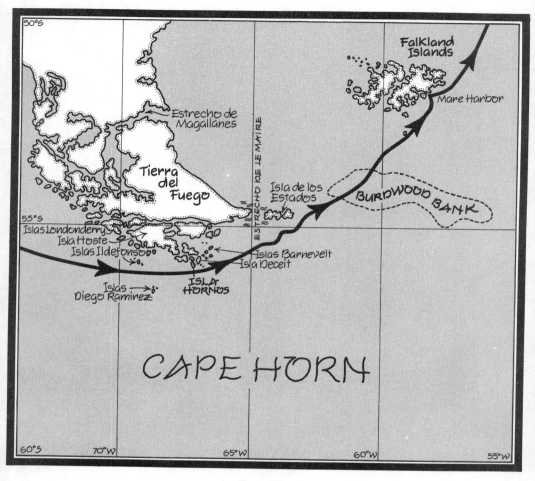

1. Cape Horn

. . . .

CHAPTER ONE

Challenges

*A*t 0530 on February 20, 1987, I was 129 miles west of Cape Horn aboard a fifty-foot yacht named *American Flag*. It was bitterly cold, and a thirty-knot wind from the northwest knifed across the deck and cut into my face like the sharp edge of a steel blade. We—the yacht and I—were logging between nine and ten knots, and headed directly east. I had three reefs in the mainsail, well eased to starboard, that was balanced by a small jib held out to port with a long spinnaker pole. I was glad that the rig was snug and strong because when a gust tore across the deck we speeded up to twelve or fourteen knots for a few seconds, and the wake of the yacht began to roar with a great whooshing sound.

I wore enough winter clothing to start a store for Mt. Everest climbers: long thermal underwear; a sweater; chest-high padded trousers and jacket; a thick woolen scarf; and finally a bright red suit of heavy, lined, overlapping outer foul weather gear. In addition, I had on special stockings, seaboots with liners, a quilted hat with earflaps, and double gloves. By the time I put all this stuff on, I looked like Santa Claus.

I climbed into the cockpit. At fifty-six degrees south latitude in the southern summer, daylight comes early. The freezing air was clear and crisp, with a kind of bluish brittleness, and I could see for miles and miles. As I did a hundred times a day, I looked carefully around in all directions. I saw nothing except a circling albatross.

I knew that Chile's big island of Tierra del Fuego lay ahead on the port bow. I tried to pick out the gray, snow-topped mountains of the southern-most Andes and the first of the fringing islands—Isla Londonderry and Isla Hoste. All I could see, however, were low and formless clouds that were full of squalls and wind. With luck and good fortune I might be able to slip past Cape Horn on this day. I held my breath and scarcely dared to think of getting around without problems. Once past Cape Horn and a little farther east, I could turn north and head into areas of gentler weather.

The gale frequency was twenty-three percent in this part of the ocean. This meant that one day in four, according to averages, the wind would be Force eight (a wind of thirty-four to forty knots) or more. My wind at the moment was Force seven (twenty-eight to thirty-three knots) with long, steady, roughly six-meter-high seas that swept past the yacht every ten seconds. *American Flag* rose as the crests rumbled past, and she eased down in the troughs. Sometimes she rolled thirty or forty degrees as a sea swept past, but her heavy lead keel quickly swung her upright.

I was worried that when I got on the shallow 200-meter shelf that extended south from the Cape Horn area for some forty miles the big following waves might break and cause a terrible sea. Or I could be battered by winds of sixty or seventy knots. At the moment, however, all was well. The autopilot steered perfectly, the yacht was tracking a straight course, and we were going nicely. Would our good fortune last another day or two?

I was competing in a round-the-world race for singlehanded sailors, that is, yachts looked after by one person. I had no crew, no mates, and no assistants. One person did everything. The captain was the cook, the navigator, the dishwasher, the sail changer, the radio operator, the plumber, and the bed-maker. When the toilet was dirty or a sail was ripped, the captain had to deal with the problem. If he got sick he had to look through the medical chest and gulp down a couple of pills. If he got depressed he had to laugh at his own jokes. Our man of all seasons wrote up the ship's log, sewed a button on his shirt cuff, and worried about overcooking the rice. He pumped the bilge, opened a bottle of wine, checked the compass deviation, trimmed the sails, tucked in reefs, watched out for shipping traffic, drew lines on the charts, repaired the electric generator, and sometimes—not often—read a book. In addition, he tried to get in six or seven hours of sleep (in short naps spread out over twenty-four hours) so that he would be rested enough to look after himself and the yacht and keep her sailing well.

Our man of all seasons had to have some administrative skills to keep track of everything. He needed a touch of fund-raising talent because paying for a large yacht was an expensive business. Sailing aside, just getting the vessel and her equipment and stores together was quite a task. The captain had to deal with the running costs, order parts and labor, and not only keep his entry going operationally but try to win the race! As it turned out, there were three quite separate parts to the competition:

1. The yacht, her sailing equipment, and stores for the race.
2. Repairs, maintenance, new gear, and supplies at the three stops.
3. The actual sailing of the race.

To deal with all this sounds impossible, but it's not, and the race was a fascinating, frustrating, maddening, discouraging, challenging, endlessly intriguing business. It also gave a person an unparalleled sense of independence and achievement.

I was one of twenty-five competitors who started in the 1986–87 race, which was divided into four parts:

1. From Newport, Rhode Island, USA, southward in the Atlantic to Cape Town, South Africa. Distance 7,100 nautical miles.

2. From Cape Town past the southern tip of Africa, eastward across the Southern ocean, through Bass strait (between Australia and Tasmania) to Sydney, Australia. 6,900 miles.

3. From Sydney eastward through the Tasman sea past New Zealand, and across the Southern ocean. Then around Cape Horn, and north into the south Atlantic past the Falkland islands to Rio de Janeiro, Brazil. 8,250 miles.

4. From Rio northward along the Brazilian coast in the Atlantic, across the equator, past Bermuda to Newport. 5,300 miles. Total for the four legs: 27,550 miles.

There were two classes of yachts: from forty to fifty feet, and from fifty to sixty feet. Except for the two classes, there were no handicaps. Everyone started together at the beginning of each leg. The first to finish in each class was the winner. The shortest total times of the four legs determined the overall winners. There were small cash prizes.

A British multinational corporation named the BOC Group ran the race. BOC's main business is industrial gases, but it runs all sorts of other enterprises throughout the world. Prior to 1982 the letters BOC didn't mean much to most people, so when a sailor named Richard Broadhead approached BOC for individual sponsorship before the first race in 1982–83, the company decided to sponsor the whole affair to publicize the BOC name. Hopefully, the executives thought, BOC would become as well known as, say, IBM, General Motors, or British Petroleum.

This is not idle industrial vanity because the financial instruments of well-known companies are easier to sell and sometimes can be marketed at more favorable rates. A well-known company's products are also more sala- ble because a history of successes and upbeat advertising means that people tend to trust the company and its wares.

"We wanted to promote the BOC name in our U.S., Australian, South African, and Latin American markets," said Richard Giordano, the chairman of the big international company. "We also wanted a high profile event that we could share with our variously named subsidiaries that trade in these markets. We liked the concept of this sailing race. We liked the idea of being associated with the qualities that the race epitomizes—courage, determina- tion, stamina, and the ability to distinguish between a gamble and a calculated risk. These are all qualities at the heart of good business management."

The BOC commitment was to sponsor the race, not the individual yachts. BOC set up a race committee, a public relations and press staff, rules and inspection committees, awards and prize ceremonies, and so on. The first race in 1982–83 had seventeen entrants and was a great success. Ten men completed the course. The fastest took 159 days; the slowest 264 days.[1]

Now, on the morning of February 20, 1987, the second running of the BOC race was underway. I was on *American Flag*, about three-quarters of the distance through the third leg, and trying to get around Cape Horn. Since 0530 I had been sailing well. At 0600 the seas had grown larger, and I shut the storm door between the cockpit and the cabin. By 1000, however, the wind had dropped to twenty-two knots. I set the full yankee jib, shook out the third reef in the mainsail, and rigged a preventer line from the end of the

American Flag, a specially strengthened Santa Cruz 50—designed by Bill Lee—in front of Table Mountain in Cape Town. Here we see the cutter-rigged yacht sailing well with the staysail, yankee, and one reef in the mainsail. The black patch underneath the main boom marks the position of the four Arco solar panels, which supplied most of the electricity during the 27,597-mile race. Note the bag at the foot of the mast with the storm trysail ready to be hoisted on its own track. The climbing steps up the sides of the mast allowed the rig to be serviced at sea. The mainsail in use at this time was a North fully battened sail (seven battens) and is pulling beautifully.

main boom to the stemhead to help keep the boom under control in the rough ocean.

[From the log]. *1030.* It's beautiful outside. Hundreds of large low formless clouds. No sign of land. Contrary to what I expected, the seas are way down on the bank (I show a depth of eighty-seven fathoms). I have been sitting in the cockpit enjoying the scene and watching a tiny storm petrel pitter-patting across the wave tops, a small bundle of dark gray with a touch of white on its tail. Plus albatrosses and a big all-brown petrel with a large yellow beak. Sitting outside in the flickering sunlight is like taking a winter walk. It's a good thing that I am warmly dressed.

At 1145 I was below in the cabin standing in front of the cooking stove stirring a pot of mushroom soup when a tremendous white squall from the northwest knocked the yacht flat. As we went over, a heavy wave thumped hard against the hull. My lunch suddenly went flying, and I was thrown against the side of the galley—now the floor—while the contents of the chart table rained down on me. The mast was in the water, and it was hard work to climb up into the cockpit. I expected to find the mast broken off and the cockpit full of water, but the rig was okay, and there was no water except for some pouring off the mainsail as the yacht rolled upright again. I was certainly glad for the heavy mast section, the running backstay, and the stout after lower shrouds that I had added in spite of the disapproval of the builder.

I rolled up twelve turns in the yankee and put the third reef back in the mainsail. It was frightfully hard work to crank the reefing winch as I knelt on the coachroof behind the mast in the fifty knots of wind that was blowing. We were still tearing along, and the mainsail was full of wind. I put both hands on the winch handle and threw my body violently against the handle. I was lucky to move it one click—one-fifteenth of a turn, even in low gear. I sobbed with the effort, and I was terrified that something in the reefing system would break. Deep reefs in the mainsail when going downwind had been a problem from the beginning. Of course, it would have been easy to have put in the reef if I could have headed into the wind, but in the seas that were running such a maneuver was quite impossible. I needed a larger winch, and it should have been mounted on the mast or in a position where I could have used the force of my entire body instead of just my arms and shoulders. It seemed to take forever to get the reef down, and by the time I was finished, I was dizzy and panting from the exertion.

There was still no sign of land or mountains. I was between Islas Il-defonso (to port) and Islas Diego Ramirez (to starboard). Each was about 30 miles away, but I could see nothing. What I did notice was another massive dark squall looming to windward. I kept an eye on it. At noon (I had taken a moment out from the reefing mentioned above to read the log) our run was

224 miles for the last twenty-four hours. We were averaging a little better than nine knots.

One squall followed another, and the wind blasted down on *American Flag*. I suppose I should have been frightened to death, but I found the sailing exhilarating and wildly exciting. Perhaps it was the challenge of being in a match with such great forces near Cape Horn. What I was thankful for was that I was going *with* the wind and east-flowing current and *not* in the other direction.

> [From the log]. *1315.* Land ho! Wonderful! The first sight of land since Cook strait in New Zealand thousands of miles ago. I can just make out dome-shaped hills and low mountains on the port bow and beam. Still far away. Dull gray color and patches of snow. The weather is cold, invigorating, and the air feels good to breathe. None of that tropical junk that rots out the lungs.

I soon worked out that if I rolled up the yankee all the way we could take the squalls with just the triple-reefed mainsail and still maintain our speed. I was worried about more wind, however, so I set the hanked storm staysail on the midstay. Now if the conditions went to hell, I would drop the mainsail entirely and continue under the tiny storm staysail, whose area was only 125 square feet. The sail was new ten-ounce Dacron with triple-stitched seams and heavy nylon tapes along the edges that I had borrowed for the race from my friend Pieter Boersma.

As the weather front passed going eastward, the squalls continued to march across the sky. Some missed the yacht. Some brushed us lightly. Some hit hard, and as the wind rose and fell I cranked the yankee in and out like a yo-yo. For a time the squalls disappeared, and I thought their attacks were over, but at 1400 another barrage, backed up with blasts of sleet, struck *American Flag*. Then the sky behind grew clear, and the wind moderated to twenty-six knots from the northwest.

I watched the landscape to the north unfold. A series of distant gray humps topped with snow rose above the horizon. I tried to pick out separate islands and identify something, but from twenty-five to thirty miles away, all I could see were general land forms mixed up with a low bank of clouds. I went below to put the charts and navigation instruments in their places and mopped up the remnants of the mushroom soup. With all the excitement and action I was so tired and sleepy that I could scarcely keep my eyes open. I set the alarm clock, pulled off my outer oilskin jacket, and stretched out on the starboard settee bunk under two thick blankets. I fell asleep instantly.

When I looked out at 1700 the sky was clear, and the wind was still twenty-six knots from the northwest. The land to the north was much closer. Now I could see different forms and contours among the hills. As I peered through my binoculars and followed the shoreline toward the east, the gray and white and black land hooked a little south and ended in an abrupt cliff.

It was Cape Horn.

Now I was at the southernmost tip of South America, and I could see the steep, 406-meter cliff that climbed from the sea and marked the border between the Atlantic and Pacific. This notorious bluff of black rock is at the southern end of a small island five miles long and three miles wide. Isla Hornos, to use its official Chilean name, is the farthest south of some four hundred small islands and rocks south of the big island of Tierra del Fuego, which in turn is separated from the mainland of South America by the Strait of Magellan. (The latitude of Cape Horn is 210 miles south of the eastern entrance to the Strait of Magellan.)

Although the passage from the Atlantic to the Pacific via Cape Horn was discovered by a Dutchman named Willem Schouten in 1616, it remained an isolated curiosity for explorers and military adventurers until 1830, when the industrial revolution fired up world trade. Within a few years, tools, machinery, agricultural implements, pottery, and textiles began to be made in quantity and could be sold for low prices all over the world. Such commodities as coal, nitrates, nickel ore, wheat, rice, wool, and cotton were carried in return. All these cargoes were freighted near and far by sailing ships of increasing number and size.

In 1848, gold was discovered in California. Soon thousands of fortune hunters clamored for quick travel from Europe and the eastern United States to the gold fields. Then, beginning in 1853, a pioneering oceanographer named Matthew Fontaine Maury showed captains how to sail more quickly by following certain wind and current patterns.

Maury suggested that ships bound from Australia to England, for example, should stop taking the slow and poky old route that went *west* through the Indian ocean and around South Africa. Instead, Maury advised ship captains to go *east* and reach the Atlantic and Europe by rounding South America. "There is a belt of westerly winds between 45° and 50°S., which are most constant and steady," he wrote. "Cape Horn may be reached under canvas from Port Philip [Australia] with these westerly winds and long swells . . . in twenty or twenty-five days."

"With these winds alone, and with the bounding seas which follow fast, the modern clipper, without auxiliary power, has accomplished a greater distance in a day than any sea steamer has ever been known to reach," wrote Maury in 1860.[2]

Ocean sailing was revolutionized. The average time for a passage between England and Australia had been 125 days; this was shortened to 97 days for the outward passage and to 63 for the return. The time for the New York to San Francisco run was cut from 180 to 135 days, later reduced to 100 days.

By 1880 there were more than 10,000 deepwater sailing ships in the Cape Horn trade: 5,000 British, 2,000 Norwegian, 1,200 each from France and Sweden, and 1,000 German. Plus those from the U.S.[3]

The familiar triangular hump of Cape Horn from the west, the most famous landfall of all.

The great years for the Cape Horn trade were from 1870 to 1900. At any time at least a quarter of a million men were involved. The seamen were often plagued by cold weather, contrary seas, adverse currents, foul winds, and short hours of daylight. In years of savage weather the toll of ships and men was high. In the spring and early summer of 1905, for instance, 130 ships left European ports for the Pacific ports of America. Out of this number, 52 arrived at their destinations, 4 were wrecked, and 22 limped into ports in distress. *Fifty-three ships were unaccounted for by the end of November.* Hundreds of men were lost fighting the worst sailing conditions anywhere.[4]

It was no wonder that such experiences quickly turned an apprentice sailor into a journeyman; in a single voyage a novice became a seaman true and true. Some of these men who waged war with Cape Horn wrote books and letters and songs. They told their families and friends and neighbors back home about their experiences. From this battlefield at sea came the legends and tales of Cape Horn, the tradition and lore that has been handed down for four generations.

I knew about all this nautical history from books, and as I conned *American Flag* along those southern shores, I felt that the ghosts of the old Cape Horn sailors were around me. When I walked along the decks I was nervous, and I sometimes wondered if people were watching me.

My wife and I had sailed around Cape Horn from the Chilean channels twelve years earlier. Now the stern black cliff looked the same except for a new light (flashing white every eleven seconds) and a tiny lookout house set up by the Chilean navy. I knew that such stations were lonely posts, and that a gunner and a radio operator took turns cooking while they fought boredom and cold and counted the days until their relief crew showed up.[5]

My watch read 1915. Cape Horn was on the port beam, about three-quarters of a mile north of *American Flag.* I took a compass bearing of the light and crossed it with a depth reading, which gave me a precise position. It was exciting to see Cape Horn, but I couldn't relax until I got away from this region of gales and storms. My immediate goal was to reach 50 degrees south latitude, about 550 miles to the northeast.

I decided to go east of Isla de los Estados, a small island separated from Tierra del Fuego by a sixteen-mile-wide passage called Estrecho de Le Maire. Going through the twenty-mile strait was a little shorter and might have saved time, but the tidal streams and overfalls in this meeting place between the Atlantic and the Pacific could be extremely severe. If the wind dropped, a sailing vessel could be swept back and forth like a tennis ball in a washing machine. The sailing directions strongly advised going through Le Maire at slack water. On my previous voyage I had sailed through at slack water before a southwest gale, and the seas had been a nightmare. I had no wish to do it again, and I thought the savings in time balanced against the *possible loss in time and risks* made a poor case for the strait.

The radio crackled with warnings about Le Maire from the others in the race who were ahead of me.

"We were nearly becalmed after the Horn, but when I got to the strait, all that changed," said Ian Kiernan on *Spirit of Sydney*. "The wind gusted up to 50 knots, and the seas were large and steep. The place was terrible! I went straight up the middle, which I thought was the right thing. But the bloody current! I was making 10.5 knots, and wasn't going anywhere. I was standing still! It took me hours to get through."

Mike Plant on *Airco* had trouble too. "By the time I got to the south end of the strait, the wind was fifty knots, which then went up to seventy knots! I had to take the mainsail down and left just the staysail up. Normally you don't keep any sail up at all in that much wind, but I had to maintain some headway because the wind was from the northwest, and Isla de los Estados was a lee shore."

To try to stay away from these problems, I aimed *American Flag* for an arbitrary point A, 150 miles northeast of Cape Horn (15 miles east of Isla de los Estados). Before I could change course for point A, however, I had to sail eastward until I was clear of various rocks south of Islas Hornos, Deceit, and Barnevelt.

At 2115 we glided along on a fairly calm sea with only thirteen knots of wind from the northwest. The weather was warmer, so I peeled off some clothes. Since we had passed the Cape Horn rocks I changed course for point A and began to steer northeast. The wind was now on the port beam so I took down the spinnaker pole, put the full yankee to leeward, and shook out a reef from the mainsail.

I stood in the cockpit and looked around while I ate a big plate of steak and onions and drank a glass of red wine. Far behind us the white shaft of light from Cape Horn pierced through the black night every eleven seconds. To the south a slash of moon curved up out of the sea. Overhead I could see the blinking dots of the Southern Cross and lots of small stars. The whole scene was incredibly beautiful and totally unexpected. It was the best evening for a month. Would such weather last?

I took another careful look in all directions, set both the off-course alarm and the alarm clock and piled into bed. At midnight I put three rolls in the yankee.

At 0200 on the morning of February 21st I felt the yacht heel and begin to labor. I got up at once, yanked on my oilskins and boots, and hurried outside. The wind was twenty-two knots from the north. I could have rolled a deeper reef in the yankee, but the more it was rolled, the worse its shape got for going to windward. Plus being hard on the sail. I decided to furl the yankee and set the regular hanked staysail on the midstay in place of the storm staysail. Fifteen minutes later I had up a small, strong sail with an efficient shape. The air was cold, and my gloves felt good while I was changing the sails. Afterward I had trouble getting warm in my berth so I got up and put on dry stockings and boot liners and zipped myself inside a down-filled sleeping bag.

At 0745 the weather was bright and sunny. The wind was up to thirty knots, and the sea was a mass of whitecaps, but the ocean was not too rough because the wind blew from the land, which was only forty miles to the northwest. A group of flat, disc-like lenticular clouds hovered low in the sky to the northwest. I put the third reef in the mainsail, and we crashed and banged as we labored northeastward.

At midmorning we were thumping along in bigger seas. The wind was thirty-five knots, but the gale was unsteady because of the closeness of the land. Tiny whirlwinds shot across the water, picked up spray from the tops of the waves, and flung it against the sails. The autopilot labored so hard to steer the yacht in the upset seas that I thought something might break. I decided to set the wind vane, but the bronze gears in the main linkage had somehow slipped past one another. I tried to deal with the gears while hanging over the transom, but the motion was too violent to use tools with any success. I gave up and continued with the autopilot. To the north I could clearly see the spiny ridge of Isla de los Estados, all thirty-seven miles of it, the dark silhouettes of a dozen craggy peaks etched against a sky of hard blue.

Even with her reduced sail, *American Flag* labored mightily. She heeled far over and pitched into seas which were mean and nasty, seas that were certainly influenced by the fierce tidal streams and overfalls around Isla de los Estados. The seas were not so high, but they were short and heavy and sometimes overlapped and rolled into one another from different directions.

Occasionally one of the cross-seas slammed into us from an unexpected angle, and the twisting comber banged into the hull with the force of a cement truck smashing into a wall. These shuddering thumps scared the hell out of me. It seemed a miracle that the hull—any hull—could take such abuse without breaking into a thousand pieces. Cape Horn was certainly the ultimate test for a boatbuilder. And a pretty fair testing ground for a sailor's nerves as well.

Clearly the mainsail needed to come down, but it was so much trouble (to take it down and put it up later) that I decided to hang on for a while. If we could just get away from the cursed land and out into the Atlantic!

At noon the east end of Isla de los Estados was prominent to port, some twenty miles away, and I worked out that we had done thirty miles to the northeast since 0745—an average of seven knots. The whine of the wind was less, and the windspeed gauge registered only twenty knots. The seas were longer, higher, and plenty nasty, but definitely more comfortable. The yacht was sailing easier.

"The storm is over," I thought. "As soon as the wind shifts a little, we can head for the Falkland islands."

I was innocently thinking about putting up more sail and whether to pass east or west of the Falklands when I happened to glance to windward. About a mile away, *I saw the sea turning white.* I raced down the side deck, dumped the staysail halyard, and clawed down the staysail. I managed to get one or two ties around the sail when the yacht was smashed over to starboard by a blast from a hurricane-force wind. All at once my legs were in midair. I clung to the partially furled staysail like a trapeze artist swinging above the abyss.

American Flag was knocked flat, and the starboard bow of the yacht was pushed into the sea. I was dunked in the icy Southern ocean a couple of times as waves washed over me. I came up spluttering and gasping. There was no time to think about the cold or my wet clothes. The wind was raging, and twice what I'd felt earlier. The yacht was quite out of control; the triple-reefed mainsail had to come down immediately. I scrambled up to windward, snapped my safety line to a shroud, leaned against the mast, and reached around the spar to find the halyard and the line jammer. While I was doing this the wind shrieked, and the yacht must have been heeled seventy-five degrees. My home on the sea felt as if a giant's hand was pushing sideways against the top of the mast. I couldn't believe the force of the wind. (I had some ties in my mouth and the ends streamed away from me like horizontal wires). The fact that we had been knocked flat had nothing to do with the design of the vessel. *Any* yacht or small ship would have been knocked flat with the same proportionate sail area up—ballast, beam, or hull sections notwithstanding. My error was not being outside earlier and seeing the approaching wind. (What would have happened at night? Even to a fully crewed vessel?)

"Come on *Flag!*" I shouted to myself. "We've got to get through this!"

I let go the main halyard, moved my safety line from the windward shroud to the windward staysail sheet so I could work aft a little, and tackled the flailing mass of the sail. Even reduced with reefs, the sail was bulky enough that I had to use long ties whose ends kept blowing away from me in the wind. I tied a bowline in one end and threaded the other end through the bowline and used the resultant purchase to yank down on the sail. Meanwhile, spray flew everywhere. Once a terrible gust blasted down on the yacht (hang on!), and I thought I would be plucked off like a leaf from a tree and sent tumbling into the sea. After what seemed like ages (half an hour?) I managed to get five or six ties around the sail and to unsnarl the halyard.

With all sail off, the yacht straightened up to forty or forty-five degrees. I got back to the cockpit and looked at the windspeed dial, but it read zero. (I later found out that the masthead indicator had filled with salt water when the mast had been pushed into the water.)

The wind continued to moan with an uncanny wail. The sea was all white, and the tops of the crests were whisked into the air and blown off into spume. There was nothing more I could do on deck, and with a wind from the northwest we had unlimited sea room. I went below, closed the storm doors behind me, and we bashed along under bare pole.

The inside of the insulated cabin seemed wonderfully quiet and sheltered. By this time I was shaking from the cold so I emptied my boots of water, stripped off all my wet clothes, and wiped myself dry with a big towel. I put on dry clothing and soon began to warm up a little, helped by a long pull from a bottle of brandy from Cape Town. (Willi Schütten had given me the bottle, and I blessed him.) I was ahead in the war with Cape Horn for the moment and felt marvelously alert and full of life. Outside, the action still raged in the trenches. Certainly the white squalls of Cape Horn were enough to send shivers down the spine of the devil himself.

By the middle of the afternoon the tempest was down to thirty-five knots or so. I had the staysail up and we were jogging along on a course of 060°M. at seven knots. *American Flag* was docile and manageable without her mainsail.

> [From the log]. February 21st.
>
> *1700.* Wind down to 25 knots from the north. Mainsail up. Astonishing how black and filthy the head of the sail and the main halyard are. There must be a lot of dirt flying around at mast height.
>
> *1800.* Wind back up. Mainsail down. Captain dead. The cockpit coamings were in running waves. Very tough conditions. Not for the faint of heart. The hardest afternoon of the race for me.
>
> *1845.* East end of Isla de los Estados 28 miles on 270°W.
>
> *2000.* 7 knots under staysail.
>
> *2200.* Black and horrible outside. The hell with it. I'm going to sleep.

The next morning we were on the Burdwood bank south of the Falkland islands. The wind was down. The gales were over. I had the mainsail up, and the staysail was in the forward cabin. The full yankee was billowed out with a light wind from the west-northwest. Soon I had untied two reefs, and I was eating bacon and eggs. The Cape Horn gales were a memory.

What was I doing here? How did I ever get involved in such a sailing race? I thought back to the beginning of the whole business.

. . . .

CHAPTER TWO

Beginnings

I can't tell you why, but I wanted very much to do the race. I don't know whether it was vanity, escapism, the zest of competition, a hoped-for sense of independence, or what. Something deep within me said that I should throw all caution and common sense aside and try it. I suppose it's the same with many kinds of endeavors. A singlehanded sailing race around the world was different, however. It was ruinously expensive and would take two years out of my life. The rules, it seemed to me, favored large and costly yachts in a thoroughly big-time operation. The little guy was aced out from the beginning. Some of my competition would be from well-financed professionals who were young, full of energy, and ingenious. A number of the entries had surrounded themselves with determined teams of builders, designers, and sponsors who were keen to dance in the spotlight of publicity. After all, good press notices and TV footage bolstered one's reputation and name, which led directly to sales and profits. For those with things to sell, the race was a direct means to an end.

Fortunately, money isn't everything. There were other attractions. The challenge. The thrill. The chase. The enterprise. The beauty of the ocean. Just imagine using the wind blowing on little pieces of cloth to make your way around the oceans of the world! Incredible!

I was fortunate to have had plenty of sailing experience. I was an engineer type and a skilled nautical mechanic, and I had been over much of the course on earlier voyages. But I had no vessel, I knew almost nothing about racing, I had no background, no organization, and no designer. Fund-raising was a complete mystery to me. If I did come up with a suitable yacht, she would be a special creature, a fine-boned thoroughbred, perhaps fit for the course but of little value elsewhere. Yet my gut feeling was that I should do it. And as I have gone on in life I have learned to pay more and more attention to such feelings because again and again my intuitive sense about something has turned out to be right in the long run. (It's the same as meeting people; if I like the person right off, generally all goes well. If the first meeting is no good, however, my relationship invariably falls apart even if I make the most determined effort to be upbeat, positive, and forward-looking.)

The event was to be a long-distance sailing race for one person. I knew a lot about ocean sailing, but I had always done it with my wife, who was tough, resourceful, and infinitely capable. When there had been problems, Margaret had always been beside me with cheerful suggestions and no end of resolution. Why then was I considering this cursed race? I was back to the basic question again. Why? Why? Why? I suppose to see whether I had the guts, the will, the resourcefulness, and the capabilities. And the technical skills. But these words are so general and unspecific.

I thought back to the days when I had climbed mountains in California's lovely Sierra Nevada. Then the mountains had had exactly the same attraction for me as the sea does now. There was always something ahead in the distance that took planning and patience to overcome. The sea was the same. Only the methods were different. *Overcome* was not the right word when talking about the sea, however. If one could arrive at a parity or an equivalence it was enough; mother nature was always the master.

"The sea is a great leveller, and quickly humbles the big-headed sailor," wrote Alex Rose after his sailing trip around the world twenty years ago.[6]

I decided to do the race, to get it out of my system, and that was that. Now it was full speed ahead.

This was the second running of the BOC round-the-world event. In the spring of 1982 I had tried hard to enter the first race. At that time I owned an excellent small vessel in seagoing condition. *Whisper* was only thirty-five feet long, but she had first-class equipment, she sailed well for her size, and she had a lot of sea miles behind her. I decided to enter the race. I was confident that with my writing and sailing background I could find a sponsor.

I sat down to write to BOC in England, but I realized that I had no address. The publicity about the race was meager, and from my remote location in Maya cove on Tortola island in the British Virgin islands I could learn nothing. What did BOC stand for? Could it have been an individual? Baron Oscar Chapman? Probably not. More likely a big company of some sort. British Overseas Corp.? Brown's Optical Computers? Barclay's Orange Crush?

The race headquarters office was said to be in Newport, Rhode Island, so I wrote to the Goat Island Marina. My letter was returned unopened. I tried telephoning, which was a major project from Tortola. Either the numbers wouldn't answer or had been disconnected. I called again and again. I telephoned the sailing magazines, but my editor friends were away on assignments. I wrote to the Royal Ocean racing club in London. The mail came back because the address on my letter was faulty. After so many failures I decided that someone was trying to tell me something.

"The heck with the race," I said in disgust. My wife and I sailed westward on a trip around the world before the gentle trade winds.[7]

In early 1985 we were back in the West Indies and anchored in the same cove in the British Virgin islands. The 1982–83 BOC race was long over, but it had been extremely successful. There had been lots of publicity, and now everyone was beginning to know the name of BOC.

Seventeen entrants from eight nations had left Newport on schedule and enjoyed a brisk race. The contestants' ages had ranged from twenty-nine to fifty-six. Their occupations included a taxi driver from Japan, a newspaper editor from Los Angeles, a deep-sea diver from Le Havre, a real estate executive from London, a restaurant owner from Brittany, and a political refugee from Czechoslovakia. A French sailor named Philippe Jeantot led the race almost from the beginning and won the competition in the remarkable time of 159 days. Two yachts had had the bad luck to run aground during the race. One was destroyed; the second was refloated and continued. Two other vessels were rolled over and terminally damaged. Both captains were rescued by other competitors in the race. Four yachts retired with various problems, but ten yachts completed the entire 27,550 miles, a remarkable achievement. Most of the captains became great friends, and a spirit of goodwill seemed to run through everything.

"This event gave us a rare opportunity to associate our company name with qualities we admire," said Richard Giordano, the chairman of BOC, when he spoke at the final awards ceremony in Newport in June 1983. "We're attracted to these sailors because they have guts, endurance, resolve, and they know how to evaluate and choose between hard alternatives." Giordano then announced that the BOC Group would sponsor a new race in 1986–87. Some of the sailors who had just completed the grueling competition promptly stood up and said that they would try again.

Maybe I would enter this time!

The rules for the next race had been changed, and now my thirty-five footer was too small. For the 1986–87 competition there were to be two classes of vessels: from forty to fifty feet and from fifty to sixty feet. A sixty-footer was a bit daunting to sail alone, but I thought I could handle a fifty-footer. The costs of a sixty-footer were very roughly twice that of a fifty-foot yacht because the volume of a vessel goes up almost as the cube of her length (L^3), which means a great deal more material and labor and sails and winch power and mast size and many other things. Since the costs might be critical, the smaller class seemed the better option.

Each yacht had to be compartmented with watertight bulkheads to make her unsinkable; a satellite position-locating transponder was to be put on board; you were required to have an emergency rudder scheme; and before the start each captain had to make a 2,000-mile qualifying run. The BOC entries were restricted to monohulls with ballast keels (trimarans and catamarans were not allowed because of capsizing problems). An important new rule was that it was permissible to carry internal seawater tanks under each side deck to modify the ballast arrangements.

I began to look at the used yacht market for something suitable for the race. First I checked what was for sale near my home on Mt. Desert island in Maine, then up and down the east coast of the United States. There were lots of almost new but outdated round-the-buoys racing yachts for sale at low prices. In general the construction was good but very light. Often thirty bags of sails were included in the price. These racing yachts had gangs of winches, all sorts of fancy blocks and deck gear, masses of electronic equipment, and had been designed by well-known naval architects.

On the negative side, the hulls had excessive midship beam, overly pinched ends, and unfair sterns. It seemed to me that the toothpick masts were far too lofty and weak for the rigors of the Southern ocean. A new mast would mean extensive sail recutting. Often these vessels had large, heavy engines for rule-beating purposes, and it was a big expense to replace the engine and propeller drive arrangement. The cockpits would have to be rebuilt for shorthanded sailing, and of course there were no water ballast tanks. So there were five counts against such a purchase (mast and rigging, heavy engine, water ballast tanks, cockpit, and sails). Without these changes—at least in my eyes—these yachts would not be suitable.

The best plan was to have a new yacht specially designed for the BOC competition. Rod Stephens sent me drawings, but I found his proposal high-sided and unattractive. At 28,195 pounds she was heavy, and the design seemed old-fashioned.

I called Santa Cruz, California, and talked with Bill Lee, a designer and boat builder whose ultralight speedsters were the rage of the downwind Los Angeles-to-Honolulu race. Lee's light displacement 50-foot design was long on the waterline (46.5 feet), which meant that she had good speed potential. Nevertheless her beam was narrow, her rig looked tall and vulnerable, and I had doubts about her weatherliness and strength. How much would that flat hull pound going to windward? No one had ever taken an ultralight displacement boat (ULDB) to the Southern ocean. Was it possible to sail such a design in hard conditions? Or would she be overwhelmed and destroyed by the seas?

"You can win the race with a Santa Cruz 50," crooned Lee on the telephone. "Remember my slogan: *Fast is fun.*"

I had grave doubts about the Santa Cruz 50. I told Lee that I would think about it.

When I had read about the earlier BOC race in Barry Pickthall's book I had been captivated by a color photograph of *Gipsy Moth V,* the late Sir Francis Chichester's last vessel, built in 1970. I thought her hull was lovely. The naval architect was Robert Clark, who had designed a long series of successful yachts that included *Ortac, Sir Thomas Lipton,* and *British Steel.* Clark's designs had the reputation of being slim greyhounds of the sea, vessels that tracked straight and true, and—best of all—they looked good, with gentle overhangs at the bow and stern and a pleasantly curved sheer line at the top of the hull. Chichester was enthusiastic about Clark's design.

Gipsy Moth V—sailed by Desmond Hampton—had been in the first BOC race and had been one of the leaders when she was unfortunately wrecked. Years before—in 1976—when my wife and I had sailed into Rio de Janeiro harbor on a trip around South America, we had had a look at *British Steel,* and I remember being so thrilled by the line of the hull. Clark's work did not reflect the latest fads of the racing rules, but I cared nothing for that because the rules changed every few years and would soon be forgotten. A pretty yacht endured, especially if she was speedy. Would it be possible to get a fifty-foot version and to put a modern cutter rig on her?

In May 1985 I wrote to a friend in London for Clark's address. I knew he had been prominent in yacht design work in 1937 (or before) so he would be elderly. I wasn't even sure he was still alive. Clark replied at once, however, and in a vigorous hand suggested that we build a largely flush-decked cutter in aluminum. We wrote back and forth.

One subject in our letters was water ballast. Fifty-six-foot *Credit Agricole,* the winner of the first BOC race, had had two 1,500-liter tanks, each of which could hold 3,390 pounds of seawater ballast (in addition to 11,000 pounds of fixed lead ballast on her centerline keel). I knew that all the new yachts favored the water ballast scheme. The idea was to use built-in tanks on the outboard sides of beamy hulls to carry a heavy weight of seawater to windward to make the yacht stiffer so she could carry more sail and go faster. Initially you had to pump the water from the sea. Then before tacking you opened a large plumbing valve, which allowed the water to run from the high full tank (toward the wind) to the low empty tank (away from the wind). There was a small risk that if the sails were taken aback and the weight got on the wrong side by mischance, the yacht could capsize. To keep this from happening, BOC rules dictated limits for water ballast which could only heel a vessel ten degrees when at rest alongside a dock. This presumably ensured that a yacht fitted with water ballast to these limits couldn't capsize. Robert—by now Clark and I were on a first-name basis—dismissed the water ballast out of hand. "Most unseamanlike," he said. "It is unnecessary, and I urge you to forget it."

It was slow writing back and forth to London. Some of my friends urged me to hire a naval architect in the United States. "Clark's good but he's an old man. His designs are dated. Chichester died thirteen years ago. Sure,

British Steel and *Gipsy Moth V* have nice lines, but they're old-fashioned and heavy. They belong in a museum. What you need for the next BOC race is a lightweight cutter with lots of beam, plenty of sail area, an elliptical-shaped rudder and keel, and a long waterline that runs right back to a skirt at the transom. The hull should be a fiberglass foam sandwich with Kevlar and triaxial cloth set in epoxy on both sides. In short, a high-tech, high-powered flier."

I had heard about a super-speed monohull yacht called *Thursday's Child* designed by Paul Lindenberg, Lars Bergstrom, and the owner, Warren Luhrs. In 25,000 miles of sailing she had averaged 200 miles a day, an incredible, simply unbelievable pace. The yacht had almost beaten the multihulls in the 1984 OSTAR race across the Atlantic. Only halyard failures and a shredded sail, it seemed, kept her from winning. Even so she had come in only ten hours after the multihulls. A sixty-footer with a draft of twelve feet and a mast seventy-five feet high, the yacht was extreme in many aspects: she was superlight, superinnovative, and superengineered. She was also superexpensive, as I found out when I telephoned Paul Lindenberg in Florida.

"What would it cost to build a fifty-foot version?" I asked.

"Oh, I guess about $300,000," said Lindenberg. "That's without sails

This photograph of the stern and cockpit of the sixty-foot *Thursday's Child* gives an idea of the complexity of a no-holds-barred custom racing yacht.

and electronics and any special goodies. Luhr's out-the-door effort was about $500,000, but there have been lots of changes since then. Things like gimbaled navigation stations don't come cheap. Special engineering and custom building take time. Good men are costly.

"You can get quite a ways for $300,000 or $400,000," he concluded.

When I heard figures like this, I thought of giving up.

I was introduced to Rodger Martin, a naval architect who lived in Newport and who talked at length about modern racing yachts and "state-of-the-art" building. He had already completed a BOC design for Mike Plant which was under construction. Rodger was full of ideas and keen to do a design for me. He promised help in seeking sponsorship and seemed well acquainted with marine dealers and boatyards. I liked his ideas and paid him to do some preliminary drawings, but Rodger was busy with several projects, and everything took too long. I began to look elsewhere.

About this time a broker called excitedly and said that the Australian yacht *Leda,* designed by Joe Adams, was for sale at a cheap price ($110,000 instead of $297,000). *Leda* had been sailed in the first BOC race by Neville Gosson, who had made his world circuit in 202 days. Neville had then sold the vessel to a new owner who had spent a lot of money to fair the hull and do a nice paint job. During a charter, according to the story, the yacht's backstay had somehow gotten in a tangle with a fishing boat, and the yacht was dismasted. The insurance company offered to pay for a new mast and two sails. The discouraged owner dropped the price.

Margaret and I hurried to Falmouth, Massachusetts, to see *Leda.* She turned out to have an extremely sturdy aluminum hull, a vast accommodation, and all sorts of winches and gear. Unfortunately, at fifty-three feet she was too large for the small class and too small for the large class. Because of her complex hull shape there was no way she could be either shortened or lengthened. She was an absolute icebreaker with a rumored displacement of 32,000 pounds (possibly more). Because of her weight and unfortunate size, we did not buy her.

Finally, on October 3rd, I telephoned Robert Clark in London and told him to go ahead with his design. Robert promised drawings in ten days. I was pleased to deal with him because I felt that with all his experience (he had designed 318 yachts) I would be in good hands. In addition, I knew that building in Europe had the advantage of a strong dollar and favorable exchange rates.

The race was to begin in less than eleven months. Already it was beginning to look as if there would be three races: one to find the money, a second to get the new yacht built in time, and a third to sail around the world and win the race.

. . . .

CHAPTER THREE

Europe

*T*o speed up things with Robert Clark, I decided to go to London. On the same trip I could stop in Paris to see Dominique Presles, a prominent French naval architect whom Claude Pittoors, a great sailing pal of mine, had been urging me to visit. I booked a cheap airline seat in New York, and eight hours later I was eating dinner at the London house of some old friends.

The next morning I walked down Oxford street to Robert's flat on Welbeck street. In person Robert looked like a tall distinguished senior politician, or a character from a John Le Carré spy novel. Robert was white-haired and very thin, a bit gaunt perhaps, because he had just lost twenty-one pounds from a bout with pneumonia in the hospital. Nevertheless he was keen to talk about the BOC design.

"I am convinced that my hull form is better and will be much faster than the others, particularly in downwind running," he said as we went over the design points one by one. He told me that before he retired he had had six draftsmen working for him. His former chief draftsman now lived in Amsterdam, and Robert traveled to Holland to use his old assistant whenever someone wanted a new Clark design. It seemed an incredible arrangement for a designer to travel to a foreign country to get a few drawings. Robert's hospital siege had slowed down everything, but he was leaving for Holland the next day and promised the plans in a few days. Meanwhile he had arranged for me to see a spar maker and several builders, each of whom Robert knew well.

During the next few days I traveled to the south of England. One morning I took the train to Emsworth, where I met John Powell, who showed me his shop and various masts and booms and gave me price quotations. He was pleasant and knowledgeable. I then called on various builders. First I went to Fairey, then Cougar Marine, and finally to Joyce Marine in Southampton, where Mark Joyce gave me a tour of a sixty-seven-foot Robert Clark design that he was building. The yacht was almost completed, and I looked at the hull with the greatest interest because my new vessel was supposed to be a smaller version. The big Clark yacht had a long overhang at the bow and also a long sloping counter stern. The workmanship was excellent, and the plating was extremely fair. I wondered how much waterline length was stolen from the overall length by the substantial overhangs.

No one was working in the Joyce shop so I presumed the owners would be anxious for a new project. Could they complete a stripped-out Clark design by April? Joyce shook his head. My first impression was that he was more interested in standing around the stove and keeping warm than in starting a new job.

"Why not hire a couple of men from among the many unemployed metalworkers here in Southampton?" I suggested. "The newspapers say there's a big employment slump."

"How would I know if they're any good?" asked Joyce doubtfully.

The next day I met Robert in London, fresh from Holland with plans. When I saw the drawings I gasped. The profile plan showed a hull that was quite different from the smaller, nicely balanced *Gipsy Moth V* hull that I had hoped for. I saw a strange hull with a long overhanging bow and a blunt, totally chopped-off stern. I immediately thought of a cat whose tail had been lopped off. The hull was not at all what I had expected, and I was sorely disappointed. I started to say something when I happened to glance at Robert, whose eyes were shining with pride. How could I—who in truth knew little about design—possibly say anything demeaning to this kind old man who was near eighty and suffering from acute leukemia?*

At Robert's insistence I took the plans to Joyce to see about an estimate. Since this would take a few days, I flew to Paris. My friend Claude Pittoors met me at Orly field. Claude had come from the south of France on the train so I rented a funny little French car and we stormed through Paris traffic to Courbevoie to see his sweet old mother (eighty-three), who had a whisky, a nice chicken dinner, and some soft beds waiting for us.

The next morning—October 21st—we drove to the studio of Domi-

* Robert Clark died on January 10, 1988.

nique Presles (pronounced *Prail*), who had designed two yachts for Claude. Dominique was slim, enthusiastic, and very bright. He was about forty or so and taught naval architecture at one of the Paris universities. His office was filled with sketches and photographs of his creations.

He soon produced drawings for *Skoiern IV*, the fifty-foot cutter that Jacques de Roux planned to enter in the BOC race. Dominique's plans and computer-generated perspective drawings of the hull were impressive. His vessel was two and a half tons lighter than Clark's and two meters longer on the waterline. We talked for two hours and went over every aspect of the yacht, particularly water ballast, which the French designer considered to be of the greatest importance. He was anxious for a second entry in the race and urged me to build from the same plans.

Dominque suggested that I look at *Skoiern IV*, which was under construction at the Garcia Brothers yard in Normandy. "It's one of the best yards in France," he said. Two hours later Claude and I were rushing through the beautiful green countryside, and we soon arrived at the boatyard, which was located next to a farm near a rural village.

The Garcia Brothers had two new hulls under construction in a big shed. Four other partially completed sailing yachts were outside. All looked smooth and sleek. The place was incredibly busy with overall-clad men on their hands and knees marking out templates on big sheets of shiny aluminum. Other men were adding new plates to partially built hulls. We saw men busy welding, clamping, measuring, hammering, and dragging scaffolding into position while they smoked one Gauloise cigarette after another. The place had a great feel of energy and movement and vigor, exactly the opposite of Joyce Marine in England.

The price for all the metal work (hull, deck, cabin, cockpit, keel, ballast, skeg, rudder, and tanks for fresh water, fuel oil, and salt water ballast) was 420,000 francs, or about $52,500 at the current exchange rate. The yard said it could deliver the completed hull at the end of February. This seemed like excellent value and timing, but Claude reminded me that the price did not include the interior cabin work, the mast and booms, rigging and winches, the engine installation, electrical parts and wiring, tank plumbing, sails, and architect's fee.

Back in Paris on the following day, I had another meeting with Dominique. His computer studies were like fairy stories come to life.

"I can predict hull performance for any sea state and any angle of heel," he said. "For example, suppose the wind is blowing twenty-five knots at seventy-five degrees off the bow." He typed in the commands on a keyboard. In a moment the moving hull of *Skoiern IV* appeared on a screen. Then waves in motion on an upset sea began to fill in. The result was a sort of continuous motion picture *("la cinéma commence")*. As the waves swept past, the hull rocked back and forth, pitching and yawing slightly. It was an incredible image, based entirely on mathematical concepts, and one that I couldn't keep from staring at with amazement.

"You should not forget water ballast," said Dominque. "My computer studies suggest a nineteen to twenty-one percent improvement."

This was a big number, and even if cut in half, it suggested a significant speed advantage.

Dominique's drawings called for a good deal of three-millimeter (one-eighth-inch) aluminum plating, which I thought was too light for the Southern ocean. When I asked him about this, he was very positive about the long life of his aluminum hulls.

"The plating that I specify is thin, but the underneath structures are closely spaced and well developed," he said. "I have used this scheme for many years, and the hulls are in perfect condition today."

Dominique looked at Clark's plans. "They're interesting relics from a bygone era," said Presles. "I have the greatest respect for Clark, but I thought he was long since dead."

I flew back to England. Robert was in the hospital again. Joyce gave me a quote of £69,200, which translated to $100,000. He said the work "should be complete by June 1st." This was too late, and even that date seemed doubtful. I needed an April 30th delivery. I had asked a second yard, Fairey Marine of Cowes, for a bid, and I got the same I-don't-want-to-work response. It seemed incredible that the British couldn't build a hull in six months when the French did it in three.

All kinds of ideas ran through my mind. I could cancel the arrangement with Clark, especially since the design was incomplete and I had reservations about the hull. I could go with Presles and get a very sleek, beamy, high-tech design.

That night, October 27th, as I flew to Boston and then went on to Maine, I reviewed my quest for a BOC yacht. So far I had looked at a number of used vessels. I had rejected the efforts of an American designer. Now I had two new proposals from Europe to think about. I was as confused as ever.

CHAPTER FOUR

The Nitty-Gritty

*M*y problem was not original. I needed money. Lots of it. Already I had spent $3,000 with one naval architect and $4,570 with a second. Plus a quick trip to Europe. Even doing things as cheaply as possible meant heavy expenses. For ocean racing, one certainly needed a rich uncle. I had been working hard for two months and so far I had no yacht at all. Not even the prospects of one!

Obviously the first order of business was to seek help. The America's Cup money-raising was in high gear and proving successful. Why not try the same techniques?

I sat down at my desk and prepared a complete fund-raising proposal. My first letter was aimed at mythical company X and described the race, its history, and what the competition meant in the way of personal initiative, daring, and high-tech sailing. I touched on the global aspects and the fact that the competitors would be from many countries. I told about the yacht that I planned to enter, and I summarized my sailing background. I explained briefly what the competition would cost and closed with a statement of why I thought I would win.

The second step in the proposal—the next letter in the package—outlined what a commercial sponsor would get out of the race. I began with a quick statistical summary that detailed the role of yachting in the recreational market (numbers of boats, people involved, money spent). Although I had named the new yacht *American Flag,* I offered to rename the vessel for a sponsor or sponsor's product. I told how the location and standing of each yacht would be known several times a day by a satellite position-finding device and how the BOC press office would send information and reports to the media. I described the hundreds of stories in newspapers and magazines that had been published in many countries during the previous BOC race and the books and films. I discussed the radio and television programs during the earlier race and the plans for greater coverage in the upcoming race. I told about an educational program in which tens of thousands of schoolchildren had followed individual competitors and had tied the race to studies in geography, oceanography, weather, international trade, world politics, and so on.

I made a detailed budget for the yacht and the costs of the race. I got two small drawings of my proposed yacht and a sailing photograph of my-self. I put together a one-page montage of a dozen press clips of the first race that ranged from the front page of the *New York Times* to *Sports Illustrated* magazine. On another page I listed eighteen major newspapers that had run stories about the last BOC race, together with a breakdown of column inches and readership. I named twenty-four corporations that had sponsored sailing events in the past. To round out these seven documents I added a small color brochure from the BOC that told of the challenge from the organizer's point of view.

I reviewed and edited what I had written until I thought it made an attractive, well-rounded package that no corporation head could refuse. I then asked several friends who were New York advertising executives for names of suitable corporate officers, and I mailed off a dozen packages, several with letters of introduction.

Meanwhile my telephone had been ringing off the hook with calls from yacht brokers who were positive they had found the perfect vessel for the race. I considered my choices to date:

1. *Swan 47.* Heavy at 32,000 pounds, but excellent for resale after the race. A big rig to handle to drive all the weight. Several for sale. One in poor condition would cost about $100,000. Plus repairs, paint, some rerigging, and new sails.
2. *Germán Frers custom 47* in aluminum. Somewhat a motorsailer. Heavy at 32,000 pounds, possibly more. She was ready for the race and would be good for eventual resale. Another big rig, but not as tall as the Swan. Some question about light-weather performance. Cost $150,000–175,000.
3. *Three international offshore rule (IOR) former racing boats* for sale at cheap prices; big conversion costs; doubtful futures. Cost $60,000–70,000 plus conversion. Weight around 24,000 pounds.
4. *A secondhand Santa Cruz 50,* the ultralight Bill Lee design. Cost

$150,000 plus substantial conversion costs. Displacement said to be 16,000 pounds.

5. *Clark 50.* Since I had the partially completed plans in my possession I asked for building estimates. I got a quotation from Maine yards of $343,000 in aluminum and $300,000 in fiberglass. A San Diego builder quoted $260,000 in aluminum. These prices were out of sight, and I was losing interest in the design since it was moderately heavy (24,500 pounds), not so long on the waterline (a little over 40 feet), and I didn't like the chopped-off look of the hull.

6. *Presles 50.* In my judgment the French design was the best and the price was good. The designer's estimate for the completed vessel ready for sea was $154,500. She would be all new and from a high-quality yard.

I thought hard about the Presles' design. She was a modern, high-tech vessel. Her displacement was 18,743 pounds, and she was almost forty-seven feet on the waterline. The building price was reasonable, and the design was by far the most advanced and seemed to me to stand the best chance of winning. She was attractive and eye-catching.

I telephoned Dominique Presles in Paris and prepared to go ahead with the building in Normandy. Besides money, another problem was how to complete the interior of the yacht and to deal with the mast, rigging, winches, sails, and finishing details. Obviously I would have to go to France to oversee this work, but I would be in a poor position since I had no language skills in nautical French. It would be hard to negotiate with suppliers and artisans, especially to get things done quickly at reduced prices if that became necessary. A foreigner buying complicated things is always at a disadvantage.

Why not put the completed hull on a truck and take it to England for completion? I discussed this with Dominique, who got a quotation for a truck and also a contract from the Garcia Brothers' yard.

"You must hurry," said Dominique on November 18th. "The job is large, and the time is short."

I did not have $150,000 for a new yacht, and I had heard nothing from the sponsorship proposals that I had sent out. Margaret and I mailed another dozen funding proposals to corporations while we debated what to do.

My wife was wonderfully supportive and keen for me to go ahead. "We'll find the money somewhere," she said. "I feel that if there's a thing that's really important to you, you must go ahead and do it. Otherwise you'll regret it for the rest of your life."

We had put our smaller yacht up for sale. We *could* use our savings as well, but both items together were hardly enough for the basic project. There would be nothing for completion costs and nothing at all for the race. We had enough nautical savvy to know that on a long ocean voyage you always needed an extra twenty-five percent for things that had been forgotten or unanticipated and for equipment that didn't work out.

Certainly in a country as rich as America, we believed, someone would want to sponsor us. I was sure I could give an advertiser a good return for his money. For a campaign that lasted ten months, I asked only for the cost of a thirty-second spot advertisement during a championship professional football game. All we had to find was the right company and a corporate executive with vision.

We sent out another dozen proposals to corporations. So far we had mailed out thirty-six solicitations.

"Why don't we appeal for private donations as well," I said to Margaret. "What we need is funding, private or corporate. We can always return private money if we find a corporate sponsor. The thing is to get money in the first place. We need help! And quickly!"

For private donors I substituted a new letter in place of the corporate funding letter. I offered to name the new vessel in honor of a private sponsor or his designee. I said that I would include the sponsor in sailing trials and in the social scene surrounding the race. I explained that I was an American sportsman who was keen to defeat the French, English, Japanese, and so on (I believe in flag-waving for international sporting events). Since the America's Cup funding was tax deductible, I began to look into the possibility of tax-deductible status for donations. I asked friends in corporate America for ideas and suggestions.

I gave a few talks about the race and what I was trying to do. From the feedback I began to realize that the idea of sailing around the world alone in a large, complicated yacht (and racing against twenty or thirty others) had a wonderful fascination for people. Especially elderly retired men, some of whom wistfully wished they were younger so they too could have entered the race. During these talks, however, I soon found out that I had to speak plainly and ask directly for money; otherwise people passively accepted my words and pictures (by now I had a few slides to show) as entertainment.

I had a lot of reservations about asking for money—something I had never done before—because it seemed like begging. There was a certain humiliation in the process that I didn't like. Most people said no. I could accept that because it was a simple black and white decision. Yes or no. However, there were wealthy people who would lead me on and on, talk nonstop about what they were going to do, and then give me nothing. I would be invited to their fancy houses to entertain their guests at large dinner parties. I would stand up and tell about the race, what I hoped to do, and answer questions. I would be kept dangling like a clown on a string. I hated such situations, which wasted an incredible amount of time, but like a blind newspaper seller I hardened my heart and persevered—and hoped for loose change from their millions.

I found out that the money of many wealthy people was invariably "tied up just now," but they had a friend "who would certainly help." I was told to "write a letter to so-and-so and give it to me." (Where, I wonder, did all those letters go?) I soon discovered that this was simply an unkind way of saying no.

Another class of zero people were those who promised me money, who made a big deal about it, and then never sent their check. I suppose a thick-skinned person might have gotten used to this sort of behavior, but I found it bitterly disappointing.[8]

Yet I don't want to carp unmercifully. Several well-off people helped me generously, for which I will always be grateful, but I had the most luck with ordinary working people, who seemed to understand what I was trying to do.

This all probably sounds like a bad case of sour grapes. Nevertheless, I had the greatest personal anguish with this aspect of private fund-raising. With hindsight I suppose I should have involved an intermediary. Yet this would have removed me from direct contact with possible donors and blunted my appeal.

I found that many people were intrigued with my passion to race around the world in a large yacht and could identify with me. Their smiles and encouragement were wonderful and somehow kept my spirits from collapsing. I received several small checks, then one for $500, one for $1,000, and then one for $1,000 from an elderly neighbor named Charlie Richardson, who began to take an enormous interest in the race. Charlie got fascinated with the whole thing and with the plans of the various yachts that I showed him. He introduced me to his friends and talked up my project. Several of them sent my proposals to wealthy friends. One thing led to another, and soon I was working all day long on fund-raising. I had to ignore my regular writing jobs. I learned that fund-raising was a hard, full-time job.

"What you need is a professional fund-raiser," said Charlie. "A person with contacts. You pay him a fee or a flat percentage and let him go. The arrangement is clean, neat, and efficient. How are you—the captain—ever going to get the yacht ready and do the race if you spend all your time hunting for money? I don't want you to turn into a banker. I want you to win the race."

As I was to find out, Charlie's observations were only too true.

I sent my prospectus to three fund-raising companies that dealt with major sports activities (car racing, football, baseball). Their replies said that my quest was outside the mainstream of their operations. Nevertheless I was commended on my presentation—which was encouraging. One company offered to hire me on a full-time basis! I met a fund-raiser in Oberlin, Ohio, who gave me some tips and leads.

I began to hear from some of the corporations I had approached. Most said no. Many declined because they had already given to the America's Cup campaign, and their advertising departments had lots of yachting material. (It was unfortunate that the America's Cup race coincided with the BOC race.) I studied each reply carefully and reshaped my funding proposal little by little. Other Americans who wanted to enter the race were also sending out proposals; the BOC competition had begun before the race. *Had the sailing race become a funding race?*

I gave my publisher an outline for a book about the race and arranged for a meeting in New York with him and a BOC official. I asked for an advance against royalties.

"I think entering the race like you're doing is wonderful," said my publisher. "I'm going to help you in every way that I can."

All these fund-raising activities delayed my response to Dominique Presles. One morning I woke up to read that the French franc–U.S. dollar exchange rate had declined substantially.

"Don't fret," said my banker. "It's probably only a temporary thing and will turn around in a day or two."

But the rate didn't turn around and instead began to drop steadily. In a little over a month the franc–dollar rate went from eight to one to seven to one, a decline of thirteen percent. This meant that just the rough hull of the French yacht would cost $8,000 more. The longer I delayed, the worse the currency exchange became. My French connection was collapsing. . . .

Meanwhile, on a cold December day, Margaret and I went to Plymouth, Massachusetts, where we looked at *Arieto,* a sleek forty-six-foot Germán Frers design with an impressive aluminum hull built by Palmer Johnson of Sturgeon Bay, Wisconsin. The yacht was nicely painted, an ex-IOR racer with masses of gear. Unfortunately, the interior was a gloomy shambles with mildewed lockers and ice on the cabin sole. The vessel had a big diesel engine that drove a hydraulic pump, which powered a hydraulic motor buried in the keel, which finally turned a shaft and propeller. All this rusty machinery was awkward and heavy and would have to be scrapped. *Arieto* had a new mast, but in my judgment it was too tall and spindly for the Southern ocean. Watertight bulkheads and water ballast tanks would have to be built, and the cockpit needed modifications. The IOR design had a thin, ribbon mainsail, which meant that the yacht sailed principally on her headsails. To get a bigger mainsail (and less headsail shifting) would require moving the mast forward, which conflicted with the water tanks. The whole project was marginal but might be possible if the vessel could be bought cheaply enough. . . .

In Beverly, Massachusetts, we looked at *Deja Vu,* a used Santa Cruz 50, the design of Bill Lee. It was the first time that I had seen an ultra-lightweight displacement boat (ULDB), and my breath came out in a gasp when I saw the hull out of the water. The Santa Cruz was simply a long skinny canoe body kept upright by a thin, wedge-shaped keel suspended from the center of the hull. A tiny spade rudder at the extreme end presumably controlled this boating torpedo. The concept was fascinating.

Everything possible had been done to reduce weight. The hull was made of balsa core with fiberglass inside and out, all put together with a high-tech system called vacuum bagging, which helped to ensure a uniform lamination and a proper resin-to-glass ratio. Instead of the usual heavy, traditional wooden interior fit for an icebreaker, the bulkheads and joinery were made of thin, high-quality Bruynzeel plywood that was carefully glassed in place. This resulted in a structure that was strong, yet extremely light. The interior reminded me of the British Mosquito bomber in World War II, which had also used innovative wood construction to make a light, tough structure. There were so many parallels with aircraft construction that I was tempted to call the hull a fuselage.

The Santa Cruz 50 was exciting to look at. I wondered how well she sailed. I thought that in light weather she might be a challenge for any of the BOC entries. What would the motion of her hull be like in a nasty sea out in the ocean? Would she track downwind or be wild and uncontrollable in big seas and gales? My common sense told me that the hull form was too extreme, too light. Yet my free spirit told me to go for it.

For a tough world voyage I had to be realistic. I shuddered at the thought of a giant cross-sea landing on top of the two dozen or more vulnerable hatches and portlights in the hull and deck structure. All these openings were wonderful for light and air on a downwind voyage from Los Angeles to Hawaii but not worth much in the Southern ocean. Most would have to be glassed shut, a big expense, and awkward to do with plywood already laminated on the inside. The mast was a three-spreader toothpick, new after the original mast had folded up in a local race when the yacht had broached under a spinnaker. If the mast were replaced, the rigging would have to be shortened and the sails re-cut. The cockpit was large and shallow, and anyone in it was at risk, it seemed to me. I worried about the spade rudder and whether the rudder stock would be strong enough. My list went on and on. Except for the rig height, however, I had no complaint about the design, only the construction details. If one had started from the beginning . . .

I had to make a decision. Probably the smartest thing was to forget the BOC race entirely. The Presles 50 was getting more expensive (and distant) every day. Deja Vu's big price plus all the modifications added up to an impossible total. Finally in despair I bid $67,000—subject to survey—for Arieto (the asking price was $210,000). The owner agreed, but he wanted to keep the mast, which was okay. Since the yacht had been made to a high specification by a prominent builder who no doubt would like publicity, I got the idea of getting the builder involved. I telephoned the people at Palmer Johnson in Wisconsin, told them about the race, and followed up with drawings and a seven-page proposal of the changes. I even made a little cardboard model of a new cockpit. Palmer Johnson was sympathetic, and talked a great game, but offered little of substance. In the meantime I went over *Arieto* with a surveyor, who found more problems. I withdrew my offer.

Sometimes in life one makes decisions based on the slightest nudges. You may be teetering on the edge of a doing this or that, you may be agonizing over things or events that are of great urgency or importance when a friend or an acquaintance or someone you hardly know says something that pushes you one way or another.

I think of the story of Ernesto Uriburu, who was walking down a street in Philadelphia when he saw a small ship's compass in the window of a store. Ernesto glanced at the compass in passing and then went back for a second look. Then a third look. Exasperated at himself, he finally walked into the

While considering the Palmer Johnson Frers 46, I made a little cardboard model to work out the cockpit changes.

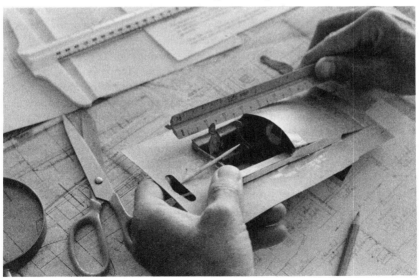

store, bought the compass, and then had to build an enormous yacht to take the compass. The yacht launched Ernesto into a whole new career of adventure and travel.

"If it hadn't been for that stupid compass, my life would have been calm and tranquil," said Ernesto years later. "Why was it that I walked down that street that I had never walked down before? Why did I look in the window of that store that I had never seen before?"

Three days before Christmas I was still wondering what to do about the BOC race when I happened to thumb through a new magazine called *Sailor*. On the inside front cover was a full-page color photograph of a J-41 racing sloop named *Smiles*. Various–sized J-boats were the products of the Johnstone brothers and had been quite successful as racing boats because they were well designed and had fast hulls. I wondered if the Johnstones had a larger model, something secondhand, or any ideas about a BOC entry. I telephoned Bob Johnstone, and we had a long talk. Bob was keen for an American to win the BOC race.

"Our stuff is really too small," he said. "What you must get is a fast hull. Not one with all kinds of hull distortions because of the stupid racing rules.

"The only really fast hull in a fifty-foot length for which tooling exists in the United States is a Santa Cruz 50," said Bob. "Call up Bill Lee and see what you can work out."

I telephoned Bill Lee. "What can I get for $100,000?" I asked. "Instead of rehashing an old boat, let's have something new."

"It may be possible by April if we start at once," said Bill. "We will have to leave a few things off. If you can get the rig, sails, electronics, radios, and winches donated, I can supply the yacht."

On the day after Christmas I flew to California, where a friend named David Allen picked me up and took me to Lee's shop. In person Bill Lee was a short, peppery, brainy man of few words. He was totally committed to a life of yacht racing, and together with about fifteen employees built boats in several old chicken sheds in the small town of Soquel in the Santa Cruz foothills. I learned that Lee was the best-known advocate of ULDBs, which had a marvelous reputation for downwind performance. ("Downwind sleds," they were called.) Lee's designs rated badly in IOR contests, but he and his disciples entered all the races anyway and usually finished hours, sometimes days, ahead of the competition. On corrected time the ULDBs generally finished last, but Lee didn't care. He was a sailing speed fanatic, and he was positive and upbeat. Since the BOC was a non-IOR race, one of his yachts might do well.

"I can offer you a super new boat with watertight bulkheads and a simplified interior," said Lee. "For where you're going we'll put in extra layers of fiberglass, ring frames, and longitudinal stiffeners. For the hull we'll

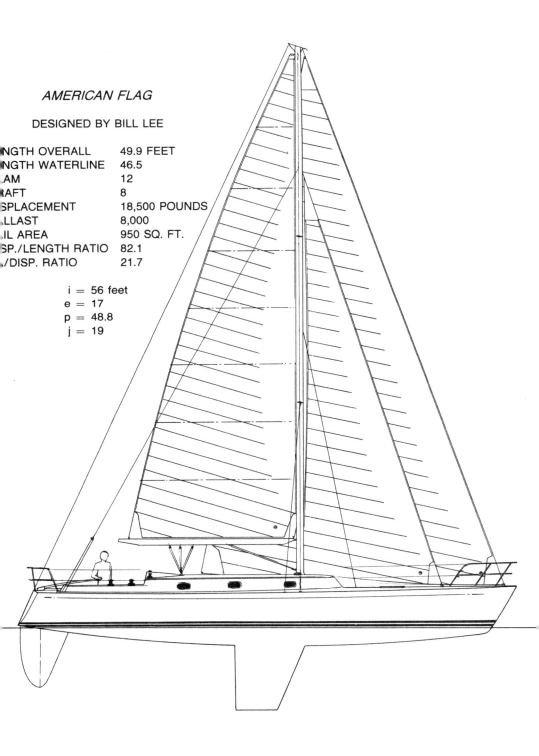

AMERICAN FLAG

DESIGNED BY BILL LEE

NGTH OVERALL	49.9 FEET
NGTH WATERLINE	46.5
AM	12
RAFT	8
SPLACEMENT	18,500 POUNDS
LLAST	8,000
IL AREA	950 SQ. FT.
SP./LENGTH RATIO	82.1
/DISP. RATIO	21.7

$i = 56$ feet
$e = 17$
$p = 48.8$
$j = 19$

go to one-inch balsa core instead of three-quarters. For the deck and coach-roof we'll use three-quarters instead of half-inch."

He took me for a sail in a Santa Cruz 50. There was little wind, but I got a chance to evaluate the cockpit (too shallow); wheel steering (I was used to a tiller and liked its simplicity); and rig height (come down five feet). During my three-day visit we discussed a hundred things, including a cockpit shelter (Lee was against it), a cockpit well (ditto), and a skeg to reinforce the rudder ("we'll talk about it").

Back in Maine I showed the drawings of *American Flag* to Margaret and our friends. My neighbor Charlie was ecstatic and in a burst of enthusiasm pledged $25,000. ("Don't tell my wife just yet," he whispered. "I'll break it to her gradually.") We had had a few nibbles from corporations. On January 8th I ordered the new yacht from Bill Lee. He said she would be completed on May 3rd—in 115 days. The search was over.

. . . .

CHAPTER FIVE

One Hundred
and Twelve Days

Now that the new yacht was underway I relaxed a bit and turned my attention to my regular job. After all, I had to make a living. Of course, I couldn't forget the fund-raising. I also had to order all the new gear for *American Flag*.

When the BOC race was announced, five hundred people wrote for a copy of the rules. The entry fee was a whopping $5,000 for sponsored yachts and $2,500 for private vessels. I could hardly believe these sums; obviously I was getting into the big leagues. I felt a little better when I found out that the Argos transmitter—the satellite position-finding device—cost the race organizer more than $5,000 for each vessel. I was to learn that it was of the greatest importance for the contestants to know the daily positions of the other yachts so that each sailor could gauge his progress and standing, and to evaluate the sailing tactics of his competitors. Additionally, it was important to be aware of the positions of the others in case another yacht got into trouble and needed assistance.

The closing date for entries was January 1, 1986. By then each captain had to send in $500 (the remainder by May 31st). According to a press release, fifty-four contestants from twelve countries had paid their preliminary fees. The list included two women—one from France and the other from Switzerland. The United States had twenty-two entries. Eleven sailors had signed up from France, Australia had five, England four, and the rest were from eight other countries. Thirty-seven yachts were actually afloat or in advanced stages of building. Only eleven of the fifty-four captains were sponsored; the others were either privately funded or—like me—were out looking for money.

One of the fifty-four captains was Dick Cross, who was also from Maine—in fact, from Mt. Desert island, where I lived. Dick was building a sleek-looking forty-six-foot high-flier called *Airforce* designed by a local naval architect named Art Paine. The yacht had a nicely curved sheer line and was constructed of laminated wood with varnished topsides and teak decks. She was certainly a candidate for the prettiest yacht in the race. Dick had begun a year earlier and had his vessel well along toward completion. He was extremely enthusiastic about the race and was working hard to find a sponsor. Dick was rumored to have the help of his wealthy mother and had surrounded himself with an eager crowd of carpenters and helpers. He hired public relations experts and had several elaborate press conferences with catered food, television coverage, and guest speakers. I had met Dick a few years earlier when he was just learning to sail, and I had some reservations about his experience. Nevertheless, I envied his progress and wished him well.

I hired Art Paine for a few days to draw a modified sail plan for *American Flag*. I had decided to lop off four and a half feet from the sixty-five foot mast used in the light-weather California conditions. After considering advice from Skip Allen in California, who had a lot of sailing experience in Santa Cruz 50s, I decided to use just three headsails:

1. Staysail (9.5 oz. Dacron) of 292 sq. ft. for heavy weather and intricate tacking. To be set on the midstay.
2. Yankee (7.5 oz. Dacron) of 565 sq. ft. for average winds.
3. Light-weather genoa (3.2 oz. Mylar-Dacron) of 915 sq. ft.
4. Mainsail (9.25 oz. Dacron) of 414 sq. ft. with three reefs and seven full-length battens.
5. Spinnaker (¾ oz. nylon) of 1,890 sq. ft.
6. Trysail (9.5 oz. Dacron) of 132 sq. ft.
7. I already owned a small storm jib and could borrow a second. Their areas were 75 and 125 sq. ft. I would fly both on the midstay.

I planned to order two of everything except the storm trysail and the storm jibs. (I owned one and borrowed the second.) This would give me a set of spares for all but the storm sails (with three I hoped I was well covered). The spare mainsail would have four short battens. In all, I would have thirteen sails on board.

I put together a specification sheet for eleven sails and sent it to nine sailmakers. Calls came immediately. Everyone, it seemed, wanted to make sails for the BOC race. And everyone, it turned out, had unique knowledge and skill. The quotes for eleven sails ranged from $18,850 to $38,482, with an average of $30,334. Discounts were possible, it was hinted, if I placed my order. For convenience, and to help local business, I preferred to use a Maine sailmaker, but when I talked about a fully battened mainsail, the eyes of the man I spoke with glazed up as if he were looking at a distant, unconquered mountain. After a lot of talking and thinking, I decided to buy North Sails.

North Sail's operation in Connecticut was big-time. In the old days sailmakers worked on their knees in tiny lofts and stuck dozens of ice picks in the floor to hold the material while it was being put together. I remember how the men grumbled when they had to get up to answer the telephone. In contrast, the North Sails loft was housed in a new 26,500 sq. ft. million-dollar building with fifty people and a sailmaking floor that measured 125 x 150 feet. The Connecticut loft was one of twenty-eight lofts which shared eight brainy designers and dozens of carefully devised programs stored on computer discs. The designers considered themselves toolmakers who fed their instructions into computers, which actuated long cutting arms (a two-inch air-driven wheel did the actual cutting) that swept back and forth on hundred-foot tables. A technician spread out and inspected a roll of cloth (Dacron, Kevlar, Mylar, or nylon) from a selection of dozens of weights and qualities and punched a few buttons. Suddenly the tiny wheel began to cut out the complex arcs quickly and cleanly. It was magic.

I watched a young woman number each triangular panel as it was sliced into shape. After the twenty or thirty panels were cut, they were tacked together with double sticky-back tape and ready for sewing. The stitcher sat in a recess in the floor so that the table of his (or her) machine was even with the floor which supported the sail and made it easy to sew. The stitchers sewed almost faster than I could watch and made pass after pass of neat zigzag lock stitches. Edge tablings, bolt ropes, reef patches, plastic windows, numbers, and various reinforcements were then sewed in place before the sail was passed on to the finishers, who knocked on hanks, sewed on leather chafe patches, and used a twenty-ton hydraulic press to put in stainless steel grommets.

What impressed me was the speed at which all this was done. The loft reminded me of a hospital. The cloth-cutting tables were the operating rooms, and the cutters, stitchers, and finishers were the surgeons who changed the cloth into new forms following the doctors' orders on the computer programs. When an old sail came in or one that needed changes, it was stretched out on the floor and its troubles diagnosed and remedies prescribed. The capital investment was high, but the yearly production was high, too. To me the miracle of the place were the computer-directed cutting wheels that worked unceasingly and never stopped zipping out the pie-shaped pieces of fabric. It was all a long way from those men on their knees. . . .

As a class the workers were young, thin, intense, nervous, mostly fast-walking intellectual types. They appeared to like their work, many drove new cars, and some flew tens of thousands of miles each year to check the performance of their sails on yachts in distant races and regattas. The pleasant manager, Bill Bergantz, gave me a favorable quotation, offered to go sailing with me to check the sails, and spoke of warranty service in lofts in Cape Town and Sydney.

I turned from sails to high finance. My neighbor Charlie Richardson was willing to make his contribution, but his accountant said that it would be easier if it were tax deductible. "Was this possible?"

I went to see a local attorney about setting up a nonprofit foundation with the Internal Revenue Service. The attorney thought that a foundation similar to the Olympic sailing foundation could be established because I merely wanted to compete in an international sporting event and not make any money from the *American Flag* effort. The attorney sent letters and affidavits to Washington and told me that the matter was underway.

I had to decide on the number and sizes of winches and on my require-ments for line (for sheets, halyards, anchor warps, guys, pendants, tackles, and so on). I had to purchase forty blocks of various types. I needed epoxy, polyester resin, bottom paint, and varnish. The race rules required radios (portable, short-range, and long-range). I had to buy an antenna coupler, sailing instruments, and an off-course alarm. On my lists were a compass (plus a second compass corrected for dip in the Southern hemisphere), an autopilot (and spare), and a wind-vane steering device, plus extra parts. The rules called for a liferaft, a ditch kit (emergency food and supplies to go with the liferaft), and an assortment of flares. I ordered 650 feet of eight-millimeter rigging wire and two dozen wire end fittings. *American Flag* needed both a cooking stove and an oil heating stove, spare parts for the engine, nautical charts, and pilot books.

I telephoned manufacturers, suppliers, and importers and asked for a donation of marine equipment for this special race (publicity means sales). If this failed I asked for the equipment at cost or at a small markup. Generally this was possible, but it was necessary to speak or write to the manager or head of the company and describe the project, what I could offer, and what I wanted. Fortunately, some of these people had read my books. A few firms were anxious for me to use their equipment and called again and again. Sometimes introductions worked wonders; other times I struck out com-pletely. My telephone bills suddenly rose to $400 a month.

Bill Lee called with a list of questions. He had spoken of a "much faster keel." When it got down to a decision, however, it turned out that this keel had never been built or tried. In addition, there was the unsolved engineering problem of how to fasten an extremely thin keel to the hull.

"How much faster is your new keel?" I asked.

"Considerably faster," said Bill.

"What does that mean?" I asked. "Ten percent? Five percent or what?"

"Oh nothing like that," said Bill. "I would say maybe one or two percent."

"Do you know positively that it will be faster?" I asked.

"Well, we don't really," said Bill. "No one knows, but we think it will be faster."

"So it could be one or two percent faster," I said. "How do you know it won't be one or two percent slower?"

"That's a possibility."

I decided to use the standard Santa Cruz 50 keel, which had worked well on the previous twenty-seven yachts. This keel was bolted to a stout, hollow fiberglass stub keel which ensured ample bilge area for drainage inside the hull. Lee fastened the keel in place with fourteen one-inch stainless steel bolts, and in addition he fiberglassed the entire keel with a thick encasement of glass. I was told that the fiberglass was strong enough to hold the keel without the bolts and that the bolts could hold the keel without the fiberglass. I liked this scheme because it gave me two ways of holding the 8,000 pounds of lead—my sole source of stability—in place. In the previous BOC race, the keel on Tony Lush's vessel began to crack off in the middle of the Indian ocean. Tony abandoned his yacht and was lucky to have been rescued by another competitor.

Bill Lee and I decided to build a skeg—a kind of permanent fixed rudder—in front of the regular rudder. The skeg would help downwind tracking, and would add to the strength of the rudder assembly. This change would mean an unbalanced, barn door movable rudder behind the skeg, but I hoped this would not be a problem. I was also keen for a fiberglass cockpit dodger and a foot well in the floor of the cockpit. Lee didn't like either idea ("I don't have the time and you don't have the money"), but he agreed to build them.

I was beginning to feel signs of panic because of the money I was spending on the *American Flag* effort. By the end of January I had sent Lee $70,000. I reduced the price of my old yacht, and the broker agreed to run advertisements. I had managed to get some equipment donated to the project, but I had to spend significant sums to buy necessary items when they were available at reduced costs.

I was supposed to be writing a book, but the BOC project was taking all my time. I spent my days ordering equipment (I had to decide between competing brands), asking for donations of marine equipment, sending out funding proposals, talking with the builder, and thinking about the race itself. Margaret made a provisional track chart of my route, collected a stack of pilot charts and pilot books, and began to study them to see what sort of wind strengths and directions I was likely to encounter.

As the construction progressed on *American Flag,* Bill Lee mailed me photographs. I had copies made and sent them out with funding proposals. I gave a few talks about the BOC race to various groups and met people who offered to write personal letters to corporate friends.

"But we've already given to the America's Cup program," was the usual response.

I learned that sponsorship of a yacht in an international sailing event was practically unheard of in corporate America. My arguments may have been slick, but the proven results of professional golf, baseball, football, basketball, and auto racing were hard to combat. One advertising man was more blunt. His words revealed a hard-boiled aspect of corporate America that I had never considered.

"If one of you sailors got into trouble and there was a dramatic rescue or collision or some big episode involving death or possible death, then we'd be interested. It would even be better if you were a beautiful young woman with long blond hair. Gladiator sports always have the most spectators. People like blood or near blood. Look at what happens when a child falls down an abandoned well and rescuers begin to dig out the child. The whole country holds its breath. That's the kind of excitement an advertiser wants. Our business return is based on a certain percentage of viewers' responses, so the more watchers the better. A race that lasts nine months is far too slow. We want all the action in an hour or two."

"The best and most skillful sailors try to stay out of trouble," I replied, no doubt the wrong thing to say. "I'm not going in this race to get killed, but for the adventure of a long, high-speed competition. I'm willing to exhibit your corporate logo or product before millions of people over a long period. I think that's an attractive offer."

I was still getting equipment for *American Flag*. I bought rigging turnbuckles, a backstay adjuster, a boom vang, mast steps, and special foul weather clothing. I got a hand-bearing compass, an inflatable dinghy, and spare galley pumps. The Bayley company in California donated an exposure suit, and a local medical supply outfit gave me a first aid kit. Although I hadn't even seen the new yacht yet, the pace was getting faster.

In early March I flew to California and hurried out to Bill Lee's shop in Soquel. When I walked in the door I was startled to see the white hull of *American Flag* propped up in the middle of the shop. She looked sleek and beautiful. The hull looked extremely fair, and the gel coat sparkled. Already the bulkheads and some of the interior furniture were in place. The deck molding—with its deepened cockpit well and oval entrance door—was propped up on stands next to the hull.

Two carpenters were installing interior woodwork. I was just in time to stop an aluminum bilge pump from going in (I had specified bronze), and I saw at once that the galley arrangement did not follow my plan (neither the carpenter nor the shop foreman had seen my drawings, which I had sent a month earlier). I had expected minor problems, of course, and this is why I went to California.

But even a skinny fifty-footer seemed big! Would I be up to sailing such a vessel? Bill Lee and I went over the budget and the schedule and discussed equipment. The next morning I ordered a stove, thirty-inch three-wire stanchions (for lifelines), and arranged for a clean-out plate in the diesel tank. We discussed the shape of the fiberglass cockpit dodger. I went to a local sparmaker named Buz Ballenger and bought a mast section two sizes larger than the normal Santa Cruz spar. Buz and I reviewed every detail of the mast, boom, spinnaker poles, and emergency rudder. I went back to the shop for a final look at *American Flag* and had a pleasant talk with one of the laminators who had worked on the hull. He told me that the laminating job was out-standing, the core matching perfect, and that he had never seen a stronger hull. He was all excited about the boat and the race and wished me good luck. Meeting him and sharing his enthusiasm was the nicest part of my California trip, and when I climbed back on the airplane for the flight to Boston, I had good feelings about the project. We would have to succeed!

Back in Maine I heard at once from my neighbor Charlie. "What about the tax-exempt status?"

I telephoned my attorney, who was out of his mind with frustration. I learned that the original application and affidavits sent to the Internal Revenue Service had never arrived. The attorney had sent a second set which also failed to reach the target. He had then sent *a third set* by registered mail. This parcel also disappeared—*registry and all*—into the IRS bureaucratic cesspool. So far the IRS bungling had cost me three months' time. I finally personally carried a *fourth* set to the IRS office in Brooklyn, New York, where I spent two hours with the head of the tax-exempt division. I was assured that my case would receive priority attention, and I got all sorts of apologies for the missing papers, "which are probably here somewhere." My attorney and I followed up on a daily telephone basis only to learn that the case had been transferred to Washington.

We began with a new set of officials, who threw one delaying block after another. Finally, I sent my attorney to Washington, where he was given assurances. . . . Still later we were told of a review procedure. By this time I was so fed up with red tape, blunders, delaying tactics, timid officials, and outright liars that I was ready to emigrate to Paraguay. How, I wondered, could a mere sailor be involved in all this?

I began to realize that I should have employed a Washington attorney who was familiar with the system. These delays had not only cost me time, travel, and fees, but had stopped the donations that I so desperately needed. I could have used tax-free foundations that already existed, but I hesitated because I thought a single dedicated foundation named for the *American Flag* project would be more direct and meaningful to donors.

In mid-April I got three high-level introductions for corporate sponsorship: I talked to Procter & Gamble; a friend arranged for me to give my presentation to Coca-Cola in Atlanta; and I spoke with the Adidas representative in New Jersey. I was working on the private sector as well. A neighbor, Lee Freedman, gave me a check and sent my proposals to ten wealthy friends. The local yacht clubs agreed to have a joint fund-raising drive for *American Flag* and *Airforce,* the two BOC entries from Mt. Desert island.

By April 25th I had received $5,600 in private contributions, which helped a little with the final payment for *American Flag,* which was almost ready for shipment. My personal funds were gone, and I owed a lot of bills. I went to see my friendly banker.

That night I gave a talk in the town of Southwest Harbor and showed the latest photographs from California. I met Fos Whitlock, a retired chief executive and sailing enthusiast who was intrigued with the concept of the race. He gave me $1,000 and pledged more.

My friend Charlie was there and excitedly talked up the race. "Let's see those pictures!" he said when he met me. Dear old Charlie was a good supporter and fervently wished that he could have sailed in such a race when he was younger.

Late that night Charlie had a very severe stroke which effectively ended his active life. I wept when I realized I would no longer have his cheerful encouragement. Charlie's $25,000 was gone too.

. . . .

CHAPTER SIX

Florida and Beyond

My long-time sailing friend Read Branch lived in Lighthouse Point, Florida, and invited me to fit out *American Flag* at the dock behind his house. Not only did Read offer his dock, but he kindly volunteered to pitch in and help with the project. Nearby Ft. Lauderdale was a particularly good area for marine supplies and services, and the May temperatures in Florida were ideal for painting.

Bill Lee completed the yacht three days ahead of schedule, and she was immediately trucked eastward. Meanwhile Margaret and I rented a small truck in Maine and filled it to overflowing with:

anchors	compasses	linens	pilot books
blankets	cutlery	logs	plumbing parts
buckets	dishes	medical kits	pots and pans
catalogs	epoxy	navigation books	sail repair items
charts	fenders	nuts and bolts	sextants
clothing	fiberglass	pillows	tools

We also took all the BOC files, stationery, a typewriter, and my word processor, printer, and paper. In early May the giant truck-trailer with *American Flag* neared Florida while Margaret and I in our rented truck rushed south from Maine. The yacht and her sixty-foot mast got to the boatyard the day before us, and when we arrived at Read's house we heard all about the great white racing machine.

Newcomers to sailing blithely think that you can buy a new yacht, step aboard with a few bags of groceries, and sail off somewhere. Nothing is further from reality. A seagoing vessel is a tiny, self-contained city and must be complete in a thousand ways. There are no supermarkets or hardware stores at sea; you have to take everything with you; otherwise you must do without or improvise. You need everything from toothpaste to diesel engine injectors, from sail needles to antibiotic ear drops, from half a dozen sizes of dry cell batteries to spare sunglasses, from a garlic press to extra rigging turnbuckles. Not only do you need masses of stuff, but it must be stowed so that it will be dry and protected, and someplace where you can find it quickly.

It was now the second week of May. We had to be in Newport, Rhode Island on August 16th to be inspected for the race, a date just twelve weeks away. Not only did we have to step the mast and completely rig the yacht, but we had to deal with the bottom of the hull, complete the interior, fit the autopilot and self-steering gear, mount all the winches, and do five hundred large and small jobs. I was well aware that some equipment would probably not work out and would require changes and further testing.

Every entrant in the BOC race had to complete a 2,000-mile single-handed transoceanic qualifying voyage. In most cases the foreign competitors sailing to Newport were able to use this trip as their qualifying run. The race committee was adamant that U.S. entrants on the east coast of the United States had to sail either to or from the Portuguese Azores in the eastern Atlantic. I planned to sail to the Azores with Margaret, who could help me shake down the new yacht, and then make the trip from Horta to Newport by myself. From Florida to Horta and thence to Newport was roughly five thousand miles. If I reckoned three weeks each way, plus a few days in Horta to deal with problems, the twelve weeks suddenly shrunk to six. It was important to sail back to Maine (say between August 1 and 15) to show the yacht to the people who were helping me and to visit Charlie in the hospital. If I reckoned to reach Newport at the end of July, I would have to leave Florida for Horta by June 15th, a date that was only about four weeks away. Was it possible to get a new fifty-footer ready for sea in a month?

Margaret, Read, and I started to work. We bolted on the pulpits, rigged the lifelines, and mounted the spreaders on the mast. I hired a carpenter to build tool drawers under the chart table, to mount insulation and thin stainless steel sheeting around the oil heating stove, and to do various other jobs. Unfortunately, the mast was slightly damaged during the transit trip, so we had to get a welder to repair a chafed area and to put a couple of guard rods around the steaming light. The welder and I used blind rivets to secure the mast wiring conduit that had broken loose.

We arranged for the bottom of the hull to be lightly sand-blasted ("dust-blasted") to remove road grease and mold wax, and then we rolled a first coat of special epoxy over the clean bottom. The dust blasting had exposed many pin holes in the fiberglass so Read rushed around with thick epoxy and a spatula filling the tiny holes. We repaired a few places, sanded down various small lumps and bumps, and under the eyes of Flip Thomsen from U.S. Paint we rolled on two additional coats of epoxy and then put on three coats of blue Awl-Grip copper paint.

In between the coats of paint, which soon dried under the hot Florida sun, Read and I began to cut the rigging wires to length and to put on the Sta-Lok wire end fittings. We hired a sign painter to letter the name and hailing port on the transom and our race number (7) on the deck and hull. Read fished various wires up the mast conduit while I put on the Fleming steering vane. Our carpenter turned out to be a dud so I let him go. Margaret and I bolted on the big cockpit winches and mooring cleats. Read began to install the autopilot. On May 24th I mailed the rest of my BOC entry fee (we heard that thirty-five sailors had paid their final fee; unfortunately, the two women dropped out). Finally on the 27th, *American Flag* was lowered into the water and her mast stepped and shakily secured with a few wires and lines. Sheldon Lake, who ran River Bend Marine, kindly reduced his yard bill when I explained what I was trying to do.

Our little three-cylinder Yanmar diesel astonished everyone by starting

Interior arrangements of *American Flag*

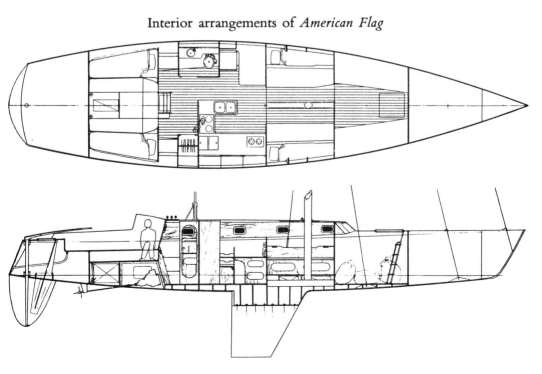

instantly, and we steamed down the New river to the Intracoastal waterway and then to Read's house at Lighthouse Point, where work was much more convenient. Jodie and little Kate—Read's wife and daughter—were glad to see *American Flag* at last. We found a good carpenter, Bill Bradley, a 6'8" giant of a man (his company was called Poverty Yacht Service, Inc., just what we needed) who set to work on a dozen small projects in the cabin. Bill Owra of Everfair Enterprises brought over two enormous twelve-volt storage batteries and loaned me a transom-mounted water-driven charging device for emergency electrical power. Six big sails bags arrived one morning, and finally the main boom came.

I began to get phone calls from the Florida Excise Tax Board, which claimed that I owed $7,000 sales tax on *American Flag*. I felt strongly that Florida had no right to claim the tax since I was a resident of another state and merely in transit so I began to fence verbally with the collector and played for time, especially since I didn't have the money for what I thought was an unjustified levy.

At night, and whenever we could find a few hours, we worked on fund-raising. By the third week in May we had sent out our sixty-seventh corporate proposal. Each had gone out with eight short documents and a personal letter. So far all we had received were polite letters of refusal, mostly written by second-echelon people. How could I motivate a big advertiser to build a campaign around a yacht race? I had the feeling that my corporate targets classified me with mountain climbers, archers, bowlers, pistol shooters, dog fanciers, chess players, and other small-time sportsmen. How could I convince a corporate sponsor that round-the-world yacht racing was big-time stuff?

The private fund-raising was doing a bit better: a few hundred dollars were trickling in, and we had indications of more. The Maine attorney called to say that the IRS was close to approving the tax-exempt foundation. I received $300 for a talk at a local yacht club.

Our heavy telephone schedule continued from Florida. Every day I spoke to manufacturers and importers in my quest for equipment and information, and there were always a dozen things to order. The UPS and Federal Express drivers soon knew *American Flag* well. North Sails had second thoughts about the fully-battened mainsail (which we had not even looked at) and told us to send it back for changes. I was impressed by such conscientiousness.

A miraculous and wonderful part of the BOC race were the volunteer workers. Whenever I gave a talk or there was an article in the newspaper, someone came down and offered to work on the yacht for free for a few days or longer. Somehow the concept of a singlehanded round-the-world competition grabbed people's attention.

"I know that I can never take part in such a race, but I would like to do what I can," were words that I heard again and again. Highly paid experts magically appeared and offered to work for nothing or at greatly reduced rates. People with limited skills volunteered to do drudgery jobs. Sailing enthusiasts gave us things—anchors, canvas bags, snatch blocks, a bilge pump. I can only explain this phenomenon by suggesting that it was the appeal of the little guy against the wild and unknown sea that intrigued people. *They wanted to help, and their assistance was wonderful. Without their strong right arms I could never have gotten* American Flag *ready for sea.*

On June 7th we were all in high gear and in great spirits. Read was on the dock assembling the Harken roller furling gear for the headstay. I was putting fittings on the ends of the standing rigging wire. Bill Bradley was in the bilge installing boxes to hold the big batteries. Two volunteers were hammering away in the forward cabin, and someone was bolting a plywood doubler on the inside of the transom to beef up the vane gear mounting. Margaret and a volunteer were bedding down the fiberglass cockpit dodger. Jody was in the house making lunch for the gang.

It was not all easy. The gear for the midstay and baby stay had not been installed on deck, and Read and I discovered that the underneath hull fittings for the below-deck rods that tied the deck plates to the hull had been put in the wrong places. I had to chisel off these fittings and glass them in new positions. The rigging company advised us to mount the deck fittings in line with the stays. This required teak wedges, which made the U-bolts too short. We had to have stainless steel extenders specially machined. When we ordered the tie rods from the rigging company we were sent the wrong lengths (twice).

We ran drain lines from the watertight compartments to the central bilge area, and I spent a day improving the Edson bilge pump mounting. When Margaret tried to fill the water tanks she discovered that the tanks had no air vents, which gave us something else to do. But little by little *American Flag* went together; gradually we replaced the temporary Dacron standing rigging with new stainless steel wires. One day we bent on three beautiful new sails.

By this time Margaret was in high gear putting food aboard for both the qualifying trip and the race. I mounted coachroof tracks for the staysail sheet blocks and began to work out the mainsheet arrangement. Read and a volunteer tried to mount the emergency rudder (which fitted on a track on the transom) only to discover that it floated and was impossible to use. I thought of lead weights, but Read cleverly took a hole saw and cut two big openings in the bottom of the rudder so that it would fill with seawater and sink into position.

Finally on June 24th, after forty-two days of nonstop work and many frustrations, but with a miraculous amount of work done, we simply had to leave for the qualifying trip. Already it was very late. Would I make the race deadline? When I shook Read's hand and kissed Jody goodbye and thanked the Branches for their hospitality and help, they graciously said they had enjoyed our stay and planned to meet us in Newport before the race. They took their Zodiac dinghy and led us out the narrow channel next to their house. Margaret and I stopped for diesel fuel and then steamed out of Hillsborough inlet into the Atlantic.

American Flag's sails had never been hoisted except at the dock so it was a thrill to put them up and to feel the yacht begin to move under her own power. I was delighted how we sped along, and I stood luxuriating in the cockpit under the warm sun with the breeze on my cheek and the tiller snug in my hand.

When I tried the autopilot, however, the yacht immediately gybed and began to go in the wrong direction. Were the compass wires hooked up backward? Margaret steered while I changed the connections. We tried it again. Yes, the autopilot was working. We stayed headed in the right direction. Marvelous!

The only problem that I couldn't handle was an incredible grinding and squeaking noise that came from the mechanical boom vang, a device (made by the Hall Spar company) used to control the main boom. Neither Margaret nor I could stand the terrible noise, and for us to be able to sleep I had to disconnect the vang and substitute two simple Schaefer rope tackles.

We were exhausted after the strain of the previous weeks and staggered around the decks like zombies for a few days until we had our fill of sleep and food. Fortunately the summer winds and seas were light, and once clear of the Bahamas the navigation was simple.

"Should we skip the race and head for Tahiti again?" I said.

Margaret gave me a big wink and pointed east toward the Azores.

There seemed to be hundreds of small jobs to do on *American Flag*. The mainsheet arrangement needed minor improvements, and I had to move the steering compass so that it was easier to read. I mounted and streamed the Walker log and arranged a preventer line on the main boom that was simple to set and stow. The new standing rigging wire was as loose as a scarecrow's arms so I tightened each shroud and stay. To do this I needed three sizes of cotter pins, but I couldn't find them in the ship's hardware drawer, which was all mixed up. I began by sorting out all the nuts and bolts and screws and washers and putting labels on each bottle and can. Then I straightened out all the tools so I could find a certain wrench or file or screwdriver quickly.

Meanwhile Margaret got out a sextant and took a couple of sun sights to work out our position. On the second day a four-engined U.S. navy Orion plane with its number-one propeller feathered made six passes over us. Since we had no radios on board I could only assume that we were a handy target for practice approaches. I hoped no one wanted to be rescued.

The trip to Faial in the Azores was poky and slow and took us almost three weeks. In my mind's eye the passage was a blur of drilling holes and plugging holes. Of bolting things on and taking things off. Of hours spent trying out the various sails. I soon knew that I had an excellent yacht that sailed well. I also knew that the sailing rig and its handling were full of large and small problems. The mounting of the mast winches was all wrong, the reefing system was a mess, the rig needed major tuning, and it was to take a lot of trial and error to perfect the location of the various sheets, guys, pendants, and halyards so they would be easy for me to deal with quickly.

Although I had a good deal of seagoing experience, it had been on smaller vessels. Much of the gear on *American Flag* was new to me. I wasn't used to such big sails or to some of the forces involved. I needed advice and help to move things around and to order additional hardware. Yet I knew I could probably neither find a qualified expert nor afford his services. While I was busy sailing I was also worrying about the pre-race inspection and a long list of mandatory safety equipment. I certainly recognized the wisdom of the race organizers in requiring a long trial voyage in these large and complicated vessels. A 2,000-mile voyage was hardly enough!

On July 11th, while kneeling on the foredeck drilling two holes for a padeye for the staysail tack, I looked up to see a large whale parallel with our course about one hundred meters away. I called Margaret, and we watched a black, glistening creature as long as *American Flag* blow seven or eight times before it sounded and disappeared.

Later we removed five turning blocks at the foot of the mast and remounted them slightly away from the mast ring so I could fit a better mast boot. I added a sixth turning block and a cheek block to lead the spinnaker pole topping lift aft. It was a day of measuring, drilling, bedding, and bolting. To stop water leaking into the cabin from around the mast, I fitted a rubber boot between the mast and a surrounding ring on the coachroof. The mast ring on the coachroof was rectangular, however, while the mast was elliptical in shape, and squaring a circle in rubber and keeping it watertight is harder than it sounds.

Can you imagine handling a spinnaker on a fifty-foot yacht by yourself? Insane. Yet I learned to do it. When I started off from Florida it took me two weeks to get up enough courage to try one of these giant sails. I carefully set up the nineteen-foot pole and sorted out the sheet, after guy, fore guy, and topping lift. Then up to the masthead went the collapsed spinnaker—stretched long and taut like a sausage and held clasped with an equally long, encircling sock that reached from the top of the spinnaker to the bottom (from the masthead to the deck).

My heart was in my mouth when I raised the sock (by pulling down on a line at the foot of the mast) and the spinnaker billowed out, a 2000 sq. ft. rainbow of colors. The autopilot steered while I rushed back to the cockpit to adjust the various strings. Margaret watched. She didn't say a word and looked nervous, figuring that I was going to kill myself for sure this time. But everything worked, and we picked up speed.

Gradually I got used to the nylon monsters, and I began to employ them regularly in light following winds. Not in strong winds, admittedly, but in moderate, say, fifteen- or twenty-knot following breezes. I was told by experts that hand steering was essential with a spinnaker. Yet I found that my Alpha autopilot handled *American Flag* reasonably well during spinnaker runs if the wind was steady. I concluded that it was simpler to do the whole spinnaker drill by myself rather than with a crew because there was no shouting, no yelling, no recriminations, and no dirty looks. Any mistakes belonged to me alone.

The passage from Florida to Horta, the main city on the island of Faial in the Azores, took us twenty days and eight hours (138 miles per day for 2,811 miles). The Portuguese were charming and put us in a lovely new marina that had just opened. I had news of four American sailors in the BOC race: Dick Cross in *Airforce* and Mike Plant in *Airco* had already left for Newport after their qualifying runs; Tony Lush was at a nearby island on his way from France to Newport; Mark Schrader, who was campaigning *Lone Star,* had also just arrived in Horta, so I got a chance to meet him.

Two days flew by while I checked in with the officials and dealt with passports and clearances. I spent a day up the mast and put more padding at the ends of the four mast spreaders and installed two after lower shrouds to beef up the rig. An American, Bill Hallstein, off the cruising yacht *Flemish Cap,* devoted a day to tightening the standing rigging. Meantime I reeved a spare jib halyard, increased the topping lift size to twelve millimeters so that it could serve as an extra main halyard, and bolted two cleats near the mast winches. The plastic through-hull fitting for the engine exhaust had leaked badly during the trip. Mark Schrader kindly gave me a bronze fitting, and after some alterations I bolted the metal piece in place. The leak stopped. While all this was going on, Margaret bought fresh fruit and vegetables. I could stay no longer. It was July 19th and time to go.

. . . .

CHAPTER SEVEN

Qualifying

*W*hen I sailed from Horta, a small trim figure on the great stone breakwater waved and blew kisses at me. It was Margaret. I waved and blew kisses back and then swallowed hard. We had always sailed together. Now I was off on a solo venture. Was I capable of such a trip without her at my side? I knew that without her help and constant support the project would have been impossible. I would do my best to succeed. I must succeed! But I would miss Margaret a lot.

I was soon ghosting slowly along past the south side of Faial, a large, green, volcanic island whose people had been extremely pleasant. It seemed a pity to leave such a lovely place after only four days. As *American Flag* headed west I saw neat fields bordered by tall hedgerows, and houses and farms with roofs of orange tiles.

Horta had little in the way of high-tech yacht services, but the men and women that I met certainly had good hearts. I had needed a machine shop to deal with the engine exhaust fitting and some other metalwork and was sent to an old big ship repair facility in several cavernous buildings just out of town. Manuel had a very red face, and like machinists on all small islands he did a little bit of everything. With diagrams, gestures, and my fleabag Portuguese I managed to tell him what I wanted, and we worked together to straighten and bend several pieces of stainless steel. Then I pulled out the bronze fitting that needed a flange ring so that it could be screwed to *American Flag's* transom. Manuel cut a heavy washer from a scrap piece of bronze, brazed it in place, machined it nicely, filled in a blowhole, and finally filed the piece smooth.

"Good enough," I said. "What do I owe you?" There had been two hours at the lathe and hydraulic press, plus hammering, brazing, filing, and a little material.

Manuel wrote out what I thought was 8,500 escudos on a scrap of paper. I dutifully counted out the money since I was at the mercy of the only machine shop on the island. However Manuel wasn't satisfied and gave the money back to me. Then he asked to see the money again and gently pulled out 850 escudos ($5.66). I could have been taken for $56.60 (Ft. Lauderdale prices) easily, but Manuel was honest and didn't cheat strangers. I was impressed.

The next morning I got a haircut from an elderly barber in a tiny shop in Horta. The barber moved slowly and was shaving an old man when I entered his little place on the main street. The man being shaved looked terrible, with a waxen face and no visible movements. The tableau suggested a dying man shaving a dead man. When the barber finished he mumbled something in Portuguese. The man in the chair began to move slowly and reluctantly, each movement a big effort, and finally got up and shuffled off. Once in the chair my long hair was soon clipped off, although before he finished with me the barber closed his shop and bolted the door (at 0800). Maybe I was enough of a challenge for the day. I tried to make a little conversation, but my efforts were useless. It was perhaps too late in the barber's life to try fragmentary Portuguese with a foreigner.

It had been fun to see Horta, to have a drink at Peter Azevedo's Café Sport, and to eat at the Clube Naval. Most of the yachts in the new marina were from France, and the atmosphere was more like a French village than a small town on a remote Atlantic island.

As *American Flag* edged past Faial, we got a light north wind and began to sail faster. I could have used the genoa, but I thought I would conserve my strength on the first day. The rig was much tighter, and the yacht was sailing better. Now that I was on my own I concentrated on just sailing the yacht, eating, and sleeping for a few days. I did mount some small blocks and light line so I could pull the slack in the lee running backstay down on deck and out of the way. I made a note to improve the lead of the spinnaker fore guy lines to reduce the clutter along the side decks. Little by little I was sorting out the jumbled running rigging.

[From my journal]. July 21st.

1715. I'm learning that handling a fifty-foot yacht is a big job. I guess the most important thing is to stay rested enough so that I can deal with the small and large problems as they come up. I have been working on the mast boot leak. I hope I have it this time. I took off all the boom vang hardware and used contact cement to glue on strips of wet suit material to increase the barriers to water.

I enjoyed meeting Mark Schrader, who is bright, pleasant, and keen on the race. When he learned that I had no radio transmitters on board he loaned me his five-watt portable VHF set. I was impressed with *Lone Star*—Mark's Valiant 47—and his meticulous preparations.

As the days passed, I got better at sailing *American Flag,* which was a new experience compared with my earlier vessels. The yacht was much faster and more powerful, but sensitive to sail trim. Downwind and across the wind in light seas she was speedy and flew along. The vessel sailed reasonably well to windward—depending on the sea conditions—but required much less sail than I first thought necessary. In twenty to twenty-five knots and hard on the wind she would punch along at seven or seven-and-a-half knots with just the staysail and two reefs in the main. She was unhandy if overloaded with sail area. I saw right away that water ballast would have been a big help. However I hadn't had the money for the tanks and plumbing so I would have to manage without several thousand pounds of water pumped up to windward to keep the yacht more upright.

Gradually I learned to become a seagoing hermit and tried to act sensibly. Unless there was a problem of some kind, I cooked three substantial meals every day, drank a glass of wine with lunch and supper, and made a point to sit down and eat slowly and enjoy the food (I was determined not to gnaw at cold food in a bunk). I took a number of one- or two-hour naps during the day and night so that my cumulative sleep generally totaled about seven hours in twenty-four. I made an effort to keep the navigation up to date and to write in my journal every day. I tried to keep my bunk made and to sweep out the cabin twice a week. Every few days I went through my work list and sorted jobs by degree of urgency. I enjoyed listening to the news on the BBC and comparing it with the same accounts broadcast on Radio Moscow. When the going was easy I took a couple of hours off and did a little recreational reading to keep from becoming a sailing drone (my first was Alan Moorehead's book on the Russian revolution, a complex story of intrigues, doubledealing, and treachery. Trotsky, to my surprise, came out much better than the much-touted Lenin).

At 0600 on the fourth day I stepped out into the cockpit to look around. I had had a red, white, and blue spinnaker up since the previous noon. Although we had passed a Romanian ship from Constanta the day before, there were no ships in sight. The wind was nine knots from the northeast but was backing to the north, so I took down the spinnaker, set the yankee, and went below to make breakfast. At 0900 I was out in the cockpit enjoying the warm sun when I happened to glance over the side. An enormous piece of bluish-green seaweed streamed slowly along in the water as far as I could see, about ten feet below the surface.

"How lovely," I thought to myself. "Sort of like a woman's tresses." I watched the seaweed for a moment and then glanced up at the yacht. We were hardly moving, yet the sails were full. I looked into the water again. Yikes! How could there be long seaweed out in the middle of the ocean where the water was thousands of fathoms deep? I knelt on the side deck and peered into the water. We were caught up in a green net of some kind that must have snagged the keel. Instead of going at six knots, we were almost stopped because we were towing a giant sea anchor. I got the boat hook and tried to pull the net on board, but it was much too heavy.

> [From the log]. July 22nd.
> *1028.* I slowed *American Flag* by rolling up the yankee and dropping the mainsail. I put on my wet suit top, face mask, and flippers. Then I tied a long lifeline around myself, clutched a sharp knife, and like a pirate, jumped into the water. The net was at least fifty feet long and caught around the propeller strut. The ship had a little forward motion, and it was surprisingly hard to hang on. I started to cut the net away—it was three mm. green nylon mesh—but I found that it was easier to slip the strands over the propeller and strut. We were suddenly free. I was *very* careful when I worked aft to the steering vane frame, and climbed back up on the yacht. I knew too well the penalty for a foolish move.

Although Margaret and I had often bathed in tropical oceans during calms, I found the experience of going over the side by myself that morning absolutely terrifying. I had a bad feeling, and I was sure that I was going to be gobbled up by a great white shark (I kept looking over my shoulder). Yet I was only in the water for a few minutes. Such fear was certainly foolish, but at the time it seemed real enough.

By the tenth day I had settled into a routine. The yacht had a number of minor problems, but I thought they could be solved before the race. The main difficulty was the headsail changing arrangement. For most sailing I used the yankee, a jib with 565 sq. ft. of area. I flew this sail (together with the mainsail with various reefs) for sailing to windward, for reaching, and for running when held out with a pole. To keep the yacht going when the wind got lighter, I changed to a 915 sq. ft. genoa, which I could also use with the wind from any direction. This sail was particularly good in very light head-winds (say five knots true) and excellent for reaching in stronger breezes.

The difficulty was changing from the yankee to the genoa and back again. I set the yankee on a Harken roller furling-reefing headsail gear. This worked well, and the sail was easy to use with either the full area or rolled up about one third. When I decided to put up the genoa, however, the problems began.

First I had to take down the yankee by easing the halyard and catching the sail as it came down. Since there were no hanks to keep the luff attached to the headstay—and the sail was held only by the clew and the tack—the sail tended to come down with a rush and keep going right over the side into the water. To get around this I led the hauling end of the halyard through a snatch block at the base of the mast and out to the stem, where I could ease the halyard and catch the sail a little at a time. This got the sail down on deck, where I tied it in place.

Then I dragged the genoa out of the front hatch, hooked up the tack and head, tied the genoa sheets to the clew, and began to hoist the sail. It was important to feed the luff tape evenly into the slot of the headfoil of the roller reefing gear to prevent jamming. It took about eight or ten trips from the mast halyard winch to the stem (walking over the slippery sail) to straighten out the genoa and luff tape since it was impossible for one person to keep such a big sail in order. After a lot of huffing and puffing, I got the genoa up.

In a squall I could furl the sail quickly and later unroll it again. The difficulty came when the wind increased suddenly. To get the big sail down in a breeze was a handful, even if I ran downwind to lessen the apparent wind. Once the wind came up I had to douse the sail *immediately* because if the wind increased to say thirty knots, it was impossible for me to take down the sail. I could have continued with the furled genoa and gone to the hanked-on staysail (set on the midstay), but then my sailing was terrible in the whole mid-range of wind strengths. Complicated, eh?

I could not carry the big genoa hard to windward in more than eight or nine knots of true wind (fifteen or sixteen knots apparent wind). On reaching and running courses the wind range was less critical. Once I had taken down the genoa and pushed it below, then I untied the lashings on the yankee and hoisted the smaller sail. The sequence was:

1. Yankee down and lashed on deck. Head and tack fittings off.
2. Genoa pulled on deck. Head and tack fittings on. Separate sheets rigged and tied to clew.
3. Genoa hoisted and trimmed.
4. To change back to the yankee, it was steps 1–3 in reverse, except that the genoa was cumbersome because of its size.

Not only did this sail scheme use up lots of energy (exhausting was a better word), but it was fairly dangerous to take down a triangle of flapping fabric more than fifty-six feet high and almost thirty-four feet wide at the bottom when the yacht was heeled over and roaring along—particularly at night when it was hard to see. I had plenty of motivation to think up a better way to deal with this monster. I knew that if the yankee could simply be rolled up and the genoa handled separately, then the physical energy devoted to these foredeck gymnastics could be halved. Ideas that I wrote in my journal on July 27th were:

1. Put up a second wire headstay forward of the existing roller furling gear and sew hanks along the luff of the genoa. Then the sail can be run up and down the wire and dealt with more easily. A good scheme, but it will require some sail handling.
2. Simply roll up the yankee on its existing gear and set the genoa flying separately in front of the yankee. Tack the genoa at the stem and hoist it without the luff being secured to a stay. I believe this is a suicidal plan for a singlehander.
3. Set the genoa flying, but keep it under control with an up-and-down sock such as I use on the spinnaker. Can a sock handle the greater bulk of the genoa?
4. Put up a second roller furling gear ahead of the present one. By far the best notion for both safety and ease of sail use, but complicated and will require deck and mast modifications. Is there enough time to do this before the race?

At noon on July 29th I was 673 miles east of the Nantucket light vessel. I had been banging and crashing along to windward in a southwest gale for a couple of days. I was surprised how well the yacht sailed in the rough sea with only the staysail and the deeply reefed mainsail. I still had a little ice in the icebox (after eleven days) so I opened a bottle of chilled Portuguese green wine (a delicious white) and sat propped up on the starboard settee berth with a book in one hand (I was rereading *The Quiet American* by Graham Greene) and a glass in the other. I could think of nothing that would improve the sailing so I relaxed and waited for a change of wind.

I pretended to read, but I fretted about the race. Would I have the money to start? Could I possibly get ready in time? It meant a month of frantic work. There were dozens of jobs to do, plus I needed extra sails, a set of radios, and with luck, some electronic gear. My only hope was enough money to hire some really good help. If I could just get my friends Tom and Nancy Zydler! It was all a question of money. I needed at least $50,000. Probably more. How did I ever get into such a situation?

[From the log]. August 2nd.

1348. At 1230 I was sitting on the coachroof taking the noon sight when I heard the sails fluttering slightly. We were being headed. I jumped below and

changed the autopilot ten degrees to starboard. While I was below I stirred
some soup for lunch. Then back to the sextant. The sails continued to rattle. I
finished the noon sight, looked at my soup, and saw many whitecaps—the
wind was increasing. I started to take a second reef in the mainsail. While
halfway through the reef, the yacht was headed so I decided to tack. I jumped
in the cockpit and let go the windward sheet and began to haul on the leeward
sheet. But something was fouled. I rushed forward. Several yarns on the windward yankee sheet had hooked on a Wichard staysail hank, something supposedly impossible (the hanks needed little cloth covers). I lowered the staysail
to reach the hank and cut away the fouled yarns. Then I finished the mainsail
reef, and started to hoist the staysail when I noticed a chafed place on the
halyard. I cut away two meters of line, tied the halyard anew and hoisted and
trimmed the sail. Now the yacht was sailing nicely. I went below to discover
that my forgotten soup had boiled over, and the galley was a mess. It's a good
thing I had a nap earlier. I thought of Alf Loomis, an earlier writer who had
had a similar morning and had written an article called "Goodbye to Single-
handing."

The weather improved, and I got to Newport on August 4th a little
before midnight. The trip had been much easier than I had anticipated, and I
was fairly rested. The next morning I saw U.S. Customs and the BOC
officials at Goat island, who inspected *American Flag's* logbook and my work-
book for astronomical sights (each entrant was required to navigate by celestial means during his qualifying trip).

I had taken a little over sixteen days for the 2,109-mile trip from Horta
to Newport. My average was a miserable 127 miles a day (best 166; worst 78).
Certainly I would have to do better in the race. Of course, I had excuses: I
was learning to sail the yacht. I had had poor winds, and the arrangements for
changing the headsails were miserable.

I bought a few groceries and left immediately for Maine via the Cape
Cod canal, where I anchored and slept while I waited for a foul tidal stream
to change. By the following afternoon (August 6th) I had a spinnaker up and
was crossing the Gulf of Maine. At sunrise the next morning I was near Mt.
Desert island, which was shrouded in light fog. The sun was visible, but no
horizon. Fortunately, there were spangles of yellow reflections on the water
toward the sun which continued to the horizon and gave me enough of the
horizon for a sun sight. The 0718 sun line for longitude put me somewhere on
a north-south line three miles east of Mt. Desert rock. Ten minutes later I
heard the blasts of the fog signal (hooray), and I laid out a course for Great
Duck island and Western Way. By 1400 I was tied to my mooring in
Somesville and surrounded by friends.

. . . .

CHAPTER EIGHT

Maine

I had selected a design. The new yacht had been built in 112 days. She had been trucked to Florida and made ready for sea. The vessel had crossed the Atlantic twice, I had sailed 5,155 miles in six weeks and had qualified for the race, which was to begin in 23 days. Already it was August 7th. I had to be in Newport by August 16th, only 9 days away, and I needed 2 days to sail there. Could I possibly get ready?

While I had been sailing, Margaret had flown from Horta to Maine and had gone to work on the finances. "The good news is that I've got $10,300 from private donors, and we'll get another $2,000 from the fund drive of the local yacht clubs this week," she said. "Several other people have promised to send checks.

"The bad news is that I've got a whole pile of cordial letters from our corporate targets, but nothing of substance," she said. "The IRS is still playing games with our tax-exempt status so I've begun to use an existing foundation. It's possible that we might get a surprise from a corporation, but I think our best plan is to press on with private fund-raising. The amounts are modest but more certain."

The telephone rang. It was Dick Cross, the other BOC entrant from Maine. "I've got *Airforce* out of the water at Bass Harbor Marine," he said. "My haulout and work are free, and the yard is willing to do the same for you. The boss, Haywood May, said to get down here. At last we've got some local support on Mt. Desert island!"

This was a wonderful gift. I accepted at once, and by the following afternoon *American Flag* was high and dry, supported by seven steel stands, and surrounded by an enthusiastic group of yard men and volunteer workers.

I soon had a welder making a more rugged stainless steel stem fitting to hold the headstay and improving the underdeck supports for the after lower shrouds. My friend, Pieter Boersma, began to mount four ARCO solar panels on the coachroof and not only loaned me a satellite navigation device but installed it as well. Dave Taylor began the fiberglass work to move the lazarette entry hatch from underneath the tiller to the port side of the deck for better access. Joe and Bonnie Darlington took off the useless genoa sheet tracks along the side decks and plugged the holes. I got a carpenter and his assistant to build stowage drawers in the interior, and a seamstress measured the sleeping berth cushions for alterations. Toby Harper made a special mainsheet reel and mounted a small pump on the kerosene tank for the cooking stove. Someone changed a through-hull valve in the hull to a handier location and strengthened the bottoms of the stowage lockers in the cockpit coamings. While Karen Boersma painted and varnished in the cabin, a volunteer polished the topsides, and a young woman in a mask and white throwaway coveralls began to roll on blue bottom paint.

Newspaper reporters buzzed around with questions, and two rival television crews from Bangor zeroed in on me with cameras and microphones. A crowd of onlookers appeared and began to climb around the yacht and take photographs. Everyone was welcome because *American Flag* had become a community effort. The yacht got a lot of skeptical looks because no one had ever seen such a long skinny hull and such a short deep keel in traditional Maine. A dockyard committee of retired experts soon collected to debate the merits of the new vessel. Their words drifted up to me.

"I reckon she'd never make the Friendship sloop society," said one man.

"She must have been designed by a cigar smoker," added a second.

"Must take a lot of fellows to handle *her*," chimed in a third. "One man you say? Impossible. Anyway, I'd never go to sea in *her*. She'd turn right over. I can tell."

Dick Cross on *Airforce* was nearby with his gang of helpers and supporters, and as friendly rivals we traded a few jokes and loaned each other tools. Dick was far ahead of me in money, sailing trials, and readiness for the race. He even had a *titanium* rudder stock. Dick looked to be a formidable competitor.

I ran around with a list of projects, things to order, checking this, complimenting someone on his work, suggesting an improvement here, talking on the telephone, and marveling that all these things were going on. Was all this happening? Or was I only dreaming that it was happening? At night there were letters to write about donations, bills to pay, and proposals to more corporations. The yard started work at 0700 so I got up early to get things going. Each day flashed by like a window shade snapping up and down. A week disappeared.

I still needed spare sails, radios (VHF and single sideband), and survival equipment (flares, an emergency position indicating radio beacon, a portable VHF radio transceiver, sea dye marker, and so forth). My old yacht had been for sale; now a buyer appeared; I was in no position to resist a low offer. The money that I received lasted about fifteen minutes, during which I ordered spare sails and paid the most urgent bills (spars, winches, batteries, life raft, and rigging wire). New donations added another $2,763, plus four cockpit cushions. On the same day Fos Whitlock gave me two radios, a weatherfax machine, and a radio beacon. The *American Flag* project was looking better, but I was completely out of cash again and $50,000 in the hole. The BOC project was sucking up money like a vacuum cleaner working on dry sawdust.

Gentlemen never discuss money until they haven't any. I was thoroughly fed up with purchases and bills and letters and pleading and scheming. I was tired of asking for equipment, of borrowing things, of favors and credit and obligations and interest payments. Of smiling at bankers and cosigners. I was weary of asking for handouts. I was fed up with hearing "yes, yes, yes," which really meant "no, no, no." It was all so humiliating and demeaning. What I needed was one big sponsor.

I was a sailor and I wanted to enter a big boat in a long race. I knew that every hour I spent scrabbling for money meant an hour away from preparing the yacht, thinking about the course, and working out long-term strategy and short-term tactics for the race itself. The days and weeks used up in my search for backing meant that the race was lost before it started. I realized that I should have recruited a sympathetic soul to have handled *all* the money and *all* the fund-raising. I was caught in the beartrap of having sufficient means to get started but not enough to finish. The marriage was half-consummated.

When *American Flag* was lowered into the water on the morning of August 14th and I shook hands with fifty smiling people who wished me luck and good fortune, my heart was a little heavy. I didn't think there was a chance of starting the race. Nevertheless, I headed south to Newport to at least try. The Bass Harbor staff and my supporters had accomplished miracles in a week, but I knew the yacht was not ready for a world race.

The 247-mile trip south was easy with Margaret. We arrived in Newport at 1100 on August 16th, one hour before the deadline.

. . . .

CHAPTER NINE

Goat Island

*S*uddenly I was in the midst of all the BOC yachts, and a bit awed. There were twenty-three of them, six or seven million dollars' worth, rafted together along two sides of a big dock, and as a group they seemed enormous, sleek, high-tech, and impressive. The vessels were blue and white and green and red. Of unpainted aluminum, varnished mahogany, and glossy fiberglass. All were cutter-rigged with tall single masts supported by needle-like wires that angled up from a dozen points on deck. The paint on the hulls was new and shiny, and each displayed a distinctive number, like horses on show in a paddock.

The masts pointed to the sky, and flags flew everywhere. I saw national flags on the transoms of entries from Brazil, Japan, and England. From South Africa, Finland, and France. From Australia, New Zealand, and the United States. High in the rigging I looked up at sponsors' flags, BOC flags, private signals, and decorative pennants. The accents of a dozen colors, patterns, and styles of flags made the fleet as showy as an Italian opera and advertised the race to a crowd of onlookers that came day and night.

The decks of the BOC vessels were cluttered with masses of control lines, polished stainless steel fittings, roller furling drums, spinnaker poles, rows of jam cleats, thin metal tracks holding fairleads for lines, and a small hatch or two for ventilation and light below to the cabin. Near the stern was the cockpit with a shelter and cabin entry at the forward end. The sides of the cockpit had high coamings to keep water out. Along the tops of the coamings were the big cylindrical drums of a dozen or so black winches (which seemed like weapons around the walls of a protective fort, ready to do battle with the winds and the sea).

Most of the hulls had high freeboard and were beamy, with almost vertical bows; at the stern a long wedge-shaped transom sloped down to the water like a shoehorn. At the end of each transom, a wind vane steering device rose up vertically for a meter or so, its pipes and tubes surmounted by a brightly painted wind blade that rocked nervously from side to side. I saw angled double rudders and lifting centerboards; I peered at wind-driven generators and flat black solar panels that from a distance looked like trays of raisins set out to dry. A dozen kinds of antennas suggested hidden electronic marvels. The biggest vessels had keels that reached down ten to twelve feet and had massive bulbs of lead at the bottom, which gave the yachts tremendous sail-carrying potential.

I was so knocked out by this display of high-tech sailboat stuff that I spent the first few hours walking up and down the dock in a daze, wondering if I fitted into this league. I soon realized that though the race was for singlehanders, the support of the yachts was certainly not limited to one man because I saw riggers, radiomen, boat carpenters, sailmakers, fiberglass experts, painters, sparmakers, electronic repairmen, and nautical mechanics of every sort hurrying up and down the dock carrying their tools and wares. In the parking lot were vans and small trucks with the names of some of the BOC entries.

There were no multihull yachts in the race because many trimarans and catamarans had capsized and turned upside down in North Atlantic races. The race organizers had decided that the Southern ocean was risky enough for single-hulled, self-righting monohulls.

The BOC race organization was good and had been planned with care. There were two BOC trailer-offices near the dock. The first was for the press; the second for the contestants. Both trailers were staffed with experts. Lois Mussell, the amiable secretary in the contestants' trailer, took messages, knew everyone in Newport, and had five hundred phone numbers at her fingertips. Her office was perfect for long-distance telephoning, and the captains and their assistants called across the world in all languages from morning till night.

I met Harry Mitchell, the entry from England. Harry, a shoestring operator like me, had elected to sail in a forty-one-foot used aluminum ex-IOR racer named *Double Cross*.

"What are we doing here, Harry?" I said. "Just walking up and down the dock is enough to discourage the little guy." At that moment three sailmakers walked by, staggering under the load of an enormous fully-battened mainsail for one of the sixty-footers.

"I know," said Harry. "I can hardly believe what I've seen since I tied up along the dock a few days ago. It looks to me as if these preparations are for a D-day invasion!"

I spoke with Mark Schrader, whose *Lone Star,* a trim blue and white entry from Texas, looked impressive. Next to him was *Airforce,* Dick Cross's boat with her beautifully varnished hull, teak decks, and masses of equipment. Earlier I had met Jean Luc Van Den Heede, a French entry who had a slim and racy-looking boat with the fetching name of *Let's Go.* Jean Luc was a bull of a man with a great mass of unruly black hair, a big black beard, and a hearty laugh. I liked him immediately.

I said hello to John Hughes, who was sailing *Joseph Young,* a skinny forty-one-foot Swedish design with an enormous Canadian flag at the end of her double cockpit. John, a small wiry man with a trim mustache, seemed to brim over with energy and nervously smoked one cigarette after another. I traded nods with Dr. Takao Shimada, a smooth-faced Japanese dentist, whose entry was named *Madonna* and whose afterdeck radio mast had enough electronic gadgets to start a discount store.

The next morning our friends from Florida—Read and Jody Branch—appeared on the dock full of determination and energy and ready to help us. Read spent the first day gazing star-eyed at the other entries. I had a feeling that he should have entered a yacht of his own.

"Why not, Read?" I said. "You've got everything. Youth, intelligence, money, sailing experience. I bet you could win the race."

"Not me," he said sheepishly, smiling at the idea. "I haven't got the guts."

That afternoon we went out for a trial sail with Bill Bergantz from North Sails. Read was pleased to steer the boat at last. I thought the sails and trim looked good in the light winds, but Bill decided to make small alterations in the yankee and mainsail and to put chafe patches on the genoa where the sail almost touched the upper spreaders on the mast. It was easy to change and remove the big sails with two extra men on board. The five new spare sails were to be delivered in a few days.

Margaret and I were amazed to discover that many of the contestants stayed in deluxe hotels and didn't appear on the dock until ten o'clock or so. We lived on *American Flag* because we loved life on board. Not only was it convenient, but it cost nothing at all, we had the best view in town, and we were in the heart of things. We were tied up next to a massive, specially modified Swan 50, sponsored by Belmont, a Finnish tobacco company. I was told later that $1,000,000 was spent on her campaign.

Read was the electrical expert and began to install the radios and weatherfax machine. I was busy up and down the mast—whipping line ends, improving the chafing gear on the spreader tips, installing a radar reflector, and moving winches from the coachroof to the mast (where I could use the power of my arms and body instead of just my arms). Margaret sorted and listed a dozen boxes of foodstuffs that she had been stockpiling for several months. She had chosen from a variety of canned foods, freeze-dried packets, pouch meals, dehydrated onions, celery, and so on.

Two more yachts appeared (each got a penalty for being late) to complete the twenty-five-vessel BOC fleet (thirty-five sailors had paid the entry fee; ten dropped out for various reasons between May 31st and mid-August). Both new arrivals were sixty-footers.

The first was *UAP* (Union d'Assurance Paris, a French insurance company), a bright-yellow high-tech design with water ballast, double rudders, concave decks, and a hull with lots of beam and flared sections. *UAP's* mast was made of carbon fiber, and she had a giant geodesic pilothouse constructed of aluminum pipe and twenty-nine triangular panels of silvery plastic. A large satellite dish covered with an enormous fiberglass dome sat on her after deck. I had met her captain Jean-Yves Terlain many years before, and he talked of his four video screens, digital radar, computers, and direct telephone system to Paris.

The other vessel was named *Credit Agricole* (a French bank) and was a green and white speedster not only of maximum length but of great beam (5.1 m. or 16′9″) that was bulged out well above the waterline so that her water ballast would have tremendous leverage and ensure that the yacht could carry plenty of sail in strong winds. She had a rugged-looking mast with four spreaders and enough rigging wires to hold up the aerial of a television station. She was constructed of aluminum and at 33,071 pounds was the second heaviest yacht in the race. *Credit Agricole* was sailed by Philippe Jeantot, who had won the first BOC race in another vessel. The new yacht came in at night to an adjoining dock, and a whole group of contestants and friends walked over to see her. The captain was handsome and smiling and busy answering reporters' questions.

"She looks like a super vessel," said someone.

"She's super all right," said Peter Dunning, an official of the race. "But these things take a superman to sail them. Look at the size of that rig! Look at the size of that mainsail! And a 3,000 sq. ft. spinnaker yet? One man? How can he do it?"

As I walked up and down the dock during the next few days I had a good chance to study all twenty-five entries. The larger class had eleven sponsored custom sixty-footers (one was fifty-six feet) and seemed thoroughly professional. The smaller class was a more ragtag group of fourteen yachts between forty and fifty feet. Only three or perhaps four were sponsored. Each of the twenty-five seemed rugged and well fitted out for hard going. I had only two qualms. *Thursday's Child* had an enviable record in hard races, but I thought her seventy-five-foot mast and rig were too light for the Southern ocean. I also had grave doubts about the mast of *Joseph Young*, the forty-one-foot Canadian entry. Both these yachts had slender, toothpick rigs, and I didn't think either mast would make it around the world. I noted in my journal at the time that I hoped I was wrong, but I didn't have good feelings about those two masts.

In Florida I had installed a Fleming wind vane steering device from New Zealand, but I hadn't been able get it to work. I thought I knew something about vane gears, but nothing seemed to help. During the sailing trials I had lubricated everything in sight, changed the vertical position of the water blade, tried air blades of different sizes, and moved the control lines up and down the tiller to change the power and travel of the steering forces. I finally removed the heavy Fleming unit and bought a competing Monitor device, whose makers offered to install it in Newport.

By now it was August 20th, ten days before the start. The race inspectors scrambled over each entry and measured and verified a hundred things. Yachts that used water ballast tanks had to demonstrate their limits. First a tank (or tanks) on one side was filled and emptied, then the other side was filled and emptied. A full tank was not allowed to cause an angle of heel of more than ten degrees. During these tests the masts assumed crazy dockside angles as the captains pumped seawater in and out. Since we had no water ballast on *American Flag,* however, our inspection went more quickly. Read's radio installation was pronounced perfect. The emergency steering, the watertight bulkheads, and the safety equipment were okay except that I needed twenty-two flares and a cockpit bilge pump. The liferaft inspection certificate had disappeared.

Every morning I spent an hour or so on the telephone calling about equipment and money. Some of my earlier appeals had begun to bring in checks—including additional help from Lee Freedman, a neighbor in Maine. I set aside enough cash for the new sails and paid the most pressing bills. We took *American Flag* to a boatyard to check her bottom, which turned out to be rough and required a thorough sanding before we sprayed on fresh bottom paint. The two owners of the Monitor company started to put on the wind vane. Dave Taylor, an expert boat carpenter and mechanic from Mt. Desert island (who had worked on *Flag* in Maine), drove down with his wife, Moe, to give a little professional help. Dave and Moe removed the propeller, strut, and shaft, and sealed up the openings. Dave then glassed in a transducer for the depth sounder and a hull fitting for a speedometer while Read wired the instruments.

A talented woman volunteer named Didgie Vrana hooked up control lines for the steering vane, rigged the trysail, began work on the cockpit bilge pump, and—miracle of miracles—found the liferaft certificate. Meanwhile Moe painted and varnished, and someone put a second mast boot over the first to stop the leaks. Margaret fed everybody and passed up tools while she unrolled twenty-three new Admiralty charts from England and sorted them into the sixty already on board. I hunted up a welder to repair a stainless steel bracket. Meanwhile Dave started to build a small hanging locker in the forward cabin. Read strung the wires for the off-course alarm and soldered all the connections, and together we got the oil heating stove into operation. While inspecting the roller furling gear, I discovered three damaged strands of wire on the headstay. It took Read and me an entire afternoon to install a new piece of wire. Two days before the race—while I went to an obligatory skippers' meeting—*American Flag* (with half a dozen captains on board) was towed back to Goat island.

The time was 0600, the dock was quiet, and I sat below stirring a cup of tea. The race was to start in a little over two days. Although I had just gotten up, I was exhausted. Completely exhausted. I had been going day and night for four months, and I was worn out. Totally worn out. Not only physically, but mentally as well. What I needed was a sleeping pill and twenty-four hours in a secret bed somewhere. Then a walk in the woods and a quiet picnic lunch. I longed for a deputy who could have taken charge. If only the yacht hadn't been so new. . . . If only there hadn't been so many details that needed refining. . . .

In spite of the most rigid price-cutting, careful shopping, discounts, free equipment, donated labor, and lots of work by Margaret and me, *American Flag* had cost $207,413, a sum I could hardly imagine. The yacht had turned out to be infinitely more complicated than I had naively reckoned, and the costs of the custom gear and outfitting had sliced through the money. The fund-raising up to the start of the race had brought in $35,233 (from seventeen donors and the two yacht clubs), a disappointing seventeen and a half percent. The remaining $166,086 represented the proceeds of my smaller yacht, my savings, and a big debt. Once I had paid for the new sails there would be nothing left for the campaign. It was madness to proceed.

I could hardly believe that in a country as wealthy as the United States I hadn't been able to find a sponsor. Sponsors should have been chasing me. Or so I thought. I suppose my appeal hadn't been broad enough. Somewhere a sympathetic and generous soul with money existed. I knew that. But where was that person? How could I find him?

It was true that *American Flag* was well prepared. I had food stores, charts, navigation gear, excellent foul weather clothing, plenty of spares, my tools, and a shelf or two of books. The sailing was easy and pleasant for me, and I thought with luck and reasonable winds I could get to Cape Town in forty-five to fifty days. If I didn't go I would disappoint many people, most of all *me*. Yet how could I possibly go off toward distant lands on a great adventure with no money? When I paid for the sails I would have $50 left.

There were no savings, no reserves, no hidden funds, no gold hoards to sell. I suppose I could compromise and try to complete just the first leg. But this would make me a quitter, which I was not.

One thing was certain. The expenses and bills would stop when the race started. I still had a dozen or more proposals out seeking money. Maybe tomorrow. Maybe next week . . .

Suddenly there was a great thump on deck that shook the yacht and woke up Margaret. I looked out. My new sails had arrived. A man from North had just thrown a large blue bag on deck.

"Can you help me carry the new mainsail from the van?" he said. "I'm in a hurry."*

The rush had began.

By 0800 *American Flag* was full of people again. The Monitor vane men were hammering away on the transom. Dave Taylor was using a hole saw to drill a route through the bilges for the new cockpit pump line. Someone delivered the container of emergency flares, and a little later a knock on the cabin top announced the arrival of a box of oranges, a box of grapefruit, and six dozen fresh eggs. Read climbed to the top of the mast to mount the wind speed and direction indicators. Fos Whitlock from Maine showed up and hurried away with a shopping list. Margaret, Didgie, and I took off the fully-battened mainsail and bent on the spare main to check the fit, shape, and reefing arrangements.

A French engineer came down the dock and handed me the Argos position-finding transmitter for *American Flag*. The device was a white plastic box about eighteen inches square and four inches high. The top was covered with solar cells except for the center, which had a small raised dome. I was instructed to mount the device on the coachroof or on the afterdeck in a protected place where I wouldn't step on it. Read and I tried several locations and finally screwed the transmitter on the coachroof just forward of the cockpit shelter.

The Argos device is known as a platform transmitter terminal (PTT) and was developed by the French and U.S. space agencies for both position-finding and collecting weather information. The Argos automatically transmitted an almost continuous signal to two polar-orbiting satellites that made a circuit of the earth every 100 minutes. During the 10 minutes or so when the satellites were above a PTT, they received the signals, which they relayed to three receiving stations on earth—two in the United States and one in France. After processing, the information was sent to Toulouse, France, where the precise location of each PTT—to within 900 meters—was calculated. Every

---

* The weight of the finished sails was: mainsail 89 pounds; yankee 66; staysail 50; genoa 50; spinnaker (with sock) 38; trysail 33; storm staysail 18. The total weight of thirteen sails was 655 pounds.

three hours the positions of the PTTs—in this case the twenty-five BOC yachts—were then telexed to the world.

The message transmitted by my Argos not only had *American Flag's* identification code but also sent out the barometric pressure and the air temperature, so we helped a little with worldwide weather reporting. In case of emergency I could pull a special lever to send a distress signal. Each yacht had an Argos set for the duration of the race, which made it possible for the race committee, sponsors, friends, the press, and the contestants (when the results were relayed) to know everyone's position. What would Columbus have thought of such an invention?

I had forgotten about the mandatory skippers' meeting until Robin Knox-Johnston, the race chairman, whisked me off to the nearby Sheraton hotel. The meeting was smoothly handled, and the twenty-five entrants had a good chance to size up one another (we all must have wondered if the same group would ever meet again). Our briefing was intense and compelling, with lots of instructions ("You must report your position to the committee once a week."); warnings to stay out of trouble ("We'll do what we can, but you're on your own."); and a weather prediction from a meteorologist ("Unfortunately, the race start coincides with the beginning of the hurricane season, but at the moment we have no tropical storms under observation."). After a session of photographs we went to a luncheon. The French entrant, Philippe Jeantot, who had won the first BOC race, spoke surprisingly well ("Why do we enter the race?" he said. "It's easy to come up with a list of reasons. The main thing, however, is the will to do it.").

I got back to the yacht just in time to help Fos Whitlock carry jugs of kerosene aboard to fill the tank for the oil heating stove. A sailmaker was hoisting my new yankee and genoa. The scene on the dock had become frantic, with perhaps a thousand people milling about. Each of the twenty-five yachts had a captain and various helpers, some professional, some volunteer, plus wives and parents. People hurried up and down the dock carrying parcels, bags, tools, food, and pieces of equipment. Television technicians were stringing wires. Sound and film interviews in French and Japanese and English were going on. UPS and Federal Express trucks were at the head of the dock disgorging rush packages from all over the world.

The three telephones in the BOC trailer sang with loud conversations in French, English, Japanese, Finnish, and Portuguese. You could spot the captains easily because they walked rapidly and always had a sheaf of papers in one hand (tourists and picture-takers ambled slowly, and generally were in the way). Sailmakers grunted and skidded their bags down the dock, and boys from the supermarkets delivered box after box of groceries. The French boats took on great loads of bottled water.

Sounds of hammering, filing, and sawing rattled through the air. Sometimes the grating whine of a grinder overwhelmed all other noises. Men and

How do things work? Just before the start of the race, I explain some of the gear on *American Flag* to Robin Knox-Johnston, Barbara Giordano, and Richard Giordano, head of the BOC Group.

women were aloft in bosun's chairs checking a dozen things and taping every sharp corner in sight. Now and then one of the engineless fleet glided out for a trial sail. On her return she slipped back to the dock under a scrap of sail, her people deftly throwing lines to sailors on the tied-up yachts.

The BOC entrants had been urged to get ham radio licenses so we could use ham frequencies to supplement the commercial radio channels. The main requirement for the license was the ability to take Morse code at thirteen words a minute. I had been studying on and off for months by listening to cassette tapes, and I had gotten up to nine or ten words. The race preparations had interfered with my practice; nevertheless, on the day before the race started I sat on deck and passed a short theory test and a code test of five words per minute, which gave me a novice license. I was ashamed not to have gotten a proper license, but there had been no time for more study.

Fos Whitlock appeared with the results of his latest shopping (including a few bottles of wine, not on the list), and I was able to fit shut-off valves on the bilge pump lines from the watertight compartments (which completed my last inspection requirement). While we were loading blocks of ice into

Is long-distance racing popular? Here's part of the mob having a look at things before the race.

the icebox, a Federal Express man ("We deliver anywhere") jumped on deck with a box of weatherfax paper and autopilot spares. Dave Taylor completed a teak coaming at the back of the cockpit to help keep out deck water. The wind vane experts pronounced their job done, and all my helpers finished up.

We had a little social visit from Richard Giordano, the chairman of BOC, and his wife. Giordano, a tall and rather intense man, asked a number of surprisingly well informed questions, and I gave the Giordanos a tour of *American Flag.* That night there was a colossal banquet and fireworks for the contestants and the BOC people in a huge circus tent. By the time the fireworks started, however, I thought they were coming out of my head. I went back to the boat and fell into my bunk.

On the morning of the start, it seems incredible to relate, there must have been two thousand people on the dock (which I thought would collapse into the sea). This enormous crowd of well-wishers and the merely curious walked back and forth, asking questions and snapping photographs. The people came to see this strange breed of men about to set off on a great adventure, the first part of which would keep them at sea for almost two months. Men and women kept passing out little gifts to me. A sun hat, a t-shirt, a Gideon bible, a cheap pocket knife—as if a small token would somehow assure my survival. A faith healer marched up and down the dock and blessed each captain. One man actually patted me on the back and said: "Are you sure you want to go? Why not stay here and be safe?"

Television cameramen aimed their bulky machines at me as the reporters jumped aboard and asked for thirty seconds of time.

"Why are you doing this?"

"It's the last great challenge."

"What are your motivations?"

"To be faster than the others and to do it with style."

The sound men with their Nagra recorders caught each word and nodded sagely (not at the words, but at the sound level). The questions were serious, but I was tempted to give flip replies.

By this time I had had enough of the questions. I was fed up with the hype. Was I a gladiator about to be thrown to the lions? A kamikaze pilot about to set off on a suicide mission against the aircraft carriers? Absolutely not. I was merely a sailor setting off on an ocean voyage.

A towboat came alongside and a line thumped on deck. "Secure it forward," I shouted to Read. "Dave, let go all the dock lines aft." "Margaret, let go the bow line and give us a shove out."

Everybody on the dock waved. I waved back. They thought I was crazy to go in the race. I thought I was leaving the asylum behind. . . .

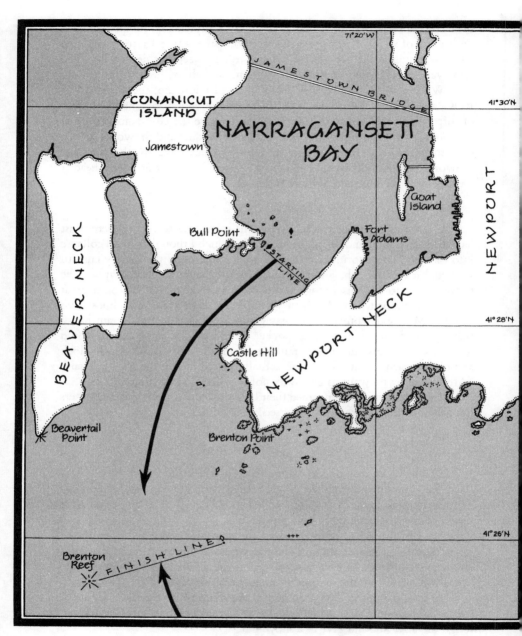

2. Newport and the start

CHAPTER TEN

The Start

*T*he fleet of small powerboats appeared at noon on August 30th and began to tow the twenty-five BOC yachts to the starting line. The race was to start on an arm of Narragansett bay called East Passage, which ran along the western shore of the city of Newport. From Goat island to the starting line was only a simple two-mile tow, but five hundred spectator boats—mostly small power boats and motoring sailing yachts—came to cheer the sailors. Though the people on the spectator boats meant well, they attacked the BOC fleet like a swarm of angry hornets.

It was a warm and sunny summer weekend, and the newspapers had been filled with talk of the race for weeks. The occasion was festive, and thousands of people lined the shores. Everyone was out and had a few beers and gathered to wave at the departing sailors. The BOC officials watched from a flag-draped stand that held the starting cannon. The public relations officials must have danced a little jig because the turnout rivaled the America's Cup crowds of earlier years.

All I saw was a mass of waving people and power boats which criss-crossed in front of *American Flag's* towboat. Fos steered, while Margaret and Moe were below stowing gear. Read and Dave were on the foredeck. Everyone around us blew horns and waved. The towing was extremely slow and at times stopped completely because of the spectator fleet and the wash from the passing boats. As we got out into East Passage I began to crank up the mainsail, but I asked Dave to finish hoisting the sail when Margaret appeared with a sheaf of papers. She produced two book contracts that I had not seen until that moment.

"Sign these," she said.

"I can't possibly sign a contract I haven't read. There may be . . ."

"Sign!" she said. "Your editor assured me that we can adjust the fine print later. We've got to have the money now."

I signed.

We talked about money-raising and a few follow-up letters. As I sat on the cabin my eyes fell on the turnbuckles for the starboard mast shrouds. Horrors! In the rush I had forgotten to put in the cotter pins that locked the turnbuckles and kept them from unscrewing. I asked Read and Dave to get cotter pins from below, put them in carefully, and check all twenty pins in the ten turnbuckles that held the wires which supported the mast. By now we were near the starting line and in the midst of all the spectator boats. I put up the staysail, ordered the towline off, and as the towboat came alongside for my passengers I shook hands with everyone and gave Moe and Margaret each a nervous kiss. The *American Flag* support crew jumped into the towboat, and I was on my own.

The start was to windward against a fifteen-knot southwesterly breeze blowing up East Passage, and a foul tide of a knot or two. The sailing itself was no problem, but getting through the spectator fleet was a terrible hazard that I had never considered. Would I be able to get past the five hundred swirling, turning, circling, joy-riding boats without being rammed and sunk? I could see plenty of destructive potential. I didn't care a whit about being first over the starting line or losing a few minutes. In a leg of six or seven weeks the thing was to get away without being wrecked at the beginning.

I grabbed my air horn and blasted away whenever anyone came close to me. It wasn't that people had bad intentions. It was just that the helmsmen who were driving the spectator boats didn't look around, particularly behind them. Once I got the attention of the other captain he quickly turned away, but it was a nervy business because I had to steer, keep the yacht sailing well in the wash from the spectator fleet, deal with the staysail sheets, and tack back and forth in the half-mile-wide channel. Soon I could feel rivulets of perspiration running down my back. Often people in powerboats paralleled my course and couldn't understand that when I blew my horn and tried to wave them out of the way, I was about to tack. The people gaily waved back and appeared startled when I abruptly turned toward them ("What's he doing?"). Suddenly I heard the boom of the starting cannon, and as I glanced toward the Newport shore I saw hundreds of colored balloons float up into the sky. Overhead, half a dozen helicopters snorted across the sky while photographers leaned out and snapped away.

Though the spectator fleet outnumbered the contestants twenty to one, I could see a number of BOC yachts immediately ahead of me. John Hughes—

who looked jaunty in a stylish canvas hat—flashed by on the opposite tack in *Joseph Young*. I saw Dick Cross on *Airforce* with the brown patches of his Kevlar-reinforced mainsail glinting in the sun. John Biddlecombe in *ACI Crusader* had very deep reefs in his mainsail and a small staysail, but appeared to be streaking along. John had particularly broad shoulders, and the silhouette of his body was distinctive against the lighter background as he tacked ahead of me. Jean-Yves Terlain in the bright yellow *UAP* was tacking under his mainsail alone. All the BOC captains looked grim and harried and peered anxiously from one side to the other. I wished for a camera, but of course there was no time.

Suddenly a power boat whizzed in front of me. I had to tack immediately. It was hair-raising to be hemmed in by these careless boat owners, but there was little that I could do except to blow my air horn. The people seemed to have no idea that I had only sails. Somehow I must have an engine and can keep out of *their* way. I passed the big green and white *Credit Agricole,* which appeared to have a sail-handling problem of some kind. My towboat was still following me, and everyone on board smiled and waved. Finally after ten or twelve tacks I worked out into the ocean, and the spectator boat traffic began to thin. My towboat pulled alongside, everyone cheered, and the boat turned back. I would miss Margaret and my friends a lot.

The ocean was not clear of traffic, but no one was near me. Nothing was ahead. What a relief after the last few hours! I set the autopilot on an east-southeast course and went below. I was ravenously hungry and cooked a big meal.

The race had begun.

I learned later that a few minutes before the starting cannon, two of the fastest sixty-foot BOC yachts had collided. The French vessel *Ecureuil d'Aquitaine,* struggling with a press of spectator boats and autopilot problems during the pre-race maneuvering, struck the stern of *Thursday's Child*. *Ecureuil* continued, but *Thursday's Child* was towed to a Rhode Island shipyard with damage to her self-steering gear, rudder, trim tab, and transom. Some twenty people, including three of *Ecureuil's* support team, worked through the night to repair the damage. Warren Luhrs, the captain of *Thursday's Child,* finally started the race the next afternoon, twenty-four hours and thirty-nine minutes late. Warren had the option of filing a protest but said that he preferred not to make an issue out of the mishap.

"This has taken off some of the pressure I felt at being the favored American at the start," he said. "It's nice in a way to be behind and know you have to work your way up. It's made me that much more determined."[9]

A second problem at the start was a collision between John Martin's

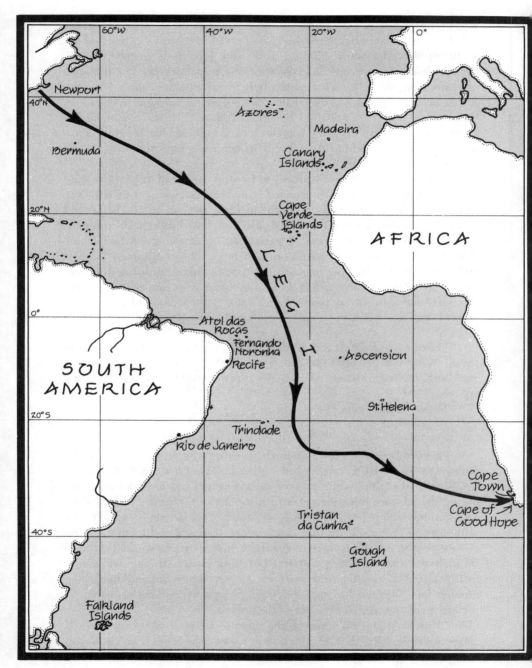

3. Leg 1

South African entry *Tuna Marine* and a spectator boat that failed to keep out of his way. The sixty-foot, thirteen-ton *Tuna Marine* caught the boom of a thirty-foot sailboat with six people on board and dragged her sideways until the smaller vessel capsized and the boom snapped off. No one was hurt, and *Tuna Marine* continued. Nevertheless, the collision emphasized the danger of an unmanaged spectator fleet.

The direct route from Newport to Cape Town is roughly 7,100 miles, but sailing vessels are seldom able to sail direct routes. The first leg of the race was tactically the most difficult part of the entire 27,550-mile course by far because of seven different wind systems and two high pressure areas whose positions change every few days. Initially—not counting the coastal breezes—I began the race in the westerly winds of the Atlantic. As I headed east and south I got into the variables, the so-called horse latitudes between the westerlies and the northeast trade wind. Eventually I would get into the northeast trade wind, which in September is roughly 1,200 miles wide from north to south. At about ten degrees north latitude I would run out of the trade wind and enter the doldrums, the mostly windless region between the northeast trade wind in the Northern hemisphere and the southeast trade wind in the Southern hemisphere. Once through the southeast trade wind would come the variables, and then finally the westerlies in the South Atlantic. The boundaries of these seven wind zones are roughly predictable but generally have to be drawn with a rubber ruler. Of course, a sailor tries to enter a wind zone so that he will have fair winds, reaching winds, or light headwinds. He tries to avoid fresh or strong contrary winds.

In addition to the wind zones there are two prominent high pressure areas in the Atlantic: the Azores high, and the South Atlantic high. Both bring special problems, and it's possible to be becalmed in these highs for days. One tries to avoid the highs, at least the center, and to enter the high in the wind quadrant where you will encounter weak or moderate headwinds.

My general plan was to head southeast toward the distant Cape Verde islands, which were at fifteen degrees north latitude, about four hundred miles west of Senegal on the African coast. This scheme was based on the sailing advice in *Ocean Passages for the World,* the great compendium of suggested passages compiled over generations by the British Admiralty. I planned to follow this book unless I had strong and overpowering reasons to do otherwise because off-the-wind sailing was what I sought.

I wanted to get as much easting as possible before I entered the northeast trade winds so I would have following winds in the northeast trade wind. I would be hard against the southeast trade wind on the port tack, but if I had worked my way east as far as possible beforehand, my distance to Cape Town would be less. Was all this wishful thinking? I would find out.

During the first BOC race, the winner, Philippe Jeantot, chose a course slightly west of the rest of the fleet. Philippe sailed south-southeast from Newport to the equator and crossed the doldrums where they were not as wide (north-to-south) as farther east. Although this route risked going closer to the area of tropical storms (it was now September, the worst month for hurricanes), Philippe's tactics were based on the windward capability of modern yachts (particularly with water ballast) and the use of on-board weather-fax charts to avoid tropical depressions. Once in the Southern hemisphere, Philippe sailed south and then west, and with the South Atlantic high on his port hand he had fair winds all the way to Cape Town. Philippe's 1982 route was dangerous, innovative, and clever, and gave all the competitors lots to think about.

> [From the log]. August 31st.
> *0806.* Wind southwest at seven knots. The ocean is fairly calm. Course 155°. Alone with nothing in sight. I just heard two tremendous bangs in the sky from the shock waves of the London Concorde letting down for New York. I am heading for a point in the ocean at 35° north and 45° west, about 1,223 miles away. I have just hoisted the genoa, something I should have done last night, but I was exhausted after the start of the race. The shape of the 915 sq. ft. sail is wonderful and pulls us along incredibly well in these light winds. It's too bad the genoa is so much work to put up. Fortunately I had a big breakfast of bacon and eggs, toast, tea, and coffee. I feel great after a couple of good naps last night.

When I had changed headsails I was aware that the Harken roller furling gear was not right. There was a terrible grinding whenever I turned the aluminum extrusion column that revolved around the headstay and held the sail. The more I used the gear the worse it got. I climbed to the masthead to check the top swivel, which was okay. I had had this problem during the qualifying trip, and now once again I found that the extrusions had slipped down the headstay wire and jammed against the lower wire-end terminal.

The problem was the two-piece collar that was supposed to hold the extrusions up in place. After a hard look I discovered that the bolts supplied by the maker to hold the two halves of the clamp collar together fitted the castings perfectly, but appeared to bottom out and put just enough pressure on the extrusions to look okay, but in truth to have little clamping power. As soon as there was a shock load on the extrusions (from pitching into a head sea), they slipped down inside the clamp collar. I found two shorter bolts among my spares, coated them with thread-locking compound, tightened them very firmly, and hoped for no more trouble.

I was dismayed at the lack of a positive locking arrangement to keep the extrusions away from the Norseman wire-end terminal. It seemed to me that the top of the entire lower assembly should have been cast or machined so that the extrusions could have rested on a strong integral lip or flange (with a clamp to hold them in place). With the extrusions resting on a solid base, all the downward thrust loads would have been transmitted directly to the excellent Harken ball bearings at the bottom of the assembly. A less elegant solution would have been to put a thrust bearing at the bottom of the extrusion column to take the torsional loads in case the extrusions slipped against the wire-end fitting. The instruction book alluded to this problem by stating that if the extrusions slipped, the furling gear would be hard to operate. Yikes! If you had to furl a sail in hard conditions with the extrusions jammed against the bottom wire-end fitting, there was a danger of turning the entire headstay wire *and unscrewing the Norseman wire-end fitting at the top of the headstay, which would mean losing the wire and maybe the mast!*

After all the advertising hype about the Harken gear, this trouble was discouraging. Fortunately the gear seemed to be okay at the moment and worked perfectly, but I had nagging doubts and would have to be careful. If I had these problems in trifling winds, what lay ahead?

In any case, I was fed up with this technical baloney. I wanted to sail, not do engineering studies on equipment. I reached over, switched on the SSB radio to 2056 KHz, and picked up the microphone.

"*American Flag,* WTV 2907, to any BOC vessel."

"Hello Hal. This is Pentti Salmi on *Colt.* How's your wind?"

Problems! The grinding noise in the difficult-to-use headsail reefing-furling gear was caused by the bottom extrusion riding down and around the bottom wire–end terminal, something that should have been impossible.

Pentti Salmi working at *Colt's* mast.

Pentti was one of the two Finnish entries, a forty-year-old civil engineer who worked in New York. He was blond, bespectacled, full of jokes, and eternally cheerful and upbeat. I pressed my microphone button and answered.

"It breezed up to twenty knots from the east in the middle of the night, so I had to change down," I said. "I've got two reefs and the staysail and am going along at seven and a half knots. Have you changed the name of your yacht?"

"Well, you see I finally got a sponsor. A Finnish tobacco company."

"In Newport you told me that you hated cigarettes. In fact you said you despised cigarette smoke. 'It's poison gas,' you said."

"That's true," said Pentti. "But I needed the money and had to make a slight adjustment to my moral principles. The money is wonderful. I don't have to smoke the sponsor's cigarettes. I just have to carry his name."

"Have you talked to anyone else?"

"No, you're the first. I did hear a radio conversation that Bertie Reed in *Stabilo Boss* is returning to Newport because of autopilot problems. I think everyone is still recovering from the tension of that terrible start."

Pentti and I exchanged our September 1st positions and agreed to talk on the following day. This was my first experience with the BOC chat hour which was to become part of my daily life for the next nine months. Each BOC entry was required to have two radios, a very high frequency (VHF) set for short range, and a single sideband or ham radio for long-distance work. According to the rules, the captains had to report their positions to race headquarters every seven days. In addition, we had to send our estimated time of arrival to the race committee forty-eight hours before finishing a leg (plus an update two hours before crossing the line). During the first BOC race, the contestants had used their radios to talk to one another and established a chat hour that became quite popular. For the present race the committee arranged a chat hour schedule and urged the entries to keep in touch with one another, both for general information and as a link in an emergency.

Of the twenty-five entries in the BOC race, everyone was a stranger to me except Dick Cross on *Airforce*. There were eleven entries in Class I. One yacht in the class, *Legend Securities,* was fifty-six feet long with partial sponsorship. The other ten were of maximum length, sponsored, high-tech, and all rather awesome, with expert assistance, vast budgets, shore-based advice, computer programs, private weather information, shipping containers full of tools and spares that went from stop to stop, and God knows what else. *Thursday's Child* was no doubt the fastest yacht and was ministered to like a newborn baby by a team of professionals who were in constant attendance, like a group of surgeons. The French entries seemed formidable, but I may have been awed by their size and unusualness. The Aussie and New Zealand entries looked tough, and certainly the two vessels from South Africa were sailed by determined men.

Class II had fourteen entries (four of maximum length) and was mostly a mixed lot with several exceptions. Jacques de Roux had *Skoiern IV,* which seemed the fastest. The two Finns had excellent yachts (Harry Harkimo had a Swan 51 cut down to fifty feet). The Americans had six entries (Mike Plant's sponsored *Airco Distributor* had made a daily run of 240 miles on her qualifying trip to Horta and was perhaps the most noteworthy). I had no idea of the potential of the other entries.

On September 2nd, John Biddlecombe, one of the two Australian entries, was on the foredeck of *ACI Crusader* changing jibs when he accidentally stepped through the open forward hatch with one leg and crashed down on his private parts. John, a former stunt man, severely injured his testicles ("an enormous groin hematoma" said the doctors later). A moment before he was in the sunlight, full of energy, happily dealing with his sails. Now poor John lay in the shade in dreadful, paralyzing pain, barely able to suck in agonized breaths. It took hours before he was able to crawl aft and head for Bermuda, the nearest port, to seek medical help.

Between 2300 and midnight on September 3rd, the prettiest yacht in the BOC fleet—*Airforce*—slammed into an unknown object in the sea 130 miles northeast of Bermuda. According to Dick Cross's later statements, he banged into something hard, perhaps a shipping container that had been lost from a commercial vessel. The wind had been increasing, Dick had rolled up his genoa, and *Airforce* was sailing at seven and a half knots under a reefed mainsail and staysail. At the moment of impact, Dick was just stepping over a cockpit coaming. The force of the collision knocked the thirty-seven-year-old captain down into the cockpit well where his back struck a winch. The blow knocked him unconscious.

"I was out for about an hour and was still in quite a bit of pain when I crawled below," said Dick. "I turned off the ship's power and used a flashlight to look around. There was water up to my knees, and the cabinet work on the starboard side was adrift. The toilet was loose, and things were floating around. The collision had punched up the area forward of the watertight bulkhead, and four or five feet aft of it. The hull had a horizontal wound along her side—a couple of feet below the waterline—near the base of the toilet.

"I tried the manual bilge pumps to remove water from both the main cabin and the forward compartment, but you have to sit and stroke the pumps, and I was in a good deal of pain. I didn't notice any progress, so I began to use a bucket. With a bucket you know you're doing something. One of the things that came floating by was a yellow pouch with my wet suit in it. I put on the suit to get warm.

"By daylight I had bailed three or four hours. Things were about the same, but I was losing ground from being tired and discouraged. I decided it was time to get off the boat. I tried the ship's power. Even though the batteries had been flooded out, I got enough juice to call Bermuda harbor radio and the east coast of the United States. I sent a distress call [at 0829] and said I was sinking. I went up on deck and found that *Airforce* was still pretty stable. I got the liferaft launched and put in my survival suit, my glasses, a hand-held VHF radio, the Argos, an EPIRB,* and the ditch kit.

"At 0930, about fifteen minutes after I got into the liferaft (I was still tied to *Airforce,* now awash), a Coast Guard Falcon jet homed in on my EPIRB, and I was able to talk to the crew on the portable radio. The Falcon told Bermuda that I was in the raft and the boat was going down. A P-3, a subchasing airplane out of Bermuda, was soon over me also. The U.S. navy base in Bermuda sent a helicopter [at 1100].

"*Airforce* began to pitch and roll, and the Falcon pilot screamed at me to cut free because he thought the yacht was going down. When the helicopter showed up [at 1205], a diver went into the water, hooked me up, and I was winched aboard. Shortly afterward I was in a hospital in Bermuda.

"About the time I cut free from the sinking *Airforce,* the Cypriot merchant ship *Allgau* appeared," said Dick later. "If I had known there was any help in the area I would have done things differently. When I left the yacht, all I could think of were the fifteen BOC yachts behind me. If *Airforce* floated just beneath the surface, she was enough of a hazard to sink or kill someone else. I felt she was nonsalvageable, so I opened up the hatches to the after watertight compartment. If I had been in a healthier frame of mind, I probably wouldn't have done it."[10]

Dick Cross's decision was expensive. *Airforce* had cost $325,000 and was uninsured. She sank in three thousand feet of water. It seemed to me that there were a number of things that could have been done to have avoided the tragedy.

1. Dick might have pulled a sail around the outside of the damaged hull area to have slowed the inflow of water. The leaks couldn't have been catastrophic because the yacht was afloat more than twelve hours after the collision; to bail and use up his energy without stanching the water first was an exercise in futility. ("I couldn't have done it because of my back.")

2. He might have plugged the worst holes with cushions jammed or nailed in place and held with shores of timber or lengths sawn from the spinnaker poles. Dick was in warm water and had on a wet suit. ("It might have been possible in a few places.") According to the official navy report made by the crew of the helicopter, the water temperature was eighty-three degrees; the air temperature eighty-one. The wind was six knots from the southeast, and the sea was almost calm.

---

* EPIRB stands for emergency position-indicating radio beacon, a small, battery-powered portable device used to find distressed mariners and downed fliers.

3. A merchant ship could have lifted the yacht aboard with a cargo crane (it was ironic that the *Allgau* retrieved his liferaft and belongings after Dick had left), or have passed him a suction line. A second merchant ship had been diverted to the scene and was nearby.

4. He could have asked the Coast Guard to have dropped him a powerful pump.

5. He could have chartered a tug from Bermuda.

6. Why he didn't stop the yacht by heaving to, or taking down the sails to reduce her forward motion and the resultant water pressure on the leak is unanswered. ("I kept sailing. I got her turned around and headed for Bermuda.") Such action might have halved the severity of the leak and, combined with a sail on the outside, have saved the vessel.

7. He could have attempted all these things.

Unfortunately none of these boat-saving ideas occurred to Dick because he was tired, injured, frightened, and no doubt apprehensive. He had had nothing to eat for twelve hours or more, and his energy—which he certainly needed in this crisis—was low. Dick had never been in such a predicament before and was perhaps bewildered. He had taken pain pills because of the injury to his back, and the medication might have impaired his judgment. ("I wasn't in great shape. I was functional, maybe fifty percent," he said later.)

When the navy helicopter picked up Dick, the yacht was clearly afloat in spite of both watertight compartments being open. The navy pilot described the situation as "man abandoning boat." It was such a pity. In the space of a few hours the romance of the great race and the excitement of Newport had suddenly become distant and remote. In Dick's eyes the sea had grown nasty and alien. "I just wanted to get off," he said.

Later Dick's friends and supporters made herculean efforts to find and salvage *Airforce*. But the yacht had sunk.

The ultimate challenge for a singlehander is the moment when he has big problems. It's easy to be critical and to pass judgment from a comfortable chair ashore. Let no one who was not there with him fault the single man against the sea.

Twenty-four yachts were left in the race.

The twenty-five competitors at the start of leg 1:

CLASS I (11)

name	yacht	size	comments
Guy Bernardin	*Biscuits Lu*	60 ft.	well-tested and modern
John Biddlecombe	*ACI Crusader*	60 ft.	fast, stability problem
Philippe Jeantot	*Credit Agricole*	60 ft.	favorite from France
Ian Kiernan	*Spirit of Sydney*	60 ft.	best from Australia
Titouan Lamazou	*Ecureuil d'Aquitaine*	60 ft.	formidable, high-tech
Warren Luhrs	*Thursday's Child*	60 ft.	good record; favorite U.S.
John Martin	*Tuna Marine*	60 ft.	South African favorite
Richard McBride	*Neptune's Express*	60 ft.	high-tech Farr design
Bertie Reed	*Stabilo Boss*	60 ft.	former Whitbread yacht
Jean-Yves Terlain	*UAP*	60 ft.	unusual modern design
David White	*Legend Securities*	56 ft.	entry from 1982–83 race

CLASS II (14)

name	yacht	size	comments
Dick Cross	*Airforce*	46 ft.	high-tech from Maine
Harry Harkimo	*Belmont Finland*	50 ft.	Swan 51 cut to 50 ft.
John Hughes	*Joseph Young*	42 ft.	narrow Swedish design
Richard Konkolski	*Declaration of Independence*	44 ft.	entry from 1982–83 race
Eduardo Louro de Almeida	*Miss Global*	41 ft.	former one-ton racer
Harry Mitchell	*Double Cross*	41 ft.	former IOR winner
Mike Plant	*Airco Distributor*	50 ft.	new Rodger Martin design
Hal Roth	*American Flag*	50 ft.	ultralight from California
Jacques de Roux	*Skoiern IV*	50 ft.	excellent Presles design
Pentti Salmi	*Colt by Rettig*	47 ft.	lengthened Sirena 44
Mark Schrader	*Lone Star*	49 ft.	Valient 47
Takao Shimada	*Madonna*	48 ft.	sole Japanese entry
Mac Smith	*Quailo*	45 ft.	Swan 441
Jean Luc Van Den Heede	*Let's Go*	45 ft.	narrow; only 4.9 tons

. . . .

CHAPTER ELEVEN

Across the Equator

*I*t had been a busy week for race headquarters in Newport. The press people thought they would have a few days of quiet after the hectic beginning which had involved three BOC yachts in two collisions. As we have seen, two of the vessels managed to continue, while *Thursday's Child* returned for repairs and restarted a day later. The next morning, however, Bertie Reed, captain of *Stabilo Boss,* 110 miles out, radioed that he was returning to Newport because of autopilot problems. Bertie spent thirty-four hours sailing back to Newport for repairs that took thirty-five hours. The genial South African finally restarted at 1100 GMT on September 3rd.

In the meantime, John Biddlecombe had almost castrated himself on the foredeck hatch of *ACI Crusader.* John was recovering in Bermuda. If that wasn't enough, *Airforce* hit something and sank. Now on September 5th came the word that *Miss Global,* the Brazilian entry of Eduardo Louro de Almeida, a keen twenty-six-year-old sailor from Rio de Janeiro, had lost both her main rudder and her emergency rudder. Eduardo was on his way back to Newport for a new rudder. He was steering by adjusting his sails, and the plucky sailor was on the radio again and again arranging for speedy repairs so he could restart quickly.

Doctors ordered John Biddlecombe to rest for two weeks, but he heroically sailed (walking gingerly) after only forty-eight hours. *ACI Crusader* soon got into forty-five knots of wind, however, and the Australian yacht was knocked down twice. Both times the mast spreaders and main boom were pressed into the water. On the second knockdown, the self-steering gear collapsed. John realized that his yacht was dangerously tender and needed more ballast, so he turned around and sailed back to Bermuda. He immediately ordered a lead bulb to be added to the bottom of the keel. The 1,260-pound bulb was to be made in the United States and shipped to Bermuda. He hoped to start again in two weeks.

Two BOC captains were now in Bermuda. John Biddlecombe was reeling under the tragedy of first his injury and then the problem of inadequate ballast. Dick Cross was trying to recover his senses after the sinking of *Airforce*. Together the two sailors went out and drowned their sorrows in dark-and-stormies, the national drink of Bermuda, a dynamite concoction of dark Gosling rum and ginger beer.

On September 7th, Pentti Salmi radioed headquarters about a nasty fire in his engine room. Before Pentti got the flames out, they destroyed the alternator, his main source of electricity. This meant a dark ship, no autopilot, no electronics, and only sparing use of the radio for the next forty-seven days. "The engine is absolutely useless now and is only a lot of extra weight to slow

Little man and a big yacht. Here Bertie Reed dances around the deck on *Stabilo Boss* while this big sixty-footer reaches eastward into the Atlantic on the first leg. This vessel previously went around the world in a Whitbread race with a twelve-man crew. "She's a bit of a handful when the wind gets over forty knots," said Bertie.

me down," said the blond-headed Finnish sailor when I spoke with him the next day. "I would throw the stupid thing overboard into the sea, but I can't think of a way to get the heavy engine out of the cabin."

A tropical depression that headed for part of the fleet was upgraded and named Hurricane Earl on September 8th. Four days later four yachts met Earl's winds in varying degrees and directions about six hundred miles southeast of Bermuda. Mark Schrader on *Lone Star* ran off before the storm in fifty-knot winds.

"I thought it would go north and east," said Mark, "but the hurricane turned west and gobbled me up. I sailed toward England for twelve hours under bare pole in steep breaking seas. At first I thought it was just a bad squall, but the wind shifted and increased dramatically, and I couldn't let go of the wheel. It was raining so hard it hurt. The wind ripped away the blade from the windvane, a hatch was open which I couldn't reach to close (my chart table was soaked), all the outside electronic equipment was flooded, and the cushions were blown right out of the cockpit."[11]

John Hughes aboard *Joseph Young*—on a better quadrant of the tropical storm—logged 200 miles in the right direction under a small headsail and three reefs in his mainsail. *Quailo* and *Double Cross* also spoke of lots of wind. Meanwhile on *American Flag*, 840 miles farther east, I glided along on a southerly heading at three and a half knots with trifling westerly winds.

By September 15th, the BOC fleet had gotten its sea legs and was spread out all across the North Atlantic. *Biscuits Lu* was in first place in Class I, with *Tuna Marine* second, 35 miles behind. In Class II, the leader was *Skoiern,* with *Airco* second. *Skoiern's* pace was unbelievable, and she sailed right along with the Class I yachts even though she was ten feet shorter. *American Flag* was third, 185 miles behind *Airco,* and 508 miles behind the amazing *Skoiern.* I was heading more eastward, however, and hoped to improve my standing with the fine off-wind capability of *American Flag* when I got to the northeast trade wind.

The Brazilian entry, *Miss Global,* got a new rudder in Newport and restarted on September 13th. However, the time spent sailing back to Newport plus the four-day stop for repairs put Eduardo 2,309 miles behind *Skoiern* on the September 15th reckoning.

[From the log]. September 4th.

1900. This morning I had the new green and white spinnaker up, a beauty, and we zipped along on a fairly smooth sea in front of a twelve-knot northwest wind on a course of 110°. The wind increased to twenty knots, but the sky was clear, and I thought the wind would gradually ease again. Suddenly the fore guy block exploded. With nothing to hold the end of the spinnaker pole down, the pole flew straight up. In about two seconds the spinnaker ballooned way out to starboard and pulled us over on our ear. The side deck, the boom gallows, and the main boom were in the water. To take off some of the heeling pressure, I eased the after guy way out. The spinnaker wrapped around itself, began to flog, got thoroughly out of control, and finally fell into the water, where the sail became a super sea anchor. I spent the next two hours winching the torn and soaked sail aboard before I got the whole mess on deck—an exhausting job. I even lost the halyard, whose bottom-end stopper knot somehow came loose in the confusion. How to reeve the internal halyard at sea is a problem. I'm sick when I think of the spinnaker, my worst ever sail-handling experience. It will take a while to dry out the sail and my spirits before I can begin repairs.

So far in the race my winds had varied mostly between southwest and northeast from eight to fifteen knots. One day the wind blew from the east at thirty knots, and another day at thirty-five knots before falling light again. Most of the BOC captains kept track of the changing winds with small onboard radio facsimile printers that picked up shore transmissions and made weather charts every few hours. If you knew a wind shift was coming, you could change your course to take advantage of it, or perhaps avoid something bad by an abrupt switch in steering. If adverse weather was about to blast down on you, you had warning. (Sometimes the wind dropped before a storm and deluded you into putting up all your light sails only to force you to change down quickly.) With knowledge of what was coming you could plan deck work and repairs for light periods, make more sensible landfalls, and in a tacking situation choose the better way. The weather information wasn't always right, of course, but with perhaps six or maybe seven correct calls out of ten chances, the odds were that a weather-routed boat would get hundreds of miles ahead and might miss a calm, headwinds, or a nasty storm. That is, if you knew how to read the charts.

Although I had done a lot of ocean sailing, none of it had been with weather charts because I had never carried a radio until now. *American Flag* had a weatherfax receiver, and every day I spent time studying the squiggly highs and lows—which looked like giant fingerprints—on the little charts. I listened carefully to the endless discussions of the weather information on the chat hour, especially between *Lone Star* and *Joseph Young*. I was learning, but I felt like a novice. I had wanted to find out more about weather chart interpretation before the race. A friend had even arranged for some private coaching, but there had been no time to follow it up.

As the race went on, I was amazed to learn that a number of the big-budget BOC yachts were linked with professional advisers on shore who not only sent out private weather advice (at confidential times and frequencies) but who plotted the positions of the leading yachts, evaluated their progress and problems, and radioed tactical advice to their clients. I thought (and still do) that the use of private shoreside advice was outrageous in a supposedly evenhanded race of lone sailors, but I soon realized that I was simply being naive. My Olympian motives were unrealistic and obsolete.

The philosophy of this "Mt. Everest of races" was that "anything goes" unless expressly forbidden. Shoreside advice was not against the rules; hence those who could afford private weather and tactical services used them to the maximum. I formally protested this arrangement at each port during the race, but my complaints were scoffed at. It seemed to me that the little guys without shoreside help weren't spitting out sour grapes, but we were riding three-legged horses in a four-legged horse race.

"We could never stop private advice," said the race chairman," because it would be impossible to moniter all the radio frequencies."

I countered with the suggestion that the race organization should get the best possible weather information and distribute it to *everyone.* Perhaps the wind information could be played on a repeating tape that would be changed

Wind directions for Leg 1 recorded on *American Flag*

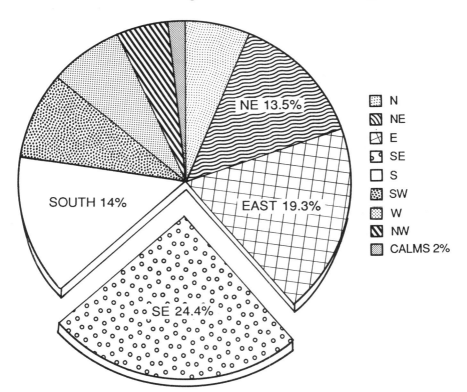

several times a day. If the best weather information were distributed freely, then—like tobacco in prison—its private value would be lost. If someone wanted additional outside information, let him have it. To get around the objection that each yacht would need a separate forecast and that twenty-five forecasts were beyond the resources of the sponsor, I pointed out that the yachts in the race tended to travel in little groupings, and that four zonal forecasts should cover the vessels. As the contestants without private help were to find out, the weather charts from a given country got increasingly useless when you sailed a thousand miles or more from a country's shores. We were to learn that adequate weather information in the Southern ocean was scanty indeed.

Some of the private weather advice was useless, of course, but some of it was incredibly good. Near the end of leg one, for example, Harry Harkimo on *Belmont Finland,* who was near me and getting information from France, said that at 1400 my wind would blow from the northeast at twelve knots. I thanked Harry but privately scoffed. At 1300 I had a light southwest wind. An hour later the wind switched to the northeast and began to blow at eleven knots or so. Magic!

Although I was busy sailing, I continued to worry about money a few levels down because it was doubtful whether I could continue in the race past Cape Town. A few days after the tragedy of *Airforce,* I wondered if I could pick up her partial sponsor. I used the SSB radio to call Margaret, who made inquiries. I then telephoned Tony McDowell at the Champion Paper Company in Connecticut. Tony told me that his company had planned to do a deluxe color book about Dick Cross and *Airforce.* Each page was to be printed on a different stock of coated paper, and the book was to be used as one of Champion's yearly promotional catalogs. With *Airforce* out of the race, the book plan was changed. It would now be in four parts, each section to be about an American. Part one would be on Dick Cross. Would I like to be part two? The pay was only a few thousand dollars, but in addition the company would give Margaret a ticket for a flight from Maine to Cape Town and return. I agreed at once and marveled that I could make these complicated arrangements while at sea.

I learned that *Ecureuil d'Aquitaine* * had not escaped unharmed from her collision at the start of the race. The hole in her bow leaked badly, and Titouan had to pump 100 liters an hour until he managed to slap a makeshift patch in place. His problems continued, however, because both his autopilot and wind vane steering device failed. Titouan said that he was spending up to

---

* Pronounced eh-cue-roy DAK-key-taine, *écureuil* means squirrel, and *Aquitaine* is a province in France. The yacht's sponsor was Caisse d'Epargne Ecureuil, a savings bank, and the yacht's name suggested that you should squirrel away your savings in this regional bank.

twenty hours a day at the wheel and was exhausted. He planned to stop at Ascension island to replace his two steering devices.

On September 17th I crossed twenty degrees north latitude and thirty-five degrees west longitude. So far I had sailed 2,380 miles southeast from Newport, and I was about 600 miles west-northwest of the Cape Verde islands off the western bulge of Africa. *Let's Go* and *Declaration* were near me, and the three of us hurried southward with fresh easterly winds. I had spoken to Jean Luc Van Den Heede twice each day since the start, and we were becoming good friends. Jean Luc was a mathematics professor who was on a year's sabbatical. Our talks were always fun to look forward to because we both made it a point to bring up one or two new things on each transmission. Jean Luc was upbeat and positive and—like the others on the chat hour—closed each radio transmission with wishes for good sailing.

Richard Konkolski was the captain of *Declaration*. He was forty-two years old and a Czechoslovakian by birth. He had come to the United States as a political refugee just prior to the 1982–83 BOC sailing race, which he entered and completed. The present race would be Richard's third circumnavigation. I knew him only slightly, but he seemed pleasant enough and keen to get to Cape Town. Richard had tried hard for sponsorship in the United States and was a bit bitter that he had not succeeded. He was sailing his old yacht from the earlier race.

On *American Flag* my biggest problem was changing headsails when the wind varied in strength. To keep sailing fast, I had to change back and forth between the staysail (292 sq. ft.), yankee (565 sq. ft.), and genoa (915 sq. ft.). The hanked staysail was easy, but taking the yankee down from the furling gear and putting up the genoa on the same furling gear was a madcap scheme. I had found this out during the qualifying trial between Horta and Newport (see pp. 76–78). I had hoped to improve the arrangement before the race, but there had been no time. I discussed the problem with the people at North Sails, but they simply didn't understand the difficulty because they usually sailed with three or four people. The situation for a singlehander was quite different.

Taking down the genoa at night in rain on the angled foredeck in a rising wind was by far the riskiest job on the ship. Going to windward I *had* to get the sail down when the apparent wind got to fifteen or sixteen knots. If the wind rose to twenty knots I was in big trouble.

My sail-lowering scheme was to rush forward, get the halyard coil in my hand, leave one turn on the halyard winch, and cast off the line jammer. Then, holding three sail ties in my mouth, I'd stand halfway along the foot of the sail, ease the halyard (led forward through a block at the foot of the mast), and gather in the sail as it came down to keep it from escaping over the side. As soon as I got the sail down part way, I threw a tie around the back section of the diminishing sail triangle. Then I eased the halyard more and got another tie farther forward. By now the drive of the big sail had lessened, and the yacht had slowed somewhat, which brought the deck level more upright. From then on the job of throttling the big sail, bundling it below, and hoisting the smaller yankee was easy. I found that my lifeline harness was impossibly in the way when I was lowering the genoa so I didn't hook on during these maneuvers.

As I sailed south in the trade wind I looked in vain for a northeast wind so I could ease the sheets on *American Flag* and get her up to ten knots or more. The wind, unfortunately, was from the east, or a little south of east. With a southerly compass course, this brought my apparent wind well forward of the port beam. While *American Flag's* performance was adequate at seven and a half knots (180 miles per day), I was getting killed by the yachts with water ballast. Jean Luc told me one day that he had spoken with Jacques de Roux, who said that he was doing a steady ten knots (240 miles a day). Even if Jacques exaggerated a little and was doing nine knots to weather (216 miles), he would massacre me on the first leg. On September 19th, *Skoiern* was 492 miles ahead of me.

The east-southeast wind breezed up to eighteen to twenty-four knots for the next three days. I dropped the genoa and put up the yankee. Soon, however, I rolled up the yankee and hoisted the staysail. In between these headsail changes I had put two reefs in the mainsail. As the wind rose and I shortened sail we still went along at seven or eight knots, well heeled. Where was that northeast trade wind?

Jean Luc Van den Heede and Richard Konkolski—who were nearby— also spoke of fresh east-southeast winds. Jean Luc reported that Guy Bernardin in *Biscuits Lu* was already in the doldrums but had a good west wind and logged nine knots. Philippe Jeantot had a problem with his mainsail and had to change the big sail, which must have weighed 100 kilos.

I had seen little bird life since Newport except for occasional red-billed tropicbirds, which are large white creatures with red bills, black bars on their upperparts, black eye stripes, and extremely long white tail streamers. These birds have a high pitched chee-chee-chee screaming call and a curious circling flight. They seem rather nervous, excited birds, with a rapid motion of their forty-inch wings. I have always wondered how they can keep up such rapid flapping without wearing themselves out. No leisurely flaps and long glides for these birds. They always seemed to be straining at the maximum.

While looking over the course ahead, I was surprised to find that the hump of South America (Natal, Brazil) is only 1,550 miles from the closest point in Africa (Freetown, Sierra Leone).

[From the log]. September 20th.
    1045. A big squall from the east. Furled yankee. Nice rain shower and bathing scene. Now underway again. On the radio this morning John Hughes

and Mark Schrader sounded a little homesick. John was obviously frightened when a nasty squall knocked his vessel flat during the night.

1200. 202 miles in last twenty-four hours. We are 672 miles north of the equator. The South African ham radio operators joined the Newport group, who were transmitting the Argos positions. It was a real thrill to hear the South Africans reaching out so earnestly.

The next day Guy Bernardin in *Biscuits Lu* slipped over the equator, the first yacht across, followed closely by *Tuna Marine,* which gradually crept into the lead. Mike Plant in *Airco* had moved up strongly in Class II and was only eighty-seven miles behind *Skoiern,* the leader.

On *American Flag* I was 315 miles behind *Skoiern* and 567 miles north of the equator. That night I arrived in the doldrums. A little after midnight a squall to leeward blocked the flow of wind, and soon I was down to two knots. The wind was quite gone, as if someone had shut a window. There was just enough moonlight to see a large cumulonimbus to port. Canopus, one of the three brightest stars, shone brilliantly off the port bow. By dawn we were in the light-weather zone for sure, with rain, squalls, fluky winds, and immensely tall, flat-bottomed cumulonimbus clouds all around. Fortunately during the night there was some moonlight so I could see what I was doing. By noon I had maximum sail up, and we were ghosting along at three or four knots under a fierce sun. I put on a long-sleeved cotton shirt, sunglasses, a big straw hat, and plastered myself with sunburn cream.

[From the log]. September 22nd.

0900. Yesterday I did a lot of grumbling when the wind dropped to six knots. Today after a night of being becalmed, six knots is "not too bad." I just finished a hearty breakfast and cleared up a stack of dishes. I had a sponge bath and put on clean clothes, all of which makes me feel marvelous.

1200. Eighty-two miles in the last twenty-four hours. Two hours of sail drill for nothing. Spinnaker poles up and down, various gybes, sails in and out, and I don't think we gained one boat length.

1450. A Brazilian ship, *Aromafa,* bound for France passed by. The officer on duty spoke only a little English, but we exchanged a few pleasantries. Still calm and hot. I finished rigging a water-catching funnel under the main boom gooseneck. I hope to top up the water tanks. It's amazing how I resent the intrusion of a ship and only want it to go away from "my ocean."

For the next seventy-two hours my daily runs averaged just eighty-four miles a day. To keep *American Flag* going meant constant sail drill. First it was a squall and rain. Then a calm. Then a good wind for an hour. Then nothing. Then another squall. And so on. It was trim, tack, change to the running rig, pole up, pole down, and back to the fore-and-aft rig. Finally I would get fed up and go below for a cup of coffee only to realize that the wind had returned! My goal was to head south, ever south, to get across the band of doldrums to the southeast trade wind.

I spent many hours in the cockpit trimming the sails, and one day I glanced over the side into the calm sea and saw a nine-foot hammerhead shark following the yacht. The light was good, and I was able to look a little way into the clear sea water. From about fifteen feet away I saw a smooth-skinned creature that was colored a dark greenish-blue with white undersides. He had five gill openings on each side, large caudal and dorsal fins that swished on the surface of the water, and an incredible, T-shaped hammerhead. A large eye looked out from each end of the hammerhead, which must have measured about two feet from one side to the other. There was a forward-facing nostril near each end of the hammer. My fish book said that a shark could sense his prey even when it was out of his sight. Did his sense of smell work the same in water as it does for a human in air?

When I called in my weekly position to race headquarters, I happened to mention Lucifer and said that he had been following me for three days and that I had no inclination to go swimming. This was put out in the bulletin sent to the thousands of schoolchildren who were following the BOC race. Months later I received letters from children who were fascinated with Lucifer, the hammerhead shark.

Dick McBride aboard *Neptune's Express* after she was dismasted near the equator. This unusual photograph of a sailing yacht with a jury rig was taken by David White aboard *Legend Securities*. David changed course and arranged to meet the disabled vessel in case Dick needed assistance (he didn't and made Recife under sail). Dick has set up a spinnaker pole for a mast and is sailing surprisingly well with a storm jib and a trysail. Sailing roughly westward with fair southeast winds, Dick made runs over one hundred miles a day.

. . . .

CHAPTER TWELVE

Problems

On September 23rd Dick McBride came on the radio in a choked voice and reported that he had been dismasted five miles north of the equator. Dick said that a three-quarter-inch Navtec aluminum fitting had sheared at the root of the second spreaders on the mast.

"The seventy-five foot mast broke in three pieces, and trying to deal with it was impossible. It damn near killed me," he said.

For a time Dick thought he could winch the broken mast and sails back on board. He almost accomplished this risky job, but his hoisting line broke and the whole works fell back into the sea. Dick's problem then was that the jagged spar ends were held next to the hull by the strong rigging wire and could easily punch holes in the hull as the yacht rolled in the ocean swell. Dick used his bolt cutters to chop away the shrouds and stays. The broken mast then sank and took with it his precious boom, mainsail, and genoa, a big loss. Dick then raised a twenty-two-foot spinnaker pole as an emergency mast, set a staysail, and headed downwind (west-southwest) toward Recife in northern Brazil.

Dick had never been to Recife and didn't have charts. Fortunately I had sailed there on an earlier voyage, and I had the requisite charts on board so I was able to radio instructions (630 miles on a course of 240°M.). I told him about the harbor, lights, and entrance and cautioned him about a few local problems (rats the size of cats, thieves in the night, and beware of the local native food, especially uncooked pork).

That same afternoon I spoke on the short-range VHF radio with Jean Luc, who was only twenty-three miles southwest of me. Jean Luc was extremely upset about the surprising progress of Richard Konkolski on *Declaration,* which was logging far better time than we were in the doldrums.

"You know that we three have been together for a week or more in the same wind zone and totally becalmed from time to time," said Jean Luc. "I have been studying the weather charts trying to understand how Richard could have suddenly pulled so far ahead of us. How could a boat that's not using an engine do so well?

Wind strengths recorded on *American Flag* during leg 1

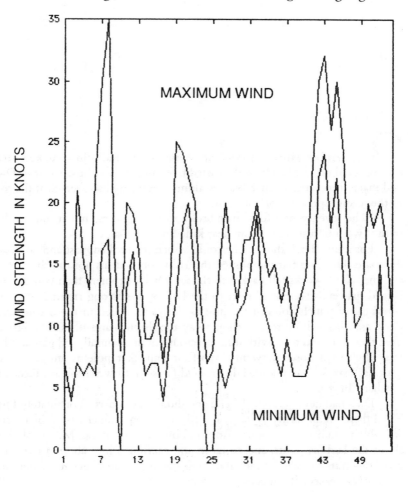

DAYS OF LEG 1

"Another point," said Jean Luc, "is that if *Skoiern* falls out for any reason, then *Declaration* could win the cash prize for the first unsponsored yacht because *Airco,* the second-place yacht, is sponsored."

I plotted the daily runs of the three yachts in the doldrums from the official Argos positions transmitted from Newport.*

	Let's Go	*American Flag*	*Declaration*
September 22	67	62	90
September 23	47	53	96
September 24	85	107	122
September 25	148	136	65
September 26	97	95	74
September 27	97	76	163
September 28	113	80	104
September 29	85	80	106
Average	92	86	102

I was astonished when I reviewed the figures and the weather charts. Not only were all three vessels in the same wind zone, but *Declaration*—being heavier and having a shorter waterline—was potentially a slower vessel than the other two yachts.

	Let's Go	*American Flag*	*Declaration*
Weight	4.9 tons	8 tons	9.8 tons
Overall length	45 feet	50 feet	44 feet
Waterline length	35.1 feet	46.5 feet	34.5 feet

The BOC race was a sailing event, although engines were allowed to be carried for routine battery charging. The propeller shafts were supposedly sealed by the race committee, and only in the gravest emergency could the engines be used for propulsion. About two-thirds of the entries had no shafts or propellers at all; however, you could make a good argument for an engine

---

* The Argos mileages were for distance made good toward a target, in this case Cape Town. Because of contrary winds or sloppy sailing, a vessel often sailed a poorer course and logged more miles through the water (the daily run) while making fewer miles toward the target.

because if you got dismasted near land, an auxiliary could be of the greatest value.

Jean Luc had no engine, and I had removed *American Flag's* shaft, strut, and propeller before the race. Konkolski had a powerful auxiliary engine and a large feathering propeller.

It seemed unlikely that someone would try to use an engine in such a race. The other competitors were not dumbbells and were well aware of the mileages that were possible in different sorts of weather. Someone might argue about the fine points of a starting line maneuver, fudge the length of his anchor chain by a meter, or be short a couple of required emergency flares, but to stick a knife in the heart of the race by using an engine was a basic insult to fair play, and as John Hughes said, "It was not on."

The race rules were specific on protests. You had to notify the committee within forty-eight hours, fly a red protest flag when entering the next port, and file a written protest on arrival. You also had to inform the person against whom you were alleging a rule violation. When I called Konkolski on the radio and told him I was going to protest, he knew immediately what I was talking about.

"You'll never prove anything," he blurted out.

I could only pity him.

Jean Luc also called Konkolski to tell him of the protest from *Let's Go*. The news of the two protests filtered through the fleet and cast a pall over everyone for a few days.

Later in Cape Town, Jean Luc and I learned that the French sailors in the race had particularly strong feelings about Konkolski from the first BOC event in 1982–83. "I had my doubts about his performance during the fourth leg of the first BOC race," said Philippe Jeantot. "In my big fast boat I was doing only 80 miles in twenty-four hours in the calm zones. Konkolski did 120 miles in his small heavy boat. Do you think that is possible?"

Another competitor, Guy Bernardin, made the same point. "I am not surprised that he did use his engine, as we did have suspicion on the first BOC on the last leg between Rio and Newport," said Guy. "This should not be allowed in any kind of sailing race."

I forced myself to put Konkolski out of my mind and got back to sailing in the race. The radios were handy for information, but when one of the receivers brought bad news I felt like taking an ax and smashing the instrument to bits. I knew this was a childish impulse, and I did like to know how the race was going and what the gang was up to, but the marvelous solitude I had experienced on earlier long voyages was gone.

Once through the doldrums and south of the equator I got into the southeast trade wind. Now the wind was stronger and on the nose. Soon I had hidden all the big sails and was bashing into fresh headwinds with the staysail and reefed mainsail. On September 29th I did 179 miles, then 178, 181, 160, and 169, all on a course a little west of south. I knew that as I worked through the trade wind I would get into the variables and finally the westerlies, and that both were strongly influenced by the south Atlantic high pressure area. My plan was to work both east and south and to approach Cape Town a little to the southwest to allow for the north-setting current and the strong southeast gales of South Africa.

On October 1st, Harry Harkimo reported that he had accidentally stuck a screwdriver in one eye while fixing something two days earlier. "This morning it's better but still painful," said Harry. "When you're stupid enough to put a screwdriver in your eye, you have to suffer."

The next morning I managed to burn my wrist while moving the steaming teakettle. The burn was painful, and I kept bumping it. I couldn't find any burn ointment among the maze of old medications in the first aid locker. Some of the stuff was twenty years old, and I resolved to find a doctor to check over all the tubes and bottles and update everything when I arrived in Cape Town.

That night John Hughes came on the radio and complained about a severe earache. He was dismayed to find no ear drops among his medical supplies. Mac Smith on *Quailo* promptly suggested a mixture of alcohol and vinegar. Two days later John reported success with Dr. Mac's home remedy. "I can now chew food without discomfort," said John.

Harry Mitchell on *Double Cross* was a bit behind most of the fleet but coming on steadily. His yacht had been built like an icebreaker for heavy weather sailing in England eleven years earlier, and her stout aluminum hull and heavy displacement (29,543 pounds) with a short rig put Harry at a big disadvantage in light airs. Harry never complained but pushed on steadily. Harry was fascinated by what people ate on sailing trips and often talked about cooking and menus when he spoke on the chat hour.

The rigging trouble on *American Flag* began just after lunch on October 3rd. I was 745 miles southeast of Recife and 2,890 miles west-northwest of Cape Town. The wind had dropped to nine knots, and I was changing headsails when I discovered that a tiny stainless steel roll pin that held two of the Harken aluminum headfoil sections together had worked partway out of one extrusion about thirty feet up the headstay. This meant that I couldn't lower the sail beyond that point because the swivel which held the head of the sail got stuck on the protruding roll pin.

How could I deal with such a problem?

My first idea was to shimmy up the fat headfoil section and knock in the pin with a small hammer. When I tried to do this I found the section was too slick and the sail was in the way. I thought again. If I couldn't go up, why not come down? I climbed to the top of the mast and considered sliding *down* the headstay foil. Gravity would be on my side. However when I looked down the headstay from sixty feet up while *American Flag* rolled in the swell, this scheme looked most unwise. I climbed down to the deck, sat on the coach-roof, and thought hard.

My third idea was to lash a small hammer to the end of the boathook. I then climbed to the lower mast spreaders, got comfortable, and tried to reach out forward with my special long-handled hammer and tap in the nasty roll pin. This sounds like a reasonable plan, but with the yacht rolling in the swell I simply couldn't guide the hammer to the pin. After half an hour of trying to thread the needle I knew this idea was no good.

My fourth plan was to hoist a bosun's chair and some tools up the mast to the lower spreaders. If I could get in the chair and swing out forward, then I could wrap my legs (and use one hand additionally perhaps) around the headstay while I tapped in the pin. When I tried this I found that I couldn't get enough momentum to swing forward. If I pushed out really hard, then I would swing back and crash into the spreaders against my back. The idea had some merit however. What I needed was a line to the headstay so I could pull myself out. I tried throwing a line around the headstay, but the rolling of the yacht defeated me. I then got the idea of hoisting the swivel (and attached sail) to the masthead and climbing up with a long light line, one end of which I tied to the swivel. I then went back down on deck and lowered the sail to the stuck roll pin area. This brought the swivel and line down to the desired place. I then carried the other end of the line up to the bosun's chair. Now there was a hauling-out line to the problem area.

It took me a few minutes to get up my nerve to continue. Once again I climbed up to the bosun's chair, got all set, and on one roll of the yacht I pulled myself out to the midstay. On the next roll I yanked myself out to the headstay. I held the handle of a small hammer in my mouth, and I managed to hold myself against the headstay with my legs and the crook of my right elbow while I tapped in the cursed pin (I am left-handed). I finally eased myself back to the mast and climbed down. I was trembling violently from the exertion of all the mast climbing and my high-wire trapeze performance. The hauling-out act took only a couple of minutes once I was in position in the chair with the hauling-out line set, but afterward I was a nervous wreck and had to sit and rest for half an hour to recover my senses.

I then lowered the bosun's chair, dropped the small headsail (the swivel slipped past the problem area okay), hoisted the larger sail, and began sailing hard again. I went below and collapsed in my bunk.

The news from the fleet (October 5th) was that Dick McBride was in Recife. He expected his new mast to arrive by air any day. He had been laid low by an acute case of diarrhea caused by the local Brazilian food and water. John Biddlecombe was still in Bermuda waiting for the lead bulb for the keel of *ACI Crusader.* The bulb was to have been made at once in Connecticut but was delayed because of an America's Cup keel. When John's lead bulb was finally ready, there was another delay because a longshoreman's strike had stopped everything going to Bermuda by ship. The bulb keel was to have been shipped by air, but perishable foodstuffs for the island had priority. Eventually the keel arrived, "disguised as a crate of fish," according to reports. After almost four weeks of waiting—with his competition thousands of miles over the horizon—John was frantic to get going.

Several of the sponsored yachts had elected to use Kevlar—a new miracle fabric—in some of their sails. Kevlar was "stronger than steel" and made wonderful high-performance sails, but it was incredibly expensive and also incredibly brittle. Warren Luhrs—aboard the sixty-foot high-tech American entry *Thursday's Child*—was gradually moving toward the leaders in Class I, and had gone from last place to sixth place following the collision at the start of the race. Warren was at 5°33' south of the equator on September 25th when his 1,240 sq. ft., seventy-panel fully-battened $11,700 mainsail suddenly ripped at the second reef point. The tear was seven feet long and parallel to the leech. Warren immediately put a deep reef in the sail to take the pressure off the torn area and continued to sail at reduced speed. The captain didn't carry a spare mainsail (to save weight) so he set to work to repair the tear in the eight-ounce Kevlar-Mylar laminate. Warren managed to keep moving, but it took him four days (during which he averaged 109 miles a day) to dry, tape, and sew the sail.

Ian Kiernan on *Spirit of Sydney* also had trouble with the Kevlar in his sails and spent many hours sewing and swearing. "I must have taken leave of my senses not to have included a few sails of all Dacron," he said. Sailmakers loved Kevlar because it was strong and held its shape well, but the brown material was so brittle that if a sail flogged for a short time it was ruined. Kevlar could not stand rough usage the way Dacron could and largely disappeared from use after the first leg.

Ian was the humorist of the fleet and kept everyone chuckling. Unfortunately his jokes stopped when he described his progress in his million-dollar boat that was sponsored by a hard rock radio station in Sydney. Ian's weatherfax machine had failed to work so he was directed by a private meteorologist in Australia, who somehow sent *Spirit* into one windless area after another.

"The bloke has put me in the middle of every bloody high in the ocean," wailed Ian. "He must be in the employ of the enemy! I wonder if he has any French ancestors?"

[From the log]. October 6th.
    1015. Problems! I was about to change headsails when I discovered that the cursed roll pin had worked out of the Harken headfoil—just like three days ago. Nothing to do but to go aloft again and play human fly and swing out to

the headstay to repair the problem. I'm glad Margaret wasn't here to watch me. She would have fainted. But now all is in order, and we are going along nicely with the big sail. Two hours completely wasted because of roll pin problems.

1600. I have been hearing a strange banging noise up forward. I started looking around and discovered that when I lowered the bosun's chair this morning, the hammer (on a lanyard) somehow got plucked out of one of the side pockets and caught on a bolthead on the lower spreaders. When the yacht rolled, the hammer tapped against the mast. It was a miracle the hammer didn't fall overboard.

At noon the next day we were going along beautifully at 8.2 knots on a smooth sea. The wind was 8 knots from the east. It was the best sailing of the race so far, especially since we were almost on a direct course for Cape Town, which was now only 2,161 miles to the east-southeast. I felt great. We were at 23°13' south latitude, or 1,393 miles south of the equator, on the north side of the south Atlantic high pressure area. If the high remained stationary (an illusory hope), we might have the same wind all the way to Cape Town.

My feelings of well-being were shattered late in the afternoon when I spotted the cursed roll pin sticking out of the Harken extrusion again. Now my problem was more troublesome because with the genoa up I was stuck with the light-weather sail. If it breezed up, all I could do would be to furl the big sail and to put up the hanked staysail on the midstay. Without use of the yankee, my mid-range sailing was ruined. *American Flag* was like a car that could only operate in first gear and fourth gear.

Since I had knocked in the offending roll pin twice, I would have to try something else. Maybe I could tap in a new roll pin coated with LocTite glue. However this would be hard to do at sea because I would need two hands. Maybe I could tie myself to the headstay when I swung out to work on the roll pin problem. For the moment, however, we were sailing well, and I had no desire to try repairs since I ached all over and had four or five nasty blue and yellow bruises from my previous attempts.

The radio brought news that John Biddlecombe and *ACI Crusader* had finally left Bermuda. The new bulb keel was in place, John was thoroughly rested, and he hoped to reach Cape Town before the BOC fleet left on the next leg. Always an optimist, John was confident that he would lead the fleet to Sydney. It was good to have him back in the race, although the distance from Bermuda to Cape Town was more than six thousand miles.

The Brazilian entry, *Miss Global,* lost her rudder for the second time. Since Eduardo was forty-five miles north of the equator, he headed for Recife to join BOC captain Dick McBride, who was pacing the decks of *Neptune's Express.* Dick was biting his fingernails while he waited for his new mast to arrive from New Zealand via a wide-body Air France plane from Paris. Somehow the mast had disappeared at the Paris airport. Dick had half a dozen international experts working on the problem, and the delivery was "absolutely promised for October 14th." By now the New Zealander had become a bit cynical: "I'll believe it when I can touch the mast," he said.

Traditionally there have been two ways to approach Cape Town from the North Atlantic with regard to the South Atlantic high pressure weather system. Theory one says that you head south from the doldrums and keep sailing south until you hit the strong westerlies around 35–37°S. Then you turn left—heading eastward—and stay south of Cape Town until your vessel gets to 15–16°E. (about 150 miles from Cape Town), when you swing northeast to the city. This is the traditional big ship route and takes into account the strong north-flowing Benguela current along the west coast of South Africa.* Also, if you get a southeast gale (likely), you are in a favorable position to reach Cape Town.

Theory two was developed by Whitbread race entries, which sailed mostly on the wind from the equator to Cape Town and stayed north and east of the high. This could be tough on body and boat but was faster when sailing from England. Four big Whitbread yachts—supposedly the best in the world—suffered grave damage trying to go to windward at speed in southeast gale force winds in October 1985 while trying this scheme. Route two is not as direct when you cross the equator more to the west as one would in coming from North America.[12]

In theory three, worked out by some of the leading BOC racers, you sail south from the equator as though you were headed for the westerlies in the south. If a high pressure area obstructs your path, you turn left and close-reach across the top of the high until it passes you headed east. Then you dip south again until the next high comes along, and so on.

Eventually you will join the course taken by the theory one boats, but you have cut the corner and greatly reduced the distance sailed. In fact, you come close to sailing a great circle course, the shortest distance between two points on the globe. To sail the theory three route, however, is difficult and demands accurate weather information and skill in reading the barometer. The Argos position information is particularly helpful because you can see if other yachts have been slowed by a high pressure system.

On October 8th I saw four small whales, each about fifteen feet long. They were shiny and black with curved dorsal fins and rolling and splashing and blowing and having a great time. They might have been false killer whales.

---

* A current is a long-term movement of water in a river or the ocean. The six-hour reversing flow of water along a coast (as in a bay) is called a tidal stream.

[From my journal]. October 9th.

Last night I dreamed that I was in a household that was keen on darkroom work but knew nothing about it. I was teaching the family, which appeared to be run by an attractive woman who was charming but quite impractical. ("How can I develop the film if I can't see what I'm doing?") At one point we all went out for a walk up a very steep hill. It was snowing hard with flakes as big as cinders (hail?). The snow crunched as we walked, and the going was difficult. Finally I got to the top and broke through to a protected area (?). Then I woke up.

That day my good runs to the southeast continued with the light weather sails and included a couple of hours with the red, white, and blue spinnaker. During the night, however, the north wind began to increase and veer,* and at 0830 the next morning I got up from a restless sleep to find thirty knots and rattling sails. I had a struggle to get the spinnaker pole down, and I tucked a second reef in the mainsail. I needed a headsail, but I felt the staysail would be too much just then so I unrolled the clew of the rolled up genoa about ten feet, which picked up the speed from 5.6 to 7.4 knots. It was much colder with a frontal system—lots of low clouds and rain—going through to the east. I put on a long-sleeved thermal shirt and a watch cap, which felt wonderful. At noon (185 miles), the wind was a little less so I rolled up the genoa and hoisted the staysail.

By noon on October 11th (172 miles), I had a third reef in the main and was crashing along in rough seas with fresh winds from the south. I was 1,465 miles from Cape Town. That evening I heard that John Martin in *Tuna Marine* had led the Class I entries across the line. John completed the first leg in a little more than forty-two days, a wonderful record, in spite of two burst water ballast tanks, which had flooded the yacht with tons of water and had to be pumped out. John was an instant hero in South Africa. *Credit Agricole* finished sixteen hours later, and *Biscuits Lu* came in the next day.

On October 12th, I learned that Mac Smith on *Quailo* had gotten into trouble. The yacht was farther south (34°03′) and west (28°22′) than the rest of the fleet.

"The yacht was rolled over in very heavy breaking seas and then knocked down when the wind rose to fifty and sixty knots from the northeast," said Mac on 4143.6 KHz on the single sideband radio. "The mast is bent, and I've lost the intermediate shrouds on one side. The masthead instruments are gone, the steering vane is damaged, and the storm jib was torn off the forestay. *Quailo* is a shambles below, but there is no structural damage. I believe the Argos emergency signaling device was turned on during the

* In the Northern hemisphere a veering wind moves clockwise; a backing wind goes counterclockwise; the terms are reversed in the Southern hemisphere.

mishap. However I do not—repeat not—need assistance. I'm bruised, but okay."

By now I had learned that *American Flag's* ICOM IC-M700 radio capability was one of the best in the fleet so I was able to relay Mac's situation to South Africa. Mac was worried that he would set off a false alarm because of the Argos device.

Poor Mac was extremely frightened, and as soon as I heard his first radio transmission, I knew he was all through with the race. It was a pity, but there

Guy Bernardin aboard *Biscuits Lu*

was nothing I could do except try to cheer him up. Mark Schrader and John Hughes set up a radio schedule every two hours with Mac to reassure him. I was sorry I wasn't aboard *Quailo* so I could have helped him. Bertie Reed on *Stabilo Boss* also spoke to the distressed sailor.

On October 13th Mac was in better spirits, but quite demoralized. "Psychologically I'm wiped out," said Mac. "It's terrible." He reported a few small leaks, but he had pumped out *Quailo*. He agonized about his broken rod rigging and how impossible it was to deal with. "It's absolutely lethal to sails when the wire whips around," he said. "The middle of my mast has a severe bend to port while the top has a hook to starboard. I'm unsure whether to sail with the mast as it is or to attempt to straighten it. In any case I'm heading for Rio," he said.[13]

The Brazilian sailor Eduardo Louro de Almeida aboard *Miss Global,* who was steering toward Recife without a rudder, now reported the loss of his forestay fitting. About the same time the Japanese sailor Takao Shimada on *Madonna* reported broken rigging and steering problems. His course had been somewhat erratic, and he was far behind. He decided to go downwind to Rio de Janeiro. Our little band of twenty-five starters was shrinking. Two had gone to Bermuda; two to Recife; and now two were headed for Rio de Janeiro. It required a stout heart and much luck to continue in the race after damage and when far behind.

I had been reading Shakespeare—Macbeth of all things—and I found that I had begun to think and talk to myself in Shakespearean meter.

> To tack, or not to tack;—that is the question:—
> Whether 'tis nobler in the mind to suffer
> The slings and arrows of outrageous weather;
> Or to take arms against a sea of troubles,
> And by opposing end them?—To tack:—to change sails,—
> No more: and, by a sleep, to say we end
> The heart-ache and the thousand natural shocks
> That flesh is heir to,—'tis a consummation
> Devoutly to be wished. To anchor,—to go ashore;—
> To sleep! perchance to dream:—ay, there's the rub . . .

When I read this bit of verse on the chat hour, there was stunned silence. Finally Harry Mitchell came on: "I do believe he's gone clean round the bend. Obviously he needs a rest cure in a private facility somewhere."

"A bit of wit from old Will Roth," said Mark Schrader.

"Does anyone have handcuffs on board?" added David White on *Legend.*

At noon on October 14th I was 1,128 miles from Cape Town. The weather had been stormy for the past three days, and the low sky was streaked with hard shades of gray. A black-browed albatross circled round and round. *American Flag* was heeled to thirty degrees and pounding along to the east with the staysail and two reefs into chilly southeast winds between twenty and thirty knots. Where was that northeast wind that the weatherman—that false prophet—had been promising for three days? It was too rough to cook so I ate crackers and canned smoked fish while I sat wedged on the port settee berth and scratched away on a magazine article about the race. The banging and crashing was enough to disconnect the satnav wires (twice). I finally taped the take-apart plug ends together.

The autopilot had become sluggish and unresponsive. When I wanted a

Daily runs during leg 1

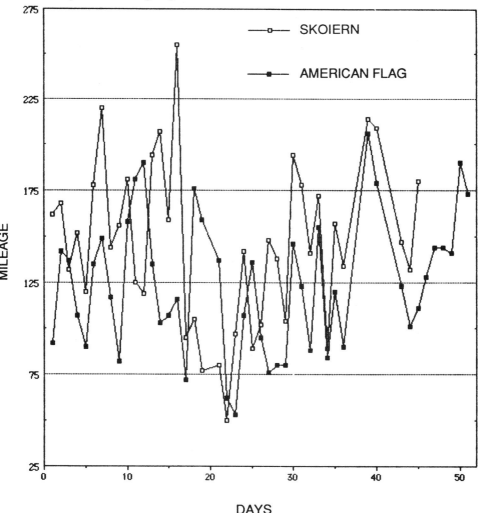

course of 125°, I found that I had to dial 150°, 200°, and finally 275°. I opened
a locker to check the components and discovered that the rough weather had
shaken out the mounting screws that held the compass unit—*which was rolling
around!* A couple of larger screws to hold the compass soon put us back on
course.

The next day the wind eased and veered to the east-northeast. I was still
stuck with the furled genoa and no yankee so when the sea eased a bit I
climbed to the masthead and tied a hauling-out line to the headsail swivel so I
could do my human fly act and get the genoa down. However, when I eased
the halyard, the big sail thundered down on deck. Apparently the defective
roll pin had come out. When I hoisted the smaller yankee headsail, I noticed
that the extrusions in the trouble zone had pulled apart several inches. I hoped
everything would hold together for the last one thousand miles to Cape
Town.

That same day, Jacques de Roux in *Skoiern IV* sailed across the finish
line of the first leg. Jacques was 250 miles ahead of *Airco,* the next in our class.
Skoiern's time of forty-five days was a smashing victory in the small class, and
more amazingly, Jacques had beaten seven of the Class I boats.

Thursday's Child finished the same day, followed on October 16th by
Ecureuil, with a jury-rigged spinnaker pole in place of her broken main boom
and a weary Titouan Lamazou, who had been hand-steering as much as
twenty-hours a day for a month. "It was not an enjoyable leg for me," said
the thirty-one-year-old French captain. "But I am not at all discouraged. I
figure I have had all my bad luck this leg, and that things will be okay from
now on."

On October 17th, Mike Plant arrived in *Airco* with the excellent time
of forty-seven days for second place in Class II. An hour later, *UAP*—the
yellow monster—crossed the finish line. Her captain, Jean-Yves Terlain, was
tired and fed up after hand-steering for nineteen days following a total
electrical failure that wiped out his autopilots and fancy electronic devices.

For the next few days on *American Flag* my winds were light and from
the northeast. When I changed to the genoa, its luff tape got caught in the
furling gear extrusions that had come apart. I managed to jiggle the extrusions together and straighten out the luff tape by working the halyard up and
down a little. New roll pins would have helped, but there was too much swell
to go aloft. On the evening of the 17th I had a spinnaker up for a few hours. I
could hardly wait to get to Cape Town.

On the morning of October 18th I sat on the edge of the cockpit
coaming while I whipped the ends of a piece of line and fumed over the
failure of the furling gear. *Declaration* and *Let's Go* were now far ahead. I had
my eye on a large bulk carrier about five miles north that was headed for the
Cape of Good Hope. It was the first ship that I'd seen for a month.

The fifty-foot *Skoiern IV*, sailed by Jacques de Roux, nearing the finish line at Cape Town. Jacques' time of forty-five days from Newport was phenomenal for the 7,100-mile leg, and he beat seven of the larger yachts. That Jacques drove his vessel unmercifully is apparent from the poor condition of his mainsail, which appears to have lost all its battens. The clouds over the mountains indicate a strong southeast wind. *Skoiern* is sailing fast with only a small staysail and a reefed mainsail.

[From the log]. October 18th.

1810. About ten o'clock this morning I got ready to hoist a spinnaker, but I found that I couldn't furl the genoa to get it out of the way. At first I thought it was because of a tangled line on the furling drum, but as I looked, the entire headstay and genoa fell into the sea.

To keep the mast from collapsing, I rushed forward with the two spinnaker halyards, which I set up as emergency headstays. I continued sailing downwind under the mainsail and staysail and managed to lift the sail and roller furling headstay on board and tie them along the starboard lifelines. *American Flag* must have looked like a swordfishing boat with a lot of metalwork sticking forward.

I spent an hour getting the sail off. It took another hour to extract the long headstay wire from the wreckage of the extrusions, which were hopelessly damaged. I found that much of the trouble was from a roll pin made of faulty metal that had split in two lengthwise; no amount of Loc-Tite glue or hammering could have kept the pin in place. All my efforts aloft had been in vain.

When the sea calms down I am ready to put up the headstay wire without the furling gear, which is in ruins.

I believe the failed roll pin allowed the extrusions to come apart and jam around the upper Stay-Loc fitting, which then unwound when I turned the roller furling gear. Or it could be that the extrusions worked down at the bottom and jammed around the lower wire terminal fitting as they have done before. Whatever happened, it's a mess.

At first light the next morning the wind was down. I cleaned the sticky graphite from the headstay wire and put a Stay-Loc fitting at one end. I sheeted the sails in and steered a course that gave the least motion. Then I hoisted the headstay wire on the jib halyard, climbed to the masthead with my tools, removed the old masthead wire-end fitting, slipped the clevis pin through the new end fitting, and put in the locking cotter pin. I was pretty tense and feeling sorry for myself and yelled down on deck for Margaret to release the jib halyard that was still tight on the new headstay wire. Of course, there was no Margaret to ease the jib halyard, and when I realized I was alone, I began to laugh at myself. I laughed and laughed while I climbed down to release the line and then back up to cast off the end and take it down to the deck. My light hysterics released the tension, and I felt better.

I put a wire-end fitting at the lower end, added a turnbuckle, connected everything, and tightened the turnbuckle. Hooray! A new headstay! I then got back on course, adjusted the sheets, and went to the galley and cooked myself a big breakfast. Two hours later I finished sewing piston hanks on every other grommet along the luff of the yankee, hanked on the sail, and we had a workable rig!

At noon the next day, October 20th, I had a run of 181 miles. The radio said that Bertie Reed on *Stabilo Boss* had crossed the finish line with a spinnaker flying. Bertie had had a tough leg. First he lost eighty-seven hours at the start because a mechanic forget to put oil in his autopilot; then near the equator he had gotten into light winds (together with *Quailo, Joseph Young,* and *Lone Star*); finally his rudder partially seized up from metal debris left by the autopilot mechanic. (Some mechanic! Was he sent by the enemy?)

A few hours later *Spirit of Sydney,* the eighth sixty-footer, got to Cape Town. Ian Kiernan had done poorly on the first leg (tenth place overall) in his million-dollar yacht. His sponsor decided to pull out (a hazard with sponsors) until Ian noticed that a mass of fish netting had somehow collected around his twin rudders and had obviously slowed him down. Ian's sponsor relented.

At noon on October 20th, *American Flag* had 237 miles to go to Cape Town. I was aiming a little south of the target in case of a southeast gale. At midnight I gybed the running rig before a good westerly wind, but twelve hours later I was whistling for wind on a smooth and very blue sea, and grumbling that *Let's Go* and *Declaration* had already finished. *Legend Securities,* the last yacht in Class I, was just slipping into Cape Town.

Pentti Salmi and Harry Harkimo, the two Finns in the race, were near me, and we talked back and forth on the radio. I was determined to beat Harry, but I needed to set the genoa to keep moving in the light airs. Unfortunately I had used up all my spare piston hanks on the yankee and had none left for the big sail. What to do?

I mentioned this to Mark Schrader, who was three hundred miles to my west.

"Do you have any large size plastic wire ties?" said Mark.

"Lots of them," I answered.

"Take the biggest and loop one through each luff grommet and around the headstay. The plastic is strong, and the ties will last for days," said Mark.

I did as directed, and I soon had the genoa up. We reached along with a light north wind. Although I tried to steer a little south of east, we were getting set north in the Benguela current. A big green tanker, *Jarrah,* passed

Faulty hardware. Part of the problem with the Harken furling gear were the roll pins which fastened together the sections of aluminum extrusions on which the sail was hoisted. Here we see a new roll pin (left) and one of the troublesome pins (right), which has disintegrated. The metal may have been faulty or have been fabricated incorrectly. Before assembly, the pin was well coated with Loc-Tite, which should have protected it from salt spray.

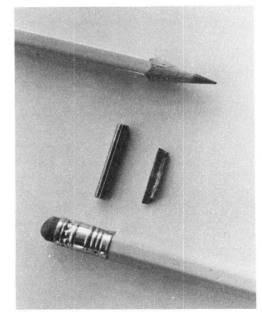

close to port. The mate reported that she was 150,000 tons, laden with oil, and en route from Mexico to Nagoya.

I had strained my left shoulder with all the mast climbing gymnastics and pulling the sail and roller furling gear back on board when the headstay came adrift on October 18th. In order to rest my shoulder I put my left arm in a sling that I made from a towel. I found I could run the yacht okay as long as I had use of my left fingers (say, to tie a bowline or whatever). The sling felt comfortable and gave my poor shoulder some rest. I would have worn the sling into Cape Town, but I thought the race committee might have looked askance at a one-armed singlehander.

I took a couple of short naps in the early evening because I knew I would be up all night. Before midnight I began to see the lights of Cape Town reflected on the clouds, and at 0145 on October 22nd, my fifty-second day at sea, I picked up Slangkop light, seventeen miles south of the Cape Town light. I sailed slowly northward along the coast, which had many lighted buildings, and as dawn broke over the city, my wind fell away to nothing. I was very excited and stood in the cockpit drinking coffee while I waited for wind, which came in trifling zephyrs. By 0700 I was near the Green Point lighthouse, but the wind headed me. When I tacked I saw *Belmont*—with Harry Harkimo aboard—about a mile away. The wind fell away to nothing, and we drifted slowly toward the finish line. Harry crossed twenty-seven minutes before me. I had reached South Africa.

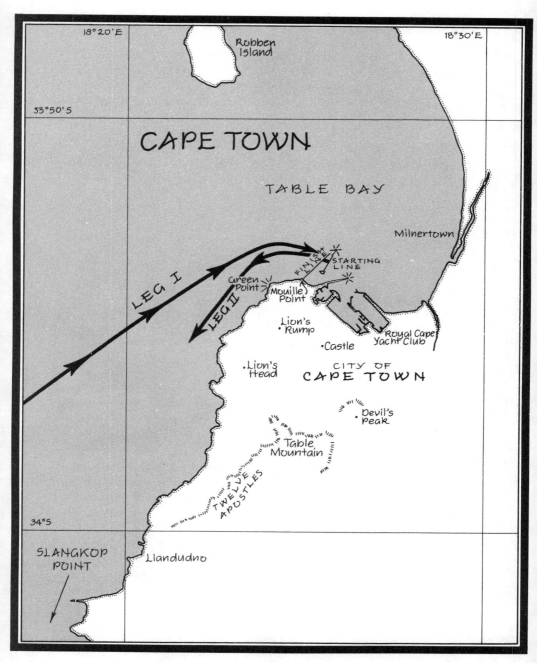

4. Cape Town

. . . .

CHAPTER FOURTEEN

Cape Town, South Africa

C ape Town is a lovely city, nestled softly along the edge of the sea at the northern foot of Table mountain, a craggy, brownish, flat-topped peak that rises abruptly from the land to a height of a thousand meters or so. From the sea you approach from the west or northwest and hope that a southeast gale is not blowing (you know immediately because of the wind and by a great white ragged cloud that hangs over the top of Table mountain and spills downward as the wind tears off its edges. At other times the cloud over Table mountain is gone, the weather is calm and still, and a sailor whistles for a breeze).

When I crossed the finish line the committee boat pulled alongside, and Margaret, race chairman Robin Knox-Johnston, and Brian Alcock, a South African cruising friend from times past, jumped aboard *American Flag.* It was wonderful to kiss Margaret and to shake hands with Robin and Brian. Robin took the tiller, Brian and Margaret dropped the sails, and I felt like a stupid spectator while we were towed to a berth at the Royal Cape yacht club. After my various problems (I reckoned that the furling gear failure had cost me three days) I had finished sixth in a minor class, and the reporters had long gone elsewhere. Nevertheless twelve or fifteen people came to see me tie up at the dock and kindly welcomed me to South Africa. Two smartly uniformed government officials cleared me in a minute, and I jumped on shore to meet Brian's smiling wife Helen and her two children. Kathy Giblin, the BOC presswoman, gave me a kiss, and I walked with the group to the clubhouse, where I sat down and ate breakfast all over again.

For the first few days in Cape Town I seemed to be floating on air. I didn't quite know where I was or what I was doing. Brian and Helen invited Margaret and me to stay at their house above the sea in Llandudno and even loaned us an old car. After I slept the sleep of the dead for a day and ate my fill of fresh fruit, I began to think of what lay ahead. Unfortunately with the *American Flag* project, the problem was always money.

While I had been sailing, some modest sums had come in from the various appeals that Margaret and I had made. During the first leg I had written a magazine article, and I expected a few checks from some other writing and photographs of the race. Would I be able to continue? It seemed doubtful. The most sensible thing was to give up the race and for Margaret and me to sail back to Maine.

During the first leg my biggest problem had been the failure of the roller furling-reefing gear on the headstay. There was no way I could race a fifty-foot yacht without the assistance of such a device (I needed two, but I could get by with one). Since I was tied up alongside *Skoiern IV,* I asked Jacques de Roux for his advice.

"By all means use the Proengin gear, which has worked well on my boat and for many of the others. If you like I will be speaking to Dominique Presles today in Paris. Dominique is a good friend of the head of Proengin and can perhaps arrange something."

The next day Jacques—who was eating and passing out wonderful Granny Smith apples from a box presented to him by a farmer—gave me the number of Proengin in Paris. I telephoned and ordered the gear, which was to be sent by overnight air freight. Even with a generous discount, however, my funds were going fast.

There were a number of additional jobs to do on *American Flag.* Fortunately Brian Alcock, our host, was a professional boat builder and a real boat nut. He was fascinated by the BOC race and loved to work on the yacht. *American Flag's* cabin sole was made of narrow strips of teak with spaces between the slats for ventilation and to save weight. Unfortunately, tools and small things kept falling under the slats, and the arrangement was impossibly difficult to keep clean at sea. Ideally I should have put a new sole of thin teak over thin plywood, but there was no time for this, so Brian found some inexpensive teak offcuts and we put these over the slats. I also needed a cockpit seat (which would cover the liferaft) and a stowage area for lines. One weekend Brian took charge of this project, and he and I built a nifty seat with line stowage underneath.

Margaret and I stayed in Llandudno for a few nights, but it was more convenient to sleep on *American Flag* because of the work on the vessel and the race activities. Also, when a strong southeast gale blew (it often got up to fifty or sixty knots), it was handy to be on board to adjust the lines and fenders.

The day after I finished, Pentti Salmi in *Colt* arrived, and the following morning Mark Schrader on *Lone Star* crossed the line. On Friday, October 24th, a fierce southeast gale screamed down from Table mountain. John Hughes in *Joseph Young* was thirty miles west of Cape Town and battling to get in. John—the Canadian sailor—was in low spirits. I called him on the VHF radio.

"*American Flag* to *Joseph Young*."

"*Joseph Young* here. Go ahead, Hal."

"How's everything, John?"

"Things are fairly grim here. The wind is a steady fifty to sixty knots. My cockpit lockers are full of water. I'm down to three reefs in the main, no jib at all, and am going slowly in big seas."

"Keep up your spirits, John," I said. "We're all waiting to welcome you. As soon as you get around the Green Point lighthouse we'll be out in the launches."

It was a fairly emotional radio transmission because our little reception committee (there were a dozen people listening) knew that John had been up for thirty-six hours. We also knew that he was nervous and upset and fairly near the end of his energy. I think a few reassuring words helped.

It was the middle of the night when we got the word that *Joseph Young* had finally been sighted. Mark, Jean Luc, Robin, and I put on our foul weather gear and jumped in the launches with the rest of the welcoming crew. The seas were big, and we all got drenched by waves that poured over the launch as we raced out to *Joseph Young*. Suddenly we picked her up in our searchlight, a tiny sliver of a yacht with a handkerchief-sized mainsail. She was almost hidden in surging waves and heeled way over while she pounded along in the appalling conditions. John, his yellow oilskins streaming with water, gamely waved a folded, soaking chart at us. We leaped aboard, shook his hand, and pulled down the sail. It was worth staying up all night just to see the smile on John's face as he crossed the finish line.

Joseph Young was the eighteenth yacht to arrive in Cape Town; there were still three others, but they were far to the north and west.

Many of the BOC yachts in Cape Town were already out of the water and undergoing extensive refits. *Ecureuil's* bow had to be repaired after her starting line collision in Newport. When the massive green and cream-colored *Credit Agricole* was taken out of the water for cleaning and painting, Philippe Jeantot was horrified to find that his yacht's five-ton lead keel had come loose from the hull and was hanging down thirty millimeters (one and a quarter inches). Philippe was lucky that the entire keel hadn't snapped off. The heads of the eight keel bolts had forced their way into the soft lead because washers of insufficient size had been used underneath the bolt heads. Philippe and his helper put in new bolts and stainless steel plates six millimeters thick (to serve as washers) and pulled the heavy lead keel back into position. Meanwhile, Guy Ribadeau-Dumas, the architect who had designed the yacht, checked over the hull and found that one weld in the upper keel structure had fractured. The architect flew back to France to calculate the extent of the problem and telexed back instructions that a number of modifications should be made immediately. Nevertheless, Philippe, worried that there wouldn't be enough time to complete the work before the start of the next leg, decided to continue and to wait until Sydney to do the modifications.[14]

Stabilo Boss's mast was also taken out (to have climbing steps added), and the hull was plucked from the water by a giant crane and put on land next to *Belmont,* which also had a crew at work. Harry Harkimo discovered that the leak that had forced him to pump forty liters every three hours during much of the first leg was caused by a hydraulic rigging expert in Newport who had removed a deck fitting and neglected to plug the hole.

Because of a siphoning problem, Jacques de Roux had lost all the water from *Skoiern's* fresh water tanks. (In order to live, Jacques had used an emergency osmosis device to extract fresh water from seawater.) Jacques was busy with improvements to his water tank plumbing.

Thursday's Child's mast had been removed, and the yacht was out of the water for painting and small repairs. I was astonished to learn that Warren Luhrs' shore crew included two prominent Swedish engineers, two expert boat mechanics, and a tactician-team manager, all flown from the United States. To hold their tools and spare parts, the shore crew had a full-size shipping container that had been sent ahead by cargo ship. My head swam when I thought of the cost of the shipping container, the wages, air fares, rental cars, meals, and lodgings for the five full-time men. (In Sydney, a sailmaker from the United States joined the team.)

The South African newspapers had story after story about the BOC race, and many people came to the waterfront to see the fleet. Since I didn't think it necessary to take *American Flag* out of the water, we stayed tied up at a yacht club slip and got to know some of the visitors. I'll never forget one nicely dressed elderly man. He walked with a cane and came thumping down the dock. When he got to *American Flag* he stopped and looked for the longest time.

"How do you fellows do it?" he said finally.

"Do what?" I replied, looking up from greasing a winch.

"Sail one of these vessels!" he said. "Around here when we go out in a fifty-footer for a day we need six or eight hearties. You fellows calmly go off on a fifty-day trip as if you were sailing a dinghy around the yacht club."

"We don't sail these things," I said. "We're just a bunch of goofy mechanics. We get towed out to where we can't hurt anybody and simply aim them at the next port. We all have some kind of self-steering apparatus. The wind does change, of course, and we need to adjust the sail area, but normally there's plenty of time, and usually the wind doesn't change that fast."

"You make it all sound so easy," said the man with the cane, shaking his head. "What about navigating? We always sailed with a navigator and tiptoed around the chart table so we didn't disturb him when he was at work. And a cook, a racing helmsman, a foredeck man, and so on."

The man turned and thumped down the dock. "You fellows are something!" he said as he left. "I just can't see how one man can do it all."

South Africa is a beautiful country, and as we traveled around a little, Margaret and I were continually astonished at its mountains and coastline and splendid farming country. One day Ken and Fay MacLachlan and their children whisked us away for a drive to the Cape of Good Hope and a meal at their home in St. James. Another time, Tuna Marine, the South African fish canning company that sponsored John Martin, chartered a bus and kindly took the contestants, wives, girlfriends, and helpers to Paarl, the famous wine-producing area about an hour's drive from Cape Town. We toured the KWV vineyard and then had a splendid buffet luncheon with the executives of the large winery. The day was a delight, and it got us away from the yachts and the sea for a change

The shadow that hovered over South Africa was the chilling effect of world opinion against apartheid, and I wondered what my reactions would be to the political and race problems. The South Africans had a craving for contact with outsiders because not many foreign visitors went to the country. Margaret and I had an invitation to dinner almost every night. Some dinners were elaborate; some were modest, but all our hosts were sincere, good people. We talked of our hopes and fears; our ambitions and failures; our dreams and aspirations. I had trouble understanding how such repressive measures could come from people who seemed very much like my neighbors back home in Maine.

Cape Town, a city of 214,000, seemed liberal in politics, and from what I observed had few racial difficulties. The people were largely involved in shipping and foreign trade, in education and the sciences, and were a long way from conservative Pretoria and the areas where large amounts of black labor were employed in mining and manufacturing. The problems in South Africa were much more complicated than I—an outsider—had realized. White people in South Africa were outnumbered by blacks and coloreds (5 million whites to 26 million nonwhites), and the population was stratified into four main groups (whites, blacks, coloreds, and Asians), whose aims often went in quite different directions. The enormous black population (22.7 million) included ten different nations made up of three thousand tribes (the Zulus—the largest—had 6 million people alone). Some of the blacks wanted peace with the whites; others spoke of confrontation. Complicating all this was the paradox that every day thousands of poorly educated, unskilled blacks tried to enter (not leave) South Africa in order to work. I thought of the parallel between those incoming blacks and the Mexican wetbacks in the United States.

In the foreign press there was much talk about the black population and its lack of voting rights. But how could a governing group that had a modern, progressive, beautiful country turn its wealth and future over to a huge majority of untutored blacks? The answer, of course, is education. The South Africans have made progress and more is planned, but it will take generations for the status of the nonwhite majority to improve just as it took a century after the U.S. Civil war for the minority blacks to rise above their status as slaves. Martin Luther King's watershed speech in 1963 in Washington, D.C., took place *a hundred years after the Civil war;* today in the United States we have thousands of blacks in leadership roles in government and industry and are proud of them, but their places in society didn't come about overnight.

The problem in South Africa was that the education reforms were going very slowly, and rapid progress was undermined by the conservative extremists who had introduced press censorship and a general iron grip on the populace, measures that seemed stupidly counterproductive to me.

On the night of the BOC awards ceremony we were to hear the mayor of Cape Town say: "We resent being the pariah of the world, an outcast among nations, simply because we South Africans have problems which are being attacked and solved."

At 0446 on November 5th, Harry Mitchell—aboard the forty-one-foot sloop *Double Cross*—arrived after a sixty-six-day passage from Newport. John Hughes, Mark Schrader, David White, Jean Luc Van Den Heede, and I went out on the launch to welcome Harry as he slipped across the finish line just before dawn.

Harry, who was sixty-two and the senior sailor in the race, was jubilant at reaching Cape Town. He was delighted to see all of us—his sailing pals with whom he had talked during his two-month trip. He immediately opened a bottle of cognac ("the right stuff"), and we toasted Harry's arrival while he sang a few verses of a Yorkshire ballad. Harry had had bad luck with Hurricane Earl ("sail damage"), calms ("my patience grew thin"), a broken boom ("the bloody thing"), and big ships ("I had three close calls").

"Did I eat breakfast on the trip?" answered Harry to a reporter's question. "Absolutely! I started each day with the full works—coffee, marmalade and toast, bacon and eggs, and 'proper' porridge. Breakfast is the best meal of the day. I can forgo the other meals, but breakfast starts the day off right."

Harry Mitchell, the enthusiastic captain of the British entry *Double Cross,* just after arriving in Cape Town. With a glass of beer in his left hand, a bottle of Nederburg champagne in his right, and a grand feeling of achievement showing on his face, Harry is a happy fellow.

With *Double Cross* tied up at the Royal Cape yacht club, nineteen of the twenty-five starting yachts were together. *Airforce* had sunk, and *Quailo, Miss Global,* and *Madonna* had dropped out. John Biddlecombe on *ACI Crusader* was on his way from Bermuda but would experience total steering failure near Cape Town and retire. Likewise Dick McBride of *Neptune's Express,* who finally got his new mast in Recife, had a nightmare series of medical, sail, and rigging problems. Since he was hopelessly behind, Dick and his sponsor decided not to continue. Nevertheless, both John Biddlecombe and Dick McBride were hard drivers and got full marks from everyone for their determination to press on in spite of adversity. No one had been keener to do the race than John Biddlecombe, whose first *ACI Crusader* had been destroyed on a reef in the South Pacific during his qualifying run.

On November 12th the prizes for the first leg were awarded at a giant party presided over by the mayor of Cape Town. A military band played, everyone was dressed up, and all the social elite of Cape Town were there. The mayor welcomed us to Cape Town, the historic "tavern of the seas" for mariners. Frenchman Jacques de Roux made a hilarious speech ("I am zee world champion of zee bad English").

I kept meeting wealthy people who assumed that because I was at the glittering party I too was wealthy. Margaret had raised an additional $1,615 from six U.S. donors, but all this was spent to get *American Flag* ready for the next leg to Australia. I was down to $200. My wife traveled on free transport, and the two of us ate off friends' hospitality. What kind of a charade was I playing? I felt that I was tiptoeing on the edge of grand larceny. Something was terribly wrong.

"Don't fret," said Margaret, passing her hand over my forehead. "Life's like a big game," she said gallantly. "Let's not worry about the cursed money. If there's something you really want in life, you have to go ahead and do it. Let's drink the champagne, dance, and have fun."

Before the start of the race I had heard vaguely about a program for schoolchildren called "The Student Ocean Challenge," a project of the Museum of Yachting in Newport, Rhode Island. The scheme—run by a wonderful, dedicated woman named Mame Reynolds—was for young people to follow the race (a textbook of the world) through weekly news bulletins and a computer hook-up which gave the latest positions of all the yachts. Many children adopted a captain and followed his progress around the world on a map which the students made themselves. Soon there was a wide-awake link between the competitors and the students. The race became an exciting, motivating vehicle to study geography ("Where is Tasmania?"); history ("Today I crossed the route of Columbus. Who was he? Where was he going? What was he trying to do?"); world trade ("What do ships carry?"); science ("Why does a ship need a compass?"); meteorology ("Today the yachts are in the Gulf Stream. How does the Gulf Stream influence the weather of Europe?"); mathematics ("If I sail 500 miles on a course of 180° . . ."); value concepts ("What if a sailor is lost?"); English composition ("Today I am writing a letter to my captain"); and so on. The children discussed such ideas as the challenge of achieving a difficult goal and what it meant.

The program became enormously popular because the race imparted a sense of urgency ("Things are happening now"), and with only the most trifling publicity some three hundred schools and twenty thousand children and their teachers in the United States and abroad signed up for the project.

When I arrived in Cape Town I began to get dozens of letters from earnest ten and twelve year olds with lists of questions. In addition, hundreds of South African schoolchildren (some in the program) trooped by to look at the BOC fleet. Many—in neat blue school uniforms—climbed aboard *American Flag*. Sometimes one of the young men would grab the tiller and pretend he was steering in a storm. His eyes would light up, and he became the new captain for a moment. The children had lots of questions.

"Do you get tired of your own cooking?"
"Did you ever hit a whale?"
"Do you ever get a headache?"
"Are you rich?"
"Have you had to dodge any rocks?"
"How do you feel about being alone?"
"Have you seen any seals or polar bears?"
"What would you do if you lost your glasses?"
"Do you think you'll die at sea?"
"What would you do if you got a hole in the boat?"
"How do you know where to go?"
"Are you scared of the dark sometimes?"
"Are you sick of sailing?"

It was fun to have the young people on board. Some claimed they wanted to become sailors. Would one of them take my place in the future?

All nineteen BOC captains were toiling away on the docks at the Royal Cape yacht club because our sailing date was only a few days away. Most of the work was centered around sail repairs, rigging, and autopilots. The slipway at the yacht club was large enough for the Class II boats, and *Colt* was out of the water for bottom painting. Mike Plant was fitting a new boom vang for *Airco*. Jean-Yves Terlain had installed an additional electrical generator on *UAP*. John Martin—perhaps worried about what lay ahead—had his mast x-rayed to check for fractures and cracks. *Skoiern* got a new spinnaker pole.

Everyone at the yacht club was helpful. Norman Maclennan took my saws and chisels away to have them sharpened. Later he brought me a can of hard-to-find engine oil. Andy Mitchell, the North Sails expert, repaired a sail and made a cover for the mast boot. A group of retired executives ran a special no-cost service that tracked incoming packages from abroad and rushed them through customs. Instead of being trapped in officialdom for weeks (a problem for foreign vessels), my rigging parts from France were delivered to *American Flag* on the same day they arrived in Cape Town. Keith Bellamy, the local mast maker, sent a rigging expert named Titch Mitchell and a helper to my vessel to set up the new headsail furling-reefing gear.

As soon as everything was in place we went out sailing to test it. The Champion Paper people from the United States had flown in for the start of the race and were keen to take photographs, so they followed us in a chase boat. In a few minutes we were out on Table bay, reaching along in smooth water at nine and ten knots, much to the delight of Brian Alcock, our Cape Town host, who was steering. The southeast wind gradually increased, however, and was soon screaming down from Table mountain at forty-five knots. The tow boat was unable to get us back to our slip, so we settled for the emergency mooring, a strategic buoy near the entrance to the yachting area. The next morning the wind was calm, and with Jacques de Roux's help, we got back to our slip. We filled *American Flag's* water tanks and put on a load of groceries (including five dozen fresh eggs and a few loaves of double-baked bread). A growers association gave each yacht two boxes of Granny Smith apples. Dr. R.D.H. Baigrie (Bags) kindly presented me with a smoked leg of lamb. ("If you don't feel like cooking, just whack off a piece. It's delicious.")

I made an arrangement with the Champion Paper people to trade a round-trip air ticket from Maine to Australia for Margaret in return for photographs and additional reporting for the Champion book.

The second leg of the race was to start the next morning. That night we had a final meal ("The last supper," quipped the cook) with Brian and Helen Alcock, who had become dear friends. My stay in South Africa had been a delight. I'd made a dozen new acquaintances, got *American Flag* in better shape to continue, and had a look at a beautiful country that I liked immensely.

The only negative element in Cape Town was the Konkolski incident, which I could not forget. I had kept careful notes on the affair.

[From my journal]. October 29th.

0830. Yesterday afternoon was the protest hearing of Richard Konkolski before a committee of four, three of whom were senior lawyers. Jean Luc and I were both convinced that Konkolski used his engine in the doldrums, and we counted on the race committee's engine seals to convict him. We were both furious when we found that the committee had simply put a wire with a seal on the engine gearshift lever. To defeat the seal, you merely had to disconnect the gearshift lever from the engine, and to shift gears with a pair of pliers. The race chairman sheepishly admitted that the technique was faulty and planned to change the procedure.

Jean Luc and I knew that without the engine seal evidence our protests would be rejected because it was simply one man's word against another. Jean Luc and I showed our logs and weather charts and told our story in a few minutes. We said we had sailed very near Konkolski in the doldrums and we believed he must have used his engine to gain thirty or forty miles a day.

Konkolski took an hour to reply. He said he had not used his engine to propel *Declaration.* The Czechoslovakian sailor boasted about his extensive experience and how he could make a yacht sail faster than ordinary sailors. He described secret German wind charts in his possession and how he made better time by sailing great circle courses. I was amazed to learn that Konkolski ran his main engine or his charging engine *seven hours a day* to power his computers, radios, eight-amp autopilot, microwave oven, and other things. He claimed that he never had calms and always did 120 miles a day or more (all the other contestants experienced calms, and every entrant except Konkolski had 60 and 80-mile days. On October 6th, for example, *Thursday's Child*—perhaps the fastest light-weather large yacht in the world—logged only 65 miles).

During their deliberations the men on the protest committee discussed the weather of the doldrums, the various yacht designs, and the determination of the three skippers. The jurists rejected the idea that lightweight, long waterline boats were necessarily faster than heavier, shorter yachts in trifling winds. The committee puzzled over the amount of fuel Konkolski must have carried to run his main engine and charging engine. If his first leg took fifty-one days and he used an engine for seven hours a day as he said, he would have needed *at least* 175 gallons of diesel oil for 357 hours of engine running. Did he carry extra fuel on board in containers and discard the containers? The jurists repeatedly faulted the race committee for not having sealed the engines adequately.

Toward the end of the hearing—which was taped—committeeman Eric Bongers said: "My feeling is that if you're asking me whether those people have proven that this guy [Konkolski] has used his engine, my feeling is no, but my gut feeling is that it must have been easy to slip the bloody thing in gear and just trickle along as they are alleging he did. But personally I don't think that they have actually proved it. That's how I feel about it. I suspect he did, and I feel that he probably did, but I just haven't had it proven to me."

The results of the hearing were: (1) the protest was thrown out although some of the committee had doubts about Konkolski's conduct; (2) the race committee got black marks for not sealing the engine shafts properly.[15]

After the hearing, the reporters were lined up outside to interview the participants. Jean Luc and I stoutly maintained that Konkolski had cheated. Konkolski said he most certainly did not. Mark Schrader who watched us all talking with the reporters suddenly spoke up: "If I had to decide what happened based on the interviews I've just seen, I would have to say that Richard wasn't telling the truth."

Jacques de Roux was particularly upset. "It's terrible," he said. "I prefer to have my engine in case of emergency, but I don't like the Konkolski affair. I am cutting my shaft and taking the propeller off *Skoiern*. Now no one can say anything." Pentti Salmi also decided to remove the propeller from his vessel ("that stops the problem for me") and hoped that Konkolski would do the same.

The next morning I saw Robin Knox-Johnston in the yacht club. "I listened to the tape of the protest," said Robin. "Konkolski contradicted himself twice during the hearing."

As I mentioned earlier (p. 124), the French sailors had strong feelings about Konkolski and his engine from the first BOC race and considered the incident nothing new. Later in Sydney, I spoke at length with Neville Gosson, who had completed the first BOC race. Neville had particularly hard things to say about Konkolski.

The comments of the race chairman and *eight* BOC captains can hardly be ignored. There was a good deal of sentiment that the race committee should have thrown Konkolski out of the race at Cape Town.

During the 1982–83 BOC race, Dr. Larry Kneisley conducted an in-depth psychological profile of all seventeen entrants. "Konkolski's behavior was extremely aggressive," recalled Dr. Kneisley. "He was a very competitive guy who had had to bend the rules in Czechoslovakia in order to survive," said the California psychiatrist.[16]

David Dellenbaugh, a distinguish sailing jurist, has written: "One of the unique things about sailing is that it's one of the few sports where rules are enforced by the competitors themselves. We don't have referees or umpires out there calling the shots, or players trying to get away with anything they can. We have a system where conscience still counts and the way you play counts as much as the final outcome."[17]

The Konkolski affair was negative and depressing. The BOC management hated it. I hated it. Jean Luc hated it. We were both revolted by the affair, which was an ethical and moral matter that shouted for attention. *The contestants simply had to police their own race.* Suppose Jean Luc and I had been wrong, and the others were in error, too. In my opinion, Konkolski could have helped his case by taking off his propeller, which would have removed doubt about his future conduct. It was suggested that he take a lie detector test to clear the air. Konkolski refused and pranced around with an air of studied indifference. He was right when he had said: "You'll never prove anything."

Konkolski was clever but not smart enough to realize that he had sown a seed of doubt and mistrust among the wonderful bonds of friendship the other eighteen captains enjoyed. Konkolski stayed in the race, but he was not popular. To my knowledge no one ever said anything to him about the incident, but he knew very well what the fellows thought. Jean Luc laughed at him. I simply ignored him.

The nineteen competitors at the start of leg 2 in order of standing:

CLASS I (9)

name	yacht	length	tonnage
John Martin	*Tuna Marine*	60 ft.	12.5 tons
Philippe Jeantot	*Credit Agricole*	60 ft.	12.8 tons
Guy Bernardin	*Biscuits Lu*	60 ft.	11.2 tons
Warren Luhrs	*Thursday's Child*	60 ft.	8.4 tons
Titouan Lamazou	*Ecureuil d'Aquitaine*	60 ft.	12.5 tons
Jean-Yves Terlain	*UAP*	60 ft.	10.8 tons
Bertie Reed	*Stabilo Boss*	60 ft.	12.5 tons
Ian Kiernan	*Spirit of Sydney*	60 ft.	9.8 tons
David White	*Legend Securities*	56 ft.	8.9 tons

CLASS II (10)

name	yacht	length	tonnage
Jacques de Roux	*Skoiern IV*	50 ft.	8.4 tons
Mike Plant	*Airco Distributor*	50 ft.	10.5 tons
J. L. Van Den Heede	*Let's Go*	45 ft.	4.9 tons
Richard Konkolski	*Declaration*	44 ft.	9.8 tons
Harry Harkimo	*Belmont Finland*	50 ft.	15.2 tons
Hal Roth	*American Flag*	50 ft.	8.0 tons
Pentti Salmi	*Colt by Rettig*	47 ft.	9.0 tons
Mark Schrader	*Lone Star*	49 ft.	12.9 tons
John Hughes	*Joseph Young*	42 ft.	11.5 tons
Harry Mitchell	*Double Cross*	41 ft.	13.4 tons

. . . .

CHAPTER FIFTEEN

The Southern Ocean

*E*arly on the morning of November 15th, the first rays of yellow sunlight floated across the harbor while I sat in *American Flag's* cockpit drinking a cup of tea and thinking of the day ahead. My most important job was to go aloft for a final check of the mast and rigging before the second leg of the race started. I climbed the mast steps to the top, caught my breath, and stopped for a moment to enjoy the splendid sight of Table mountain, which towered over the city. In the warm and pleasant sun the mountain seemed almost like a golden plateau floating above the sea.

I began by looking at the condition of the new headstay rigging wire where it entered the terminal fitting. I climbed down immediately.

"That was quick," said Margaret. "Is everything okay?"

"It most certainly isn't," I said. "The new headstay wire has somehow gotten untwisted for three inches where it comes out of the wire-end fitting. I can't possibly go to sea with such a wire, the most critical piece of rigging on the yacht. We must change the wire."

I hurried down the dock to the clubhouse, where I telephoned Keith Bellamy and explained the problem. With the race start just a few hours away, there was no chance to do the job myself. Keith sent his two ace riggers, Titch Mitchell and Billy, who took down the entire headstay assembly, replaced the stainless steel wire, and hoisted everything back up. Just before noon *American Flag* was operational again. While this was going on, Eric Bongers volunteered to overhaul a couple of winches. Brian and Marga-

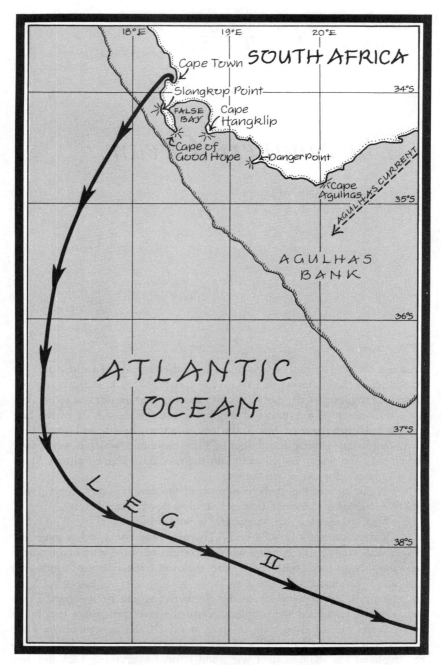

5. Leg 2 start and Cape Agulhas

ret were busy below. Meanwhile I had cleared customs and immigration and put some last-minute stores on board. I got a diver to give the bottom a light scrub, had a weather briefing, and laid out courses on my charts. I was ready to go.

At 1230 I shook hands with the people on the dock. Margaret, Brian, and I cast off *American Flag's* lines, and we were towed from the yacht club. An hour later we were under sail in Table bay, munching sandwiches and drinking coffee. The day was lovely, the sea calm and blue, and it seemed that half the population of Cape Town was out in sailboats, launches, tugs, naval vessels, runabouts—anything that would float. At 1430, half an hour before the start, I said goodbye to Margaret and Brian, who were taken off by a spectator boat.

Unlike Newport, the start of the race at Cape Town was easy in the light wind. The contestants—a bit worried about a southeast gale—began with reefed mainsails and small headsails, but it wasn't long until the reefs were gone and the fellows were on the foredecks dragging out genoas and light-weather sails and shouting jokes across the water.

The start was as much a spectator event for me as for the South Africans around us because I had never seen half the BOC yachts close up under sail. All nineteen of us glided along southward in a loose grouping a couple of miles offshore while the Saturday pleasure fleet circled around and wished us good luck. The sail plans of the cutter-rigged BOC fleet looked surprisingly similar except for the huge 1,240 sq. ft. mainsail (with 6½ ft. of roach) on *Thursday's Child* and the top six feet of *Colt's* sails, which had been painted bright red. A few of the captains had put up battenless, short-hoist mainsails for the hard days ahead.

For a time I sailed alongside Jacques de Roux on *Skoiern* and Ian Kiernan on *Spirit of Sydney.* I was surprised at the amount of banging and reverberations from the two aluminum hulls as they crashed through tiny waves. How, I wondered, did the captains stand the noise on board during a storm?

Our little fleet sailed southward for four hours with John Hughes in *Joseph Young* leading the pack ("My moment of glory," said John later).

[From my log]. November 15th.

2250. As night fell, the wind continued light. One by one the masthead lights of the BOC fleet came on. Soon I was able to count sixteen, and they moved as if in a ballet. A nudge to the right. Then a move to the left. One light would slip up close to another, and then fall back. It was hypnotizing to watch the lights, and I must have dozed in the cockpit. Suddenly wham! A hard southeast wind funneled down from the night sky. We were on our ear. I have rolled up the yankee, and we are going along with the staysail and two reefs in the mainsail. The fleet has scattered.

By 0200 the next morning the wind whistled at forty knots; the seas were soon big and nasty. I dropped the staysail. The sea was hard as we headed toward the South Pole under the triple-reefed mainsail alone. We had been promised fair weather for a few days, but the meteorologists had done it again. At 0600 the small white coaster *Africans* steamed by headed for Cape Town. The master reported winds gusting to forty-five knots and that he had seen one other BOC yacht. On *American Flag* we thumped on a wave from time to time, but the seas had evened out a bit and were not too bad. Since land was far away and we were going okay on a rough course to the south-southwest, I said the hell with it and climbed into the starboard pilot berth. I padded myself with pillows and went to sleep.

I was headed into the Southern ocean, a sea you won't find on any maps. Nevertheless, all voyaging sailors know about this distant sea, which is the band of frigid water at the southern part of the world below the land limits of Africa, Australia, and South America. This vast ocean of the south runs unimpeded entirely around the bottom of the globe at latitudes of fifty and sixty degrees south, its lower boundary marked by the pack ice of Antarctica.

A century ago the Southern ocean was a great sailing highway for crossing the world. Today, however, most seagoing commerce is carried in ships of ten or twenty times the tonnage of the old square-rigged sailing vessels. Instead of slugging it out around Cape Horn, modern traffic slips through the Panama canal; instead of the Cape of Good Hope, most ships go via the Suez canal and the Red sea. These days not much is down in the Southern ocean except storms, icebergs, whales, sea birds, and lots of isolation.

One weather depression after another circles the southern part of the globe. These powerful storm centers move from west to east and often spawn violent winds, which in turn generate big seas. Some storms are slow-moving and cause large, reasonably regular seas. Other storms are fast-moving depressions with intense lows and swirl through the varying latitudes with winds that change direction and force rapidly. Often during a westerly gale the wind swings from the northwest to the southwest. Since seas are caused directly by winds, these wind shifts can produce terrible cross-seas that can batter and bludgeon a vessel to death.

Over the years, hundreds of big ships have been swallowed up by the storms of the Southern ocean or have come to grief by running into ice. Not many yachts have ventured into the Southern ocean, and of those that have gotten into trouble, few have come back to tell their tales. One that fortunately survived to sail again because of her plucky crew was the forty-six-foot ketch *Tzu Hang,* which was picked up by a tremendous sea on February

14, 1957, and somersaulted stern over bow and then rolled sideways. Both of her masts were destroyed, and her doghouse, cockpit coamings, and rudder were ripped away. Even the bowsprit was broken in two. Only by the most herculean efforts did her crew bail out the water-filled hull, cover the deck openings, construct a rig from boards taken from the woodwork below, make a steering oar, and sail her to Chile.[18]

Most of the BOC race was to be run in the Southern ocean. Each of the nineteen sailors knew the risks and dangers. Each was ready for combat with the greybeards. Each thought (or perhaps hoped) that he would be equal to the problems of the sea. To tackle the Southern ocean singlehanded was a daunting challenge.

I was headed for Sydney, Australia, 6,247 miles to the east (the mileage depended on how far south I went). For planning, I broke the course into three parts:

1. From the Cape of Good Hope to King island in Bass strait (5,650 miles).
2. Across Bass strait (320 miles from King island to Gabo island).
3. Finally, northward up the east coast of Australia to Sydney (240 miles from Gabo island).

The distance from Cape Town to the Cape of Good Hope is 37 miles. (Cape Agulhas, the actual southern tip of Africa, is 82 miles farther to the east-southeast). Then it's a straight shot to Australia. Well, not quite straight, because for a 6,000-mile polar run, the curvature of the earth becomes a factor. The mileage from the Cape of Good Hope to Australia's Cape Wickham at the north end of King island in Bass strait was 6,042 miles if I sailed a straight course on a Mercator chart. However, a great circle course dropped the mileage to 5,432, a savings of 610 miles. This meant I had to go to 58°47′S. I could sail a composite or partial great circle route at varying latitudes. The figures looked like this:

rhumb line	6,042 nautical miles
41°S	5,804
45°S	5,646
50°S	5,516
55°S	5,447
58°47′S (true great circle)	5,432

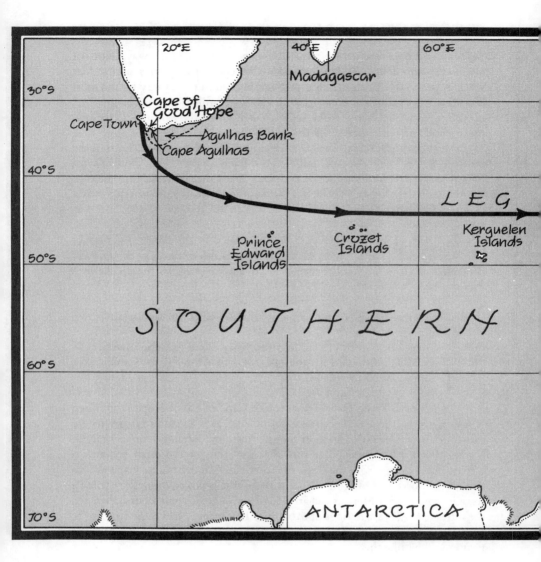

Did I want to go as far south as 58°47'? There were two considerations: good winds, and danger from ice. *Ocean Passages for the World* recommended that I sail between 42° and 43°S.

"In summer," said the authoritative voice of the Admiralty, "many vessels take a more southern route, some going as far south as the parallel of 52°S. latitude, but the steadiness and comparatively moderate strength of the winds, with the smoother seas and more genial climate north of 40°S., compensate by comfort and security for the time presumed to be saved by taking

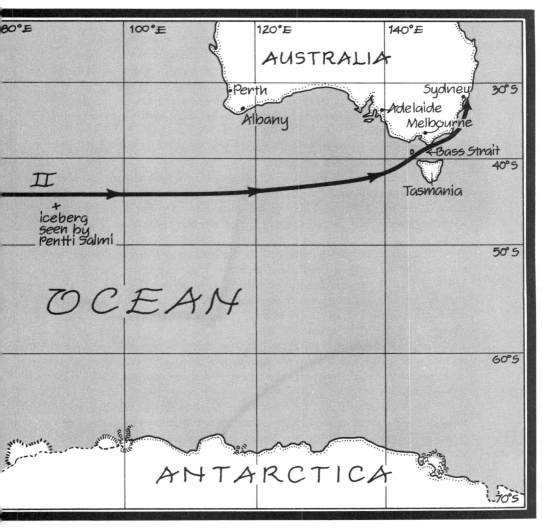

6. Leg 2, Cape of Good Hope to Bass strait

a shorter route. Tempestuous gales, sudden violent and fitful shifts of wind, accompanied by hail or snow, and terrific and irregular seas are often encountered in the higher latitudes; moreover the islands in the higher latitudes are so frequently shrouded in fog that often the first sign of their vicinity is the sound of the surf beating against them."

Although I knew the Admiralty books always discussed the worst possible situations, the information on ice was even more daunting: "The lengths of many of the Southern ocean icebergs are remarkable; bergs of 5 to 20 miles in length are frequently sighted south of the 40th parallel, and bergs of from 20 to 50 miles in length are far from uncommon. It may be gathered from numerous observations that bergs may, in places, be fallen in with anywhere south of the 30th parallel, that as many as 4,500 bergs have been observed in a run of 2,000 miles, that estimated heights of 800 to 1,700 feet are not uncommon, and that bergs of from 6 to 82 miles in length are numerous."

When I finished reading this I rushed up on deck and looked carefully in all directions. Nothing was in sight.

I was still sailing south, and even a little to the west, because I had been repeatedly warned to avoid the shallow Agulhas bank that extended 120 miles south of the tip of Africa. The Agulhas current (two to five knots) sweeps southwestward down the east coast of Africa and out onto the huge shallow bank.

"If a southeast gale catches you on the bank, you'll get clobbered by the seas. By all means go south and then east," the people in Cape Town had told me. The sailing books underscored this advice: "Should a south-easterly wind be blowing on leaving Table or Simons bays, stand boldly to the southwestward until the westerly winds are reached or the wind changes to a more favourable direction. In all cases when making for the 40th parallel southward of the Cape of Good Hope, steer nothing eastward of south, so as to avoid the area south-eastward of the tail of Agulhas bank, where gales are frequent, and heavy and dangerous breaking cross-seas prevail."[19]

The southeast gale blew for twenty-nine hours. Then the wind fell away to nothing. By the evening of November 17th, the sails were slatting, and *American Flag* rolled idly on a calm sea. Nothing was in sight. No other yachts. No icebergs. No ships.

[From the log]. November 18th.

   0600. An hour ago it was dead calm. Suddenly we were heeled sixty degrees when a white squall from the southwest pounced on us. I leaped from the port pilot berth, rushed outside, and let the staysail and main sheets fly. Fortunately the yankee was not set or else it would have blown out in a twinkling. We had been standing still; suddenly we were going ten knots. In a few minutes the severity passed, and I had time to go below and put on my heavy oilskins. It's much cooler—cold is the word. Now I have put the staysail down and let the yankee fly while I watch a line of squalls to the south. The sea is absolutely flat. I see that the mast is bent a little to starboard in the middle. I must adjust the lower shrouds. I feel quite good after a big meal at 0100 and a sleep till 0500. Albatrosses are around all the time.

The news from the fleet was that three yachts had turned back. John Hughes on *Joseph Young* reported damage to his upper shrouds. He sailed back to Cape Town, where Lars Bergstrom, one of the engineers on the *Thursday's Child* team, repaired the rigging. John started again eight hours later.

Thursday's Child had also returned to Cape Town with autopilot failure and water ballast tank problems. Though the yacht had three new autopilots, none worked, and it took sixty hours for the five-man shore support team to sort out the problems and get Warren Luhrs underway again.

Jean Luc on *Let's Go* reported that his headstay wire was unstranding. "I cannot fix it," radioed Jean Luc to Alistair Campbell, who was in charge of the ham network. "It's too dangerous to continue because if the wire breaks, the mast will come down." Jean Luc was headed for Simonstown for repairs.

Additionally, John Martin on *Tuna Marine* radioed that he blew out his new mainsail on the first night. The South African captain had put up his spare. Bertie Reed on *Stabilo Boss* had problems with halyard wraps on his Hood furling gear, and his genoa had blown out when he was unable to furl or lower the sail. In order to get a new sail to furl properly, Bertie finally went aloft and tied the swivel to one of his mast steps. *Lone Star* and *Belmont* told of major sail damage as well. Harry Harkimo was near the Cape of Good Hope on Sunday night when his main halyard had parted ("The sail came crashing down"). Harry climbed his mast to deal with the problem.

I gradually learned that of the nineteen yachts in the race, at least seven—principally in the larger class—got private weather information every day. A little of this data was quietly leaked to several of the other vessels so about half the fleet was armed with special assistance from land-based meteorologists. Most of the weather information was radioed from France on confidential frequencies at certain hours, although specialists in the United States and Australia also were involved. As I wrote earlier, some of the weather information was sent via tacticians on shore who plotted everyone's position and then radioed suggested courses and plans to their clients.[20]

To be sure, in port no one had talked about his special arrangements. Smug, noncommittal looks masked a background of carefully bought information. Presumably the captain with the most money could buy the best weatherman. Was the next step to jam your competitors' radios? Was I crazy or were there parallels with industrial espionage? Had the race become a subject for a spy novel by John Le Carré? What had happened to an amateur sport? Or more correctly, what was a dumb amateur doing in a professional circus?

With hindsight it's easy to see what the tactical ploy for the yachts in the race without shoreside weather advice should have been. Each day I got the Argos positions of everyone; I should have shadowed the leaders, who presumably received the latest information on the movements of highs and lows. Yet instead of doing this I stupidly stuck to the charts that came over my weatherfax machine and tried to work out what my weather would be. I reckoned that the public information was as good as the private advice. I was dead wrong. Also in retrospect, I didn't drive the vessel to the south as hard as I might have during the first few days because I wasn't aware of a critical weather change.

All of the savvy weather-receiving group (and the close followers)— who used water ballast to the maximum—had pushed hard to the east and south on the first few days and had avoided a high pressure system coming from the west (a move not forecast by the South African weathermen). The yachts that had gotten away moved into a different weather pattern and were soon making good easterly runs while the tail-end Charlies languished. I found myself bashing into twenty- and twenty-five-knot headwinds; my runs for November 19–21 were only 148, 129, and 133 miles. Private weather information and better windward performance for the others coupled with stupidity on my part had wiped me out.

In Cape Town I had forgotten to rig a safety line for the chart table seat, which ran athwartships on the port side of the cabin. During the sail from Newport, I discovered that when the yacht was heeled to starboard, I tended to slide off the seat. I countered this by propping my right foot against part of the galley furniture, but I had to sit partially sideways, and it was hard to work with both hands. Since I often spent hours at the chart table, I installed a pad eye outboard of the seat and made a safety line with a snap hook. It took only a moment to put the line around my waist and snap the hook into the pad eye; then I could sit comfortably no matter what the angle of heel and not worry about becoming airborne.

At noon on November 22nd I was down to 42°20′S. and 28°45′E., or 680 miles southeast of the Cape of Good Hope. I had done 146 miles in the last twenty-four hours against east and northeast headwinds of fifteen to twenty-two knots. I was still stuck on the north side of the high pressure area that was moving east at about the speed I was sailing. Playing the prudent seaman and sailing south and south-southwest before heading east had certainly not worked.

Meanwhile the chat hour had become the newspaper of the day:

Spirit of Sydney: Ian Kiernan reported the loss of his main electrical power because of a fire in his auxiliary engine. The problem was in the water cooling system, which Ian was trying to improve.

Let's Go: After heading back toward Simonstown for eight hours because of broken strands in his headstay, Jean Luc decided to continue and turned back to the east. "If I go back, it will be the end of the race for me," said the French captain. "I won't be able to start again."

Jean Luc headed for Sydney and planned to use his staysail stay for most of his headsail setting. I worried a lot about Jean Luc's decision to push on with poor rigging. By now I knew him well enough to realize that if he had turned back, his rigging must be in desperate shape.

Belmont: Harry Harkimo had hired a chap in Cape Town to clean his water tanks. The man dumped in detergent but failed to flush the tanks properly. Harry pumped out all the foul water and was hoping for rain. Meanwhile he was drinking milk and fruit juices and dreaming of coffee.

Lone Star: "I thought I was buying freshly ground coffee. However when I opened the package it was full of coffee beans. If I smash the beans with a hammer, can I use the pieces to make coffee?"

Joseph Young: "I almost hit a whale. It was at least 150 feet long."

This immediately brought out all the whale stories of the fleet, including Ian Kiernan's yarns about the 500- and 600-foot Bass strait monsters. I was soon laughing so hard that I almost embarrassed myself.

Often after everyone had finished speaking on the chat hour, the two Finns, Pentti and Harry, would have long talks in Finnish, a strange and utterly incomprehensible tongue that was as alien to me as Basque or Urdu. It was fascinating to listen to Pentti and Harry speaking, and I always strained to pick out a word or two. The only phrase I could recognize, however, was an occasional *son-of-a-bitch!*

By the afternoon of November 23rd the high pressure area had imprisoned *American Flag* in a cocoon of calms and zephyrs. I was at 42°07'S. *Ecureuil,* in the lead, was at 49°21'S. (434 miles south of me) on the north side of a big low and logging a steady ten knots. At noon the next day I had done just eighty-four miles, and on the 25th only sixty-seven, my poorest twenty-four-hour run of the race so far. The barometer read 1025 millibars, the sky was clear, and the sun bright. The roaring forties were as quiet as a swimming pool at dawn.

Since the sea was calm, I climbed to the masthead to inspect the new headstay wire. I was relieved to find it perfect. The view of the Southern ocean from the highest point of *American Flag* was wonderful, and I wrapped both arms securely around the masthead while I took a careful look in all directions. According to table 8 in Bowditch, the distance to the horizon was 8.9 miles from the top of the sixty-foot mast. This meant that I could see a circle whose area (πr^2) covered 249 square miles, a figure I could never quite believe.

Harry Harkimo

The blue and peaceful ocean rose and fell in slow motion as the long swells ran endlessly from the west. Because there was no wind, the ocean was quiet, and the surface of the sea rose and fell in slow, steady breaths, like a quilt tossed over a sleeping person. I knew the ocean would soon wake up and become alive when the wind came.

Somehow as I looked around, I thought that everything I could see belonged to me. It was mine alone. No one could take it from me. I held the title and ownership to this patch of sparkling ocean. The sea, the earth, the spirit of life—whatever you call it— seemed filled with energy and vitality and reflected the spirit of the universe. How lucky I was to be on this great voyage. Sometimes one had to do many humbling things to be able to undertake such trips, but no one could ever take away the golden memories. This bit of water in the vastness and isolation of the Southern ocean was perhaps best of all. When I climbed down from the masthead I was almost hypnotized with calmness and tranquility after so enjoying the beauty and immensity of the ocean.

During the trip I ate four kinds of food: fresh, freeze-dried, meals from retort pouches, and cans. *American Flag* had a big icebox which held four or five good-sized blocks of ice. Surprisingly, the ice lasted ten or twelve days, depending on the outside temperature, and the fresh refrigerated food gave me a good start for each leg. I took lettuce, cucumbers, carrots, beans, squash, tomatoes, celery, various cuts of meat, bacon, and so forth. My unrefrigerated fresh food included apples, oranges, onions, potatoes, very fresh eggs greased with Vaseline petroleum jelly, and lots of oranges and grapefruit.

For the first few days I made salads and cooked the fresh meat, usually with rice or sometimes with potatoes, spaghetti, or noodles. When the fresh food began to run out, I used backpackers' freeze-dried foodstuffs (Dri-Lite) and had such things as chicken and rice, vegetable stew with beef, turkey tetrazzini, beef stroganoff, and several shrimp dishes. Usually the directions called for me to pour two or three cups of boiling water over the contents of one or two packages, to stir carefully, and then to wait ten minutes. The portions were generally adequate for two meals; however the food tended to be somewhat heavy and overseasoned. On a scale of one to ten, I'd give the small freeze-dried packets a rating of four or five. (The shrimp dishes were poorest of all because the tiny shrimp seemed more suited for tropical fish than for humans.) Nevertheless, the freeze-dried packets were easy to fix, nourishing, and filling.

The Dri-lite selections also included vegetables (green beans almondine; peas and carrots) and desserts (chocolate mousse; hot apple cobbler) that were tasty and handy to eat. A special treat was freeze-dried neopolitan ice cream (yes, that's right), which came in little blocks something like tiny candy bars. You ate the little blocks right out of the package. Delicious!

Two special freeze-dried foods (Mountain House) in a somewhat different class were beef stew and chicken stew, which came in large number ten cans. To fix a really good quick meal, I merely had to dip out a cup of the dried preparation, pour a cup of furiously boiling water over it, stir, and wait ten minutes. These quick stews were excellent, smelled good, and looked appetizing as well.

The retort pouch meals were new to me and a complete success. Mine came from Yurika and consisted of a small flexible foil pouch filled with beef, herbs, spices, vegetables or whatever. After the ingredients were put inside, the air was withdrawn from the pouch, which was sealed and the contents cooked. The manufacturer claimed that since the contents were cooked in their own juices, the taste was better. To prepare a pouch for eating, I merely had to drop a pouch into boiling water and wait five minutes. The pouch meals were excellent, and on a scale or one to ten, I would rate them eight or eight and a half. I had things like canneloni, cabbage rolls, salisbury steak, sweet and sour pork, and trout almondine (my favorite). I usually cooked rice to go with each entrée. Prior to the race start we were given pouch meal samples from another company, which I found poor. I learned that it was best to sample these foodstuffs before buying in quantity.

Pentti Salmi

I took a variety of the usual cans along—everything from anchovies to zucchini—including small cans of roast beef, tuna, and chicken (packed in water, not oil) and tins of peaches and pineapples. The French yachts had some particularly good canned sport food in which choice bits of excellent meat, spices, and vegetables were cooked to perfection.

These flat-shaped French cans were not only tasty, but the food inside was arranged so that it looked nice as well. There were half a dozen varieties and included one of shellfish. Jacques de Roux passed me a few cans, and later Philippe Jeantot gave me a case and a half. I would rate the French sport food cans about seven on my one-to-ten scale.

Of course I mixed up the various foodstuffs to give my meals variety. Since at sea one never knows what will happen, I put in plenty of extra food. The freeze-dried packets and the retort pouches took up little space and were lightweight so I took lots in case of an emergency.

For quick energy during moments of crisis I had a couple of large cans of a special high-protein powder called Neo-Life Super Ease, which was based on fructose and special ingredients. I put two tablespoons in a cup of milk (made from powder) and drank the mixture, which was nicely flavored with black walnuts. My second high-energy crisis food were small candy bars called Pak-A-Meal from Yurika, which were not only good to eat and filling but also gave my energy level a boost. Though I had both of these foodstuffs available, I seldom used them.

I learned to make a big effort to prepare proper meals with several courses and to sit down and eat slowly and leisurely. Gulping meals in a rush simply didn't work for me. Not only was such eating inelegant, but I found that for the long haul it was important to eat a proper meal while I was relaxed and comfortable.

While I waited for the wind to return I read the autobiography of Baron Philippe de Rothschild and sat chuckling over this irreverent multimillionaire's look at the French wine industry, World War II, and his adventures with dazzling women.

I slept. I worked some crossword puzzles. I did a few boat jobs. I wondered why the head sink emptied so slowly. After taking half the head furniture apart I found that the drain hose had somehow gotten blocked by a large bolt cemented in place with something that appeared to be a mixture of old soap and toothpaste. It took two hours to clear the line and put things back together.

From the Argos reports I learned that *Skoiern* and *Airco* were almost 500 miles ahead of me and doing about 170 miles per day. Would they run into calms too? According to my weatherfax chart, the high I was sitting in didn't exist. So far every weather forecast from Cape Town had been wrong. On November 25th, *Belmont* was only a few miles from Marion island (Harry could see the island) and sailing in a fifteen-knot southwest wind while the island talked about thirty to forty knots. So much for voodoo weather forecasts.

As usual, the radio was full of lamentations about fickle winds, blown

Far south in the Southern ocean aboard *American Flag,* I adjust the topping lift on the mast. I took this photograph with an automatic Nikon camera, which has focused the lens on the mainsheet instead of on the captain. The small square-sided box with the white knob on top is the Argos device, which sent out weather information and position reports.

computers (laughter), gripes about overheated autopilot parts, instructions about fixing a broken Nagrafax weather machine, advice regarding a bent Aries wind vane gear, suggestions for a broken pump impeller, and other assorted wisdom. Someone had made a call to the United States via Cape Town. "The charge was eighteen gold francs. Does anyone know how much that is?"

A few days earlier Cape Town radio had warned of an iceberg at 43°S. and 47°E. This had gotten everyone thinking about icebergs. Why, we wondered, can't icebergs and pack ice be charted by satellites? We vigorously pressed the matter with various national authorities and got the jarring answer that in truth no one went to the Southern ocean these days. There was no demand for ice information and hence no arrangements to collect it. Someone said that ice didn't show up on satellite photographs, but I doubted this.

Jean Luc reported on a conversation with the Crozet islands, five tiny bits of land in the southern Indian ocean. The Crozet group belonged to

France, and thirty scientists were in residence. Most dealt with wildlife and the natural scene (botanists, geologists, geophysicists, ornithologists, etc.), although one man was a submarine expert. A ship came occasionally and transferred men and supplies by helicopter. There were no women.

One of the handiest sailing instruments is a speed and distance recorder. Unfortunately mine wasn't working. In Cape Town I had called Brookes & Gatehouse to calibrate the unit, and the local expert had pronounced it perfect. It may have been perfect, but the dial read zero for the next month (in Sydney, a repairman found that a reconnected wire wasn't making contact). I got out a spare unit—a Stowe log—which used an odd-sized nine-volt battery that I hadn't been able to buy in Newport or Cape Town. I finally managed to solder together several smaller batteries to get the log into operation. The simplicity of a kerosene lamp began to seem appealing.

By November 26th *American Flag* was sailing well on a southeast heading with sixteen knots of wind from the north-northeast. I recorded 170 miles at noon in a light misty rain. The next day—with twenty-four knots from the same direction—I logged 211 miles at noon. In this wind strength I had a little trouble keeping the yacht on a straight course because even with three reefs in the mainsail, she tended to round up. The magnetic variation was now 37° west, which meant that to go east (90°), I steered 127°.

The leaders in the race had problems. *Credit Agricole* reported one broken spinnaker pole (later shortened and repaired), and *Ecureuil* radioed about *two* broken spinnaker poles, which showed how hard the leaders were driving. Obviously they must have been running hard with fair winds. Philippe Jeantot also said that radio transmissions affected his autopilot (a frequent complaint with the unshielded Autohelm units). David White on *Legend* was making excellent time and radioed: "Nobody goes slow when the wind blows."

On *Tuna Marine* all of John Martin's autopilots had stopped working. His Fleming wind vane gear was unsatisfactory. For self-steering, John ran the staysail sheet (plus shock cord) to the wheel, but this arrangement required endless adjustments. Pentti Salmi on *Colt* told of total engine failure. He was sailing too fast to use his water-powered electric generator so his batteries were going down. He asked me to relay a message to his wife that he was okay and all was well on board. On *Stabilo Boss* Bertie Reed's autopilot failed. He rushed on deck just as the mainsail gybed. The mainsheet slammed him in the face and "roughed me up quite a bit. Blood and skin and a mess. Another eight inches and I would have been in real trouble," said Bertie.

[From my journal]. November 28th.
    1225. North of the Crozet islands. Nasty outside. Wind north-northeast at thirty knots, down from thirty-six. Heading southeast by compass (true heading is east). My run at noon was 218. *Skoiern* did 251. Incredible! I have three

reefs in the mainsail, the storm staysail on the midstay, and ten or twelve rolls in the yankee. I don't see how I can carry any more sail with this much wind on the beam and such rough seas.

I lie on the lee settee berth and wonder whether the yacht is going to turn over. We are going along at nine knots, but the course is wild and erratic as we lurch off big waves and yaw from side to side. Rain is pouring down, and the sky is as gray as navy paint.

For the first time I have shut both the top and bottom halves of the storm door between the cabin and cockpit. Every locker is latched shut. Part of a wave roll rolls across the top of the cabin every few minutes, and I am glad I don't have ventilators and leaky hatches.

I am dressed in three layers of Musto foul weather clothing except for the outer red jacket, which I can put on quickly if I need to go on deck. For lunch I had biltong (beef jerky from South Africa), a few dry crackers, and just now I am sipping some Jack Daniel's bourbon with a little water. A few drops of liquid courage is not a bit out of place in the Southern ocean.

. . . .

CHAPTER SIXTEEN

Only Four Thousand Miles To Go

The wretched weather improved as the cold front passed going eastward. By 0100 of November 29th the wind had veered to the southwest and dropped to twenty knots. With a fair wind and the seas behind me at last, I set up the running rig and began to sail rapidly east. The night was clear but much colder, and my heavy jacket, a thick woolen watch cap, and gloves felt good when I went on deck. After the yacht was sailing well (*American Flag* must have been relieved to have had a fair wind) I turned in and had a wonderful sleep, and at dawn I cooked a big breakfast. I sat on the starboard settee berth and ate bacon and eggs while I drank a steaming cup of coffee and began to read *Ways of Escape* by Graham Greene.

The westerly variation was now 43°, which meant that to go east (090°) I steered a compass course of 133°, which seemed crazy. Later I switched on the radio and heard Philippe Jeantot say that he was racing along in front of good winds and surfing up to twenty-two knots. "It is frightening sometimes," said the French sailor. He sounded nervous.

[From the log]. November 29th.

0930. During the last storm, Harry Mitchell got thrown across the cabin of *Double Cross* and cracked or bruised some ribs. Harry says that his chest is very painful. He radioed that he lay on his cabin floor for an hour—stunned—until the worst of the pain passed. He is better, but quite unable to crank a winch. He is using a hot water bottle and hopes to be better soon. A good deal of pain however. Poor Harry!

I had been at forty-four degrees south on the northern fringes of the low, and the strongest wind that I had measured was thirty-six knots. Most of the BOC fleet ahead of me was farther south, and when the east-going low had struck the yachts, their winds were a good deal stronger. Harry Harkimo in *Belmont* was 350 miles south. "When the front came through, the wind was fifty knots, and the waves were like houses," said Harry. He had been surprised by a sudden wind shift that had slammed his mainsail from one side to the other, took out a running backstay, and damaged the sail.

When the low reached *Ecureuil*—traveling at eleven and twelve knots and leading in the race—the yacht was knocked down twice, that is, she was momentarily rolled sideways into the ocean, which dunked her mast into the sea and put her fin keel and rudder out of the water. Waves swept over the vessel and broke all the long fiberglass battens in her mainsail. A special running headsail was swept overboard and lost. Another sail was damaged, and the Argos transmitter was broken loose and thrown into the sea. When the people at race headquarters began to get Argos reports that *Ecureuil's* progress had dropped to only one knot, they feared the worst. At 1530 on December 1st, however, I heard Titouan Lamazou speak to ham radio operator Alistair Campbell in South Africa.

"I am okay," said Titouan in a deep, confident voice. "There is some damage, and the Argos machine has been lost overboard. Maybe the Argos will continue the solo voyage by itself and beat me to Sydney," he joked. Titouan then arranged to broadcast his position each day by radio. (The Argos device, which floated and had solar cells, continued to send out position reports and showed a movement of three-quarters of a knot to the east.)

Later I learned that Titouan was scared that *Ecureuil* would break up. "I was frightened most of the time," he said. "The trip was very rough. The first time I was knocked down, I was under autopilot. The seas were huge, and one big wave pushed the boat sideways. The next wave turned the boat right over.

"The second knockdown was my mistake because I was trying to change a sail. I was stopped in rough seas, and in rough seas you must go fast. If you go fast, you are safe. But if you are stopped, you are not safe at all."

Back on *American Flag* my weather was falling apart again. My fair wind had lasted only twelve hours. I then had calms for eight hours followed by a high barometer (1018 millibars) and light northeast winds. I had been overtaken by a high-pressure area moving southwest.

I loved to watch the birds in the Southern ocean. I usually had an albatross or two in sight, circling around and around the yacht. These great fliers often soared below mast height, and each circle took five or ten minutes. There were two kinds of albatrosses that I recognized. The first was the black-browed, a bird with a long dark eyebrow, bright yellow bill, and a chunky three-foot white body with a bit of black at the tail. The wings were eight feet from tip to tip, and white with black edging.

The second bird was the great wandering albatross, the king of the Southern ocean, with a wingspan of eight to twelve feet. These birds also had short white bodies with black tail edging, but extremely long, white, high aspect ratio wings edged with black along the trailing edges and wingtips (the leading edges were white). Close up, the albatrosses were very wooly and white, and I always felt that they'd be good for stroking. I wondered how such a short fat body could possibly fly, but the birds soared for hours with only an occasional wing flap, and wheeled around and around. Their appearance was faintly comical with a small beady eye and an enormous pinkish bill with a blunt hooked end that was used for taking squid, their main food. Three out of four albatrosses that I saw were the black-browed; the fourth was the less frequent wandering albatross.[21]

During calms the birds didn't fly and would land on the water and paddle around the yacht. I tried feeding them bits of crackers, but—believe it or not—I had the best luck giving them pieces of apple. I can't imagine that black-browed albatrosses often feasted on Granny Smith apples from South Africa, and I am sure that the agency that handled the advertising for the growers' cooperative could have made some wonderful copy from this information.

I began to see small blue-gray petrels—hundreds of them—flitting about near the water. Each of the little birds was about a foot long with two-foot wings and had a white breast, a bluish-gray head, black along the leading edges of the wings, and a black tail tip. The birds seemed delicate, timid creatures that belonged along a shoreline somewhere instead of being far out at sea. Their flight was fluttering and erratic; sometimes the birds hovered above the water and let their legs touch the surface, apparently after microscopic food particles. The birds seemed to have their own busy society and paid absolutely no attention to the yacht as we hurried past. I worked out that these were fairy prions, often called whale birds by sailors.

[From my journal]. Sunday, November 30th.

0845. Yesterday was the pits. While the leaders surged eastward at up to twenty-two knots, I slatted and rolled in a near calm. *Lone Star, Joseph Young, Let's Go, Double Cross,* and I are in roughly the same area, and we all have had miserable winds. The start was followed by a sharp gale. Then four days or so of near calms. Somehow the leaders got east and have had nothing but favorable winds. All this should average out, one would hope. The leaders should get the calms we have had because the weather moves eastward.

According to the current weather forecast, I should have southwest winds of forty knots; the wind just now is northeast at twelve knots. Ho hum!

Only four thousand miles to go to Cape Wickham on King island in Bass strait.

I learned later that *Credit Agricole,* far ahead of me and driven to her maximum in heavy seas and fifty knots of wind, had been knocked down three times in less than twenty-four hours. During the second capsize, when the mast was in the water, the spinnaker pole broke in two. The jib blew out, and the three meters of broken pole—whose outer end was still attached to the clew and the remains of the sail—began to flail around like a wild demon, ripped the yankee, and smashed its furling gear. Philippe had to move carefully to clear up the mess because the flogging pole could have killed him in an instant. The knockdowns strained the weakened keel, which began to leak more and more. It was an ominous circle: the faster he went the more he risked knockdowns, which in turn made the leaks worse. Could Philippe make it to Sydney?

On December 1st the sea was covered with fog, the first I'd seen in the Southern ocean. I had the distinct feeling that land was nearby, but I knew that was impossible. Nevertheless I couldn't shake the notion (was I thinking of icebergs?) so I kept a careful watch for a few hours until the fog cleared. The wind continued to increase, and soon I was down to small sails. By the afternoon of December 1st things were very nasty (Crozet reported fifty to sixty knots from the north). My barometer read 1007 millibars, and the northeast wind (true north) rose to forty knots. In a few hours the sea had become extremely rough. I had to be careful to hang on and to go from handhold to handhold when I moved around. Poor *American Flag* was being shoved sideways into the sea. I changed my course more to the south and hoped I could continue with the triple-reefed mainsail, but the squalls were slamming us down violently. I had no choice but to take down the mainsail, a job I didn't like.

In a violent storm at sea, the motion on a ship—large or small—is generally awful. A deeply reefed mainsail on a sailing yacht, however, stabilizes the vessel quite a bit and makes life tolerable. With no mainsail, the motion tends to be grim, even with a headsail pulling hard. Besides this, there's something negative about taking down the mainsail when you're trying to get to a distant place.

An icy rain pounded into my face while I stood on the coachroof and clawed down the sail. The full-length battens made the job troublesome. Three battens were already down and tied to the boom with the deep reefs, but the top four battens jammed against the starboard after lower shroud, particularly the topmost batten, which was quite flexible. After I got the sail down I had to climb two mast steps (hang on!) to get above the stacked battens to grab the halyard, which I needed to keep a little tension on so it wouldn't get caught around the spreaders and upper mast steps.

Heavy going in big seas with the staysail and three reefs in the mainsail.

(Some people might ask why I didn't head into the wind to drop the mainsail. In a quiet bay somewhere that's no problem, but as a practical matter out on the oceans of the world it's a doubtful procedure. Certainly in the big seas of the Southern ocean, heading up is out of the question. A singlehander or a short-handed crew must be able to reef on all points of sailing, particularly when running hard downwind.)

Once the halyard was made fast, I turned my attention to tying up the flapping sail. With three reefs already in the sail, its area was sharply reduced. Nevertheless, it took half an hour of fumbling on the wildly rolling coach-roof to work five or six ties around the boom and sail. As I mentioned earlier, my only hope was to use long sail ties with a loop at one end. After getting the tie around the boom, I fed the other end through the loop and heaved on the resultant purchase to cinch down the sail. This was one job where I wore my safety harness and moved from secure point to secure point.

Guy Bernardin on *Biscuit Lu,* nine hundred miles ahead of me on the same latitude (44° south), also had some excitement. The French captain reported three knockdowns and said that he was lucky to have stayed on board because he had been on deck when the yacht had been rolled. Harry Harkimo on *Belmont* told of a raging snowstorm at 50°35′ south.

Bertie Reed on *Stabilo Boss*—who was always ready with helpful advice, a smile, and a joke—radioed that he had been treating his scratched face with Oil of Olay, a special beauty cream for women. "By the time I get to Sydney, I'll be a raving beauty," predicted Bertie. (How he happened to have Oil of Olay on board was not mentioned.)

Meanwhile the great storm from the north raged on. I was warm and dry below, but it was hardly the weather for cooking gourmet meals. I surrounded myself with pillows and munched some crackers and fruit in my bunk. It was the first time in my sailing career that I tied myself in my berth to keep from being thrown out.

We continued reaching at high speed across big seas with the storm staysail and a tiny bit of the yankee unrolled. Although I managed to stay on a southeast course, *American Flag* was taking some fairly heavy water on board. We seemed to be going at terrific speed (the log had given up), and the waves crashed and banged against the hull. As I lay in my bunk I wondered how strong the hull was. No one had ever taken such a light yacht into the Southern ocean before, and every time a cross-sea walloped into the hull, I fervently hoped that boat builder Bill Lee and his crew of hearties on that sunny hill in California hadn't forgotten any essential glue or bits of fiberglass. The Southern ocean is a great testing ground; only the successful return to complain.

At 0400 on December 2nd the wind dropped to twenty-four knots from the north-northeast. I went on deck and hoisted the triple-reefed mainsail, taking great care to keep the halyard from wrapping around something. How the sail stabilized the yacht! We picked up speed at once. An hour later a cold rain was falling; I expected a wind shift, but a twenty-two-to thirty-two-knot northeast wind continued for the next thirty hours.

At noon I found that I had done 240 miles in the last twenty-four hours according to a noon satnav fix. This was my best run so far in the race. I was astonished that I had made such a run with the mainsail down for eight hours. No wonder the motion had been lively!

That evening Pentti Salmi on *Colt* reported an iceberg at 45°23′S. and 69°07′E. I passed the ice information to Cape Town radio, which began to broadcast the sighting on its regular weather and shipping information channels. John Hughes on *Joseph Young* was quite close to Pentti's iceberg and tearing along in fog. John sounded as nervous as a seal surrounded by polar bears. I suggested that he take down some sail and slow down until morning.

The seas that ran past *American Flag* were large and regular. Occasionally one came along that was bigger than usual, but my little vessel seemed light and buoyant and rose easily as the great waves whooshed past. A few weeks of progress like this and we would be in Sydney.

On the morning of December 3rd I heard a surprisingly high-pitched hiss coming from the port quarter. A moment later a big wave seized the yacht, scooted her forward at great speed, and broke across the vessel. As we rolled, the yacht was suddenly smothered in white water and foam, and the jib and mast must have dipped into the sea. I was in the galley cooking breakfast. All at once my frying pan and cup of tea were airborne, and I found myself sitting on the side of the galley. Then the wave was gone. As the heavy lead keel righted the vessel there was a tremendous flapping noise. I also heard water running off the coachroof and decks and sloshing around in the cockpit. I rushed outside and found that a jib sheet had come off its winch. I quickly dealt with it, took a fast look around (all clear), and went below to start breakfast again.

That afternoon as I passed the Kerguelen islands—which lay three hundred miles to the south—the reports from the fleet were scary. There was talk of fifty- and sixty-knot winds. I heard that *Airco* had gotten rolled upside down. *Airco's* Argos had come adrift, her floorboards had fallen to the ceiling of the cabin, and things were a mess below. Mike Plant said that he was okay, but spoke of a terrible sea. Just after the *Airco* report, *Stabilo Boss* was laid on her side. Richard Konkolski on *Declaration* radioed that he had broken a spinnaker pole during a savage roll. *Belmont* capsized the night before. Harry was thrown overboard, but he had had his harness on and managed to pull himself back on board.

"I was just coming to the crest of a wave—or so I thought—when it kept coming and rising," reported Harry. "It took the boat and turned it right over, about two hundred degrees, and when the boat came back up I wasn't on board anymore. I don't know what happened. I tried to keep my hands on the wheel, but I found myself hanging over the stern pulpit. There was water everywhere. I couldn't breathe. Everything was mixed up. It took me about ten seconds to pull myself back on board. If you put me there now, I'm sure I couldn't pull myself up. Where I found the strength I'll never know.

"I didn't have time to be scared then, but I had more knockdowns during the day," said Harry. "When night came again, I thought I'm never going to make it. I steered for twenty-three hours and was totally wet—I was a solid block of ice. I simply couldn't leave the wheel."

That same December 3rd, far to the north and west, *American Flag's* wind veered to the west-southwest and steadied at thirty knots. As I eased the mainsail and poled out the yankee, we sailed into dense fog. Again I expected to see icebergs, and I stood a careful watch. The sea was gray and rough, and a cold wind whistled across the deck. I was thankful for my three layers of special clothing and stayed up until 0115 the next morning when the fog vanished.

All of a sudden I could look up into the clear night sky and see the Pleiades, my favorite constellation. We had been roaring along, but the results appeared to be more roar than speed because the yacht was yawing somewhat in big seas. At 0245 on December 4th we had a series of squalls that pushed the eased main boom into the water and made a lot of noise. I rolled up most of the yankee to slow us down. Astern were some tough-looking swells. Orion twinkled overhead as the blue fingers of dawn began to push back the night. I was tired and sleepy and tumbled into my berth.

At noon I worked out from satnav fixes that we had done 207 miles in the last twenty-four hours (677 miles in three days). The wind began to slacken, however, and by the evening we were becalmed.

I spent many hours at the chart table writing in the log, talking on the radio, and working out my courses. I am strapped in (a line clipped around my waist) to keep from becoming airborne when the motion was violent.

That night I telephoned Margaret. The conditions were good so I used the single sideband radio to contact AT&T high seas station WOM in Florida. Once the operator heard my feeble call and position, he directed his large antennas to my location and put my call through to Maine. It seemed a miracle when Margaret answered the phone. I had told her that I would try to call, and we each kept a list of things to cover. It was wonderful to hear her voice from almost ten thousand miles away. She told me the news from Maine. I spoke of the race. She reported on the fund-raising. We talked about her flight to Sydney, and I asked her to bring a few things for the yacht. We planned to meet for Christmas. I blew her a fast kiss, and our twenty-minute call (cost $99.59) was over. It was immensely cheering to have heard Margaret, and I felt wonderful afterward.

My good feelings were countered by the grim reality that the fund-raising had failed to keep up with even the modest expenses of my campaign. My money had run out. The only thing to do was to sell *American Flag* in Sydney.

John Hughes, Pentti Salmi, Jean Luc Van Den Heede, Mark Schrader, and I had been talking regularly with Harry Mitchell on *Double Cross*. We all took turns trying to cheer up Harry, who was in low spirits because of the injury to his ribs. Now we got additional bad news. Harry reported that he had slipped and fallen as he stepped from the companionway hatch into the cockpit. The yacht had lurched, and Harry—already a bit unsteady from his rib injury—had fallen and struck his head on a cockpit winch. Apparently he had knocked himself out and had somehow tumbled or staggered down into the cabin, where he collapsed. Harry woke up many hours later with his eyes and face covered with a great deal of dried blood.

"I can hardly open my eyes because of the congealed blood," he said. What bothered Harry more than the blow to his forehead was that he had no memory of the previous afternoon.

"What happened to those hours?" said Harry. "It's the strangest thing. Will I ever get them back?" Harry also said that the pain in his chest had increased. "I have had to take tablets," he said.

I knew that Harry's high frequency radio was poor; by luck mine happened to be particularly good. I also knew that Harry would never ask for medical assistance and that he was in no condition to spend hours fiddling with weak signals across 2,250 miles of ocean. So on December 4th I called Alistair Campbell—who ran the ham network—and sent the following message:

> Harry Mitchell on *Double Cross* has some fairly severe medical problems. I hope that Harry won't think I am meddling in his affairs if I ask you to arrange a radio schedule between a doctor and

Harry. Frankly, Harry's symptoms have scared us all to death. Those of us in the tail end of the fleet need to be reassured. I only mention this because we're all fond of Harry and wish him well.

Harry—who is listening in—is a tough Englishman, but he is perhaps reluctant and a bit diffident about speaking up.

Alistair Campbell immediately put me in touch with ham operator Nick Moon in Johannesburg, who had a powerful signal that stretched across the Indian ocean. I relayed Harry's symptoms to Nick, who in turn relayed a doctor's questions and advice to Harry via *American Flag*. I practically wept with relief when this complicated relay was completed. Harry got lots of essential advice, and his spirits were immensely buoyed. The interchange of medical information on the ham network was a wonderful thing. I couldn't thank Nick Moon enough for his help.

Later when Harry got better he was able to speak directly to South Africa. Unfortunately during this time Harry's sailing times were poor. *Double Cross* gradually dropped behind the fleet.

On December 5th Jacques de Roux was rolled twice in a hurricane force wind that reached sixty-five knots. The culprits were breaking cross-seas. The first capsize was not too bad, but during the second *Skoiern* was rolled right over and suffered major damage. Her antennas and wind vane gear were torn off, and her entire steering wheel and pedestal were ripped from the cockpit. The autopilot was ruined, there was a lot of water in the yacht, and Jacques was *very* discouraged. The French captain rigged an emergency tiller to the rudder post and began to steer by hand. According to Jean Luc, who spoke to him twice every day, Jacques planned to go to Adelaide for repairs.

Credit Agricole's leaks continued to increase after her knockdowns. "I am not able to stop the shivers of anguish, because if my engine-driven pump stops, I will not be able to keep up with the leak with the hand pump," said Philippe.[22]

Belmont and *Tuna Marine* also reported being rolled twice on the night of December 5th. *Belmont* had some damage, but the stoutly built Swan yacht and her Finnish captain kept going. On *Tuna Marine* every bit of gear on one side of the interior of the sixty-foot South African yacht was thrown to the other side, and her spare mainsail was blown out. (She had already lost her new mainsail, her self-steering gear, and autopilots.)

"That night was unreal," said John Martin later. "I was surfing at twelve knots, and it was blowing so hard that I had only a small jib up. I closed the hatch when I went below. Thirty minutes later all hell broke loose. It was a pitchpole, roll, and nose dive.

"I tried to piece it all together afterward, looking at the damage," said John. "I really don't know what happened, except that I was suddenly on the roof, then I was on the engine, and then I was walking on the side of the engine casing. Meanwhile water poured through the cabin. I decided to go up on deck and see what had happened. A mass of running rigging was stuck in the wheel, and enormous waves were breaking over the boat. I grabbed the wheel and held on. I was wearing no oilskins, and I steered the boat that way for five hours. That night was the first night of the whole trip I had taken my boots off! 'Well,' I thought, 'I'm either going to die by being rolled again, or I'm going to die of hypothermia.' It was some night!"

John considered going to Albany, Australia, but he cleverly set a storm jib back to front in place of his ruined mainsail and pressed on.

During the same storm, Ian Kiernan on *Spirit of Sydney* was knocked down two times. The Australian captain reckoned that his wind got up to sixty-seven knots.

"The seas were like mountains with snow avalanches," said Ian, "but the old girl loved it all and we sped on. My main trouble was trying to sleep. The ocean made so much bloody noise that it kept waking me up."

Thursday's Child had been moving up steadily in the fleet after her poor start and was eighth in her class and going well. On December 6th Warren Luhrs reported two nasty gybes when big waves shoved the stern of his lightweight sixty-footer the wrong way. On the second gybe, the main boom broke where it was held rigidly in place by the unyielding hydraulic vang. Warren reefed his mainsail, sheeted it to the deck, and set about putting the boom back together with a special Kevlar splice that he carried for such an emergency. He completed the repair the next morning. Unfortunately the boom broke again. Warren then rigged a spinnaker pole in place of the broken boom and pressed onward with the clew of the third reef taken to the end of the pole.

As the BOC fleet sailed farther and farther into the distant reaches of the Southern ocean, the public weather information got poorer and poorer and finally fell away to almost nothing, no doubt because of limited demand. John Hughes and Mark Schrader were particularly enraged when two weather fronts they were watching on a South African weather chart suddenly disappeared on the next chart. The weather information existed; it was a question of getting it on board; hence the success of private advisories.

On December 6th I had snow and a high barometer. When a forty-knot northeast wind of the day before dropped to twenty-four knots from the southwest, I hoisted the mainsail—which I'd taken down—and increased the headsail area. The southwest wind felt as if it was straight from the Antarctic ice cap. By the evening I was becalmed. At 0100 the next morning I got a trace of wind from the southwest again and was soon sailing nicely. By noon the breeze was up to seventeen knots, but I showed a run of only 114 miles because of the calms.

Aboard *Credit Agricale* things were not good. Philippe was worried that one more knockdown would be fatal to his keel. He was pumping at the rate of 400 liters of water an hour. "The keel disturbs me more and more," he said. "I hear water running all the time. I have located new cracks." Philippe had all his survival gear at hand, but his vessel was sailing fast, and he hoped to finish the leg before she sank.

And so it went day after day. Ever onward and ever eastward across the endless sea. Another gale, another hard night, another cold front, another blast of icy squalls, and finally the bright sun. Sails up, sails down, sails from one side to the other, sails tight, sails loose—on and on we went.

Our little mosquito fleet was gradually being destroyed by the savage ocean. Pentti Salmi on *Colt* told of a torn mainsail, roller furling problems, and bad standing rigging wire that was breaking strand by strand. Mark Schrader on *Lone Star* reported that during a squall the spinnaker track on his mast was torn off and the spinnaker pole punched a big hole in his mainsail.

Running hard before the big seas of the Southern ocean.

One day I spent two hours sewing on the yankee after the leech of the sail caught on seizing wire at the end of the spreaders.

John Hughes spoke to the container ship *New Zealand Pacific,* which was on a great circle course to Melbourne. The officer on watch knew all about the BOC race, and everyone on board kept a keen lookout.

On December 10th I heard a strange noise forward in the middle of the night. I dressed, put on the deck light, and discovered that one of the spinnaker poles was half over the side because the forward pole holder had disintegrated. The aluminum crossbar had come off the Forespar chock, which was okay for San Francisco bay but not nearly strong enough for the Southern ocean. I lashed the forward pole end to the mooring cleat.

During the height of the spinnaker pole problem I was hurrying to put on my oilskins when a roll of toilet paper escaped and began to roll back and forth on the floor of the cabin. In a jiffy, paper was criss-crossed all over the place. You can't believe how quickly a roll of paper can unwind on the cabin sole of a wildly rolling yacht. A kitten would have had a great time.

Bertie Reed radioed that he was heading for Albany on the southwest coast of Australia. During his capsize on December 2nd, his diesel generator—Bertie's sole source of power—had quit, which meant no autopilot, no lights, no instruments, and only enough battery juice for a last gasp radio message. During Bertie's attempt to repair the generator, he got exposed to diesel oil, to which he was allergic. He began to take antibiotics, but he needed medical attention.

I picked up a message for *Skoiern* on the ham network that a man in Sydney with a French name wanted to assist Jacques de Roux with repairs, help, and money. What good luck! I passed along the message to Jacques via Jean Luc, who spoke regularly to *Skoiern.* Both Jean Luc and I commented that we hoped *our* messages would come tomorrow.

The news from *Double Cross* was that Harry Mitchell's chest was better, although he was stiff and creaky. Harry said that his rib cage was extremely painful if he bumped into anything. The English sailor got the clever idea of wearing a life preserver to pad his chest. Following the directions of the doctor in Johannesburg, Harry had carefully bathed his face and eyes, and the swelling was going down on his forehead, although he still had quite a lump where he had struck the winch. Harry mentioned that his wind generator had fallen into the cockpit after the bearings (lifetime bearings) had worn out in the winds of the Southern ocean.

There was much earnest cursing from all sides about so-called ocean gear that was useless and bad and obviously designed by Sunday sailors for Sunday sailors.

On December 11th I passed three Japanese fishing boats that bristled with radio antennas. Each of the steel vessels was about a hundred feet long, and white with light green decks and a cream-colored superstructure. The letters JJJJ were prominent on the sides of the deckhouse of the first boat. (The letters JAGD and JBEE were on the others.) I saw no sign of fishing gear or the usual following birds. Guy Bernardin had broadcast a warning of the fishing fleet a few days earlier. I guessed that the boats were engaged in fisheries research.

The next day Mark Schrader on *Lone Star* reported an 800-foot, 101,000-ton bulk carrier from Melbourne that was headed west for Houston. Later I heard an engine running and went on deck to see another Japanese fishing boat, *Eisen Maru #72* (JANF), about a quarter of a mile away. She was stopped and broadside to the swells but rolling very little, which made me suspect that she had stabilizers. There were a few floats on the after deck, but no other signs of fishing gear. I waved and two men responded. At the stern was a Japanese flag painted on a piece of plywood.

I cured some portlight leaks by putting a thick coating of Vaseline petroleum jelly on both mating parts. To improve my sleep and to stop the brain-deadening clatter of the staysail blocks, I hammered small pieces of hard plastic between the slider and the block.

[From the log]. December 12th.
   2000. Yesterday at dusk Jean Luc Van Den Heede on *Let's Go* had his big running booster sail up when the wind began to increase. Jean Luc tried to pull the sail down, but the top hanks caught on the wire U-bolt clamps that he had used at the top of the wire for his earlier repairs. The wind continued to rise, and the sail would not come down. By now the wind was thirty knots, and the sail had wrapped around the pulpit four times. The only thing to do was to go up the mast to release the sail at the top so Jean Luc climbed the mast with his special wire climbing rig. "I was quite afraid that if the forestay broke it would be all over for me," said Jean Luc. "Already I had repaired the wire. Indeed, the clamps were the reason the sail was jammed. While I was at the top of the mast, two or three brown birds flew very near to me to have a look. Maybe they were waiting for me to fall! However I released the sail and everything was okay." Although I have climbed *American Flag's* mast many times, I always do it when the wind is light and the swell is down. Besides, my steps make it easier. I don't think I could have done what Jean Luc did. He's a tough guy.

At 0100 that night I saw a searchlight in the sky far off to port. I began to feel spooky about Japanese fishing ships. At noon I heard that Bertie Reed had arrived in Albany, where he saw a doctor for his medical problem. A mechanic found twenty-five liters of fresh water in one of Bertie's diesel tanks, no doubt the cause of his generator failure. There was also the news that *Ecureuil* had arrived in Sydney after a twenty-eight-day passage, during which Titouan had averaged 240 miles per day, a phenomenal record for the thirty-one-year-old French captain.

The next day (203 miles) squalls and hard winds continued from the south. I saw a very delicate blue sky to windward toward Antarctica and wondered if the weather would ease. In the morning I played cobbler and repaired a pair of shoes. The stitching had disintegrated along one side of each shoe. I used heavy sail twine, followed the old holes, and pulled a needle through with pliers. The job was easy once I got down to it, and I was pleased with the result.

I finished reading the autobiography of Charlie Chaplin. The first part about Chaplin's struggles as a comedian were excellent. When he became rich and famous, however, he turned into a society type and a name dropper. The second half of the book was a bore.

I wrote down 195 miles at noon on December 15th. My wind that day was 14 knots from the south and it was cold, so cold that I put on a second thermal underwear top underneath all the rest of my clothes. My average for thirty days over 4,852 miles had been 161.7 miles per day, or 6.73 knots. At 1400 I had a chat with Bertie Reed, who had just left Albany for Sydney after medical treatment for diesel poisoning and various repairs. I learned that during an earlier accidental gybe, two winches had been torn off the deck of *Stabilo Boss.* "She's a bit much for one man at times," said Bertie. He made it clear that his partially converted IOR Whitbread boat (formerly crewed by twelve men) was impossible for a singlehander unless he had a powerful autopilot.

[From the log]. December 15th.

1615. Thirteen miles from *Joseph Young.* John Hughes and I have been speaking on the VHF radio. We are trying to find one another so we can take photographs. John told me that he and Mark continue to be astonished at Konkolski's progress on this leg, especially on November 24th and 25th. Konkolski did 124 miles while *Double Cross* did 60; *American Flag* 49; *Lone Star* 40; *Joseph Young* 69; *Colt* 74; and *Let's Go* 37. The seven yachts were all together in the same high pressure area south of Mozambique. In fact, Konkolski was north in the absolute center of the high; yet he logged roughly twice the mileage of the others. The guy is unbelievable. If he keeps at it, someone is going to throw a flower pot at him.

1930. I finally sighted *Joseph Young* off the starboard bow about seven miles away. How small a yacht is at seven miles! Without a precise heading there is no way I would have seen John.

That night I heard a strange rumbling sound. At first I thought it was the autopilot. I hunted everywhere. A submarine? No, the sound was on board somewhere. Later when I was coiling a line on the afterdeck, I happened to put one hand on the water-driven generator, *which was running and being driven by the ship's batteries!* (To make electricity in an emergency, I had an Everfair water-driven generator bolted to the port transom deck. The generator was driven by a small propeller towed in the sea at the end of a thirty-foot length of braided line. I never used this device or towed the propeller, but kept the generator in reserve.) Anyway it was running in reverse, being driven by the ship's batteries. Had the generator been running ever since Cape Town? What had the electrician done with the diode that was supposed to make a reverse current flow impossible? I disconnected the wires.

On December 16th my noon run was 156 miles. The wind was north-west at sixteen; the sky was clear and blue with a bright sun, by far the best day since Africa. *Joseph Young* was three or four miles astern and barely visible in the swells.

I had a careful look at the mainsail, which was eased with the fair wind. The full-length battens tended to push forward. Since they had no slider or mast attachments at their forward ends, the load was entirely on the luff slides *between* the battens. This put a strong bending load on each slide and a heavy strain on the cloth seizings that held the metal sliders to the sail. It seemed to me that a slide with a mechanical pivot (or maybe two slides) should be placed at the forward end of each long batten in a sail of 414 sq. ft. I could see that the bronze slides were severely abraded and worn. Several were broken.

The next day the news from Australia was that two more Class I yachts had crossed the finish line. Philippe Jeantot—with one eye on the water in *Credit Agricole's* keel—had come in just under six hours behind the winner. Jean-Yves Terlain in *UAP* had been becalmed for thirty-six hours only thirty miles from Sydney. All of *UAP's* big sail inventory except a staysail had been blown out. Jean Yves could not sail to windward so he poked along back and forth until he got a fair wind. It must have been a frustrating time for the French sailor.

On December 18th at three o'clock in the morning another strong front overtook *American Flag,* and the wind was soon whistling at fifty knots from the northwest. As I started to put the third reef in the mainsail, I stupidly fouled one turn of the reefing pendant when I put the line on the winch. The over-ride jammed tight. The more I pulled the worse it got. I knelt on the coachroof with a hammer and a screwdriver and flailed away at the fouled line. Water was flying all over the place. I put my tools down for a moment while I pulled the drawstring of my foul weather hood tighter, and as I did I looked around me.

The night was as black as the heart of a bat. The yacht was going ten or eleven knots, and the great waves roared as they swept past, their white tops eerily luminescent in the weak glow from the electric light up on the mast. Several times big waves broke almost on top of the yacht; water exploded in every direction. I could feel the power of that raging sea. What a scene! If ever a person wanted high adventure, this was the place. I must have been mad to have taken my toy boat into the heart of a furious storm in the Southern ocean. I felt like a minnow being chased by a troop of hungry crocodiles.

I finally managed to loosen a loop of the fouled line with my tools. I then threaded a small line through the loop and took the small line to a second winch which had enough power to strip the fouled reefing line from the first winch. Success! It had been a near thing because I needed that third reef. With three reefs in the main and the tiny storm staysail we showed 213 miles at noon.

During the afternoon I heard that *Thursday's Child* was dismasted south of Sydney. The fleet was falling apart.

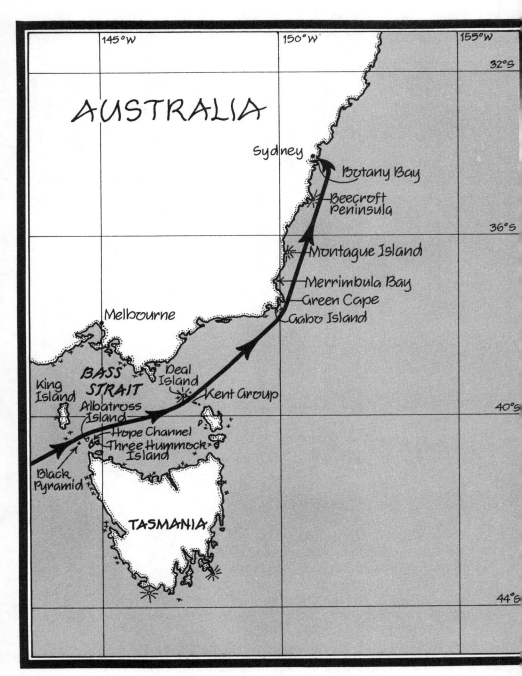

7. Bass strait to Sydney

. . . .

CHAPTER SEVENTEEN

Bumpy Water

*F*rom high in the sky, the big island of Tasmania looks roughly like an equilateral triangle with its base toward the north and its vertex pointed south toward Antarctica. This little-known island—which measures about 190 miles on each side—is separated from the southeast corner of Australia by a stretch of wild water called Bass strait. It was through this 130-mile-wide passage that we were to sail on our way to Sydney. The place had an ominous reputation for upset water, obstacles, and gales, and the Australians all shook their heads and called Bass strait "awful, terrifying, and treacherous." The fellows in the BOC fleet thought this talk was more of the usual Australian exaggeration and hyperbole. Once on the scene, however, we found that the Australians were right.

From King island in the west to Gabo island in the east, Bass strait is 320 miles long. Then once around the southeast tip of Australia at Gabo island, the run to Sydney is 240 miles. Only 560 miles in all. But first I had to get to King island.

[From the log]. December 19th.
   0140. It's been a terrible night with a west wind of forty knots. I have been in and out of the cockpit a dozen times because of gybes caused by getting slewed around in enormous seas. Sailing in the high southern latitudes is certainly not for the faint of heart.
   0315. Frightful squalls. I should have taken down the scrap of mainsail, but

I must keep going. Spume is blowing along the tops of the waves. Sort of wind wrinkles. I am trying to sail northeast with a west wind, which should be easy with the mainsail eased to starboard. The problem is that random swells from the south and southwest keep pushing the stern of the yacht around, and we gybe.

0415. Wet, cold, and tired. Can I ever get on course and sleep?

0620. King island is 405.6 miles. Sleet is rattling on deck.

After a nap I talked to John Hughes, whose weather was "diabolical." John had been studying one of the Australian weather charts we had begun to receive. "According to the official chart our wind waves are ten meters, and the swell height is eight meters," said John. "When a wave gets on top of the swell—often enough—we have eighteen meters or sixty feet!"

Sixty feet? I went outside and looked at the seas. During the moments when *American Flag* was down in a wave trough we were surrounded by walls of gray, angry-looking water that climbed up steeply on every side. Then a few seconds later we rose up on a crest, and I could see for miles and miles to distant horizons.

This was not as dangerous as it sounds because when the wind was steady, the waves and swells were long and reasonably steady, too. The problem came when the wind shifted abruptly and began to make cross-seas that were out of sequence with the main wave train. It was the cross-seas that were the dragons of the sea and caused such damage to small vessels.[23]

At 1015 I heard that *Thursday's Child* was underway again toward Sydney with a jury rig. Bill Biewenga and Courtney Hazelton—two of the yacht's six-man shore crew—had heard about the dismasting the day before. The rules of the race allowed helpers to go on board if a yacht was in a port or anchored. Bill and Courtney chartered a plane and flew to Merrimbula in New South Wales, where they hired a small boat and went out to *Thursday's Child*. Meanwhile Warren had managed to sail his injured sixty-footer close enough to shore to anchor (the captain tied all the spare lines on board to make a warp long enough to anchor in 300 feet).

Bill, Courtney, and Warren lashed the tops of two spinnaker poles together to make an A-frame, which they erected athwartships with the bottom ends secured to the side decks outboard of the cockpit. They then ran a long wire stay forward from the top of the A-frame to the stemhead and set the luff of a small jib along the wire. The low, skinny triangular sail that resulted was strange-looking, but useful as an emergency rig. Bill and Courtney then got off, Warren pulled up his anchor—and in light winds—headed for Sydney.

At 1015 on December 19th I also heard the worst news of the race. Sydney radio said: "*Skoiern* is possibly adrift or disabled southeast of Gabo island." On the day before when I had had my daily talk with Jean Luc he

Thursday's Child with her jury rig heading for Sydney after being dismasted. The arrangement we see is based on two short poles erected as bipoles at the sides of the cockpit with a wire stay running forward to the stem. An upside-down jib is hanked to the wire stay. Compare this setup with that used on *Neptune's Express* on p. 120. *Neptune's* rig seems clearly superior. The poles on *Thursday's Child* need to be longer or at least erected vertically. Perhaps the main boom could have been used as the jury mast.

said that he was "very, very worried because Jacques has missed two radio schedules. Jacques has always been meticulous about coming up at the right time. Guy Bernardin has not been able to contact Jacques either."

Without saying a word, I knew, and everyone in the race knew, exactly what these things meant: Jacques de Roux was probably overboard and lost. He might have been sick and been below. *Skoiern* could have lost her rudder or had some other problem. But these things were unlikely because Jacques was in a shipping lane with plenty of coastal traffic. He would have called on his VHF radio if he had needed assistance. My eyes filled with tears, and a shudder went through my body as this terrible message sank into my consciousness.

The ultimate risk of short-handed or singlehanded sailing is falling over the side. We all went to extreme lengths to avoid even the slightest chance of this happening. We had high lifelines made of strong steel cables. We had sturdy fittings and frames and rigging and masts and booms to grasp or to lean against. A sailor learned from his first days to always hang on with one hand while he did something with his other hand. If both hands were needed, he could lock his feet around a winch or jam his body against the mast or whatever so that he was firm and secure. Besides that a sailor had good balance and even if he got jerked or knocked about, he knew to drop to his knees and to grab something. After a few years a sailor got very good at running around the decks with complete freedom. In addition to these basic skills, the singlehanders all had strong lifeline harnesses which they usually (not always) wore when the weather was bad or a man had to take an unusual risk (like working on the self-steering gear or hanging out over the side to repair something).

When the news of Jacques came over the radio, Harry Harkimo was near Gabo island. He immediately offered to drop out of the race to search the area (it was decided that airplanes were better). There was some discussion whether Jacques could have made his way to shore (his last position was five miles from land, a little north of Gabo island). It was possible that he was along the remote coastline. Titouan Lamazou and Guy Bernardin had arrived in Sydney. Almost crazy with grief, they borrowed a helicopter and scouted the coastal beaches for their friend. The *Thursday's Child* plane and another chartered light aircraft also searched. No one found Jacques.

I learned later that Bill Biewenga and Courtney Hazelton, the two men who had helped set up the jury rig on *Thursday's Child*, had telephoned race headquarters (at 0956 on December 19th) to report that Warren Luhrs was underway for Sydney. Robin Knox-Johnston, the race chairman, asked the two sailors to take their airplane and search for *Skoiern*, which was nearby.

Let Bill Biewenga go on with the story: "Robin told me that *Skoiern's* course made no sense, that Jacques had missed all his radio schedules, and that headquarters and his friends were concerned for his safety. Our charter flight was scheduled to go back to Sydney so we changed our plans and searched the area where *Skoiern* was supposed to be. We found the boat in the early afternoon. Although the wind was only fifteen to twenty knots, when we looked down we saw that *Skoiern* had three reefs in the mainsail and a small booster sail poled out to weather. The yacht was on a beam reach heading west—away from Sydney. The headsail was backed and contributed nothing to the vessel's progress.

"We asked the pilot to circle and fly low over *Skoiern*. There was no sign of anyone on board. We then did a triangular pattern to see if we could spot anything in the water. We circled once again and then flew back to the airport on the coast at Merrimbula, a distance of 42.5 miles.

"Back on land, Courtney and I learned that *HMAS Freemantle* was going out to *Skoiern,*" said Bill. "We went aboard to help and hurried out to the scene. We found that *Skoiern* had been boarded by men from an ore carrier [there was an all ships alert], who had lowered the sails and taken charge of the ship's log and last chart. The men found no one on the French yacht.

"Courtney and I and the executive officer from the *Freemantle* then boarded the drifting vessel. We discovered that *Skoiern's* steering was not working. Many of the lifeline stanchions were bent. One was out of its base, which caused the starboard lifelines to be slack. A broken spinnaker pole was lashed to the foredeck. The masthead instrument unit was missing. From the way various lines were tied off and the reef had been put in, we judged these actions had been done in a hurry.

"Below in the cabin we found clothing and various articles along with two sets of foul weather gear and a safety harness," said Bill. "Food and some of the dirty plates in the sink weren't more than two or three days old. There was ample food, water, and diesel fuel. The generator and single sideband radio were working. The VHF radio did not work properly because its antenna was missing.

"Since the yacht couldn't be steered we got a tow from the *Freemantle* and took the vessel to the small port of nearby Eden, where we arrived at 0330 on December 20th.

"I didn't know Jacques personally," said Bill, "but I was aware of his reputation as a methodical seaman. When I boarded *Skoiern* the conditions I found indicated that some extremely stressful situation had occurred which more than likely caused Jacques to either fall or be washed overboard."

Courtney Hazelton's observations were similar: "When we flew over *Skoiern,* she was headed west at about four knots. I estimated the wind was ten knots from the north. However, the yacht was rigged for strong winds, and the sails were set for a completely different point of sailing. Lines and sails were over the side. No one was visible. We searched the area around the yacht for about forty minutes, saw nothing, and returned to the airport.

"We were asked by the fellows from the Australian sea rescue service to go with *HMAS Freemantle,* which we boarded on Friday afternoon," said Courtney. "We got to *Skoiern* about 1900. The sails had been taken down by men from the ship *Iron Carpentaria,* which was standing by. I spoke to the ship and learned that the officers had Jacques' logbook, passport, and the last chart which had been in use.

"Once on board we found that the main steering was unusable," said Courtney. "The decks were littered with lines, and a broken spinnaker pole was tied down on deck. The lifelines were slack, and one of the stanchions on the starboard side was not in its base, which meant that half the guard rails on that side were down. The cabin was a shambles with clothing and gear scattered everywhere. The ship's power had been turned off at the main switch. Because of rudder damage, the self-steering gear was inoperative. The VHF radio did not work.

"During the tow to Eden, Bill and I cleared up the deck," said Courtney. "While doing this I noticed that several things had been done in a very rushed manner, the mainsail reefing for example. I am an experienced sailor, and to have done things this way indicated that Jacques must have been in an extreme hurry. Something must have taken place which caused danger to the vessel.

"Back in Eden I saw that the safety harness, foul weather gear, two cold weather survival kits, and the liferaft were still on board. All this told me that whatever happened, Jacques must have been in a terrible rush when the incident took place. The French sailor had a reputation for being a good seaman and keeping a neat and tidy vessel. What I saw on board reflected none of this. Something extraordinary must have taken place."[24]

When *Skoiern* was taken out of the water by John Majewski, the Australian who eventually bought the vessel from the de Roux family, she had considerable underwater damage, although her aluminum hull plating had not been holed. The yacht apparently struck something unyielding and metallic in the water while traveling at nine knots on an easterly course (learned from the manual inputs to the satnav). The vessel hit on her port side; the impact was severe enough to swing her 180 degrees counterclockwise and slam her into the obstruction a second time. The second impact bent the skeg and jammed the rudder 20 degrees to port. What did *Skoiern* hit? It could have been a metal container lost from a ship or a moving submarine. It might have been heavy metal tanks or a wreck with just enough buoyancy to float beneath the surface. Probably no one will ever know for sure.

Most of the damage to the yacht was on the port side of the hull and included two long dents, 18 to 24 inches below the waterline, made by a 12-inch circular object passing down the 5-millimeter metal plating of the hull. The first dent was forward of the keel and about 10 feet long. A second dent—5 or 6 feet long—was aft of the keel. In addition there was a deep dent in the front of the keel (made by a round object 18 inches in diameter) plus lesser damage along the bottom of the keel, 7'9" below the surface of the sea.

Such a collision might be attributed to rocks, but *Skoiern* was miles from land and in clear deep water where no one would expect such a thing. An analysis of the damage suggested *two* impacts. The first brought Jacques rushing from the cabin to see what had happened. A second violent impact tossed him over the side, just when he did not expect it, a cruel mockery to a careful sailor's concern for his vessel. This explanation is based on inconclusive evidence, but I believe it's reasonable, particularly when the damage was assessed on a hull that I personally saw in perfect condition in Cape Town.[25]

Several months after I wrote the above, I received the following letter—dated May 20, 1988—from Dominique Presles, the designer of *Skoiern IV*.

> Dear Hal,
> . . . I have now a bit more information than when I wrote to you earlier, and perhaps we can imagine an explanation quite different from the previous ones. As you know, John Majewski sent me some damaged pieces of the keel for analysis. Although there is no official report on these investigations, I have been informed that the analysis did not show any metallic particles on the gashes but rock particles (quartz and silica) plus—which is more strange—some particles of glass and resin.
>
> From other sources I got more accurate information on the Argos positions and on the weather at the time of the accident. I have noted this information on a chart that you will find enclosed. It clearly shows that on the morning of December 18th *Skoiern* was sailing a normal course: about north, reaching on the port tack (i.e. with the spinnaker pole on the port side, as it was when the boat was found later). Then, in the afternoon, the wind—which was not light: twenty to thirty knots—revolved from southwest to southeast and the boat gybed (perhaps roughly?). We can imagine that Jacques at this moment (about 1530 local time) leapt out to handle the vessel and fell overboard. Then *Skoiern* was pushed by the wind to Green Cape and beached (roughly with the waves, which can explain several gashes on the keel and damage on the rudder) before drifting out to the deep sea.
>
> This seems to me more credible than an impact with a floating container? But in all cases, who will ever know?

I sent a copy of Dominique's letter to John Majewski, who replied (August 5, 1988) as follows:

> Dear Hal,
> . . . I spoke to Paul Kelly, who did the repair work on *Skoiern,* and we still both feel that *Skoiern* hit something at sea. Otherwise there would have been far more damage to the bottom of the keel. It's strange that the skeg and rudder were badly damaged and not the lower part of the keel, which showed sliding marks. Obviously the boat had gone over something and created a secondary impact at the stern of the boat. Had it been a rock or grounding there would have been considerably more damage to other areas of the boat because the boat would have been forced on its side.
>
> The silicon or rock particles may have been embedded in the

aluminum when I had the boat slipped. I had to pick the pieces off the gravel [in the boatyard], and since this area is so filthy perhaps something was picked up in the samples. Or the cutting tools used to cut the section out could have been a stone cutting tool or a grinder. However, this is conjecture.

A man unfortunately lost his life. It appears that until the day we go to the pearly gates, exactly what happened will remain a secret.

Jacques was gone. The fellows in the fleet were terribly upset, and a cloud of despair settled over each of the eighteen remaining BOC yachts.

There was a lot of soul-searching and gloomy talk on the December 20th chat hour. Bertie Reed said that he was disappointed in *Stabilo Boss*. "She's a handful and too much for a single guy when it gets to be forty knots." Bertie said that the systems aboard his yacht were a nightmare. He admitted getting overboard twice. "I said goodbye to Pat and the kids and to all you guys. It seemed an eternity before I was able to pull myself back on board. I barely made it." Bertie had on a safety harness, but it took all his strength to overcome the force of the rushing water.

Jean Luc discussed the risks the winners took. "The leading sixty-footers went way south where there is great danger from ice. Guy Bernardin lost a few places by refusing to go so far south.

"In the first race the entrants were pioneers," said Jean Luc. "Now the people in the race are out to win with special boats and plenty of money. The leading boats have been driven unmercifully. Most have been upside down. If you want to win, you may exceed your limits. Then the problems begin," said the French sailor.

I could hardly stand to think of the terrible accident that had happened. Fortunately I was so busy sailing so that I didn't have time to brood on the matter. My immediate problem was to navigate through Bass strait.

When I looked over the charts I thought back to Francis Chichester's circumnavigation of 1966–67 in *Gipsy Moth IV*. During his trip through Bass strait, Chichester had laboriously tacked along the Australian shore with all its hazards and changing winds. What I wanted as a singlehander was to stay in open water *away from the shore* as much as possible and to go from point to point. Such sailing was much safer and easier, and the winds were likely to be steadier away from land. If the capes and islands were suitably separated, then I'd have chances to sleep to keep alert.

The recommended route for Bass strait was to go north of King island and then east. However since my borrowed Walker satnav was working perfectly (and I was quite capable of taking celestial sights if it failed), I saw no reason not to go south of King island on a route that was more direct.

I planned a landfall on a tiny islet called Black Pyramid. Then to Albatross island 15 miles northwest. From Albatross I had clear and unobstructed water for 135 miles to Deal island in the Kent group. Then 170 miles further northeast to Gabo island. Both Deal and Gabo islands had powerful light signals. With this plan I would stay south of a number of hazardous offshore oil rigs. The only pitfall in my scheme was a night landfall on Black Pyramid. Fortunately the days of summer were long, and the odds were that I would not arrive at Black Pyramid in the middle of the night. In any case I would plot a line of fixes to keep track of my position. If things looked bad I could always sail north to the lights on King island.

On the evening of December 20th I cooked a hearty meal and had a good sleep. It was an anxious night for me because I was about to make a landfall on a strange, unlighted shore after a six thousand-mile passage.

[From the log]. December 21st.

0110. A line of nine fixes since yesterday morning shows us right on course for Black Pyramid. There's a ring around the moon (high cirrus for the next depression?). Earlier tonight I saw Saturn and Mars almost together.

0305. The water is definitely smoother. Those huge waves are gone. It sounds like an exaggeration to speak of eighteen-meter waves, but I have seen lots of them during the past weeks. Fortunately their length from crest to crest is generally long—and they present no problem except when one breaks on board. This is what happened a few days ago—when for the second time one pushed the yacht hard enough so that the mast went in the water and bilge water was thrown on the overhead in the cabin.

At 0400 I was on deck and carefully looking ahead. The wind was twenty knots from the west-northwest, but the weather was unsettled. Clouds rapidly scudded across a waning moon just above us to port. A few streaks of whitish clouds were in the east, and the dawn was dim and bluish. Half an hour later we were overtaken by some hard-looking clouds. The wind picked up to thirty-five knots, a heavy rain pelted down, and I rolled up the yankee. When the rain squall passed, I looked ahead. Black Pyramid island was clearly visible about ten miles ahead of *American Flag.*

It was exciting to see land. The island was unmistakable and really did look like a black pyramid. The place reminded me of Diamond Rock off Martinique in the West Indies. I took over the steering by hand and went close to the island, which was 240 feet high. From half a mile away, the black island was slightly greenish. Thousands of birds were in the air, and the smells of nests and fish and vegetation pricked at my nostrils.

I began to see the islands off the northwest corner of Tasmania and the distant blue of the big island itself. By 0820 I was abeam of tiny Albatross island, but I had to head up thirty degrees to leave the island to starboard because of the tidal stream pouring through nearby Hope channel at Three

Hummock island. I was sailing at nine knots and rapidly left the islands behind. More squalls pummeled down on the yacht. The sea increased substantially as I got out into the main part of Bass strait and left the gray smudges of Tasmania behind. My next land was Deal island, 120 miles northeast.

Below in the cabin I cooked a big breakfast of eggs and bacon and potatoes. Then with nothing in sight I lay down for a ninety-minute nap. At 1035 I heard from Pentti Salmi, who was east of King island. *"Colt* is falling apart," he said. "My rigging problems are terrible. Half the wires are unstranding. I hope the yacht will hold together to Sydney, otherwise I'll have to go into a bay somewhere to fix things." Bertie Reed was approaching King island from the west and in good spirits. Mark Schrader was a little ahead of me in Bass strait. "I feel the heat from you guys," he said.

At noon I worked out that I had done 197 miles in the last twenty-four hours. I heard on the radio that eight of the eighteen BOC yachts had crossed the finish line at Sydney Heads.

The most spectacular finish was *Spirit of Sydney,* which came in fourth. Australian Ian Kiernan—a local sailor who wanted to show off a bit to the fifty boats and helicopters that had come out to welcome him—tried to cross the finish line with an enormous spinnaker flying in a twenty-knot southeast wind. Unfortunately the finish line was tucked a little behind the entrance to Sydney harbor and required a short turn south, more into the wind. Ian knew this, but thought he could just make the line with the spinnaker sheeted in as much as possible. "I decided to take a chance," he said later.

Everything worked perfectly, the yacht looked spectacular, and the television cameras covered every moment. As Ian turned southwest to cross the line at an angle, he came closer to the wind. The sail luffed. Suddenly a gust filled the giant sail with a bang. *Spirit of Sydney* was out of control and among the spectator fleet. Ian let the spinnaker sheet fly, the sail collapsed, and he ran forward to throttle the sail with a sock he began to pull down from the masthead. At that moment a gust filled the huge sail a second time and began to drag the yacht sideways. With the sail filled, it was impossible to pull down the sock. Pandemonium! The yacht careened until her rudder was out of the water. It was a spectacular broach in crowded waters! The television cameras ground on.

By the time Ian got things under control, the spectators—and millions of television viewers (the footage was repeated again and again)—had seen an incredible finish to a 6,500-mile run all the way from Cape Town. Ian—smiling with embarrassment—became an immediate celebrity and in a dozen talks said: "It was a bit of grandstanding gone out of control. I got my ambitions mixed up with my capabilities!"

Back on *American Flag* I continued to sail rapidly toward Deal island. Unfortunately, the wind and seas were dead aft and increasing. Instead of being able to change course to get the wind on one quarter or the other, I had to steer directly for my target. With the wind behind me, the yacht rolled terribly. Bands of squalls marched across the sky from west to east and threw whiplashes of wind at *American Flag* as they passed. At 1400 I ducked below for a nap. When I woke up I switched on the radio and listened to the local Australian fishermen, who—apparently tied up at the docks—were fed up with the weather, fed up with fishing, fed up with their wives, and fed up with their boats. Some fishermen spoke of selling out. ("But who'll buy, mate?")

At 1805 Jean Luc (along the coast south of Sydney) reported no wind at all. Richard Konkolski (on the east coast of Tasmania) said that he had fifty to sixty knots and that the sea around him was all white. John Hughes (near

Here Ian Kiernan demonstrates how to get a spinnaker down correctly by hauling on a line running to a sock that throttles the big sail when collapsed. Note that Ian is holding on to a lifeline with one hand while he pulls with the other. He is also in a crouched position and can easily drop to his knees. The curious appendages on deck just forward of the mast are part of a complex retractable centerboard scheme (with solar panels mounted on the sides) that unfortunately was found to be more of a weight penalty than a sailing advantage. At each stop Ian removed weight from *Spirit of Sydney* and she went faster. "If we'd gone around again and I kept taking off weight, I'd have beaten those wily Frenchmen," said Ian.

King island) talked of "diabolical swells, one of which broke on top of me and sent its spray over the top of the mast."

My wind continued at twenty-eight knots from the west, and as the daylight began to fade in the early evening I picked up the powerful group flashing light on Deal island. I took careful bearings of the light because I had to approach on a certain compass course to avoid several small islands to the north. The planets Mars (small and yellowish) and Jupiter (large and bluish) were almost together in the western sky behind me. At midnight I passed Deal island, a pyramidal rockpile a thousand feet high with the light at the top. I watched carefully for several small islands to the northeast and then changed course for Gabo island, 170 miles northeast.

The swells and seas running through Bass strait continued to be extremely high and rough. I was running hard with three reefs in the main eased to starboard and the full yankee poled out to port. I took one-hour naps during the night and kept a watch for ships and oil rigs but saw nothing. I was amazed to learn later that one of the sailors had attempted to stay awake all the way from King island to Sydney. After three or four days he began to hallucinate badly and in the sloughs of fatigue almost walked over the side. Certainly with reasonable sailing management he could have taken half-hour naps from time to time.[26]

At 0830 the next morning the west wind increased sharply and was soon up to forty knots. I put the yankee on the leeward side and began to roll it up. Squalls and heavy rain blasted *American Flag*. Some of the seas looked nasty, and I closed both storm doors. Jean Luc reported passing Warren Luhrs in *Thursday's Child*, who was proceeding toward Sydney at one knot under jury rig. Warren was very discouraged. At noon I showed 214 miles for the last twenty-four hours. My average for thirty-seven days over 6,237 miles was 168.5 miles a day.

Four hours later I looked out to see the gray and hilly coastline of Australia about fifteen miles ahead to port, and as we continued sailing northeast I gradually worked into the lee of the land. The sea conditions improved hugely. Soon I was in smooth water with a west-southwest wind of thirty-five knots. The sailing was marvelous. I couldn't believe how calm the sea was. Since I had several deck jobs that I had put off because of the hard going during the last few days, I got busy with my tools. Nearby were several coasting ships that were headed south for Tasmania.

I sat on the coachroof just aft of the mast with my feet on the starboard side deck while I sprayed lubricant on the gooseneck reefing lines sheaves and tried to get them to turn easily. A small red-orange ship with containers on deck passed a half-mile west of me. I turned to see the coaster's name so I could write it in the log. Because my attention was on the coaster instead of on the sea and my business, it was almost the final act of my life.

The yacht suddenly rolled heavily, and a large, totally unexpected wave *from the east* swept on board and thundered down the starboard side deck going aft. The wave was thigh-high and moving rapidly and washed me down the deck. I dropped everything and threw my arms around the four-part boom vang and lifelines, which were on the downstream side of the water as the surging waterfall shot me along. The experience was all over in two or three seconds, but I almost went overboard. I was wearing my harness, but I was not hooked on because the sea had been so smooth. I got completely soaked and went below to change clothes and to try to calm down. This moment was by far the most dangerous incident of the entire race for me and demonstrated for the thousandth time that a sailor can never let his guard down.

Fast-moving ankle-deep water is no problem. Fast-moving knee-deep water is no problem. But fast-moving thigh-deep water is lethal!

At 1900 I was abeam of Gabo island and its high fingerlike lighthouse at the southeast corner of Australia. This was the place where Desmond Hampton was wrecked in *Gipsy Moth V* in December 1982 during the first BOC race when he overslept while the wind changed and his vane gear steered him to disaster. I remembered how impressed I had been when I saw the BOC film in which Desmond had forthrightly told how the stranding had been his fault and his responsibility.

Just three days before I arrived, Jacques de Roux had lost his life here. I thought back to Cape Town, where Jacques had been so jubilant and had worked on his boat, which was tied up next to *American Flag*. I remembered how he had talked of visiting a farmer who had presented him with a box of apples ("Here, have one"), how he had helped me with my new headsail furling gear, and how he had given me some tins of the special French sport food ("It is quite good, really") to eat on the next leg.

I wept bitter tears.

By the next morning, December 23rd, my entire world had changed. The Southern ocean was behind me. The gigantic waves and swells were gone. The weather was warm, hot even, and for the first time in almost six weeks I stripped off my three layers of heavy foul weather clothing. Without my long johns and the Santa Claus suits, I was able to move twice as fast. I felt as nimble as a gazelle without the layers of elephant clothing and danced up and down the side decks.

I poked along a coast with trifling winds of two knots or eight knots or fifteen knots. I even flew my green and white spinnaker for two hours. Hooray! This sailing seemed like a vacation after the stupid Southern ocean. Playing with the sails was a lark, and I navigated from point to point. Gabo island to Green Cape. Green Cape to Montague island.

At noon on December 23rd, Sydney was 120 miles away. I was 5 miles offshore on a course of 015°, and close-hauled on the starboard tack into 15-knot wind from the east-northeast. The sea was flat. I had the full yankee up and one reef in the mainsail when I spotted a mast far ahead. I did my best to overtake the single-masted yacht and gradually pulled up on the vessel. I saw that it was *Declaration*. Richard Konkolski had his vessel strapped in as hard as he could, but I sailed past him, pointing higher and going faster. Since Konkolski had boasted so much of his fabulous skills and wonderful yacht at the protest hearing in Cape Town, I was surprised that on a perfectly even match, *American Flag,* a pig to weather according to her detractors, easily beat him. As I pulled away from the Czechoslovakian sailor, he tacked out to sea—away from Sydney, his target. I smiled at my small victory.

Following race instructions, I radioed Sydney with my estimated arrival time and also secured a medical clearance from the authorities. In the early evening I tacked past the Beecroft peninsula and worked slowly northward along the coast. At midnight the wind changed to the west-southwest and freshened. I immediately put up the running rig and began to move fast. I knew Konkolski could never beat *American Flag* with a fair wind on a flat sea no matter what he did. At 0300 the wind was up to twenty-four knots. The yacht was flying along and made a great roaring sound at her transom. By dawn I had begun to work inshore in a south wind of thirty knots as the great yellow shoreline cliffs south of Botany bay hove into view. I was soon running by the lee and had to gybe the rig in near gale conditions, a tricky job near shore.

After I gybed and got sailing well again, I looked ahead and saw a yacht in the distance (which I later learned was *Lone Star*). I then made a stupid navigational error. I still had ten miles of sailing before I got to Sydney Heads. I should have continued running at high speed. Somehow I misread the scale of the chart and thought I had only *two* miles to go (I had begun to see houses and apartments on top of the cliffs). Because of the near gale I reckoned that it might be gusty and squally when I turned into Sydney Heads. Since I had never been there before and didn't know what I might be getting into I took down the running rig, tucked in a reef, and reduced the headsail area (and so failed to overtake *Lone Star*).

A little before 0800 I passed Macquarie lighthouse high on the cliff at the south entrance to Sydney Heads. Instead of squalls and raging winds, however, the area was calm and quiet; Sydney was enjoying a hot summer day. The horrors of the Southern ocean, Bass strait, and ocean gales were a million miles away. I cursed at myself for my bad performance the last two hours. At 0843 I headed south inside the great harbor of Sydney and crossed the finish line. A gun went off. I had sailed halfway around the world in ninety days and twenty-two hours.

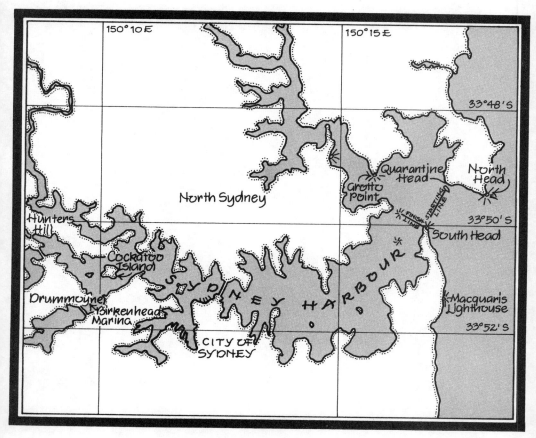

8. Sydney harbor

. . . .

CHAPTER EIGHTEEN

Sydney

*A*ustralia's greatest harbor is seven miles long, perfectly protected from the sea, and the center of a bustling population of five million people. I arrived the day before Christmas, the focus of the great summer holiday season. The sun was out, the sky was clear and blue, and everyone was in a joyous, festive mood.

A police launch pulled up and threw me a towline. A BOC official boat came alongside, and Margaret jumped on board, smiling and pretty, wearing a fresh summer dress and bubbling over with pleasure at seeing her husband, who was falling asleep. Another launch appeared with health, customs, immigration, and agricultural quarantine officials, who climbed on board and—believe it or not—began to fill out their own papers (of which there were plenty). "Sign here, mate," said one of the uniformed men. "We'll make short work of these forms."

The launch pulled us down the great harbor at five knots. We passed bays and marinas and docks. I looked up at shoreside houses, wide green parks, modern apartments, and tall office buildings. We glided in the shadows of giant warehouses, went under a noisy bridge, and crossed wakes with big ferryboats and sightseeing launches (everybody waved). We slipped past the enormous opera house with its layered, shell-like, winged structure. Finally almost seven miles west of Sydney Heads we got to Birkenhead marina in Drummoyne, where we were to stay for three weeks.

Fourteen of the eighteen BOC yachts were now in Sydney. Three of the sixty-footers were already out of the water at Cockatoo island for major repairs. The rest of the fleet was clustered around a small dock at the Birkenhead complex, which had once been a factory but was now an enormous shopping center with several hundred small stores and shops near the water.

Sydney was filled with sailing enthusiasts, and the BOC people had made arrangements for each captain to be adopted by a host family while he was in Australia. This was a great idea, and as we tied up at the dock I met Ian Hansen, a prominent marine artist, who put Margaret and me into his car and whisked us away to nearby Hunters Hill, where I met Ian's gracious wife, Kaylene. The Hansens—who were sailing nuts like Margaret and me—lived in a big old comfortable house with two children, lots of rooms, dogs, cats, gardens, flowers, a pool, and a totally relaxed ambiance. Ian had a studio in one room, and his wonderful paintings were everywhere. I was fed and then led to a bed, where I collapsed for a day.

The next morning—Christmas—Pentti Salmi and John Hughes were both due in. I wanted to welcome them. Margaret and I borrowed an old truck from Ian and drove to Birkenhead, where we did a few things on *American Flag* and then went out on a launch to meet *Colt*. Pentti was jubilant at getting to Sydney. I jumped on board and steered during the tow to the marina. *Colt* was in poor condition. Her entire steering pedestal had almost been ripped out during a roll. Worse yet was the rigging wire. There were about *forty* broken strands on the twelve main shrouds and stays. Obviously the wire was faulty and would have to be completely replaced. Pentti was absolutely enraged at the engine, which had supposedly been rebuilt in Cape Town (it was new in Newport and had never run). To even mention the engine was forbidden. "It makes me think of murder or sick jokes," said the smiling Finn, who was so pleased to be in port and united with his wife.

One of the tragedies at Sydney was Jacques de Roux's girlfriend, a pretty Indonesian woman who had flown to Australia to greet her hero. She was nicely dressed in new summer clothes and wandered around the docks aimlessly. She kept peering out to sea as if secretly watching and hoping that Jacques would somehow appear. The slim young lady spoke no English and only a few words of French so it was impossible for me to say anything of substance to her. Guy Bernardin and his wife, Mitzi, looked after the Indonesian girl. It broke my heart to see her, and I wanted to put my arms around her and comfort her. I offered to take up a collection if she needed money, but Mitzi said that the girl was okay. There was nothing to do but to walk away. I felt stupid and helpless. I didn't even know her name.

Back at the Hansen house we met a whole houseful of relatives who had come for a big Christmas dinner. Margaret and I were introduced to everyone and made part of a splendid family celebration. To be taken to the heart of these people in a faraway foreign land was a wonderful thing, and when the champagne was opened, my sailing venture seemed far away. I loved the whole human race.

The next day we tried to welcome Bertie Reed, but—incredible enough—the big wooden launch that a group of us went out on caught fire. The engine had to be shut off. We drifted about helplessly. Someone called for assistance on the radio, but no one paid the slightest attention to our messages or to our frantic waving (people merely waved back). It was uproarious. "Sailing is safer than engines," observed Pentti. Bertie crossed the finish line and was towed right past the welcoming committee. He never saw us. After a while the fire went out, and we returned to Birkenhead, feeling rather foolish. Bertie had already left.

Credit Agricole had been taken out of the water at the naval shipyard on Cockatoo island immediately after finishing the race to keep the vessel from sinking. Her keel was a sorry sight. The lead ballast was held by only three of the eight keel bolts; the other five had sheared, and it was possible to put your hand in the open space between the lead and the keel. The shipyard workers and BOC onlookers could not understand why the lead ballast hadn't snapped off completely, which would have meant disaster in the Southern ocean. Philippe Jeantot's architect said the twenty-millimeter (three quarter-inch) bolts had sheared because they had been overtightened in Cape Town. This explanation didn't satisfy Philippe, who summoned a French expert who worked for the local insurance companies. "Your keel has been held on by a miracle and not by any mechanical means," said M. Jacob.

Philippe hired the engineers at the naval shipyard to calculate the loads on the entire keel structure, to review the strength of the keel itself, and to look into the attachment of the lead ballast. The engineers inspected the keel and agreed with the others that "It was only by luck that the the keel hadn't fallen off." The engineers thoroughly reviewed the problem. They changed some of the upper keel reinforcements to stainless steel, added more keel bolts of a larger diameter, and used finer threads on the bolts. Philippe had no further trouble.[27]

His difficulties highlighted one of the design problems of these extreme sixty-foot racers. With a draft of 3.6 meters—almost twelve feet—and a thin, ribbonlike keel with a bulb of heavy lead ballast at the very bottom, the engineering problems were horrendous. Fortunately, *American Flag* was smaller, lighter, and her 2.4-meter keel was held by *fifteen* 25-millimeter bolts plus lots of fiberglass. I was confident that her keel structure was sound.

By now I had been in Sydney for several days. I was well rested. It was time to think about what lay ahead. *American Flag* needed a modest amount of work, a haulout, and a few supplies. But there was simply no money. I had four choices:

1. Drop out of the race and sell the yacht in Australia.
2. Sell some of the yacht's gear to get cash.
3. Attempt fund-raising.
4. Do something to earn money.

I desperately wanted to complete the race. There was not much on board to sell because the radios, sails, winches, and spare parts were necessary if I was to continue. Could an American raise money in Australia on short notice? Other than a few acquaintances, I knew no one. I had no office, no papers, and no telephone. Still, I could appeal to American companies in Australia. But curses! The whole country was shut down because of the summer holidays. People were off on vacations and simply unavailable. Maybe I could talk to Australians through television and radio and raise something. It was not a very hopeful outlook, but I could try.

Finally, maybe I could earn some money. What could I do? Talk about sailing, of course. Margaret had brought along a 16 mm. lecture film of an earlier trip that she and I had made around Cape Horn. I arranged to show the film at a nearby hall. There was scarcely time for publicity, and the hall was small (one needed to work ahead, get lots of publicity, hire large halls, and arrange a string of lectures). Nevertheless it was something. I would have to get my song and dance act together.

What was aggravating was that instead of chasing dollars, I should have been using my time to work on *American Flag* to get her ready for the next long sea passage. I read in a yachting newspaper that the budget for the shore team of *Thursday's Child* started out at $250,000, which represented just one part of the project.[28] This was more than my entire effort—yacht, sails, campaign, and all—had cost. How could I possibly compete with such an operation? Yet I had to tell myself not to be covetous of the others but to be thankful that I had gotten this far. *American Flag* was not the only yacht short of money; six others shared my problem in varying degrees.

Kathy Giblin and Kim McKay, the two publicity women in the BOC office, did everything they could to help. They arranged for me to appear on a morning national television show, where I talked about the race and my money problem. The interviewer assumed that all the BOC boats had million-dollar-plus budgets. He couldn't understand how anyone could be in the race without a sponsor. "You're putting me on!" the interviewer said over and over. ·

Meanwhile the girls in the BOC office had made an arrangement with the boatyard at Birkenhead for inexpensive haulouts of the smaller yachts. We took *American Flag* out of the water to clean and paint her bottom and to deal with several through-hull fittings and other jobs. I decided to put the shaft and folding propeller back on because of the difficulty of going out for trial sails. The BOC berths were excellent but tucked back in constricted marinas that were extremely hard to get in and out of. I was fairly good at sailing in restricted waters, but dealing with an uninsured fifty-footer in a foreign country where there was a lot of boating traffic seemed unwise. Tows were possible, but inconvenient. (Also, putting the propeller on, meant one less expense when I got back to the United States.)

One of the miracles of the BOC race was the help from volunteers in all the ports. In Newport and Cape Town, people had come to the yacht day after day and slaved away at drudgery jobs with no expectation of pay. These

A look at *American Flag* out of the water in Sydney. Normally the Santa Cruz 50 hull has a balanced spade rudder, but I added the skeg to give the rudder additional support and to ensure good tracking. All through the race I was amazed at how well the yacht performed on different points of sailing including going to windward, when she pounded surprisingly little. Her only failing was excess heeling when sailing to windward. This could have been lessened with water ballast tanks (or perhaps a lead bulb on the keel), which were not installed because of cost. The holes at the bottom of the transom are for cockpit drains (there were four drains) and a bilge pump outlet. The vertical track on the transom is for the emergency rudder.

volunteers just wanted to be part of the great competition. In Sydney various sailing enthusiasts stopped by to see the yacht, we got talking, and sometimes one of them wound up on board doing something. Three men joined Margaret as my shore crew in this way. These fellows worked long hours, chased down parts, drove me around on errands, and even brought me small presents. Jim Nisbet, Geoff Errington, and Gil Forrester became good friends, and with their expert help, work on *American Flag* progressed nicely.

I was amazed at the damage to some of the yachts and the amount of reconstruction at each stop of the race. *Credit Agricole's* keel was undergoing major repairs. The two Finnish yachts were in the hands of professionals who had flown in from Helsinki. A gang of hard-working French mechanics swarmed around *Ecureuil* for two weeks, and one day she appeared from the shipyard with a gorgeous paint job and much new gear. An enormous box of sails from Technique Voile had just arrived and sat on the foredeck. Her new fully-battened mainsail was superb. *UAP's* refit was complete, and she was towed around from the shipyard to the BOC dock, where her professional shore crew began to bend on her new sails. Ian Kiernan was determined to make *Spirit of Sydney* (original cost: $1,400,000 Aus.) faster. Ian junked the $60,000 hydraulically operated twin centerboards to reduce weight. Experts were going over the entire yacht to see what else could be thrown out. Sailmakers brought down a special new spinnaker and a high-tech reaching sail. *Thursday's Child's* mast had been repaired, and shouts came from aloft, where someone had a noisy electric drill going.

A look at some of the rigging on *Let's Go* would have turned the Devil into a Christian. Fully half of the wires on Jean Luc's headstay had broken and had bunched up about three-quarters of the way up the length of the stay into something that looked like the head of a mop. Jean Luc bought a coil of wire and hired a rigger.

On January 9th there was a memorial service for Jacques de Roux in the navy chapel in Watson's bay on South Head at the entrance to Sydney harbor. The chapel was small and exquisitely located on navy grounds on a quiet knoll high above the sea. Jacques' family, the French ambassador from Canberra, friends, BOC officials, and fifteen of the competitors attended the requiem high mass. The service was conducted in both French and English by a French priest and an Australian chaplain, both of whom wore magnificent vestments. As the priests intoned the solemn prayers, we in the congregation were able to look past the two men of God, across the altar, and out at the sea. That Friday afternoon was sunny and calm, the water was intensely blue, and the Southern ocean that had claimed Jacques was far away. The service was short, touching, sad, beautiful, serene, and eminently fitting.

By now seventeen of the eighteen BOC yachts were in port. Only Harry Mitchell was still at sea. It seemed axiomatic in the race that once you fell behind, you invariably got into poorer and poorer weather systems. Harry had been plagued by severe injuries and headwinds and spent a long time tacking across Bass strait. He finally arrived at 0356 on January 10th, fifty-five days after leaving Cape Town.

Harry's wife, a gang of the captains in the smaller class, the race committee, the press people, and Margaret and I all went out to meet Harry, who was delighted to arrive in Sydney. He had recovered from his rib injuries, and his nose and forehead wounds were healed except for small scars. Harry's eyes were bright and twinkling, and he was full of smiles.

"My best days were the first few out of Cape Town," said the sixty-two-year-old captain. "I clocked 180- and 190-mile days and was ahead of some of the others, but it didn't last long. My boat needs ten strong men all sitting up on the weather side. Then I could put up some canvas, and I bet you she would fly. But singlehanded and without water ballast it is difficult. If I put up too much sail, I heel over much too far, and then I have to reduce the sail area, which cuts my speed. It was pretty frustrating."

Harry's main problem in getting ready for the next leg was the condition of his sails, which looked poor and were quickly sent off for repairs. His wind generator had worn out, and he had the usual long list of small jobs. Soon half a dozen volunteers were busy on *Double Cross* while Harry slept, ate, talked to his pals, and slept again. Harry was immensely pleased to have made Sydney and to be with the fleet.

I told Gil Forrester—one of my volunteer helpers—about the problem with Richard Konkolski and his engine. Gil, who was a senior consulting engineer, said that he knew a simple and foolproof way to detect engine shaft movement. I introduced Gil to race chairman Robin Knox-Johnston, who quickly adopted Gil's scheme.

The procedure is to wrap ordinary painter's masking tape around and around the engine shaft for six inches or so and then to continue wrapping the tape further aft over the engine stuffing box (a part that does not revolve). The slightest movement of the engine shaft will break the tape. To keep anyone from tampering with the tape, one or two people on the race committee sign their names (in ink) down the length of the masking tape. Then the masking tape and signatures are covered with transparent sticky paper-mending (cellophane) tape. It's impossible to pull the transparent tape away from the masking tape without destroying the signatures. This scheme is simple and foolproof, can be inspected instantly, and takes longer to describe than to do.

It is notable that Konkolski's placings in the final two legs of the race were poorer than in the first two legs. I wonder if he knew that only his shaft was treated in this manner because only he was suspected of wrongdoing.

In early January I showed the Cape Horn film to a small audience and made $800. Titouan kindly gave me some Dacron line that I needed, and

Philippe presented me with a supply of French sport food. A sympathetic sailing couple made a donation of $500 to the *American Flag* project. Margaret's fund-raising in the United States brought in $594. The $1,894 may have been small change to the other competitors, and it's certainly peanuts in the ocean racing game, but it meant that I could continue in the race. I also managed to trade the rights to some art work for the Champion book for a round-trip air ticket for Margaret from the United States to Rio de Janeiro.

By now *American Flag* was out of the boatyard and sailing on Sydney harbor, a wonderful body of water. It was great fun going out with my shore crew. They were thrilled, and the sailing was easy for me.

I got the electric log working and calibrated. I checked over the seven Dacron halyards (twelve-millimeter Samson braid) on the mast; all were in perfect condition after half a circumnavigation. Carl Seipel from the Monitor company made adjustments to the wind vane gear. With the Southern ocean ahead of me again, I knew I had to improve the deep reefing arrangements for the mainsail. A local sailmaker substituted short battens for the long battens and replaced the bronze sail hanks (all of which were severely worn or broken). For the top of the mainsail he made a new double-length hank of stainless steel that he fastened to the headboard with two quarter-inch bolts. I needed more power for the reefing pendants, but since I couldn't afford a larger winch, I mounted a block on the mast so that I could stand and use a halyard winch and get more power from my back and shoulders. All these things seemed to work well during trial sails.

My stay in Sydney certainly wasn't all work. One afternoon Margaret and I went to a picnic sponsored by the BOC. A few days later everyone went to a luncheon put on by the Cruising Club of Australia and—while everyone roared with laughter—heard Ian Kiernan tell how to fly a spinnaker. Most nights we stayed with Ian and Kaylene Hansen, our host family, who treated us grandly. I discovered that Ian was not only a fine painter but had once been a boat builder; he was soon on *American Flag* improving a few things.

A week before the race was to start on January 18th, we went to a gala evening of prize-giving where we drank champagne, ate well, saw a multi-image video show of the contestants and their boats, watched fireworks, and danced to the music of a Brazilian band.

The formal briefing for the third leg of the race was held on the morning of January 15th. Someone had found out that this day was my sixtieth birthday, and the skippers' meeting opened with the girls from the office marching in with a big birthday cake. I was quite touched when the cake with its lighted candles appeared. Everyone applauded. (Before the day was over, three other birthday cakes appeared, and Ian Hansen presented me with a birthday card with a painting of *American Flag* that he had done specially for me.)

We heard that the prime minister of Australia would visit the yachts at Birkenhead before the start. Then we got detailed instructions about the actual start at Sydney Heads. Robin Knox-Johnston told about the towing arrangements and the recovery vessels to take off crewmen. A meteorologist spoke about the weather, and a radio expert gave us a list of frequencies for New Zealand, Chile, and Brazil.

The next morning—two days before the start—*Thursday's Child* went out again for a sailing trial, as she had for the past week or so. Her seventy-five-foot mast had been repaired and thoroughly checked. The yacht was all ready for the start on Sunday and the second half of the race. Suddenly while she was gliding along in light airs, her slim spar collapsed. As it fell so did the determination of Warren Luhrs. Although Warren's shore crew was willing to make further repairs or to find another spar, Warren was not. He withdrew from the race. Seventeen yachts were left.

The seventeen competitors at the start of leg 3 in order of their standing:

CLASS I (8)

name	yacht	length	beam
Philippe Jeantot	*Credit Agricole*	60 ft.	16 ft. 8 in.
Titouan Lamazou	*Ecureuil d'Aquitaine*	60 ft.	15 ft.
Guy Bernardin	*Biscuits Lu*	60 ft.	14 ft. 9 in.
John Martin	*Tuna Marine*	60 ft.	14 ft. 9 in.
Jean-Yves Terlain	*UAP*	60 ft.	18 ft.
Ian Kiernan	*Spirit of Sydney*	60 ft.	15 ft.
David White	*Legend Securities*	56 ft.	14 ft.
Bertie Reed	*Stabilo Boss*	60 ft.	16 ft. 8 in.

CLASS II (9)

name	yacht	length	beam
Mike Plant	*Airco Distributor*	50 ft.	13 ft. 9 in.
J. L. Van Den Heede	*Let's Go*	45 ft.	8 ft. 4 in.
Harry Harkimo	*Belmont Finland*	50 ft.	14 ft. 8 in.
Richard Konkolski	*Declaration*	44 ft.	13 ft.
Hal Roth	*American Flag*	50 ft.	12 ft.
Mark Schrader	*Lone Star*	49 ft.	13 ft. 10 in.
Pentti Salmi	*Colt by Rettig*	47 ft.	12 ft. 5 in.
John Hughes	*Joseph Young*	42 ft.	8 ft. 10 in.
Harry Mitchell	*Double Cross*	41 ft.	12 ft. 6 in.

. . . .

CHAPTER NINETEEN

Back on the Blue Highway

*S*unday, January 18th, was a gorgeous summer day, and a little after noon-time the BOC fleet began to leave Birkenhead for Sydney Heads. The towing arrangements had gotten behind schedule because of the visit of Prime Minister Bob Hawke, who had gone around the assembled fleet beforehand and shook hands with each captain. There had been enormous publicity about the race, and thousands of people were jammed together on the docks, on the ramps, and on the surrounding roads and shore.

Finally, however, the police boats maneuvered into position, took our lines, and began to tow us the seven miles to the start. Each captain was supposed to have only one or two helpers to assist with the tow, hoist the sails, and tidy up the dock lines, but a few friends climbed on board all the yachts and went along for the ride. There were so many spectator boats that the towing went very slowly, and we didn't arrive in the starting area until an hour before the 3 P.M. gun. I had *American Flag*'s mainsail up, so I dropped my tow, hoisted the staysail, and began to sail back and forth across the great channel between the headlands.

The race committee had arranged for a number of inflatable dinghies with large outboard motors to take off the helpers from the seventeen yachts, but because of the press of more than five hundred spectator boats, the men running the inflatables had trouble finding the BOC vessels. I never saw a single one of the inflatables, although I was astride the starting line ten or twelve minutes before the gun. There was a terrific amount of noise and confusion—engines, whistles, foghorns, shouting—and a lot of fumes from the gasoline and diesel boats. While I steered, I used my portable VHF radio to call the race committee. "Please send someone to take off my people," I pleaded. Five minutes before the start, a police boat pulled alongside. It was expertly handled and came to within a foot of *American Flag*'s port quarter. A burly policeman stood at the bow and helped Margaret and my passengers who quickly scrambled on the police boat.

It was a difficult moment just then. I had to look forward and deal with steering because an enormous, high-sided ferryboat—filled with shouting, screaming sightseers—suddenly crossed directly in front of me *on the starting line*. I had to bear off sharply to avoid a collision. When I glanced behind me, I realized that I still had one passenger on board—a lady psychiatrist, of all things—who was terrified.

"I can't do it," she said meekly. "I'm afraid to jump to the police boat. I'll have to go with you."

"Not this time," I said.

With visions of stowaways, international incidents, and hysterical women flashing through my mind, I motioned to the police launch, which again closed to within a foot of my port quarter. The lady psychiatrist was terrified and held her shoes in one hand. I dropped the tiller, jumped up on the after deck, picked up the woman, and handed her to the big policeman, who seized her as if she were a sack of corn. Unfortunately at that moment we pitched into the swells from the idiot ferryboat, which caused the police boat to run into *American Flag*. The bow of the police boat tore off my stern light and the port stern pulpit. I had to steer away from more spectator boats, continue to blast my air horn at others, and try to fill away on the other tack. It was a nasty time, and all because of the uncontrolled spectator boats—particularly the big ferry, which had no business being across the starting line.

At the moment I was handing the psychiatrist to the policeman, the starting gun went off. "It's too bad my mother isn't still alive," I thought to myself. "She'd have loved this story, but wouldn't have believed a word of it."

I had to gybe downwind to get clear of the spectator boats. By the time I got turned around and sailing properly, I was the last vessel to cross the starting line. I waved to the assembled officials on *HMAS Geelong*, the moored warship that served as the north end of the line. I made a mental note to petition the race committee for a time allowance to cover the starting line fiasco.

A few minutes later I was clear of all problems and sailing nicely on the port tack headed east in a fifteen-knot northeast wind. I remember unrolling the yankee and picking up enough speed to scoot ahead of *Joseph Young* and *Double Cross*. As I passed Harry Mitchell, I shouted, "Good luck." Harry looked around, startled.

A sleek Australian yacht came close to me. Ian and Kayelene Hansen, my hosts in Sydney, were in the cockpit. They had come out to wish me bon voyage. I gave Ian a big wave and blew kisses to Kayelene. They were nice people, and I would miss them. But already they were getting small. Good-bye Australia!

I turned the tiller over to the wind vane steering gear and trimmed the sails. Some of the yachts headed east; some south. I saw spinnakers going up and coming down in the fluky coastal wind. Meanwhile I got out my tools to make repairs to the damaged port stern pulpit and the stern light. It was a relief to be at sea.

The start of each leg of the race was absolutely hair-raising. The first hour was a nightmare of confusion and unbelievable tension and pressure on the captains, who were busy tacking fifty- and sixty-footers in crowded conditions. So much money and hope and work and the expectations of others rode on these little ships. The main difficulty, of course, was the spectator fleet, which came because of the publicity generated by the race sponsor and the sponsors of the various entries. The sailors didn't object to the publicity or to the presence of a controlled spectator fleet. Indeed, people and publicity were vital to the race. The problem was an *uncontrolled* spectator

Joseph Young leaving Sydney Heads at the start of the third leg. The Canadian yacht is sailing nicely, with her stem cleaving a big bow wave. The pennants at the right are the racing flags on *American Flag,* from where I took the photograph.

fleet at the start and the chances of serious collisions. The BOC vessels were outfitted for 10,000 voyages and were well suited to the dangers of the sea; however they were extremely vulnerable to damage from spectator boats. It was an issue that would have to be resolved somehow, particularly as the races got larger. I can tell you that after undergoing the gauntlet of the Sunday starts in Newport and Sydney in moderate winds, I gave some thought to starting a few hours late (and accepting the penalty) so that I could sneak out quietly *and in one piece.* I can't imagine starting a race in gale conditions. The BOC yachts could do it, but the spectator boats might sink the fleet!

Nevertheless, as we headed out and the coast of Australia gradually got smaller behind *American Flag,* I calmed down. My trembling and agitation soon disappeared. With almost two months of sea time to look forward to, what lay over the eastern horizon?

The distance from Sydney to the southern tip of New Zealand (to the Snares islets south of Stewart island) is 1,098 miles. The course is southeast (141°T.). From New Zealand (48°02'S.) to Cape Horn (56°S.) is 4,679 miles to the east (096°) on a rhumb line course—a straight line on a Mercator chart. For a great circle course dropping to the south, the figures are:

to 70°48'S. (true great circle)	4,000 nautical miles
to 65°S. (modified great circle)	4,057
to 60°S. (modified great circle)	4,207
to 56°S. (modified great circle)	4,417
rhumb line	4,679

I had some time to decide how far south to go. But for now I accepted the 4,679–mile figure. Once I got to Cape Horn, the next leg was northeast (course 053°) into the South Atlantic. The distance from Cape Horn to Cape Pembroke on East Falkland is 427 miles. Finally, from the Falklands to Rio de Janeiro is 1,851 miles to the north-northeast (021°). The total of the four parts of the third leg of the race was 8,055 miles if I traveled in straight lines. However, because of storms, headwinds, and God knows what else, I was looking at 8,300 or 8,400 miles, a long drink of water, as my grandfather Knapp used to say.

To summarize roughly, my course from Australia to Brazil was:

southeast for 1,098 miles
east for 4,679 miles

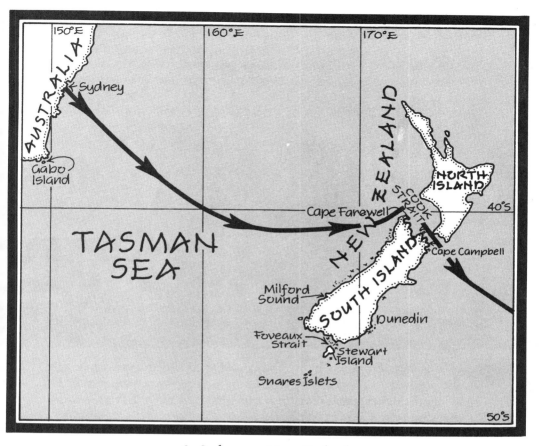

9. Sydney to New Zealand

northeast for 427 miles
north-northeast for 1,851 miles
course irregularities, say, 345 miles (?)
total: 8,400 miles

    The Tasman sea—the thousand-mile stretch of the Pacific between Australia and New Zealand—has a nasty reputation with sailors, and even during the summer months the pilot charts are zigzagged with the red tracks of fifty- and sixty-knot storms. On the first night out from Sydney a southerly buster arrived while I was asleep. In the space of a few minutes a nine-knot wind from the north changed to thirty-eight knots from the south. Somehow I had been lulled into thinking that Sydney's summer weather extended east; I was totally wrong, of course, and like a fool I went on deck wearing ordinary clothes and got soaked while shortening sail.

Let's Go reaching along in the Tasman sea. This Leif Angermark design displaced only 4.9 tons—the lightest in the fleet—and was just 45'3" in length. Her captain drove the yacht very hard and achieved remarkable results.

"We're back on the blue highway," said Ian Kiernan the next morning on the chat hour. The news from the fleet was that everyone was okay, but the fellows groused about the abysmal headwinds. I heard that *Legend Securities* had returned to Sydney for a few hours with autopilot problems. David White unleashed a great blast to the newspapers about the crowding at the start. "I can't believe the yachting public, knowing we were out there single-handed on sixty-foot boats, was doing such dumb things," he said.

That night my wind fell away to nothing. I was becalmed and at noon showed a twenty-four-hour run of only 64 miles, one of my poorest days in the race so far. In the first forty-five hours I had gotten only 192 miles southeast of Sydney. We had warnings of a westerly gale, but the trifling winds continued.

[From the log]. January 21st.

0850. At 0700 there was a big squall—dark and purplish-blue—on the port quarter. The wind was northeast so I set up the port spinnaker pole and lines and got ready to wing out the yankee. Just as I was ready to trim, I saw that the wind had changed to the northwest so I put the port pole away and hoisted the starboard pole. Since the light wind was steady and the horizon to windward was clear of rain and squalls, I decided to put up a spinnaker. I got the sheet and guy and pole all ready and was about to set the chute when I noticed wind on the starboard bow! Wait a minute! I put the pole away and tidied up all the strings. Was I into the westerly gale that the radio had been warning about for two days? I tucked in a reef, raised the storm staysail, and set the yankee, but the wind continued to veer. I eased off to 090°—east—and could barely fill the sails. Now (at 0850) I have tacked south and am steering 170° at 6.9 knots. In less than two hours the wind has shifted 300°. Oh for the sailor's life!

An hour before noon I saw a sailing yacht in the distance on my starboard bow. There was no sign of activity (or word on the radio) on the other yacht, but it's surprising how exciting the presence of another sailing vessel becomes when you're at sea. I rushed around and hoisted the big staysail in place of the storm staysail, trimmed all the sails carefully, tidied up lines, and drank a fast cup of coffee in anticipation of a friendly meeting and a private race. However the other yacht soon disappeared.

At noon the next day I was at latitude 38°S. and on a line with Bass strait four hundred miles to the west. The weather had become terrible. Savage squalls had begun to blow from the south, and in the late morning I had to take down the mainsail when the blustery wind got up to forty-five knots.

[From the log]. January 23rd.

0840. The combination of a double-reefed mainsail and the storm staysail with twenty-knot squally beam winds is good. We can take squalls of forty knots or more without trouble. The next step is to run off and triple-reef the mainsail. The barometer is dropping. Jesus, all this and we're only at 38°S.

1055. Mainsail down after a terrible struggle. Wind 50 knots from the south. The sea is all white. Jogging along at 7.5 knots on an easterly heading with only the storm staysail up. Pretty severe outside.

1325. I was putting up the triple-reefed mainsail when another squall hit out of a clear blue sky. Very heavy and no warning at all. I must be careful not to get any broken bones with the violent motion.

Early that morning I discovered that while I was asleep we must have rolled to about eighty degrees—enough to dump the bilge water into the lower tool locker, a chart table drawer, and a storage bin below. The small tape recorder I had been speaking into for Champion was ruined. I put the tools in the sink for rinsing, wiping, and oiling. Later in the day the autopilot stopped working. The wind vane air blade had broken in the storm, so I replaced the blade and got the unit to steer the yacht. I had a spare autopilot. Changing it was a big job, however, and involved not only swapping up to

four units but feeding two cables through a watertight bulkhead and soldering five wires.

I was becoming increasingly concerned about getting pinned against the
western shore of New Zealand's South island. The gales were all from southerly quadrants. I wanted to get south, not east, but everything was driving me
toward the lee shore of South island. Tacking to windward in strong gales
was not my idea of paradise at all. Once clear of New Zealand, I could sail
east with southerly gales and gradually work south in suitable weather. Now,
however, I had a problem with a lee shore, a sailor's worst nightmare.

There was another way to get east of New Zealand. I could go via
Cook strait between North and South islands. I had brought along the charts,
and I was intrigued by the challenge. It would mean staying awake for the
entire transit, but the strait was only 120 miles long, well lighted, and reasonably clear. I might even slip ahead of the fleet, which perhaps would be mired
down in dreary windward sailing in gale conditions.

At 1700 on January 23rd, with the wind thirty-five knots from the south

David White in Sydney.

and the barometer at 994, I changed course for Cook strait. The bad weather continued, but at least my heading was more favorable. The wind shrieked all day, and a wandering albatross circled around and around *American Flag*. I cleaned and oiled the tools and began to work on the autopilot. The biggest job was changing the drive unit in the after watertight compartment. I spent several hours at this, and while working away I discovered the source of all the seawater that had been leaking into the compartment. During poor weather a lot of water ran around the decks, and an astonishing amount of this got past the top Harken rudder bearing, which I found had no seal at all. I estimated that the bearing leaked at least a gallon an hour when the decks were wet—some twenty-four gallons a day. I had long wondered where all the water had come from, and I made a mental note to plug the bearing or somehow block the water to the bearing. Meanwhile I changed the autopilot drive unit and strung the wires through the after watertight bulkhead.

By noon on January 25th I was 234 miles from Cape Farewell, the western entrance to Cook strait. The weather had been foul and stormy all night again with the wind from the south at thirty-five knots. When I checked around the deck at first light, I was horrified to discover that the port spinnaker pole was gone! The second Forespar deck fitting had collapsed because of faulty welds, and the pole had vanished during the night. This was a serious loss because it was impossible to handle my downwind rig without a spinnaker pole. I would have to move the single remaining pole from one side of the deck to the other, which was a dangerous business for one person because I had to balance the nineteen-foot pole and slide it past the baby stay, the midstay, and the headstay. I felt an absolute blind fury. Why did a manufacturer make such a simple and basic fitting so flimsy and then pass it off as ocean gear? I had never argued about the cost; only the quality. Now look what had happened!

During the afternoon I got the rest of the spare autopilot assembled and hooked up. It worked a short time and quit. Since it was unlikely that two autopilots would malfunction, I began to look further. After a while I found that the obscenity of an electrician in Cape Town had not rewired the compass light on a separate wire to the main power panel as I had directed but had simply tapped into the convenient autopilot power (why is it that people so often do the *easy thing,* rather than the *right thing?*) When the compass light had shorted out, it killed the autopilot. All my work changing the autopilot had been wasted! However, at least the autopilot was working. I decided to stand myself a whiskey, to forget about technical things for a while, and to get rested for Cook strait.

I finished Heinrich Boll's story *The Train Was on Time.* The novel was quite good with two strong characters and reflected the gloom and desperation of war and lonely people. I found that the story of the German enlisted man and the prostitute grabbed me because the characters showed fear, doubt, uncertainty, hope—all the foibles of mankind.

Late in the day the weather improved. The seas were large but moderating and steady from the south. I cooked myself a steak from a box of selected meats that Kayelene Hansen had presented me with before I left Sydney. My big icebox was half filled with ice and then topped up with fresh fruits and vegetables and all sorts of goodies that Margaret had found. Another Sydney

10. Cook strait

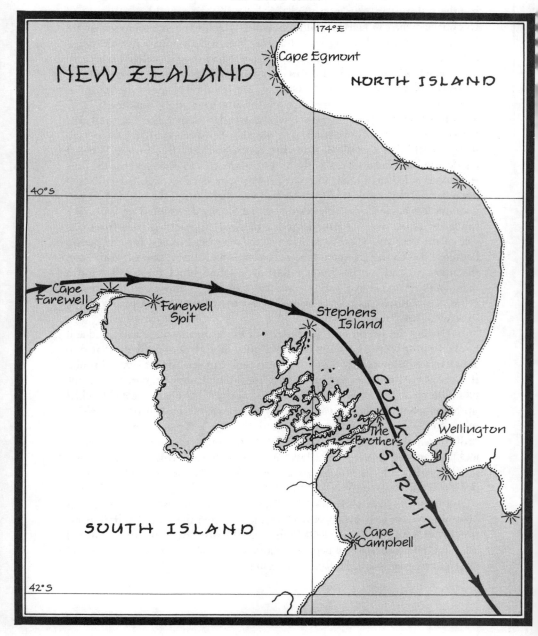

sailing friend, Mike Retallack, had brought down a large block of dry ice, which we pushed in on top of all the food. For an improvident sailor, I was certainly eating well.

The news from the fleet on January 26th was that seven of the eight Class I yachts were already around the foot of New Zealand and racing eastward. Mike Plant on *Airco* was leading Class II and 180 miles southeast of Stewart island. *Let's Go* was 65 miles south of the Snares. *Legend Securities* and the rest of the smaller yachts were approaching the foot of South island. Harry Harkimo on *Belmont,* 50 miles northwest of Cape Providence, said that he could see snowy mountains to his east and was worried about a westerly gale.

Harry Mitchell on *Double Cross* reported that his steering pedestal had been twisted by a big wave that had swept across his vessel. The same storm also damaged the upper part of his Fleming wind vane steering gear—a device that he relied on heavily. The steering pedestal was still operable, but the vane gear was not, even though Harry—a clever mechanic—tried every sort of repair. Several critical parts simply had to be welded. In addition, two of the sails on *Double Cross* needed patches and sewing.

At first Harry talked of going to Milford Sound for repairs, but I told him that it was an extremely remote place, certainly not where he'd find a sailmaker and welding shop capable of dealing with stainless steel repairs. Westerly gales could pin him there for weeks. Harry then spoke of heading for Dunedin on the east coast of South island via Foveaux strait. Unfortunately, he had only one very small scale chart of the strait and had never been to the area. I heard Mark Schrader giving Harry—who was only three hundred miles west of me—detailed instructions for Foveaux strait. I was tempted to suggest to Harry that he follow me through Cook strait and put into Wellington for repairs, but I was afraid I would only confuse Harry so I kept quiet. It was a pity that I didn't speak up.

I found that I was eating heavily to make up for the stormy days when I'd eaten almost nothing. Three very large albatrosses were around the yacht. It was hard to realize that the wingspan of these birds was as much as twelve feet. Out at sea it was hard to get a sense of scale. Were they small birds close up or giant birds some distance away? I had a good sleep and began to read the pilot book for Cook strait, which was marked by seven lighthouses and seemed straightforward. I brought up two anchors and warps from the bilge and put them on deck in case I got into a calm and foul tide.

Seventy miles west of Cape Farewell I ran through a fleet of Japanese boats fishing for squid. I spoke with Bertie Reed on *Stabilo Boss,* who told of a propeller shaft leak that he cleverly stopped with a plastic bag and hose clamps. The ingenuity of these fellows was amazing. Sometimes it was fix fix fix all day long to keep the damned boats running.

I found it pleasant to speak with the other sailors in the race. Six or seven of us generally talked twice a day for a minute or two. On January 26th, John Hughes was in a particularly foul mood because he had wasted three hours getting his mainsail up after a halyard problem. We all tried to cheer him up.

At 1910 on the 26th I began to see prominent blue mountains on my starboard beam. I was forty-six miles from Cape Farewell. The wind was seventeen knots from the south. I had one reef in the main, the storm staysail, and the yankee with six rolls. The water was smooth, and I was making eight to nine knots. It was exciting to try the strait under sail by myself at night. Would I be successful?

By 2110 the flashing light on Cape Farewell was in view. At 2325, however, I was not up to the light and it was obvious that the tidal stream was against me. A little after midnight I picked up the second light—on Farewell Spit—but my wind was dying. By now I had full sail up and was five or six miles north of the southern shore. Since I was going only one or two knots, the sea was flat, and there was no traffic, I set the autopilot and my off-course alarm and took a forty-five-minute nap. At 0300 a small ship passed far to the north, bound westward.

By 0700 a light breeze began to fill in from the west-southwest. I soon had up my green and white spinnaker and continued east-southeast. Two hours later the wind backed to the west at thirteen knots so I gybed the spinnaker in a wind that gradually rose to twenty-three knots; the sea was calm, and I surfed along at speeds between eight and fifteen knots. At 1255 I arrived at Stephens island, where I took down the spinnaker, changed to a southerly course, reefed the mainsail, and poled out the yankee to starboard in twenty-three knots from the northwest. By the late afternoon I was at The Brothers lighthouse and approaching Wellington and the eastern entrance to the strait. The wind was now up to thirty knots from the north. *American Flag* raced along in smooth water as I steadily reduced sail.

All the time I was in the strait I had gazed to the south at the most appealing mountains and inviting-looking sounds, where I knew there were dozens of marvelous anchorages. I could have easily spent a month in the intricate waterways south of the area between Stephens island and The Brothers. But there was no time for that now.

As the huge ball of a yellowish sun sank in the west behind me, I passed two large ferries running between South island and Wellington. I thought the wind would ease once clear of the islands, but no! It blew harder than ever. Soon I was racing along along at ten, twelve, fourteen, and sixteen knots for a few seconds as we surged forward on small waves. The autopilot steered perfectly. I hung on, waiting for the wind to ease, and dozed on the starboard pilot berth. We broached a couple of times, and at 0145 on January 28th I dressed for the battle of the third reef.

The weather was shocking, a real screamer from the north-northwest. I had a deuce of a time getting the deep reef in the mainsail, and I was glad that I had removed the full-length battens in Sydney. A fully-battened mainsail was very good in light airs, but I had found it extremely hard to tuck in deep reefs when going downwind in gale force winds, which jammed the battens against the shrouds. Even with short battens the deep reefs were not easy. I began to realize that I needed to haul down the luff reefing lines with a winch instead of trying to pull them down by hand. It was, of course, quite impossible to round up and head into the wind to reef in the big seas of the Southern ocean. Somehow the sailmakers never seemed to understand the difficulties of downwind reefing in winds of forty knots or more.

We broached again when I was on my way back to the cockpit and took lots of heavy water aboard. I was lucky not to have been swept away. I wore my safety harness, but the safety line between the cockpit and the foredeck to which I clipped myself was fouled by various running rigging lines that led along the deck. In order to move around, I had to hook and unhook my safety harness, which was not a good arrangement when seas were thundering on board. (One of the jobs on the work list was to improve the run of the lines along the deck. I had gotten started in Sydney, but there had not been enough time.)

The power of boarding seas was a hundredfold more than I had reckoned. I got soaked and could feel the water sloshing around in my boots. Fortunately the seawater was not cold. I needed a bath anyway. Once below I stripped, dug out fresh clothing, and turned in for a long sleep. The wind continued at thirty-five to forty-five knots (steady, no squalls) and blew out of a star-filled, cloudless sky. During the last twenty-four hours I had been becalmed, ghosted along under a light spinnaker, and now was hard-pressed in a strong gale. How we ran on hour after hour was a wonder.

I was headed a little south of east and took my departure from Cape Campbell. The next land was Cape Horn. Distance 4,723 miles.

CHAPTER *TWENTY*

. . . .

The Longest Ocean

*T*he captain of every ship—whether she is twenty feet long or a thousand feet long—makes hundreds of large and small decisions every day. Most are trifling and become routine. How much power (sail or engine) shall I use today? Will my route take me too close to those islands? Do I need to change course because of an approaching vessel? Is my dead reckoning okay, or should I try for another position line? Will I arrive on schedule? What about the shore arrangements? Which jobs on the work list are most important? Shall I confer with the cook about the spaghetti sauce for dinner? Do the batteries need charging or can I go another day? Is it wiser to shorten sail (or reduce power) now, or shall I press on until the storm comes? And so forth.

One tough decision in the BOC race was how far south to go in the Southern ocean between Cape Town and Bass strait, and between New Zealand and Cape Horn. The mileage difference while skirting around the bottom end of the globe is significant. The numbers between Cape Campbell at the east end of Cook strait (that I had just left) and Cape Horn are as follows:

rhumb line	4,723 nautical miles
true great circle to 66°54'S.	4,160
composite great circle to 65°S.	4,166
composite to 60°S.	4,244
composite to 56°S.	4,391

These numbers suggest that by sailing south to the latitude of almost sixty-seven degrees a mariner would save 563 miles. Such a course, however, would put the vessel either in pack ice or very close to it. There would be great danger not only from icebergs, growlers, bergy bits, brash ice, fog, sleet, sea smoke, and freezing temperatures, but from an endless series of gales, some of them from the east. Certainly it takes a very stout heart and reckless nature to venture farther south than that needed to pass Cape Horn at fifty-six degrees south.

"The usual route in the Pacific Ocean, all the year round passes S of New Zealand in about 48°30′S," says *Ocean Passages*. ". . . inclining slightly to the S, the route assumes, as a mean track, the parallel of 51°S from the meridian of 150°W, across the ocean to 120°W; keeping about 60 miles north of this track from December to February (so as to be more clear of ice). . . . From the meridian of 115°W, incline gradually to the S, to round Islas Diego Ramirez and Cabo de Hornos.

"The alternative route, which is only recommended from December to February, runs on a more S'ly track from the position S of Tasmania . . . to cross the Pacific Ocean between 54°S and 55°S.

"This course would, clear of ice, and with favourable weather, doubtless ensure the quickest passage, as being the shorter distance, but experience has proved that at nearly all times of year so much time is lost at night and in thick weather, and even serious danger is incurred on account of the great quantities of ice normally met with in these higher latitudes, that a parallel even as far N as 47°S and 50°S will provide steadier winds, smoother water, and less ice; and that a quicker passage may be expected in better weather, and with more security than in a high latitude."

Much of the material in *Ocean Passages* was based on facts collected a long time ago, and it appears that today there is less ice than formerly. Nevertheless, the experiences during the recent Whitbread round-the-world yachting races make gritty reading for a singlehander. During January 13–14, 1974, for example, the yachts *Kriter* and *Grand Louis,* when midway between Australia and Cape Horn at fifty-one degrees south, both saw ice.

"At dawn [wrote Patrice Quesnel, the captain of *Kriter*] we beheld a fantastic spectacle in front of us: icebergs 300–400 meters long and 40 meters high with perfectly vertical walls. The morning sun danced on these islands of ice and reflected a rainbow of colors from the bluish walls which accentuated the depth and grandeur of the crevasses. Needless to say, all the crew [twelve men] were on deck and looking to their hearts' content. . . . That night we set up special watches and relieved each other every fifteen minutes. We certainly didn't want to run into an iceberg! Happily the nights were short and clear, and an iceberg shining under the moon was visible at 300 to 400 meters which gave us plenty of time to maneuver. However we had to keep our eyes open in order not to have an accident."[29]

Between Cape Town and New Zealand in 1977, *Condor*, *Great Britain II*, and *King's Legend* all reported icebergs (one was at least 700 feet long and 150 feet high) at fifty-four degrees south. *Debenhams* ran into severe pack ice at fifty-eight degrees south and had to reverse her course to escape. ("We were now embayed in a huge area of loose ice surrounded by bergs of all shapes and sizes. Ahead lay a great wall of blank white some 10–15 feet high and stretching to the north and south horizons. This was pack ice; there was no way through. We were forced to head northwest until we cleared it.") Later in the Pacific the yachts, attempting to sail a great circle course, regularly saw icebergs (as many as five at one time, plus growlers breaking off the parent iceberg) at sixty-two degrees south.[30]

Robin Knox-Johnston, describing the action aboard the big seventy-seven-foot sloop *Condor* on her way to Cape Horn wrote (January 8, 1978): "Whilst the wind remained light and westerly the icebergs provided a pleasant attraction, but the moment the wind got up and visibility was reduced by driving rain or snow, they became a real hazard. A hundred yards of warning is very little in which to gybe or alter course radically to avoid a big berg, and one never knows which part of the berg you have in front of you, so it is a gamble as to which way to go."[31]

In the mid-Pacific *Debenhams* sailed to sixty-three degrees south and encountered many bergs, some of which were enormous and sculptured in incredible forms. Since most of the ice is underwater, the total size of the icebergs was astonishing, judging from the photographs, *because only about one-ninth of the mass of an iceberg is above water.*

Clare Francis, aboard *Accutrac* at fifty-nine degrees south, wrote: "We saw two or three icebergs every day, all of them magnificent. One was shaped like a giant ice-cream wedge with ripples of ice down the sides. Another had a tall, thin finger at one end which slowly broke away from the main berg as we watched. For one moment it balanced precariously in the air, then it fell in a mass of spray and turned turtle, its round, smooth, underwater section showing watery white above the surface."[32]

Again in 1986 the Whitbread yachts saw ice on the third leg. Three of the vessels avoided bergs by keeping a radar watch. Padda Kuttel, the captain of *Atlantic Privateer*, spotted an iceberg a half mile long and called for the helmsman to harden up to avoid the danger.[33]

None of the yachts in the Whitbread races came to grief because of ice. However they had radar and big crews (*Lion New Zealand* had twenty-two men, and Captain Peter Blake was able to keep one or more fresh lookouts on constant duty). All this, of course, is a far cry from a singlehander, who can in no way keep a lookout more than half the time on a long voyage. Already during the second leg of the BOC race, Pentti Salmi had seen an iceberg as far north as 45°23'S.

Because of the ice danger I made the decision to stay at fifty degrees or so for most of the Pacific run and to drop down to the latitude of Cape Horn (fifty-six degrees) only toward the end of the crossing. In my judgment it's madness for a singlehanded sailor to go anywhere near ice because if you run into it you have absolutely no defense. By sailing far to the south you might gain a few miles on the other contestants, but you also might find an instant watery grave. In a race, of course, you try everything to get ahead, but to attempt to win miles with ice around seems to me like dating a mafioso's girlfriend: the rewards hardly seem worth the risk. After all, a principal object of the race is to get back in one piece; you can't win unless you cross the finish line.

I fully expected that one or two of the yachts that went so far south would come to grief. I'm glad that no one had any problems, but I think the odds were not on their side. Sooner or later in these singlehanded races there are going to be casualties from sailing near ice unless some sort of a warning scheme is developed or a southern sailing limit is specified.

During this leg *Credit Agricole* went to 62°40′S., only 1,700 miles from the South pole. *UAP* dropped down to 61°04′S. *Ecureuil, Airco,* and *Belmont* sailed to 57°S. (After the race Philippe Jeantot told me that running in strong following winds with a spinnaker up at night and in fog and sleet was absolutely crazy. "I knew the ice was out there. But what could I do? The others were doing it. I needed to win. How do you think I slept? It was terrible.")

To me this sort of reasoning is like Russian roulette. Certainly there are enough dangers in singlehanded sailing without pressing an unloaded (?) revolver to your forehead. I, for one, had no desire to end my days impaled on an iceberg. Guy Bernardin, a keen competitor in *Biscuits Lu,* did not hesitate to speak up. "I'm not going down there," he said, "even if I lose a few places. It's too dangerous."[34]

Since *Ocean Passages* clearly mentioned better weather between forty-seven and fifty degrees south, I relaxed and got set for a three- or four-week passage to Cape Horn along the latitude of fifty degrees south, a line that I thought would be reasonably safe. I would have to see how I did with the winds. I was aware that the weather information would be scanty, but I hoped to get limited help from my weatherfax machine. I would have an indication from the Argos reports how the other BOC vessels were faring and could adjust my course accordingly. Above all, I wanted fair or reaching winds and as few headwinds as possible. This meant staying on the south side of the high pressure areas and on the north side of the lows. Cape Horn was 4,600 miles away, or twenty-three days at 200 miles per day. Was I up to it? I don't mind saying that I was nervous and full of doubts after such a hard first night east of New Zealand.

I suddenly realized that in the confusion of the last storm I had applied easterly compass variation the wrong way. Instead of subtracting when going from true to magnetic, I had added. No wonder I had gone south so fast! As soon as I realized my mistake, I altered course. Henceforth when I wanted to go east (the variation just then was 23°E.), I needed to steer 090° *minus* 23° or 067° magnetic.

The news from the fleet was that David White's satnav had packed up, and he was navigating with a sextant. Pentti Salmi had gotten confused about the English words and had ordered a case of grapes instead of a case of grapefruit when he was putting food aboard in Sydney. "Of course all the grapes have ripened and are going rotten," he said.

I had the New Zealand pilot book for South island so I radioed information about entering the town of Bluff on Foveaux strait to Harry Mitchell. Among other things the recommendation was for a daylight approach. Mark Schrader reported that during some hard going the spinnaker pole track had torn off *Lone Star*'s mast. The pole then stabbed a hole through the mainsail, so Mark was busy patching and sewing and wondering how to strengthen the track fastenings since this was the second time the track had come off. Bertie Reed and John Martin talked of autopilot problems. Harry Harkimo said that his Navtec hydraulic rigging controls were broken and that his main generator was out of order. Harry had a gasoline-powered Honda generator for a spare, but he said he had only forty liters of gasoline. I suggested that he take the generating unit from the Honda and mount it on his big diesel engine, for which he had plenty of fuel. "My price for this advice is one bottle of red wine in Rio," I said to Harry.

"My problem is that I have a degree in economics, not mechanics," said Harry.

During the afternoon of January 29th I crossed the international date line and gained a day (I had *two* January 29ths). Henceforth *American Flag's* longitude was reckoned in degrees west of Greenwich. My strong northerly winds and hard gray skies gradually changed to light southeasterlies and a clear and sunny sky. The sea was calm; the weather bright and sunny. I walked around the decks in shirtsleeves and adjusted my biggest sails. Was I in the Gulf of Maine in summer? The barometer read 1018, and by evening I was becalmed.

"Light wind is my friend," said John Hughes that night. "A flat sea and ten knots."

"Picnics on the decks and nice girls," replied Pentti Salmi. "But then you have thunderstorms and strong winds and never see the girls again."

"It is good to have a bottle of wine with the girls," added Jean Luc.

That night I relaxed with a marvelous book called *The Tenth Man* by Graham Greene. Certainly, I thought, this book together with all his others ought to qualify him for the Nobel prize. I liked the quote (p. 84): "When you reach a certain age you don't care about the future: it is success enough to be alive: every morning you wake with triumph."

Later I had a conversation with a radio operator on Endurbury island, a northern islet of Auckland island (51°S.; 166°E.), an obscure dot of land south of New Zealand, about six hundred miles southwest of *American Flag's* position. Four wildlife experts were doing a sea lion census and installing tiny radios on the animals to track their migrations. Another party was trying to find out whether any changes had taken place in goats that had been released many years earlier. Jacques Cousteau and his vessel *Calypso* were at the island filming, and the ship's helicopter had seen a group of thirty goats. The biologists—who grumbled about their meager rations on the remote island— were following the BOC race and wished us well.

The next morning I had a big breakfast and got busy on various jobs. While I was in Sydney I had installed a large, heavy-duty pad eye in the middle of each side deck to take the lower boom vang block. Moving this block and its lines inboard helped reduce the clutter of running rigging lines on the side decks. Unfortunately, both the deck and pad eyes were not up to the high loads. After a week of hard sailing, the stainless steel pad eyes were bent out of shape, and the decks clearly showed that they needed reinforcing where I had mounted the hardware. To stop leaks and further trouble, I removed the pad eyes and again led the boom vang to the reinforced deck rail.

I tightened both after lower shrouds and adjusted the autopilot linkage on the rudder stock. Next I drained the lazarette, pumped out water from the main bilge, and packed the leaky top rudder bearing with a ring of marlin and a thick coating of Vaseline petroleum jelly. I hoped this would stop the water that leaked into the rear compartment. Then I shortened various lines and whipped the ends. Meanwhile I listened on the radio for news of *Double Cross,* which was approaching Foveaux strait and Bluff. The ham operators had been in touch with local mechanics who were ready to help Harry Mitchell.

My daily runs since New Zealand had been 196, 180, and finally 110 miles after a night of calms. By now I felt I was getting the hang of sailing *American Flag* and was learning not to press her. Often with reduced sail, the yacht went just as fast with less heel and more comfort. As I've mentioned, my main sailing problems continued to be (1) deep reefs in the mainsail, and (2) the difficulty of hoisting the big genoa, which was a nightmare to drag out and put up after dropping the yankee to free the single headstay (and later to do it all in reverse in a rising wind). I was sure that before the end of the race I would be found dead, slumped over that big sail, my final shroud.

At 0830 on January 30th the radio crackled with the distressing news that *Double Cross* was aground in Foveaux strait near Bluff. Harry Mitchell had anchored and dragged ashore. At 1700 that afternoon a message from a New Zealand ham operator said that *Double Cross* was on a beach nineteen miles east of Bluff at a place called Fortrose. According to the reports, a boat had gone to assist Harry (who was okay) but failed to get a line aboard the yacht. The attempt to pull the vessel off had been postponed because of unfavorable tidal conditions and a rough sea.

That night the talk on the chat hour was gloomy and morose because of Harry's mishap. I heard Mike Plant on *Airco* speak with Ian Kiernan on *Spirit of Sydney*. It was the first time that I had heard Mike—who was leading Class II—on the radio. He said that he was at 56°25′S. and that both his weatherfax and satnav had stopped working. *Airco, Belmont,* and *Legend* were now navigating with sextants.

My mileage run the previous day had been 209, and at noon on January 31st I showed 185 miles mostly in front of southwesterly winds of twenty-two knots or so. I was at forty-nine degrees south. During the night when I changed sails in a heavy rain I got chilled and couldn't seem to get warm. I

A sailor's worst moment. *Double Cross* aground at Fortrose beach on New Zealand's South island. This mishap occurred to Harry Mitchell because of a combination of bad luck, darkness, lack of charts, a lee shore, and an anchor that failed to hold.

finally put on thermal underwear and my heavy outer (red) oilskins together with lined boots and a storm cap. I drank cup after cup of hot tea and gradually warmed up.

I spoke again with Chris Thomas on remote Endurbury island. When I commented on his stronger radio transmission, Chris said that he was aboard *Calypso* with Jacques Cousteau and his party. "The exquisite French cooking here is certainly better than our poor camp rations," said Chris. "Isn't life amazing sometimes?"

The latest word on Harry Mitchell was that the *Savannah,* a vessel owned by a Mr. Leech (sp?) tried and failed to pull *Double Cross* off the sandspit at Fortrose. At 1000 I spoke with Ron (ZL4MK), who had talked with Harry, who was staying with a local farmer. Harry, according to the relayed message, said that the grounding was his fault because of his lack of proper charts. He and the locals planned to use a mechanical excavator to dig a channel to the water at low tide and then to attempt to get the yacht off at the next high water.

Though Mark Schrader, John Hughes, Pentti Salmi, and I repeatedly tried to speak to Harry (we had the number at the house where he was staying), we found that the commercial radio stations in New Zealand— unlike all other countries—refused to accept normal credit calls from ships at sea and required special advance credit arrangements. Since none of us had anticipated commercial radio traffic with New Zealand, we were unable to talk with Harry, which was disappointing because we knew he needed cheering up. Normally it's possible to patch through a call to a third party via a ham operator, but this is not done in New Zealand. All we could get were relayed messages from the hams, which contained the words "doubtful" and "marginal." We knew how much the round-the-world voyage meant to Harry, and we felt sure that if one of us could have talked with him he would have redoubled his efforts to get off the beach. I kept trying to get a call through to New Zealand via commercial radio station KMI in California, but I had no luck.

According to the Argos reports, *Credit Agricole* and *UAP* were at 59°S. Philippe Jeantot said that it was "foggy and cold." It worried me to hear about these sailors so far south.

[From my journal]. February 1st.

1445. Today at noon we showed 199 miles. Now at fifty degrees south, I wear the blue Musto foul weather gear all the time.

Sometimes the smallest improvements bring the most gratifying results. The little safety strap that I made for the navigator's seat means that though *American Flag* is well heeled to starboard (like now) I can sit comfortably and write, use the radio, and work with the charts and instruments.

The weather is nasty again. A gale from the north with forty-knot winds.

Squalls, a rough sea, and lots of flying spray. Last night at 0330 I pulled down the third reef in the mainsail and put the spinnaker pole away. I have gradually rolled up the yankee, which is now furled. I set the storm staysail (which looks a bit tired). It's not a nice day.

Yesterday I began my first *Inspector Maigret* book by Georges Simenon. Somehow I thought such stories beneath me. Ha! They (at least the first one) are simply excellent ("She was the typical tart, ordinary and vulgar, healthy and cunning."). Much better than Raymond Chandler, who writes crisply but always has the same plots and people.

I had a wash, shave, and change of clothes and feel quite fit. I picked up a mass of laundry and stowed it in a duffel bag. One of Margaret's shoes is caught on an engine control lever near where the laundry bag is stowed on the starboard quarter berth. Whenever I see the shoe I think of Margaret.

The next day I heard that Mike Plant on *Airco* had almost collided with an iceberg at 56°40'S.

"After the initial heart attack I got control of things," said Mike. "I had a sail stretched out along the cabin for repairs to the foot, and when I saw a white reflection in the cabin windows I thought it was the sail. Then I looked again and rushed outside.

Onions, potatoes, and eggs for breakfast on *American Flag*.

"The iceberg was right next to me to port," said Mike. "I could hardly believe it. The sides were really sharp—vertical and cliff-like, a magnificent sight. I thought I was looking at a ghost. If my course had been a little different I would have scraped some of the red paint off the side of Airco's hull. A half-hour later the ocean was covered with sea smoke, and there was no visibility at all. A strong easterly blew me south thirty to forty miles the night before last. The water has completely changed color, and it has gotten a lot colder."

February 2nd was bright and sunny. I had a fair wind and moderate seas and sat in the cockpit with my breakfast of bacon and eggs, toasted pumpernickel bread, and tea. I had been listening to the Voice of America (the only station I could receive), but all the news stories were so negative that I turned off the radio. At noon I showed 191 miles. *American Flag* was sailing a bit faster, however, and I thought we would break 210 the next day. We had come about 2,400 miles from Sydney and were 1,150 miles east of New Zealand.

That evening the fellows in the fleet heard that *Double Cross* had gotten off the beach and was under tow for Bluff. We were overjoyed and hoped that Harry would soon be chasing us. However, in succeeding days the reports grew gloomy ("her rudder is bent; she'll have to be slipped"). We knew that time was not on her side, and eventually we learned that Harry Mitchell had withdrawn from the race.

Four months later in Newport I heard the story from Harry in person. "To begin with," said Harry, "my tiny chart of South island [scale: 1 to 6,016,000] was totally inadequate. The small chart suggested that Invercargill was the port, not Bluff. I sailed past Center island with no problems. Unfortunately, when I got near Invercargill I talked to a radio operator who knew nothing of the sea or details of the coast. She advised me to go to the port of Invercargill, which has been silted up for years. The woman meant well, but her suggestions were worse than none at all.

"At first I had a ten- to fifteen-knot northwesterly wind and ran along nicely in daylight. When I got near Invercargill it was obvious that the west-facing entrance was breaking and unapproachable. I continued to the southeast, rounded the high land southwest of Bluff, and picked up the light on Dog island, which had been turned on for me. Somehow I thought that the Bluff peninsula was an island. I got to Dog island and continued east. It was unfortunate that no fisherman or ferry came out of Bluff just then because I looked right into the harbor at one point and saw the tall smokestack of the fertilizer plant.

"I thought I was looking for Invercargill and that its entrance was farther east," said Harry. "By now I was past Dog island and in Toetoes bay. At dusk I saw a pipeline to the north. I didn't realize it, but the pipeline was

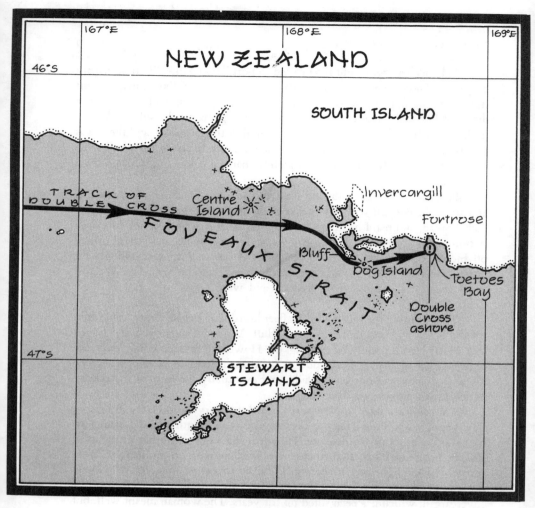

11. South island and Foveaux strait

the shoreline. Suddenly in the dark I was in a depth of only six fathoms. I put out an anchor at once, but the west wind veered to the south. I was on a lee shore so I put up my foresail to sail out when the vessel struck the bottom and went up on a beach on a very high tide. When the water fell, we were way up on the sand.

"As bad as it was, I couldn't have found a better spot to have been shipwrecked," said Harry. "Everyone from Fortrose, Bluff, and Invercargill was kind and generous. The local farmers were marvellous chaps. They took me into their homes and helped me all they could. After the wind and seas from the south eased off, a man brought down an excavating machine and dug out a trench at low water between *Double Cross* and the sea.

"It took twelve men to carry the heavy wire rope for the tow along the sands. A two-man dinghy and skindiver then went through the surf to link up with a fishing boat that was standing by to pull me off. When *Double Cross* and I finally bounced free from the beach and went through the surf, a tremendous cheer went up from the crowds of people on the cliff top. There wasn't a dry eye in sight. Several boats have gone ashore along that coastline. *Double Cross* is the only one to have gotten off.

"It was a marvelous moment," said Harry. "We raided the grog locker, and all my helpers and I had a drink or two to celebrate.

"Since the yacht's rudder was damaged, I was towed backwards to Bluff, fifteen miles away, where the local engineering works set about to repair the rudder, autopilot, and vane gear—all free of charge. I was rushing to get the various sails put back in good condition before starting again when I spoke on the telephone with a member of the BOC race committee, who told me that I was in trouble because I had been towed more than the two-mile limit in the race rules. And since I was so far behind everyone— those who might help me in an emergency—it was suggested that I withdraw from the race.

"This was a terrible blow to me," said Harry who had sailed more than halfway around the world and was wildly keen to complete a world circum-navigation under sail. "I knew I'd broken the rule. My resolve suddenly crumbled."[35]

Sixteen men were left in the race.

. . . .

CHAPTER TWENTY-ONE

Why Do We Do It?

On February 3rd *American Flag* was 2,702 miles east-southeast of Sydney. Cape Horn lay 3,162 miles to the east. My run that day was 217 miles, or 9 knots for twenty-four hours. However my average for the seventeen days from Australia so far had been only 159 miles a day—some 6.6 knots, principally because of calms on three days. Of the eight yachts in my class, I was in sixth place, not very good.

As long as I had wind I could keep *American Flag* going, which meant that in light airs I had to hoist the genoa promptly. However, I found that it was so energy-sapping to put up the big sail that I tended not to do it unless the conditions were favorable. It wasn't that I was lazy; it was simply that I got exhausted because of the cumbersome and hazardous arrangements to change the big headsail, principally to get it down in a rising wind. Most of the entries had two roller furling headsails, or one furling headsail and a second separate headstay wire that could be used to put up a light sail. I had known about the shortcomings of *American Flag's* rig before the race started, but I had never realized what a handicap it would be. I felt like a failure when I wasn't driving *American Flag* to her maximum.

Additionally, water ballast would have helped going to windward, but the tanks weren't on board. The lack of tanks and the poor sail changing arrangements were certainly my fault and clearly reflected inexperience and bad management, although I could have solved both problems with more time and money before the race.

My third difficulty was the shortage of weather information. I studied the weatherfax charts carefully each day and tried to pay attention to the progress of the other yachts in the race. When an east-going low pressure system passed a little south of *American Flag* we had gray skies and northwest, west, and southwesterly winds. When an east-going high moved to the north of the yacht we had clear skies and west, northwest, and northerly winds. The closer I sailed to the center of a low, the stronger the winds. I knew that I would have no wind at all in the middle of a high pressure area.

The only axiom that was always true is that the weather was not simple and clear and predictable at all. The highs and lows sometimes traveled east, but they went in other directions as well. Some highs were enormous— hundreds of miles in diameter—and influenced my weather for days. Some lows were small and intense and passed quickly. Whenever things were not as predicted, however, the weather bureau people had excuses. "A rapidly moving secondary low has slipped under the high." "A strong flow of polar air has upset everything." "The high has unexpectedly stalled." "Two lows have blocked out the high." "The front moved faster than our predictions." And so forth, plus laments about the lack of reporting stations, faulty equipment, and manpower shortages.

I had learned that once a thousand or two thousand miles away from a shore station, a weatherman's interest in distant mariners dwindled and collapsed. Yet if a competent *private* weatherman concentrated his talents on a certain moving point on the globe and used all his resources to deal with a single problem, he could come up with consistent, helpful advice. Maybe not nine times out of ten, but perhaps seven or eight times out of ten, which was significantly better than a crapshooter who based his moves on public weather charts.

The leading yachts received continual weather updates, advice from tacticians on land, and used computers both on land and at sea to coordinate the weather information with the vessel's performance on different points of sailing. The most usual was an on-board Apple Macintosh computer with the $3,000 MacSea program, which related a yacht's polar performance curves (under various sails and headings) with wind strength and direction information. *Credit Agricole, Ecureuil,* and *UAP* used this system, and these three speedy vessels were far ahead of the rest of the BOC fleet.

"When racing I receive radioed weather information from a friend in France who inputs data into a computer and calculates the fastest route from one point to another, based on the weather forecast and the boat's speed potential on different courses," wrote Philippe Jeantot on *Credit Agricole.* "The system is called 'routing.' The biggest and best sponsored Class I boats all have shoreside assistants who do their utmost to divert us away from the calm fronts. But the weather changes quickly and forecasts are not 100 percent reliable . . . which leaves room for uncertainty. Such weather assistance is

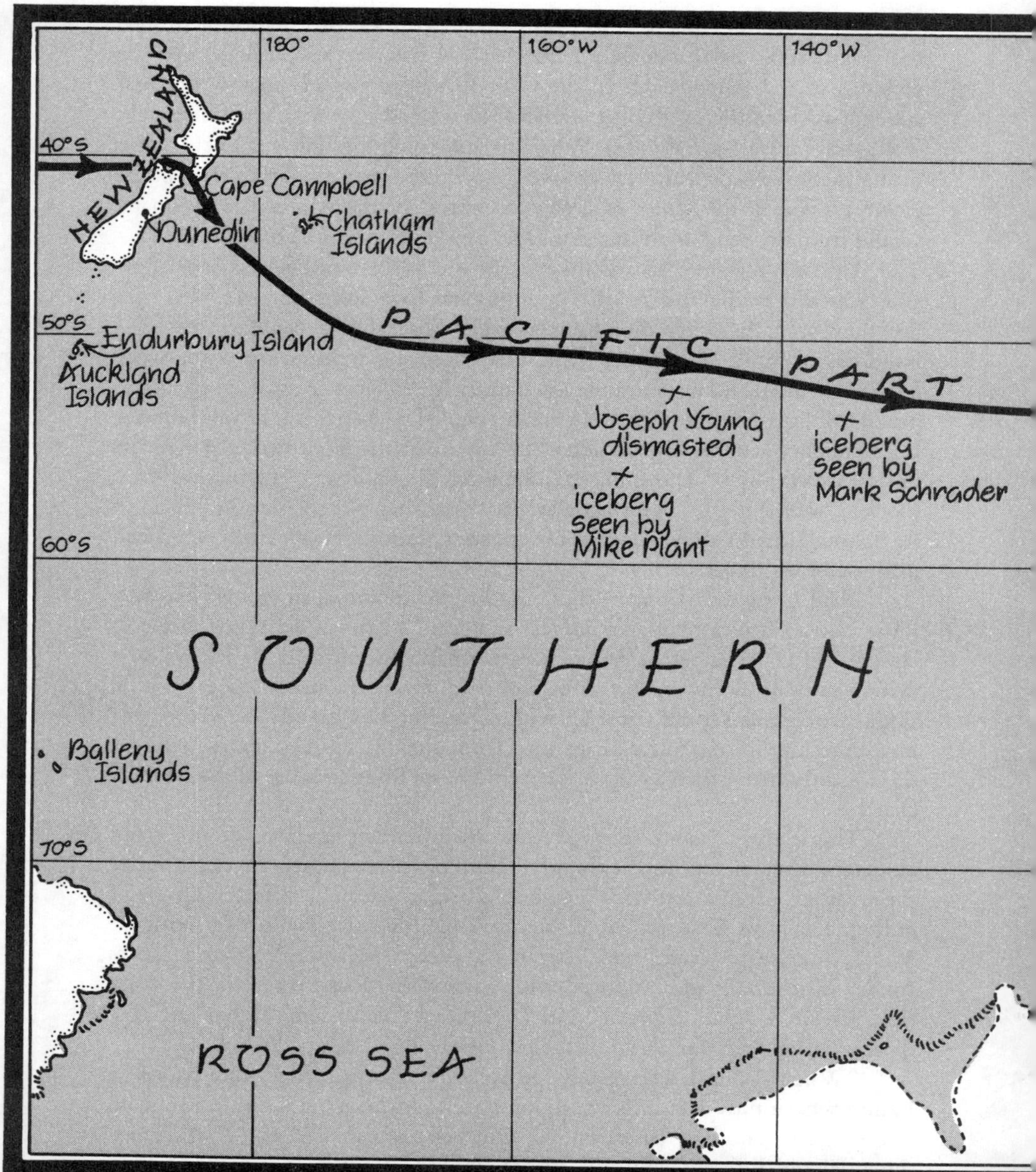
180°
160°W
140°W
40°S
50°S
60°S
70°S
NEW ZEALAND
Cape Campbell
Chatham Islands
Dunedin
Endurbury Island
Auckland Islands
PACIFIC
PART
Joseph Young dismasted
iceberg seen by Mike Plant
iceberg seen by Mark Schrader
SOUTHERN
Balleny Islands
ROSS SEA

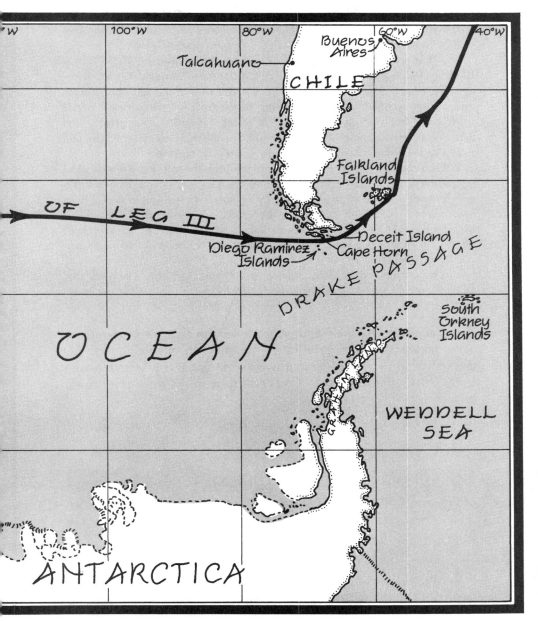

12. Leg 3: New Zealand to Cape Horn

indispensable if you want to place well in the standings. I still receive on-board weather maps through a facsimile recorder and still study the best possible routes. Yet the computer works in a more scientific way."[36]

What would the singlehanders of old—Joshua Slocum, Vito Dumas, Blondie Hasler, Al Petersen, and Francis Chichester—have said to such space-age technology? On *American Flag* I had access to nothing like this. Yet, in spite of my complaints, and my feeling that there were really two separate BOC races, I was going fairly well. The yacht was sailing wonderfully, and her steering was a dream. Navigation was no problem. I was snug and dry and eating and sleeping okay. Everything on board was working.

On February 4th we logged 182 miles with light following winds and a big westerly swell that caused heavy rolling. The radio brought news of a new hazard: a series of large, free-floating buoys (with drogues) had been launched at various high latitudes in the Southern ocean by the International Meteorological Council. As the buoys drifted ever eastward, radio equipment on the buoys sent out basic weather information. I hoped not to crash into one of the steel buoys.

That evening we sailed into dense fog. At midnight it was so black that when I looked around I thought I must have my eyes closed. Were the buoys

Here I adjust the backstay tension while we run along in the Southern ocean on the starboard gybe in seas of only ten or twelve feet. Although the sun was out, the southwest wind felt as if it were blowing directly from the South pole. I was glad to wear my three-layer storm outfit.

out there? Where was the nearest iceberg? I closed my mind to these problems, poured myself a welcome cognac, climbed into my bunk, and began to
re-read a favorite book (*Maquis* by George Millar, a compelling story about
the French underground in 1944). Afterward I had a wonderful sleep.

After noon the next day (202 miles) I looked in the lazarette to lubricate
the autopilot drive arm and discovered a thirty-inch ball of twisted lines from
three reels of line, half a dozen fender bumpers, and *the wires to the autopilot*.
This mess was rolling around in seawater. I quickly extricated the electrical
wires and tucked them up out of trouble. The fender lines took a while to get
clear. I then pulled the rest of the tangle up on deck and spent two hours
sorting out the lines, which I tied carefully and stowed elsewhere (how line
can get unwound from a spool at each end is beyond me). I pumped out the
compartment and tried to improve my homemade seal around the leaky top
rudder bearing. What I needed in the lazarette were some simple shelves with
high fiddles to keep stored things out of trouble.

[From the log] February 6th.
1045. Bad news! *Joseph Young* was dismasted about four hours ago at position 52°47′S. 149°08′W. "The mast broke at the gooseneck and went over the
side," said John Hughes, who is busy setting up a jury rig so he can start sailing
again. "I'm not leaving the boat," were almost his first words. Good for him!

Of the twenty-five yachts that started the race, three had been dismasted.
I thought that a twelve percent rate was quite unacceptable, although two of
the rigs had what I would call toothpicks for spars. Neither mast broke
because of rolling over but during moderate sailing when the spar simply
fractured and collapsed. So far on *American Flag* I had been lucky, although I
was glad that I'd increased the section of the spar significantly and lowered it
slightly. Additionally, I'd added running backstays, after lower shrouds, and a
midstay. I *always* kept one running backstay set up at sea. Nevertheless, if I
had had a section failure as John Hughes had, my mast would have come
down too.

Like the other fellows in the fleet I felt very sorry for John, whose first
job was to set up a jury rig—both to get somewhere and to stop the terrible
motion of a mastless sailing yacht out on the ocean. By noon we heard that
John had raised one of his eighteen-foot spinnaker poles in the cockpit and
had put up a small sail and an antenna for his radio. Mark, Pentti, Jean Luc,
Bertie, and I all made suggestions about a jury mast, but it was David White
on *Legend* who came up with the most sensible idea: "Set up an A-frame,"
said David. "Put your two spinnaker poles together at the top and lash the
bottoms to the chainplates on the side decks. Then all you need are a headstay
and a backstay plus halyard blocks and halyards for a storm jib and trysail."

At 1325 we heard more details: "The weather was not unusual, and I was
broad-reaching with fifteen to twenty knots of breeze with the number two

jib and the main with two reefs," said John. "I had a running backstay set up along with the windward check stay. The boom was not in the water.

"The Isomat spar just collapsed. There were two breaks when I got up on deck. One clean break at deck level, and the second just below the goose-neck where the section was bent and completely flattened. There was a lot of confusion, a ten-by-twelve-inch hole got knocked through the coachroof, and a shower of fiberglass, fittings, and foam core material flew everywhere. I was lucky to get the Argos out of the way. The spreaders and wire seemed okay, and I saw that the break in the mast was new, not from an old crack.

"Initially the mast was lying over the starboard side," said the twenty-six-year-old Canadian captain. "I spent the first half hour trying to save the boom, which I hoped to use for a jury rig. The mast worked back and out of the deck and the top started to go deeper into the water. I got scared of getting caught so I cut away all the halyards and backstays—everything but the forestay. I then tied a piece of half-inch Kevlar line to the eye [?], but with the rig adrift the turnbuckle worked back and forth, fractured, and broke. The Kevlar let go and the lot disappeared. The starboard stanchions and pulpit are gone, but the steering vane is okay."

John was absolutely shattered by his misfortune, which happened in the worst possible place. Yet he was smart, clever, completely optimistic, and determined to continue in the race and to complete the last two legs, even if it took him six months. He soon passed messages to the race committee that he intended to carry on and gave the committee no chance at all to recommend withdrawal.

I was sure that John would prevail over his misfortune. He considered various options, and our little group of six or seven captains earnestly discussed his best moves. There were four choices:

1. Dunedin, New Zealand	1,632 miles to the west-northwest.
2. Papeete, Tahiti	2,115 miles almost directly north.
3. Cape Pembroke, East Falkland, via Cape Horn	3,300 miles east (then northeast).
4. Talcahuano, Chile	3,361 miles east-northeast.

Dunedin or one of the other ports along the east coast of New Zealand was the nearest place to get help and assistance. If John could have simply turned around and sailed a reverse course it would have been direct and the quickest route. Unfortunately, there was little chance of heading westward into the teeth of the prevailing westerlies with the tiny rig on *Joseph Young*. Everyone agreed that New Zealand was out.

Tahiti (or one of the islands in the Australs or Society group) was another possibility. Papeete—the main city of the islands and the only place where a new mast could be fitted—was about 2,100 miles north and a reasonable choice. John would be sailing in easier weather and once in the trade winds could expect enough rainfall to replenish his fresh water supply, which was an important consideration. For a good slant in the southeast trades, however, he should have been farther east, particularly with the tiny rig on *Joseph Young*. David White suggested sailing north into the shipping lanes, where John could either get off his vessel or perhaps have the yacht lifted aboard a cargo ship. John would have to sail through the variables, however, and with his small rig this might be tedious. One problem with sailing in the French islands was the prevalence of coral close to land. A singlehander with little experience in coral pilotage and a handicapped vessel would be at significant disadvantage. In addition, John had no charts.

Bertie Reed and I had both sailed in Chile and knew about the extensive naval facilities in Talcahuano and the receptive and helpful people. John could arrange to have a mast (in two short sections) sent by air to Santiago and forwarded to Talcahuano. The Canadian embassy would probably assist him. But best of all, John should have fair westerly winds to the coast of Chile and then the strong Humboldt current to boost him northward. The approach to Talcahuano itself was easy and straightforward.

New Zealand was out of the question. Tahiti and Talcahuano were possibilities, and John talked of continuing in the race because he desperately wanted to complete the four legs and get back to Newport. Could he stay in the race with sails that only reached fourteen feet above the deck? How could anyone go around Cape Horn—a savage place where the average winds were Force eight some twenty-six percent of the time—in a severely handicapped vessel?

Talcahuano was a reasonable compromise because with favorable winds and current, John might be able to do the 3,361 miles in thirty-three days— say, four to five weeks, which was possible with the food and water supplies on *Joseph Young*. If a new mast were shipped and got to Talcahuano before John arrived, he ought to be able to have it stepped and be headed for Cape Horn in another week. All this would put him behind the fleet, but not by too much.

I thought this was a good plan and so did Bertie Reed. I told John about two other yachts that had gotten dismasted in the Pacific and had managed to sail to Chile. I said that I would search among my charts for coastal plans of Chile and start trying to recall details of the coastline. Bertie cautioned John to be careful to sail east before heading north to keep away from a high pressure area and related calms in the central South Pacific.

On February 7th it breezed up again. At 0120 I found myself kneeling behind the mast while I cranked in the third reef. The barometer was high and the west-southwest wind veered to the south, increased slightly, and felt much colder. Later that morning the conditions for long-range radio transmission were perfect, and I got through a call to Margaret in Maine about fund-raising. Then I spent two hours telling John Hughes about the Chilean coast and relaying calls to his supporters in Halifax.

John was depressed and in low spirits. "I had a little cry last night," he said. "I'm going to miss all you guys."

Pentti cleverly changed the subject and suggested to John that he might be able to capitalize on his unfortunate predicament. "I know that you had no luck getting a sponsor in Canada," said Pentti. "People always like to read about troubles and potential disaster. I can see the headline now. 'Valiant Canadian Battles To Stay in the Ultimate Sailing Race and To Show the Canadian Flag.'

"It's the ghoul complex in people," said Pentti. "Don't minimize this thing. It may be worth more than you realize."

At 2020 someone reported an iceberg at 54°58′S., 135°18′W., about 220 miles south of *American Flag*. The ice was said to be one hundred feet high and half a mile long. About then my wind fell to a few knots from the south. The yacht was soon crashing and banging around in a heavy swell. I ran up full sail and made a course change to bring the wind forward a little. By the next morning, however, the light wind had switched to the north. I gybed, took down the spinnaker pole, and trimmed the sails for a reach. It was chilly iceberg weather and at 51°22′S. I looked for ice. I wore my lined Musto sea boots continuously now.

A little before noon Mark Schrader saw the sun glinting on a large iceberg and sailed *Lone Star*—at 54°27′S.—close for photographs. Later I listened to a discussion about hull insurance between David White and Ian Kiernan. I was amazed to learn that *Spirit of Sydney* was fully covered, which was quite unusual for a shorthanded vessel on a world trip.

John Hughes had his A-frame mast up and was experimenting with sails. During the afternoon he reported that he was going along at four to five knots with his A-frame jury rig. Up forward he flew his smallest headsail with a knot at the top, which reduced the hoist by six feet. Aft, he set his trysail with four or five feet of the head tied off. He was in good spirits and heading northeast. Since my radio capability was good, John passed along his shopping list for his new rig. I began trying to contact Halifax.

The next morning—February 9th—I had the misfortune to burn my left hand when the yacht lurched while I was making coffee. I sprayed on some burn ointment I had gotten in Cape Town, cursed myself for clumsiness, and slapped on a bandage. Three of the yachts farther south complained of strong adverse currents (at fifty-five degrees south) that cut into their light-weather performance. I heard that Titouan Lamazou had gotten violently ill from a reaction to antibiotic medicine he took to combat salt water boils on his hands. The French captain spent a day flat on his back, too sick to get out of his bunk. Fortunately the crisis didn't last.

From *Stabilo Boss* came the word that Bertie Reed was having a few problems. "Why do we do it?" he lamented, which seemed to sum up the frustrations of the fleet.

At noon I took stock of my position. My runs for the last four days had been 202, 194, 132, and 207 miles. In twenty-three days from Sydney I had come 3,821 miles. My average run was 166 miles per day, or 6.9 knots. I was in fifth place in my class and within shooting distance of third place. Cape Horn lay 1,989 miles to the east.

I sometimes wondered why I was making this trip around the world. I had long wanted to attempt a solo circumnavigation in a small vessel to see whether I had the fortitude, the personal discipline, and the sailing skills to pull it off. I liked the freedom, the freshness, and the vitality of the sea. I liked the out-of-doors, the pleasure of sailing, of living in a neat and tidy home afloat, and of making a small vessel go anywhere under sail. I liked the endless challenges, the surprises behind the next headland, and the people in the port beyond the horizon. It was a series of unending adventures and delights. I embraced a life that I loved.

I found that the sea gave me a wonderful sense of tranquility. My life had a sense of form and dimension, and I knew precisely the size of my world. From the cockpit, my horizon was four miles away, and the sea that I saw belonged to me. It was *my* sea. The vessel was *my* responsibility, and I knew the height and width of my life. If I was neat and tidy, then my world was precise. If I was sloppy and did something badly, then I suffered directly.

It was exciting to make *American Flag* sail well; to feel her heel when the wind came; to leave one port for another and to watch the miles change as I crept across the globe. I looked at the clouds and the sun, the birds and the fish, the moon and the stars. For me these pieces of my life were the diamonds of my existence.

I had looked forward to the challenge of the Southern ocean. The BOC race was a convenient and pleasant structure on which to base such an adventure. It was immaterial to me whether I made the voyage in company with others or by myself. Nevertheless, the race was a good way to pitch my performance against the rest of the fleet, and by studying the twenty-four BOC yachts and preparing my own, I learned an enormous amount about light displacement vessels, ocean racing, and sailing in general. In addition I made a whole set of wonderful new acquaintances. Many became good friends.

In no way did I intend to stretch myself over the cliff edge of irresponsibility during the race. I wanted to come back, to complete the course, and I tried to conduct myself as a prudent deepwater sailor. I had the guts to carry on and push the yacht, but I knew when to ease off and try on another day. The main thing was to finish; dead sailors never make port.

Unlike the first BOC competition (1982–83), by the time of the second race (1986–87), sponsorship had taken an iron grip on the event. Naive entrants like me who had based their entries and thinking on the pedestrian pace of the earlier race were stunned by the new designs and the extent of equipment and support.

The BOC race was arranged for two classes of yachts, but as the competition progressed, the publicity and press attention concentrated on the larger class (all sponsored). In addition, the rules and reporting favored the sixty-foot vessels. The winner of the large class would be declared the victor. He would be feted and featured on all the book jackets and magazine covers. He would be sought for interviews and press conferences. He would be the hero in films and videos, asked to make the speeches, and his views would be solicited on many subjects. His sponsor would be delighted and would agree to pour millions into the next venture.

The public and the sponsors wanted to know who won the race and cared nothing about subclasses or minor victories. The way the competition shaped up, it was smarter for a middling small-class entrant to add a foot or two to his overall hull length and enter the large class, where at least he would be in fifth place or seventh place or last place rather than be lost among the confusion of classes. In a big race like this, it seemed to me that a single class would have made more sense for many reasons.*

Sixteen of the twenty-five starting yachts were partially or fully sponsored. Some had budgets over $1,000,000, which made an equable competition with amateur sailors a laugh. In both Cape Town and Sydney I had watched *major reconstruction and total sail renewal* on some of the large yachts. Many of the captains went on deluxe vacations while large shore parties of professionals flown in from abroad put on rigging and instrumentation and dealt with other essentials.

Nevertheless, I was not the sponsor of the race. I had had no hand in shaping the rules. I was only a sailor trying to get around the course in one piece and trying to do as well as I could. I would have gone along with any rules because I wanted to make the voyage.

It had been an enormous undertaking to select and equip a large new yacht in a short time. I could never have gotten *American Flag* ready by myself. I owe my luck to have reached the starting line to Margaret, Fos Whitlock, Read Branch, and Dave Taylor—all wonderful people who overstretched themselves to help someone chasing an idea. Secondly, the financing of *American Flag* was hopeless. It was crazy to have put all my personal assets into a new vessel. I should have turned over the fund-raising to someone else a year or two ahead of time so I could have concentrated on the yacht, her equipment, and the race. By trying to wear several hats at the same time I had fatally diluted my strength.

> [From the log]. February 10th.
>
> *1200.* 189 miles. I had a good sleep and a big breakfast after I got the yacht sailing well again. The gale yesterday was nasty and I about killed myself cranking down the third reef. God help me in fifty knots. I am eating the last piece of ham, which will finish the fresh meat. It's amazing that the ice lasted until a few days ago.
>
> I am still trying to sort out the birds. I believe the hard-to–identify bird is a white-headed petrel. I may be seeing Antarctic fulmars as well. This morning some grayish-blue prions were fluttering around the yacht. The sky looks different today, very wintery. I need warm clothing all the time and wear both a neck scarf and my storm hat when I go out.

I had a long talk with John Hughes and Bertie Reed regarding the new mast for *Joseph Young*. Bertie thought it would be cheaper and easier to get a new spar from Bellamy in Cape Town. I made a big effort to speak with John twice a day to cheer him up and to let him know that someone cared about him.

---

* Based on a BOC press release, my hometown newspaper in Maine ran a headline which said: "Martin Regains Lead in BOC Race; Roth Chugging Along in Thirteenth Place," when actually I was in fifth place in my class.

Late that afternoon, at 52°08'S., *American Flag* reached along nicely with twenty-two knots of wind from the south-southeast under a sky with low broken stratus. The weather was cold and clear and beautiful with patches of blue sky here and there. It felt good to take deep breaths of the fresh clean air.

Three of the French yachts had taken what I thought was a terrifying gamble with ice and had sailed far to the south—one to 62°40'—seeking shorter courses and hoping to find powerful west winds. *UAP, Ecureuil d'Aquitaine,* and *Credit Agricole* had fast sailing, but they also ran into piercing cold and fog. ("Some days I could not even see the top of the mast," wrote one.) The men were sorely afraid of smashing into icebergs, and they nervously peered at their radar screens with bloodshot eyes while they raced eastward and gained thirty to sixty miles a day on the rest of the fleet. The three Frenchmen were fully aware that if they struck ice at twelve knots (one yacht logged 295 miles in twenty-four hours) their chances for rescue and returning alive were slight; nevertheless, they pressed on like blind men on a battlefield and somehow avoided the dangerous ice floes which they all knew were out there. It was a knife edge gamble, not a calculated risk, and the other thirteen BOC captains refused to follow. I thought the decisions of the three men who went south of 60° were reckless and foolhardy.

Nevertheless, the French trio got away with their desperate game and gradually worked to the east-northeast. By the evening of February 10th, Philippe Jeantot, who was slightly ahead, sent out a radio message:

> I am thirty-five miles from Cape Horn. The wind is twenty-five knots from the west-northwest. The sea is calm and everything is okay. I wish all the competitors the same. I hope to see the Cape in the light; otherwise I will have to come back in four years.

CHAPTER TWENTY-TWO

Hello Atlantic

A t noon on February 11th I calculated that in the last twenty-four hours *American Flag* had traveled 184 miles. I'd been in the Southern ocean for three and a half weeks. The winds showed no signs of stopping, and my daily average for 4,194 miles had climbed to 168 miles a day, or seven knots. I was now at 52°S. and heading a little south of east to clear Cape Horn. Once at 56°S. I could presumably continue sailing eastward forever and just keep on going round and round the globe until I got dizzy and fell off. Forget the race; forget sanity; just keep going!

American Flag could have done it. All her sails were intact, and I had a complete second set. There was plenty of food on board. The solar panels would have driven the autopilot, and if it stopped breathing and died, the Monitor steering vane could have taken over. There was a weird fascination in the thought of continuing on for another circuit. . . . On earlier voyages I'd experienced the feeling that once I got settled on a long passage and fell into the swing and rhythm of a seagoing routine, each day got shorter and shorter. I wanted the trip across the ocean to go on forever. . . .

There was lots of news to write in my journal. I'd been watching a group of remarkable birds called diving petrels, which not only flew in the air (with whirring wings) but flew through crests of waves and dived into the sea with ease. These amphibious birds were small (nine-inch body; fourteen-inch wings) and colored gray and black with white underparts. The diving petrels

Deck work on *American Flag*

paid absolutely no attention to me and often dove into the water at full speed, disappeared for a time, and then suddenly flew out of the sea as if a magician had waved his wand.

For several days I spoke on the radio to solo sailor James Hatfield on *British Heart III,* who was north of the BOC fleet and sailing from New Zealand to the Strait of Magellan. James was on a global voyage to raise money for heart research and had had many adventures, including being picked up by a container ship after the sinking of *British Heart II* (whose rudder shaft had fractured). James asked a lot of questions about the Strait of Magellan at the southern end of South America.

Hatfield to *Colt:* "Do you believe in God?"

Pentti: "He may be around."

Hatfield: "On this trip I suddenly became aware of being surrounded by a powerful force."

[From the log]. February 12th.

0925. A long hard night with squalls from the southeast and icy rain. It's a battle to keep going to the east. I am surprised at the power of only fifteen or twenty knots of cold wind. Is the air more dense down here? And where is my fair west wind?

1016. Alert! Heavy low clouds with ragged bottoms to windward. Look out for those ragged bottoms, which always mean trouble! At the moment we are hard on the wind in 22 knots and traveling at 6.5 knots with the tiny storm staysail and double-reefed main. I continue to be amazed at how easily this hull is driven.

1200. 157 miles today. Onion soup for lunch. I sorted through the bag of onions and heaved an arm load of rotten onions over the side. The albatrosses showed no interest at all.

1800. A successful call to John Sanford in Halifax regarding John Hughes' new rig. Isomat will supply a free mast. Everything's going well. 110 items on list. One or two men will accompany the shipment and help put up the new spar.

1930. I relayed all the information from Halifax to John Hughes, who was delighted.

2100. Becalmed. A radio warning of a seventy-knot low at 53°S. and 77°W. near Cape Horn.

I tried to speak on the radio to John Hughes twice each day. Mark Schrader, Pentti Salmi, and Bertie Reed also talked with John. I was a little surprised that some of the others in the fleet didn't take a few minutes each day to have a word with John, who was in a tough spot. I had learned that the radio conduct of the BOC captains varied widely and represented a whole range of humanity. Some of the sailors didn't talk on the radio at all and kept to themselves except for the mandatory position reporting once a week.

Others listened carefully to everything to see what race intelligence they could sift from the conversations. One fellow tried to ask sly questions about weather and the plans of the others. Some totally ignored any talk of dismastings or big problems as if by shutting out such subjects they would insulate themselves from trouble. Several of the fellows concentrated totally on the race and—like Trappist monks—appeared to sail entirely around the world with blinders on to all else.

Yet Ian Kiernan, for example, was always upbeat and full of laughs and jokes ("My weather bloke has done it again. This time he must have given me the wind information for the wrong week!"). David White was good at making technical suggestions, and he repeatedly came up with clever ideas to help others. Amiable Bertie Reed was the fleet weather consultant and must have dreamed about highs and lows in his sleep. Ever since Cape Town, Richard Konkolski had spent a lot of time on his radio trying to be extra-friendly.

Some of the captains had radio failures; still others—the strong silent types—lived in their own private worlds and neither needed nor wanted to talk. Fortunately for me, half a dozen of the sailors—were we too chatty?— were outgoing types who talked about books, birds, weather, shipping, the sailing, their hopes and fears, technical problems, and even how they looked forward to seeing their wives and girlfriends.

While all this light talk went on, Harry Harkimo on *Belmont Finland* was living his own private hell. Harry was sponsored by a Finnish tobacco company in a million-dollar campaign. He had done well on the second leg of the race, and his progress was reported by all the newspapers and magazines in Finland, which ran endless stories about the country's new thirty-three-year-old sports hero. Because of all this we heard that Belmont sales were up in Finland. Since Harry was doing better as the race progressed, the reporters wrote stories that suggested he would win the third leg. Unfortunately for Harry, the winds were light, just what he didn't want for his 15.2-ton Swan 50, the heaviest vessel in the BOC fleet.

"The pressure was terrible," said Harry later. "I was crying all the time, and I got nervous. I was probably close to a nervous breakdown. I don't know where the edge of a breakdown is, but when you start crying for half an hour and you cry and cry and have to talk to yourself to get over it, it all adds up to a bad sign. Especially when each session gets worse. At that point you are probably close to a nervous breakdown. And all because of the pressure on me to win."[37]

On February 13th my winds went around slowly in a great clockwise circle, and the barometer began to drop. At 0400 an enormous low cloud first brought wind and then took it away as it passed. The moon was so bright that I could read the compass. Since I had only five to seven knots of wind, I took advantage of the lull and made breakfast. Meanwhile the rest of the fleet raced eastward. It was incredible. *American Flag* was in one of the stormiest places on earth, and we had had no wind of consequence for days.

At dawn I saw five towering cumulonimbus clouds. Was I back in the doldrums? Later in the morning I ran nicely before a light south-southwest wind that would have been perfect for a spinnaker, but I counted eleven squalls spaced around the horizon. The weather was sunny, but it was chilly, and I was glad to pull on gloves. My run at noon was 145 miles.

The next morning there was a great discussion of barometer readings. *American Flag's* read 990. *Lone Star's* was 982 ("There may be no sunrise," said Mark). *Colt's* dropped to 967. "Mine's down, too," said David White. "What's coming?"

Mark passed along a report that French journalists had hired a Chilean boat to photograph Philippe and Titouan at Cape Horn. Apparently the journalists lured Titouan too close to the shore because *Ecureuil* struck a rock with terrific force. Later I got the story from Titouan.

"The collision stopped me dead in the water," said the thirty-one-year-old French captain. "The shock broke the forward part of the keel away from the hull and pushed the aft part into the underbody of the hull. I thought it was all over for me at that moment. But the keel bolts held, and in spite of a loose keel and a gap between the keel and hull, the boat kept going.

"I managed to sail the boat by tightening and loosening the keel bolts (on opposite sides of the hull interior), depending on the tack I was on," said the plucky Titouan. "When I was on one tack, I would tighten one bolt and loosen the other. Then when I changed tacks I would tighten the loose bolt, and loosen up the tight one. I could do it with my bare hands!"

Jean-Yves Terlain on *UAP* was in third place in Class I. He also had had a nasty accident near Cape Horn, but of a different sort. "I was cutting a piece of bread," he said. "I had done it so many times before without paying much attention, but I had just spent an hour sharpening the knife with a stone. I wasn't looking at what I was doing, and the knife slipped and cut my hand through to the bone." Jean-Yves managed to stem the flow of blood by keeping the hand tightly bandaged for days, and padded it heavily so that he could still use the hand for some things. "I didn't put up the spinnaker poles for the rest of the leg," he said.

Back on *American Flag* I continued to worry about the low barometer readings, which soon turned into real wind.

[From the log]. February 14th.

0500. We're tearing along at a steady nine to ten knots under the double-reefed mainsail, but the wind is increasing. I need a third reef. Can I do it?

0710. I am wringing wet from the inside out getting the third reef down. I must get a bigger winch or rig a purchase on the reefing pendant. The weather is simply frightful (a steady northwest forty plus squalls).

1200. 206 miles today. Barometer 982, the lowest I recall since a typhoon alert in Japan many years ago when Margaret and I sailed there in *Whisper.* Today I sailed on to a new chart, which at last shows Cape Horn (1,255 miles on 100° true).

1415. A long talk with John Hughes on 12 and 16 megahertz. He was at 45°30′S., with 3,170 miles to go to Talcahuano. Everything okay. He had a south wind at ten knots and was sailing eastward. He figures twenty to forty days plus seven days on land to step the new mast. He plans to fly his spinnaker as soon as he has a fair wind (a spinnaker with a knot in it to reduce the hoist).

1500. Colt's barometer reads an unbelievable 962; yet Pentti, who is 210 miles south and 256 miles west of me, has blue skies and fifteen knots from the southwest.

1840. Weather much improved, although the ocean is still quite rough. Set more of the yankee (all but five rolls). Slept much of the day in the port berth, where it was safe, snug, and warm. Just had dinner of chili, coffee, and brandy.

The next day I checked off another 204 miles. The wind had settled in the north at eighteen knots, but there was still a big sea running plus a lot of rain here and there. I had a strange rig of three reefs and the full yankee, and we were reaching along at nine to ten knots (sometimes more) with no weather helm and almost perfect balance. Should the mast be moved forward a little? Perhaps the skeg and barn door rudder changed the balance of the yacht. John Hughes reported 110 miles in the last twenty-four hours. In the evening I heard that John Martin had pulled into the lee of Deceit island after rounding Cape Horn to rig new running backstays on *Tuna Marine.*

Aboard *Biscuits Lu,* Guy Bernardin heard a noise, rushed out into the cockpit, and was astonished to find that an overtaking wave had washed a baby seal up on the transom skirt of his vessel. "I don't know who was more startled, me or the seal!" said Guy, who fed cookies to the animal.

Because of the ice danger, Guy refused to go farther south than 56°30′. "I give the others credit," he said, "but it was not my plan to follow them. I went only as far south as Cape Horn."

At 0105 on February 16th the wind collapsed again. I thought of my friend Don Straus in Somesville, Maine, who had said before the race that once I got to the Southern ocean and the westerlies, the race would be a piece of cake. "A good place for you to read *The Decline and Fall of the Roman Empire,*" said Don. "You'll have nothing to do down there except to run before the eternal westerlies." Eternal westerlies indeed. Infernal westerlies should have been the words. There were west winds all right, but only after the winds went around in a circle with the usual sail drill and spinnaker pole game and calms. I wish Don had been along to reef and unreef the sail and to have maneuvered the spinnaker pole from one side deck to the other.

Six hours later I was rolling heavily and crept along in dense fog and cold rain at fifty-four degrees south. I anxiously peered ahead and half expected an iceberg to appear out of the gray gloom. The seas were confused and upset. One of them slammed into the steering vane and gave it a hard knock, which separated the bronze gear train. Although *American Flag* was still rolling heavily, I wanted to fix the gear so I carefully hooked myself to the yacht with my safety harness, leaned out over the transom, and started repairs. During the work I went below to get a large cotter pin from a jar of cotter pins I kept with all my nuts and bolts and screws and discovered that several of the hardware containers had gotten upset. The fastenings were in a terrible mixup. It took an hour to sort things out. Mixed in with all the hardware containers and nuts and bolts, however, was a box of delicious South African cookies that had somehow gotten in the wrong locker. The bolt sorter got a surprise dividend!

By noon (152 miles) the wind was up to twenty knots from the northwest. We rushed along to the east, although an occasional swell from the north thumped on board with a heavy crash. *Joseph Young* reported 96 miles. Late in the afternoon the sky to the north turned the color of pewter, the wind increased and switched to the north, and a line of low clouds rolled down from the north. I shortened sail in a hurry. Even so we were going eight to ten knots with twelve rolls in the yankee, the tiny storm staysail, and three reefs in the mainsail. At midnight the wind veered to the northwest and by 0500 was a steady thirty-three knots. The prospects looked nasty so I rolled up the yankee entirely, closed both storm doors to the cockpit, and went below to make breakfast (tea, a dish of figs, two boiled eggs, an orange, and cheese and crackers). By noon (197 miles) the wind had eased to twenty-five to thirty knots, but it was not steady. A big sea was running.

I hoped that an eastbound low south of *American Flag* would bring southwest winds. By noon (197 miles) the sky had cleared, and the sea was bright blue with a mass of whitecaps. In the late afternoon Pentti mentioned that he had had a feeling he should go up on deck. He did and saw a Japanese fishing boat, the *Queen Mary,* one mile ahead. After a lot of hilarious attempts to communicate on their VHF radios, the Japanese spoke to the Finnish yacht in Spanish. Pentti learned that the ship was bound for the Falklands.

Early the next morning we were still charging along in front of a southwest wind. For the first time in my life I saw snow and rainbows at the same time. The air was cold, the seas large and ominous, and the yacht rolled heavily. Because of the violent motion I was careful to keep a preventer line rigged from the end of the main boom to the stemhead. The line helped keep the boom under control and reduced the banging and crashing. At noon the mileage was 204; Cape Horn was 493 miles away.

With all the gybing because of wind shifts, I'd learned that it was extremely dangerous to move the spinnaker pole from one side of the foredeck to the other when the boat was rolling heavily. I had to juggle the nineteen-foot aluminum pole around the baby stay, the midstay, and the head stay while trying to keep my balance. Sometimes I felt like an acrobat on a high wire. The loss of my second pole because of the collapsed Forespar fitting had been a big blow. I suppose I should have had a secondary attachment scheme, but you have to trust *something*. I wish Mr. Forespar could have been with me for a few days.

The news from the west was that *Joseph Young* was becalmed. John Hughes was in good spirits. I was afraid to ask how much drinking water he had on board.

[From my journal]. February 19th.

0345. I can scarcely write because the spinnaker pole end fitting nipped the little finger on my left hand. Already the nail is turning blue. Very painful. I awoke at 0130 with the yankee slatting. The wind had veered a little, and I had been on the edge of a fore-and-aft and running rig change. I got dressed and looked outside. I could dimly see a squall in the distance so I made some hot chocolate and boiled two eggs which tasted good. I then put on my heavy oilskins and went out to deal with the sails. A streak of weak blue-gray was the front-runner of dawn at about 0300 (today I will move the clocks forward another hour). I could see quite well. I wrestled the pole from starboard to port, tied the outer end to the pulpit, and hooked up the mast end. Then the four control lines—the topping lift, fore guy, after guy, and sheet. As I worked, the clouds brightened a little, and the gray-blue became stronger. An albatross circled around, no doubt laughing at me struggling on the foredeck. I was surprised how white the breast of the big bird appeared in the early light. I finished with the pole, winched it into position, and set the yankee to windward. Our speed picked up from 7–8 to 9–10. My poor little finger hurts like hell. Mark Schrader just passed on a doctor's tip to drill a hole through the nail to relieve the pressure underneath, but I don't feel up to that. Besides, how will I hold the eggbeater drill and turn the crank while I drill a hole through myself? No thanks.

During the morning I had a long discussion with David White about generating electrical power. He used a twelve-inch diameter, six-inch pitch, two-bladed bronze propeller permanently mounted under his hull a little aft of the keel. The propeller was on a strut and drove a stainless steel shaft, which entered the hull through a stuffing box and was coupled to a small Bosch generator. "Nothing much happens until seven knots, but in a sixty-footer that's no problem," he said. David got enough electricity to run a dozen electrical devices plus lots of lights. He thinks a twenty-amp alternator with a ten-inch feathering propeller would be ideal.

American Flag's run at noon was 203. Cape Horn was 275 miles east. The radio crackled with the voice of Ian Kiernan on *Spirit of Sydney*, who had just rounded Cape Horn. "It was wonderful," said Ian. "I was in awe. The rock showed up at sunrise, and it was simply stunning. Fantastic. I spoke with Marcello, one of the Chileans at the light on Horn island."

The best sailor in the race was Jean Luc Van Den Heede, a hearty and jovial mathematics teacher from Lanester, France. Jean Luc was always full of smiles and jokes, but one level down he was a tough and determined sailor who did remarkably well with *Let's Go,* the lightest yacht in the fleet.

Later Mike Plant, the leader of Class II, passed Cape Horn in *Airco*. "I felt like I was in another world for a day. It was very enjoyable. I glided by Cape Horn about two miles off the land and some rocks. Then the wind went light and stopped. It filled in after about three hours. . . . My satnav has been out this leg. I spend half the time looking for the sun and the other half worrying about where I am."

That evening Jean Luc talked enthusiastically about rounding Cape Horn. His deep bass voice crackled with emotion as it boomed over the speaker of the single sideband radio: "At daybreak I saw the islands of Diego Ramirez and a little later I saw Cape Horn. It was *fantastique*. Waves from port passed in front of the boat, but one wave from starboard was going in the wrong direction and hit and heeled *Let's Go* to about eighty degrees. The spinnaker pole dipped in the sea and snapped. I broke the other one near New Zealand so now both are gone.

"Cape Horn was my best souvenir of the race," said the French sailor. "Fifty knots of wind. I was surfing at twenty-four knots. It was unbelievable. *Fantastique!*"

I have described my rounding of Cape Horn in Chapter 1. Briefly, I had an excellent run of 224 miles on February 20th and slipped past this shrine of all seaman at dusk in the late afternoon. The weather had been boisterous all day, but the west wind dropped to eighteen knots when I passed the great black rock. *Legend* ("At last I can cross it off the list.") and *Belmont* ("Wonderful.") were just ahead of me. *Declaration* was a little behind. *Lone Star* and *Colt* were closing fast. Only John Hughes in *Joseph Young* was still in the middle of the Pacific (the evening before he reported 2,896 miles to Talcahuano and "two to three knots in very light winds").

Of the sixteen sailors still going, fifteen had rounded or were about to round Cape Horn, which was clearly the most important mark of the race. It was a turning point geographically because we were about to leave the vast reaches of the Southern ocean. Additionally, Cape Horn was the emotional high point of the race because sailing one's own small vessel past this great mark of the sea after working our vessels across 12,000 miles of the Southern ocean from Cape Town was a wonderful moment.

The pages of this book do not chronicle a history of seafaring but are simply the notes and thoughts of one man. My book is a narrative of the daily life, small happenings, and things that concern the lives of long-distance sailors. I have no sermons for statesmen, no revelations, and nothing to shock people. My account is filled with trifling things because from these paragraphs I can recall the fellowship of the race. We were all comrades of the sea, and we felt a togetherness because we knew what it was to run our little ships before the mighty winds on the great sweeps of the oceans.

We felt the sunlight and the salt tang while we hauled on lines and hurried to adjust our sails. We tasted the excitement of fierce winds. We fretted over icebergs. We cooked our solitary meals, scribbled in our log-books, and tried to do nothing foolish. Our race around the world was a ridiculous whim, but it intoxicated us and made us glad that we'd come. In a long life of much dullness and tedium, these were moments of wonder and delight, perhaps never to be repeated. We had staked all we had on our long crossings, and they were wondrous adventures. The experiences could never be taken from us.

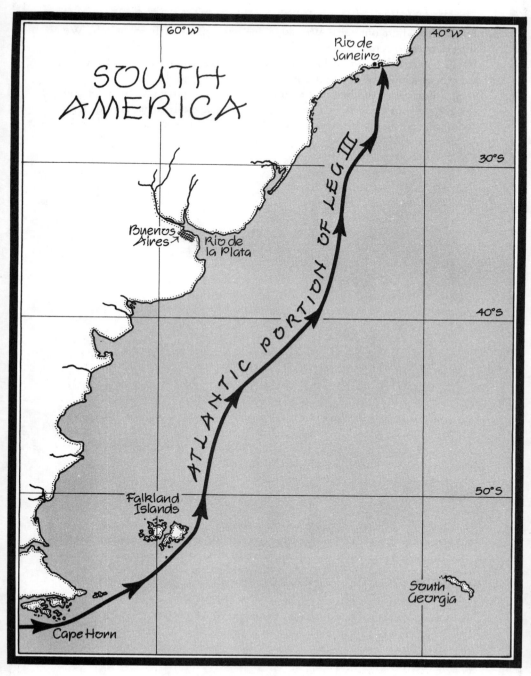

13. Falklands to Rio de Janeiro

CHAPTER TWENTY-THREE

North

*A*merican Flag had two drinking water tanks of forty-five gallons each. Instead of being located low down in the bilge area of the main cabin where they belonged for the best weight placement, however, the tanks had been installed higher up along the sides of the hull directly beneath the pilot berths. One tank was on the port side, and one was to starboard. The slightly elevated tanks made pumping water to the galley easy, but when the yacht heeled a lot, gravity caused the water to run out of both the galley sink hand pump and the small hand pump in the head compartment. During nine months of sailing I had learned to deal with this niggling little problem with a tiny shut-off valve at the end of the galley outlet pipe, and I stuck a small tapered wooden plug in the outlet of the head sink pump.

When *American Flag* dipped her mast in the sea during the violent storm south of Isla de los Estados after rounding Cape Horn (described in chapter one), the wooden plug somehow came out of the head sink pump. I failed to notice this, and during an hour or two when I took a nap, fresh water poured out on the cabin sole and into the ship's bilges. When I awoke, I discovered water sloshing around everywhere. Pandemonium! I didn't know what had happened. I got busy with the big Edson hand bilge pump and soon got rid of the water. After it was gone, however, I discovered that I had pumped most of my drinking water into the sea.

I sat down to reflect on my situation. It was February 22nd. I had been at sea for thirty-six days and had sailed 6,200 miles. I still had 2,000 miles to go to Rio de Janeiro in Brazil. Normally at sea a person needs about two liters of water per day for drinking, cooking, and light washing (or sixty liters or fifteen gallons a month). In the thirty-six days from Sydney, I reckoned that I had used eighteen or twenty gallons. I should have had seventy gallons left (or at least thirty-five, because normally the outlet valve to one tank was *always* kept closed; somehow, however, both valves had been open). Now except for a few jugs with emergency water, my drinking water was gone. I still had two solar stills and some cans of food packed with water. In extremis I suppose I could have cobbled together a still and made fresh water from salt water using my kerosene stove to boil the water, but this would have been time-consuming and interfered with sailing. I recalled that in the first BOC race, Bertie Reed had gotten water from the Chilean navy in the lee of the Cape Horn islands. I was already east of this area. The next possible stop was Port Stanley in the Falkland islands, about 200 miles to the northeast.

While I thought about all this I had my big green and white spinnaker up and was sailing nicely toward the northeast. The wind blew from the southwest at eleven knots, the sea was smooth, and not a squall was in sight. Was the hard Cape Horn weather behind me?

At noon I crossed 54°S. Since I had been almost stopped during the mighty storm of the day before, we showed only 129 miles for the daily run. We were over the greenish-blue waters of Burdwood bank, and the depth sounder read sixty-seven fathoms. Small albatrosses, shearwaters, and storm petrels flew everywhere over this fertile feeding ground.

[From the log]. February 22nd.

2035. For the last six hours we've had a bit of foredeck drama. The spinnaker got back-winded, and we have the spinnaker wrap to end all spinnaker wraps. An incredible mess. Five trips up the mast. I finally disconnected the sheet and after guy from the clews and even untied the halyard at the head of the sail. The problem is a dozen wraps around the midstay. I managed to slide the mess down the midstay a little, after taking a line aloft and leading it down to a winch. What frustration! Somehow part of the sail got caught between the midstay and the midstay halyard. Then the sock line wrapped around and around everything. The whole thing is mind-boggling. Anyway, after a big effort I have the sail down on deck but still wrapped—horribly wrapped—and jammed on the stay, halyard, and sock line. The staysail, of course, is useless, which makes me vulnerable to bad weather. What a mess! I have visions of taking a knife to the $4,000 sail or going to Port Stanley. I am exhausted.

Spinnaker wraps are a terrible problem for singlehanders. The difficulty is that if a big balloonlike spinnaker gets back-winded in light airs, or if the wind shifts for a moment, the sail can wrap itself around the headstay. To prevent this, one usually hoists a net made of half a dozen pieces of webbing or light line, which acts as a barrier in the area between the headstay and the mast. If the spinnaker tries to wrap itself around the headstay, the net stops any fouling. Spinnaker nets are difficult to rig with roller furling headsail arrangements, however, and the lofty BOC rigs and various baby stays, midstays and headstays often made nets impossible to use.*

I knew that my wind was getting too light for the spinnaker. I had just gone forward to douse the sail, and I had my hands on the line to pull down the furling sock when the wind changed direction. The sail blew back against the midstay, which stopped the forward half. The rear half began to wrap around and around the midstay wire. Then the wind changed and the forward half went the other way and began to wrap around the already wrapped aft part of the sail in the other direction. This—and more—happened in a few seconds while I watched—unbelieving—with my mouth open.

In retrospect I should have put up and poled out the genoa, a step that would have been much more practical in the light and failing wind. However, I was keen to fly the spinnaker, the macho step, and this sail was usually much easier to handle than the genoa. But there wasn't enough wind, and eventually the chute wrapped. I was learning that spinnakers had a very limited range on fast sailing yachts because the apparent wind moved forward.

At twenty minutes past midnight on February 23rd I was only thirty-four miles southwest of Beauchêne island, a tiny dot of land thirty-three miles south of East Falkland island. I was close-reaching with two reefs in the main and six rolls in the yankee in twenty-two knots of wind from the northwest. I began to see fishing boats and by 0145 had ten in sight. At dawn I passed close to a Polish fishing trawler, whose captain advised me to get weather information from Port Stanley.

[From the log]. February 23rd.
0635. Sea Lion islands (dull-yellow, flat, dangerous-looking slabs of rock) to port. We are hurrying along at eight to ten knots up the southeast shore in the lee of East Falkland in fairly smooth water. No sign of land. Wind north-

---

* This is a big subject which we haven't the space to detail. The solution for a lightweight yacht is to use a hanked sail of some sort. The French employed booster sails, which are double jibs with hanks along the central luff of the sail. The booster can be unfolded to double the area (one side to port; one to starboard). The weather sail is held out with a spinnaker pole. With hanks securing the booster, there is no wrapping problem, and the sail can always be pulled down a wire stay if it breezes up. Two or four sheets are used for control. The French sailors generally carried three sizes of boosters which they changed, depending on the wind.

west twenty-four knots. The air has the tang and smell of the seashore, an essence of iodine. Many small albatrosses. We're heeled at twenty to thirty degrees. The sky is clear. During the night the sky was clear too. The stars, those windows into the heavens above, were out by the hundreds, and a new quarter moon hung in the crisp black sky. I am very sleepy.

Later in the morning I began to see a low and formless dun-colored sliver of land to port. I called Port Stanley and spoke with the Royal Navy ship *Green Rover*. I identified myself and asked for fresh water and a place to make rigging repairs for a few hours. *Green Rover* directed me to Mare harbor on Choiseul sound halfway up the southeast coast of East Falkland. "We've got a tug en route to Mare that will pick you up," said the officer on watch."

A cold thirty-two-knot wind poured across the island from the west. I slowly tacked back and forth (through about 100°) with three reefs in the mainsail and part of the yankee. The sea was reasonably smooth, but there was a lot of water flying around, and I was glad for my heavy foul weather clothing. I had expected mountains and low hills; what I saw, however, was a bleak and somewhat forbidding, flat, brownish island covered with hay-colored grasses and small shrubs. There were no trees at all. Years before, Margaret and I had sailed among the Aleutians islands and Bering sea in far western Alaska; somehow I expected similar islands. But the bit of East Falkland before me was prostrate and drab; not high, mountainous, and vibrating with green like the Aleutians.

By late morning I was five miles from Mare harbor when the *Irishman*, a squat and powerful-looking 139-foot seagoing tug, hove into sight. Her captain, Paul Cavanaugh, offered me a tow. Since the BOC rules restricted tows to within two miles of a harbor, *Irishman* agreed to escort me while I continued toward land. Finally a little after noon (165 miles) and two miles from Mare, I handed the sails. *Irishman* backed down to me, and a crewman heaved across a monkey's fist and a light line. I hauled across a two-inch manila hawser and away we went, a mosquito pulled by an elephant. Captain Cavanaugh was extremely proficient and towed me gently at six knots. As we headed into Mare harbor, dozens of small black and white Commerson's dolphins raced through the shallow water.

Mare harbor was well sheltered, but the wind whistled over the low land. I expected a military harbor to have docks and buildings and roads. It had all three, but the docks were minimal, the buildings were few and rough, and a Land Rover crept over a solitary dirt road. Instead of warehouses, a hundred or more cargo containers from ships were stacked in a long low row near the shore. The place had the look of a temporary wartime installation.

A small crowd of servicemen took my lines as *Irishman* eased me along-side a modern new dock. Unfortunately, the dock had large protruding

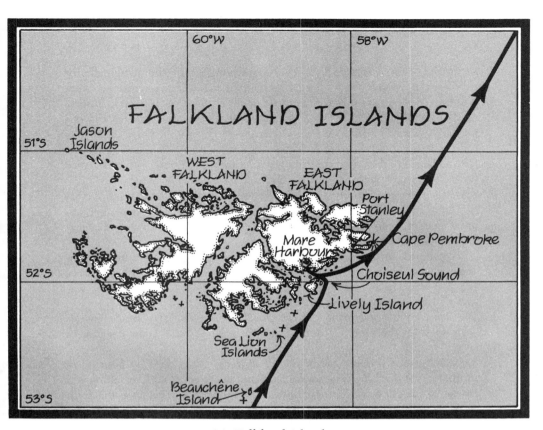

14. Falkland islands

rubber bumpers of a design that made it impossible for *American Flag* to stay there. Nearby was a small boat facility in a more sheltered place. "Can I get a tow?" "Of course." A launch appeared. I gave the man in charge careful instructions because the wind was thirty-five knots, and I knew the hazards of such tows.

The coxswain nodded approval, but he failed to pull when I shouted at the critical moment as the dock lines were cast off. *American Flag* drifted backward, and a groan went up from the people on shore as the starboard stern pulpit slipped under one of the rubber dock bumpers and was torn off. The steering vane gear also got a hard knock. The port stern pulpit had already been destroyed by the Australian police boat in Sydney. A mass of twisted, useless pipes rose above the transom of *American Flag*.

Suddenly the coxswain applied power and with difficulty towed me to the small boat area. A large high-sided engineering service ship (originally for oil rig work) was nearby with a compliment of engineers with nothing to do. A group of them had watched me drift helplessly into the big dock. Instead of wringing their hands, seven engineer-mechanics climbed aboard and immediately started repairs ("We'll soon have you set right."). Three of the men took away the pulpits to the welding shop on the repair ship, and two other fellows began to deal with the damaged steering vane. I put another two men on the spinnaker wrap problem ("We don't see many yachts here. This is fun."). Meanwhile I climbed to the masthead to replace a burned out navigation light bulb and to check several things. An hour later the spinnaker was unwrapped; I hanked on the big staysail. A petty officer heaved aboard a large jug of fresh water.

I became aware that a lot of soldiers were engaged in some sort of maneuvers on shore. They carried automatic weapons, wore full battle dress, and had their faces blackened underneath their eyes. "We're having war games just now," said one of the engineers.

I pulled out a camera. "Excuse me." An authoritative English voice boomed from the shore. "I don't think we'll have that." I put the camera away.

By now it was late in the day. The petty officer finished pouring in another jug of drinking water and handed me a sack of bread. Everything was set except for the work on the pulpits. The engineers hurried back and forth between the service ship and *American Flag* to check on the bending, base plates, and welding. The wind began to ease.

Captain Cavanaugh from the *Irishman* and I walked toward the harbormaster's office, which was on the third floor of the tallest building. On the way I saw soldiers in battle dress rushing around everywhere. Apparently the harbormaster's building had been taken over for a command center. At the door we were stopped by a mean-mannered guard who carried a large club, which he swung in the most menacing manner. The upstairs office had windows all around, but they were covered with blackout curtains. A somewhat daffy woman officer was in charge and agreed to call for a vessel to tow *American Flag* out of Mare harbour before nightfall. The scene in the harbormaster's office with the blackout curtains, the British officers, the lady lieutenant, and the guard with the club seemed a re-creation of a World War II motion picture. I expected Gregory Peck (an American general) and Erich von Stroheim (the Nazi high command) to walk through the door.

Once on the telephone the woman officer droned on and on. Captain Cavanaugh and I finally arranged for a tow and left the building, escorted out by the club-carrying soldier.

Back at the yacht the engineers were just finishing the pulpits, which looked remarkably good considering what they'd been through. The bent and twisted stainless steel pipes had been straightened. Kinked bits had been replaced. The base plates had been rewelded. Certainly the repairs were a miracle in the few hours that I had been in port.

I was nervous because it was already twilight. The petty officer finished pouring in another jug of fresh water, the launch appeared, I shook hands all around, and away we went while someone in the service vessel sent an Aldis signal of "good luck." By the time *American Flag* headed south out of the harbor, I had the reefed mainsail up, but it was almost dark. I had been told about a lighted buoy that marked a shoal, kelp, and a turn to the east. The towboat cast off. A British major shouted, "God speed, sailor." Then I was alone.

The wind was light. I unrolled the yankee and headed for the yellow (I hoped) buoy to leave it to port. Once in the main waterway I steered east. There were no lights, and I could hardly see. Had I turned too soon? Suddenly I felt the yacht slow as we glided into a bed of kelp, which gently swished along the hull. Was I about to run aground and be wrecked? I eased a little to the south, toward the middle of the channel I hoped, scarcely daring to breathe. I was terrified that each minute would be the last moment of life for *American Flag*. I could feel the sweat running down my back underneath my oilskins. It had been madness for a stranger to attempt the channel so late in the day.

By straining to see through my 7 × 50 binoculars I was just able to pick out three small islets that I had passed coming in. I had laid out compass courses before starting, but these depended on a pair of leading lights (not seen) and another yellow buoy (invisible). I slowly pushed eastward, hardly breathing, trying to stay in the middle of the dark channel, tapping the white cane of the echo sounder, which was fortunately working. In an hour—which seemed like fifty—the depths increased from four to twenty fathoms. I had been crawling over the knife edge; never had deep water been so welcome.

Finally out of danger, I set a course to pass east of Cape Pembroke and collapsed into a bunk. (I set my alarm clock and got up every thirty minutes to check for fishing boats). Unfortunately, the powerful navigational light on Pembroke, the easternmost point of East Falkland, had been discontinued, which was a pity because the night would have been much easier if I had had a mark to leave to port. Little by little the lights of Port Stanley gradually got closer, and I finally edged past Cape Pembroke, which was dimly silhouetted against the lights of the settlement to the west. I set a course northward into the open sea and crawled into my bunk and slept the sleep of death, exhausted from the nervous strain of the day and the harrowing passage out of Mare harbour.

The British engineers had been wonderful—quick, pleasant, and eminently practical. However the stop had cost me about thirteen hours in all, instead of the three hours I had figured. Later, when I discussed my spinnaker wrap problem with Bertie Reed on the radio, he suggested another idea that might have helped. I could have disconnected the midstay at the deck fitting and worked the wire out of the sail, something I had never considered. The miracle of seafaring is that you always keep learning.

On the same day that I stopped at East Falkland, Philippe Jeantot in *Credit Agricole* crossed the finish line at Rio de Janeiro. The French sailor completed the Sydney-to-Rio leg in thirty-six and three quarter days, a remarkable run that was eleven days faster than his same passage during the 1982–83 BOC challenge. Just three and a half hours later, Titouan Lamazou arrived in *Ecureuil*. Although Titouan had sustained keel damage at Cape Horn and had had to pump every two hours, he felt he could have won the leg if he hadn't bungled a critical message from his private meteorologist in France.

"I had been on a more easterly course than Philippe and was gaining on him each day, but then I got instructions—or so I thought—to head west, towards where he was," said the thirty-one-year-old artist. "I should have stayed east instead of cutting west; I had more wind, and a better course to Rio. But I cut inside, and that, I think, cost me the leg."

Both sailors reported that leg 3 had been easy compared with leg 2 and their experiences in the southern Indian ocean. Philippe said that except for a knockdown in fifty knots of wind (which blew out a headsail) during the passage of a cold front on the second night after leaving Sydney, his winds had not been over forty knots.

On February 24th, *American Flag's* noon run was only 110 miles because of the stop at East Falkland. Pentti Salmi on *Colt* was a little behind me with a few problems. He also wanted to call at the Falklands so I was able to tell him exactly where to go and what to expect. By midafternoon I had crossed fifty degrees south. Already the weather was warmer. I put away my heavy Southern ocean foul weather gear. I was sailing nicely on the port tack when I saw an enormous wave approaching from the west. I quickly ducked into the cabin and shut the storm door just as the sea walloped into *American Flag*. Life's small victories: for once I avoided getting soaked! Ha!

My hands were quite sore and felt like claws after six weeks of line handling and mast climbing. I had an imaginary conversation with my imaginary manicurist: "Oh, Mr. Roth. What *have* you been doing?"

Birds that I had never seen before flitted around the yacht. Dark brown on top with all brown wings and a rounded tail tip. White underneath the body. Face white with dark eye areas and a dark throat ring. Medium-sized (body thirteen inches) with long thin wings. After studying the bird books I decided I was seeing soft-plumaged petrels.

[From the log]. February 25th.

0320. Some difference from last night when I was so tired. Now with lots of sleep, good food, and easy sailing, life is pleasant.

0703. Lovely and warm in the sun. No oilskins at all! No long underwear!

1040. Becalmed. Busy cleaning galley. Scrubbed mud from Mare harbor off the afterdeck with 409 cleaner, followed by detergent, and then lots of seawater. I mounted a snapshackle at the tack of the staysail to make sail changes easier.

1200. 161 miles at noon. My wind has collapsed. Big genoa up but only four knots of wind from the north-northwest.

1310. Calm, unruffled water, a disc of hard blue reaching away on all sides. A few soft-plumaged petrels.

2100. Wind 6 knots from the northeast. Making 6 knots on a course of 350° with an apparent wind of 10.8 knots. In these light headwinds, the performance of North's big genoa is magnificent. The shape is like a huge bird's wing.

I sent a message to ham operator Sergio CE3BEQ in Chile for relay to Newport: "American Flag diverted to Mare harbor, East Falkland on 23 February for 13 hours for rigging repairs." My hope is to beat *Declaration* and *Belmont,* which are only twenty-six and seventy miles ahead. *Let's Go* has gotten ahead of *Airco.*

2330. John Hughes announced that he's going to head for Cape Horn in *Joseph Young* and try for the Falklands. "I've had no wind over ten knots for twenty days," he said. "My solution is less than ideal, and there's the possibility of being overwhelmed by a severe storm. I've thought about this decision hard and even made a list of pros and cons. So my decision is not rash.

"I see another twenty days to Port Stanley," said John. "It's so depressing to realize that in three weeks I've gotten 2,500 miles behind everyone else. *I think my only hope of ever seeing land again is to go for Cape Horn.* I've tried not to be silly but rational in my decision. I'm sure I will be heavily criticized. My tiny rig is not the easiest to sail, and I cannot go to windward at all. About eighty degrees true wind off the bow is the best I can do."

Pentti said that he'd had steady forty-knot winds near Cape Horn and gusts up to fifty-three knots. He pleaded with John to reconsider. "The only heroes are dead heroes," said Pentti.

"I think my decision is rational," replied John. "I am not suicidal. I hope it works out for the best."

The next day the winds were light and fluky from the north-northeast, and I showed 90 miles at noon. On the 27th the winds moved to the northwest, but continued to come and go, as if a giant were breathing in and out. At dawn there was a light rain. Then as a warm wind blew across the cold sea, dense fog covered the ocean while soft-plumaged petrels circled and dived close to the yacht, a scene that seemed unreal. *American Flag's* run at noon was 108 miles.

For several days I had variable headwinds and seemed to be changing sails all the time. I would just get the yacht sailing well when the wind would increase and put us over on our ear. Then after a shortening of sails, the breeze would fade away. These wind and sail changes invariably occurred just after I had cooked a meal and was about to eat.

Pentti reported that he had put into the Falklands for six hours to repair a headstay foil and to refasten his autopilot drive connection to the rudder shaft on *Colt.* "A good stop and pleasant people," he said. Mark Schrader was trying to start his diesel generator, which had water in the fuel system. "No joy so far," he radioed. Ian Kiernan was building a mythical airplane with bad yachting gear and various rejects from each yacht including broken autopilots, inoperative vane gears, bum spinnaker pole fittings, poor sails, etc. Everyone in the fleet had a few clinkers for Ian's airplane.

According to Harry Harkimo's private weather information, which he passed along, the competitors north of the Falklands were scheduled to have light weather for the next four days. There was a high pressure area over the Falklands and a second over St. Helena.

That evening at forty-four degrees south, the sea was a strange green color. I had a good dinner of chicken and dumplings. Afterward I began to read a detailed history of the Crusades, which apparently were some of the most idiotic missions of all time.

A little before midnight I had a long talk with *Joseph Young.* John was 2,200 miles west of Cape Horn, which he hoped to make in three weeks. That day his wind was only five knots out of the north; often the sea was absolutely calm. During the last twenty-four hours John had made 70 miles; the day before he did 80. John said that he had run out of cigarettes ("Good, I suppose.") and would probably be short of stove alcohol before reaching Port Stanley. I relayed a message to John from Mark Schrader: "Don't try Cape Horn. I had about the worst night of my life the night before the rounding." John acknowledged this and realized that we'd all be saying such things.

Once John's decision was made, I tried to be supportive. Obviously the radio chats were extremely important to him, and he seemed to live for news of the fleet. There was the aspect that once dismasted he could not be dismasted again (or at least it would be hard to tear off his tiny bipole rig). So *Joseph Young* should be able to weather very heavy gales. I warned John about the heavy tidal streams around Isla de los Estados and told him I would pass along information on the Chilean channels on our next talk. Harry Harkimo, Mark, Pentti, and I all spoke with John, who seemed ecstatic at the radio contact from the South Atlantic.

On the next three days (February 28, March 1 and 2) I had runs of 172, 164, and 145 miles in light north and northwest winds while I tried to get north as fast as possible. Jean Luc had moved into first place in Class II and urged me to head east for better winds. I spent an hour trying to telephone Margaret via Portishead, England, but I stupidly gave the operator my social security number instead of my phone number. Obviously I had been at sea too long. North of forty degrees south and in steadily climbing temperatures, I began to wear shorts and light shirts.

The news from Rio was that *UAP, Biscuits Lu,* and *Tuna Marine* had finished. John Martin reported a near collision with a ship off the Brazilian coast while *Tuna Marine* was running with a spinnaker up.

"It was a crystal clear night—just beautiful, one where you can see forever into the black night—and I saw a ship on the horizon. I watched it, watched it, watched it . . . took a position on it, and knew that we were on a dead-center collision course. When the ship was one mile off, I called him on VHF and said: 'I'm on your starboard side. Do you see me?' 'Sure I do,' he said. But he just held course anyway, and at the last moment, I had to broach-to, flattening the boat out, and let the guy go by; he was only 250 yards away." It was a nasty incident, particularly because the ship's officer was clearly obligated to change course, implied that he would, and then didn't.

Most of the other BOC competitors were out of easy radio range with John Hughes, but with patience I spoke with him twice each day on 16 or 22 MHz. I was beginning to feel that these daily talks were vital to John way out there in his tiny, handicapped vessel. The problem in the Southern ocean is that if you stay in the high southern latitudes long enough, you will certainly get smashed by fierce storms. The faster the passage the better.

On March 1st, John was still two thousand miles west of Cape Horn and being thrashed by a forty-knot wind from the east. "The seas are unbelievable, worse than any since Sydney, and I'm waiting to get rolled over," he said. "It feels like a punishment." March 2nd: "Earlier today a couple of seas picked me up, and the vertical acceleration was remarkable. It's a good thing that I was strapped in my bunk. It's a credit to the boat builder that I'm still here."

John had gotten a call through to Vicki, his girlfriend in Halifax, who complained that reporters were annoying her ("John will die. What's your reaction?"). This made John furious, and he was a little disheartened. "I would commit hari-kiri if I were Japanese," he said. "This gale has been a good test for the rig. Very very rough seas. I hate to complain every time I talk with you, but this is simply physical abuse. . . . If I ever see land again it will be a welcome sight."

On March 3rd (184 miles), *American Flag* sailed through a patch of crude oil residue pumped out by a ship. The black, oozy oil was in small, soft lumps that made a frightful mess on the lower parts of the staysail and yankee. I scrubbed the oil splotches off, but some of the oil apparently combined with the Dacron and will never come out entirely. While I was up forward with my bucket and scrub brush, a big flying fish slammed on deck next to me and half scared me to death.

During the day the light northwest wind veered to the southeast and increased to twenty-four knots. For a lark, I tried running with no headsail and the full main, and we scooted along in great style. From 1200 to 1400 we logged 19.9 miles with no headsail (and no pole) on a moderate sea and steady wind. Once we touched 18.6 knots and another time 17.5 knots for a few seconds. At these high speeds the water at the transom made a great roaring, whooshing sound, and I felt that I was really getting somewhere. Unfortunately these momentary surges, while exhilarating, actually meant little in the way of hard mileage.

Although the yacht tracked perfectly straight, I was very nervous about gybing, or rounding up and broaching under such a rig, and kept a strong preventer line rigged between the stem and the end of the main boom. The autopilot worked the tiller a trifle to windward, and we sped along hour after hour. But the strain of the high speed running was too much. Every time we surfed for a few seconds I was sure I was going to have a heart attack. I finally threw a couple of reefs in the mainsail and poled out the yankee opposite the main. I felt much better.

At midday on the 4th, Rio de Janeiro lay 650 miles to the north. The news was that Bertie Reed and Jean Luc were both becalmed near the finish line. On *American Flag* we showed 198 miles, with 7,699 miles behind us since Sydney. We were at thirty-three degrees south. Rio de Janeiro and the finish line were at twenty-three degrees, only three days away at 200 miles a day. Now, however, my winds grew light and vaporous, and sometimes were nonexistent. The sea was smooth; the silence complete; the sun hotter each day. Finally I was able to open the front hatch and all the portlights to dry out the damp cabin below. I put up my largest sails and ran around the decks in shorts and bare feet while I heaved on lines and checked the horizon for signs of wind.

I managed a weak contact with John Hughes. *Joseph Young* was 3,200 miles to my west-southwest if I measured straight across Argentina and Chile into the Pacific. John said that he was okay, but that his satnav had failed. He had a wind from the south at twenty-five knots and was 1,900 miles west of Cape Horn according to a fix some hours earlier.

[From the log]. March 5th.
     0920. All the flashlight batteries got wet in the supposed sacrosanct compartment outboard of the navigator's seat. I am trying to dry the batteries.
     1105. I must beat *Belmont* and *Declaration*.
     1210. 145 miles at noon. Terrific heat.
     1310. Just now 8.5 knots with 6.5 knots of wind, thirty-five degrees off the

bow. I can hardly believe these numbers. Are they real? I have rigged a second sheet so I can use the genoa reefed (I hope). Another albatross, black-browed, certainly the last that I will see.

1450. The most beautiful day of the race. A flat sea of deep blue, a gentle azure sky filled with cottony tufts of clouds in a checkerboard-perfect pattern, a few circling shearwaters, and a trifling wind from the north. The sun is hot, the front hatch and portlights are open, and the yacht is filled with fresh, dry air. The genoa, almost a thousand square feet of sculptured Dacron and Mylar, seems a magical towrope that pulls us along at six or seven knots hour after hour. It's wonderful that man could have fashioned a contrivance that harnesses the wind so well.

2350. A good talk with John Hughes who is 1,700 miles from Cape Horn, but becalmed again. He had no weather picture, but he thinks that clouds indicate wind is coming. John has decided that he can handle gales with his jury rig. "It's the calms that get you." He was eating fruitcake for breakfast and has run out of bacon, milk, bread, and butter. "I wonder if I'm going to crack up?" he said. "I suppose it's only natural to get a little despondent. I honestly don't think there is any danger with the jury rig, which is good and strong. The yacht is quite controllable. I just need to be careful near land."

The news came through that Jean Luc had crossed the finish line at Rio at 2300 on March 4th. The French sailor had certainly turned into a formidable opponent and did remarkable things with his featherweight flier *Let's Go,* which displaced only 4.9 tons (the average tonnage of the sixteen yachts still in the race was 10.78). Also he did it in style and good humor. If Jean Luc had had a sixty-footer he certainly would have been in first place overall.

"It was fantastic to arrive first in Class II and ahead of three of the Class I yachts," Jean Luc said later. "I wanted to win this leg more than anything— more than any other—because it was the leg with Cape Horn.

"When I bought my boat and was preparing for the BOC race, all my thoughts and preparations were aimed at being first," he said. "But when I got to Newport at the start and saw all the other boats in Class II, I was very, very afraid. All throughout the race I have seen the differences in the boats and how everyone is doing. In this kind of race, it is a couple between the boat and the skipper. I think some of the couples might be better pairs than others. I think my couple is good; I am in love with my boat.

"Cape Horn was simply fantastic," said the forty-two-year-old mathematics teacher. "I could not dream of a better passage. The day was just dawning. I could just see the light coming. Then a low came through, and the wind changed to the southwest. The conditions were perfect, so I decided to go close to the Horn.

"By the time I got close it was midday, and there was beautiful sun. The wind began to pick up—it went to thirty knots, then thirty-five, and the waves became shorter and shorter. The wind kept increasing, up over fifty knots. I was making tremendous speeds, surfing at more than twenty knots. My top speed was over twenty-four knots! I covered 160 miles during the daylight in thirteen hours and averaged more than twelve knots. . . . What a memory!"

Jean Luc, like many of those who placed high, benefited from private weather information (passed on by Titouan Lamazou) that guided him through the Southern ocean and up the coast of South America. "Toward the end of the leg there was a lot more wind farther east so I thought I would head east first, then go north," said the French sailor. "My actual progress toward Rio was much better than the Argos reports were showing. I went as much as ten degrees farther east than some of the others."

Bertie Reed on *Stabilo Boss* and Ian Kiernan on *Spirit of Sydney* followed Jean Luc into Rio, and in the early hours of the next morning—March 6th—Mike Plant sailed *Airco Distributor* across the line.

Mike's time of forty-seven days was excellent, and although he placed second in Class II, he was still the overall leader of the smaller class. The long slog from Sydney had been a frustrating time for the thirty-six-year-old American sailor from Rhode Island. At the beginning of the leg, two of his three autopilots broke down.

"That left me with only one autopilot to go the whole way to Rio, all through the Southern ocean," he said later. "I did manage with it, however, in spite of its many quirks. On its own, without any provocation, the autopilot would flash into another mode, and the boat would go hard over. It was deadly when I had a spinnaker up." Mike's satnav and weatherfax devices also packed up, and he was dismayed to learn that his Fleming wind vane wouldn't sail *Airco* for more than a few minutes without adjustments.

Mike Plant and Jean Luc had a duel not only across the Southern ocean but up the South Atlantic as well. "At one point Jean Luc was four hundred miles behind me," said Mike later, "while I sat becalmed in the middle of the Southern ocean. Meanwhile my opponent had steady winds. It was very frustrating."

After both yachts rounded Cape Horn—with *Airco* still one day ahead of *Let's Go*—Mike headed west of the Falklands while Jean Luc went far to the east, where he found better winds that suited his lightweight Swedish-designed cutter. While the heavier *Airco* languished in calms in the west, *Let's Go*—with an ear tuned to a French meteorologist—kept going and finally slipped into the lead of Class II.

Back on *American Flag* I was still 390 miles to the south. The light winds began to affect my daily runs, and for the next two days we showed only 126 and 125 miles at noon. During the early hours of March 6th the weather breezed up for a few hours, and I changed to the yankee in the dim light of Venus in the east. It was surprising how well I could see with only the light of the planet. Because of the unsteady winds I changed to the Monitor vane gear, which followed the wind instead of a magnetic course. I spent hours studying the Rio approach charts and couldn't wait to get across the finish line.

It's incredible how one's senses get attuned to things. One night I was tired after a lot of deck work. I was in a bunk and sound asleep when something in my head sensed an unusual sound: water running in an odd way. What had happened was that water was draining from the fresh water tanks into the galley sink because I had forgotten to turn off the shut-off valve at the end of the tap. *My precious fresh water was going over the side again!* I got up, secure in the knowledge of what was happening, twisted the tiny valve shut, and went back to sleep in a single involuntary action without even putting on a light. It was remarkable that I heard the sound of the tap water when there were so many other water sounds (the sea swishing along the hull, the slap of waves on the hull, water in the bilge, waves meeting outside, the contents of the water tanks slapping back and forth, and so on). I was a mother listening to the breathing of her child.

At 0245 on March 7th the wind veered ten degrees in the right direction. The vane gear followed it, and the Hadrian off-course alarm detected the change. Such technology was amazing. During the afternoon and evening I was becalmed for ten hours, which showed up in the next day's run of only 92 miles. I sent a required message to the race committee that I would cross the finish line at Rio in forty-eight hours. John Hughes' news was that he was 1,476 miles from Cape Horn, in good spirits, and had had an 80-mile day.

My weather was hot and humid, and the breezes were six or seven knots from northerly quadrants. In the light and halting winds the autopilot was preferable, but it had suddenly gone crazy and swung the tiller violently first one way and then the other while demanding ten amps of power. I began to replace the components one by one.

Early on March 9th I was still struggling along in trifling and unsteady headwinds and sometimes sailed into unpleasant short seas. According to the Argos reports, *Belmont, Declaration,* and *Legend Securities* were about twenty miles ahead of me. I thought I might be able to pass *Belmont* and *Declaration* because I knew my light-weather performance was better. I was unsure about *Legend. Lone Star* was 250 miles back, and *Colt* was 308, but both were coming on strong since I had sailed into the almost windless zone. (Pentti on weather: "They tell us that all men are equal, but some are luckier than others."). Since I was getting close I had a great bathing scene and washed my hair, put on decent clean clothes, and felt quite respectable. I knew I would probably be up all night so I made an effort to eat a good lunch and supper and have several naps during the afternoon and evening.

Toward midnight—with sixty miles to go—I saw a ship to starboard and a flashing strobe light far ahead of me. The wind increased a bit from the east-northeast so I changed down from the genoa only to discover that when I had the yankee set and drawing the wind collapsed. I nursed *American Flag* through the night, playing the wind shifts and running the sails up and down. At 0525 I had twenty-nine miles to go, and as the new day brightened, it was a thrill to see the incredible green of the Brazilian coastline.

At the latitude of Rio de Janeiro, the coast runs east and west and is high and mountainous with tropical beaches and coconut palms reaching into the Atlantic. Just offshore there are a number of small, rocky islets, and I knew from an earlier visit that the winds got fluky and uncertain when the sun heated the coastal area and the islets. As I passed close to a reef called Laje da Redonda, I became aware of a strong east-setting current.

I tried to get through the required VHF calls to the race committee on the channels specified in the race instructions, but all I heard was Portuguese, in spite of the printed notices of bilingual announcers.

[From my journal]. March 10th.

1030. I completed leg 3 of the BOC race an hour ago after running entirely out of wind one and a half miles from the finish line near the west end of a little stony islet called Ilha de Palmas. After about fifteen minutes, a trace of west wind came up so I set up the running rig quick as a flash because I suddenly noticed David White in *Legend* approaching from the southeast (I came from the south).

David appeared to have a completely different wind, and he was sailing steadily toward the line. Just as I got the port running rig up, the paltry wind switched abruptly from the west to southeast. Curses! I had to gybe the rig and to move the spinnaker pole from one side to the other. Meanwhile David was coming closer, sailing well, and seemed like a train on a track.

By now the sweat was streaming off me, and my breath was coming in gasps. I got the starboard running rig up only to have the southeast wind switch to the north. I quickly dropped the forward end of the spinnaker pole down on deck, unhooked the yankee sheet from the end of the pole, and we took off for the finish line close-hauled on the port tack.

I had to locate a certain yellow buoy off the east end of Ipanema beach, and when I did, I saw that it would require a tack to fetch it because the current was setting me eastward. When I tacked (David was coming on strong), the yankee sheet of course fouled on the spinnaker pole topping lift, which I hadn't had a chance to tie out of the way. I raced forward, whipped out my knife, cut the line in a flash, and hurried back to the tiller. I then sheeted in the sail, continued on the new tack until I could clear the yellow buoy, and finally tacked across the line. Nine minutes later David crossed the line. He had not been as close as I thought, but the finish had been wildly exciting for me. Imagine only nine minutes between two sailors after almost fifty-two days at sea!

15. Rio de Janeiro

CHAPTER TWENTY-FOUR

River of January

Rio de Janeiro is a city of hills and domes and mountains that surround one of the finest natural harbors in the world. From a viewpoint high on Corcovado, where a colossal 120-foot statue of Christ raises his arms benevolently over the city, you look down to beaches and the tropical Atlantic to the south, mountains to the west, a throbbing, noisy city to the north, and a wonderfully sheltered harbor to the east.

Five million people live in Rio, a hot, crowded, bustling mélange of the super-rich and the desperate poor. Downtown in the early morning, clerks (in yellow and blue sport shirts) push past chattering typists (in dresses of bright reds and greens). A banker rubs shoulders with a bootblack, bond salesmen pass shoelace peddlers, the limousine of a corporate treasurer honks past the pushcart of a fruit juice hawker, and a police sergeant lectures a boy who stole an apple. In Brazil, an enormous class of mulattos does much of the blue collar work; the Negroes and Indians reap the dregs. The country is a federal republic where in theory everyone has the same rights, but in fact the society is totally segregated by wealth, education, and color into five or six classes, each of which knows its precise limits and bounds. Those who are unhappy with South Africa should take a look at Brazil.

A few hours after crossing the finish line, *American Flag* was tied up at the Rio yacht club with the other BOC vessels. Of the seventeen that had started from Sydney, eleven were in Rio. *Double Cross* had retired in New

Zealand. *Belmont* and *Declaration* were nearby and about to finish. *Lone Star* and *Colt* were one day away. *Joseph Young* was approaching Cape Horn.

As I was towed into the yacht club, it was a thrill to see Margaret standing on shore waiting to take my lines. In spite of the shelter of the great natural harbor, there was a nasty swell called a *ressaca* rolling into Botafogo bay, which made tying up to the yacht club docks a dangerous business. All the BOC yachts lay at right angles to the shore with one or two stern anchors out on long nylon warps and bow lines to the shore. I put out two stern anchors and ran bow lines ashore, but if I adjusted the lines so that the yacht was far out enough to be safe, it meant a risky jump to get ashore.

Once on land I was whisked off in a high speed taxi to the police and customs offices downtown by a pretty, bilingual blond girl who worked in the BOC office. My passport and visa were quickly approved. I signed a pile of forms, smiled and shook hands with various officials, heard a lot of machine-gun Portuguese, and was declared fit and proper to stay in Brazil for a few weeks.

Back at the club I relaxed under a shaded veranda and had a long lunch with Margaret while we exchanged all our news. We sat at a table set with a starched white tablecloth and a bowl of fresh blue and yellow flowers while we looked out at the water and distant mountains. Meanwhile a deferential waiter served a salade niçoise and poured white wine into tall chilled glasses. After almost two months at sea, the lunch seemed like heaven.

"Can I afford this?" I asked Margaret. "Are we bankrupt?"

"Relax," said Margaret. "I've got a fistful of cruzeiros in my purse because the exchange rate is favorable. We got a few donations to the project. Just eat and talk and then you can have a long sleep."[38]

Now, finally, I didn't have to leap up at the slightest change in wind. I didn't have to think about the way *American Flag* was sailing. I didn't have to jump when I heard a strange noise. In a twinkling I was relieved from concern about the weather and how it was going to change, where I was and possible dangers, how the competition was doing, and my list of repairs.

The next morning my long sleep was interrupted by the sickening crunch of a yacht slamming into the seawall. The swell had picked up *Stabilo Boss* and had hammered her violently into the wall. *Belmont* (with no one on board) broke all her dock lines in the surge and began to drift away. Margaret and I managed to lasso the Finnish yacht and tied her up again. I decided to go out in the bay and anchor, and one by one the yachts followed. There were nice views, the breeze was better, and it was easier to sleep in the sweltering tropical heat. Unfortunately, the holding ground was particularly bad in Botafogo bay, moorings were not available, and we had to go out a half to three quarters of a mile to anchor. We could have used help from the race chairman, but Robin Knox-Johnston was involved with heavy visa problems for himself and John Martin from South Africa. The BOC yachts did not carry dinghies; in order to get ashore we had to rely on the yacht club launch service, which was poor beyond belief. The abysmal launch service and lack of moorings didn't concern everyone because many of the BOC captains had flown off to Europe or America and had left their vessels in charge of others. Only five or six captains lived on board.

On the second day in Rio, a familiar figure sculled alongside *American Flag*. It was my old friend Remo Casasco, an American who lived in Argentina. When Margaret and I had sailed around South America some years earlier, we had become the greatest friends with Remo and his wife Pelusa. Remo was a real sailing nut and totally dedicated to small boats. He had pooled all his money and bought a handsome wooden forty-foot double-ended ketch named *San Juan de Luz* in Buenos Aires. Remo's idea was take Pelusa to the United States on his yacht and settle down and find a new career. When Margaret and I had sailed north from Buenos Aires in 1976, Remo was about to leave. "Just a few things to get ready," he said. "I'm planning to follow you in less than a week." Now many years had passed during which I had not only sailed around the world with Margaret in our former yacht and written three books, but I had almost made a second circumnavigation in the BOC race. In the intervening years, Remo had only sailed from Buenos Aires to Rio, a distance of 1,151 miles. However his smiling enthusiasm hadn't changed a whit. "I just have a few things to perfect on *San Juan*," he said. "Then I'll be following you to the United States."

In the meantime, Remo pitched in and helped enormously with the work on *American Flag*. He was knowledgeable, a hard worker, and spoke the local languages to perfection. He knew all the locals, the best places to eat, the sources of hard-to-get items, and where to change money at the most favorable rates. He asked logical questions, earnestly listened to your advice, and appeared to be really trying. Yet he never got off his rear end and went anywhere in his own vessel. I wanted to grab Remo by the shoulders and shake him with rage; yet he was so charming and his excuses were so logical and disarming that when you seized his shoulders you wound up embracing him because he was such a pleasant fellow. Remo was a grown man with a wife and two children; yet I could always see a trace of the boy in him. I liked him very much.

The days passed quickly because I had many jobs to deal with on *American Flag*. One of the most important was to get a new spinnaker pole. I was assured by various people that this would be easy, but when I got down to it I ran into the old story of South America. It was delay, out of stock, the man is on vacation (or away, or dead), the company has moved, or "we don't do that anymore." Excuses, excuses, excuses. It generally wasn't a question of cost because the prices were often modest when you finally got the goods. The problem was getting delivery of *anything*. I had expected the spinnaker pole to be a problem so I had told Margaret to bring new pole-end fittings.

All I needed was an aluminum tube 100 millimeters in diameter and 5.8 meters long. Remo set to work on the problem.

The Rio yacht club (Iate Clube de Rio de Janeiro) was a prestigious social organization with magnificent waterfront property. The club was an expensive operation, and it was obvious that its members were well off. The club had several splendid restaurants with world-class chefs, a free coffee bar, lounges, various stores and shops, beauty and barber services, gambling rooms, banquet halls, an enormous swimming pool, tennis courts, private apartments, a dinghy fleet, almost constant sports fishing tournaments, and about one hundred power and sailing yachts on moorings plus service shops, a haulout facility, and dry storage. To run all this required a staff of 500.

While the club was ostensibly a yachting organization, its main function was a meeting place for businessmen and their families. There were several very keen senior members and officials who afforded us the greatest help and hospitality, but after a few weeks you had the inescapable feeling that the club as a whole didn't give a damn about foreigners and their toy boats.

In general—with a few exceptions—the Brazilians were very private people who were involved with their own affairs; the members liked to go to the club for a drink and a nice meal, but yacht racing and hospitality to cruising vessels were simply alien to their interests. They said yes, yes, yes, but they really meant no, no, no. In both Cape Town and Sydney, the yacht clubs were madly in love with foreign sailors, and we had enjoyed incredible hospitality. In addition there were local sponsoring organizations that were part of the BOC Group. Rio offered neither.

I continued to talk to John Hughes, who was making steady progress in *Joseph Young*. "Everything's fine," he said on March 19th. "Seven hundred miles to the Horn. I have a fresh breeze and feel reasonably good, although I was knocked down pretty badly and got a lot of water inside. Unfortunately I had the hatch open and was cooking breakfast when a big sea came from nowhere and pooped me. I took lots of water below.

"One of my water tanks is empty," said John, "and my food's getting a bit unusual. My position is 54°38′S.; 87°25′W. With luck I expect to get around on the 20th. The last two days I did 140 and 133 miles running before southwest and northwest winds. At the moment I have twenty-five to thirty knots. I spoke to John Sanford [his manager] in Halifax yesterday. The new mast and sails will be in the Falklands shortly. I could be in Port Stanley by March 25th."

I told John that if he got into trouble, he could go to Puerto Toro and Puerto Williams in the Chilean islands for assistance and supplies. I suggested that John head north immediately after Islas Hornos and go between Islas Herschel and Deceit to the east end of Isla Navarino. If he stayed up to windward as much as possible in the prevailing westerlies he ought be able to make the sixty-mile trip northward to the Chilean bases. We both hoped that he could get to the Falklands without such a stop.

The water in Rio's Botafogo bay was warm—over 80°F.—and incredibly polluted. Already I could see a big crop of hard barnacles and other marine growth on *American Flag's* bottom. I wanted to get the yacht hauled out to paint the bottom. The BOC had made vague arrangements with the yacht club, but when I went to find out about actually using the Travelift I ran into the usual South American baloney.

First I was told that because of my draft—2.4 meters—"It is out of the question. You will have to go to the Navy Arsenal." When I looked into this I found that the arsenal would cost $700. Remo then checked around the yachts already hauled out at the yacht club and found several with a draft of 2.5 meters.

Next we were told that we could not be hauled out because we had no cradle. We knew the answer to that one because both Remo and I had often been hauled out in South America and had propped up our vessels with timbers and wedges. We found some that were not in use.

"Okay on the draft and props," we were told a few days later. "The real problem is that we have no space. We're full up. There is no way you can be hauled."

I went to see Admiral Roberto Mario Monnerat, who was serving as the liaison man between the Rio yacht club and the BOC, and got him to intervene about the space problem. "Wait only two days," said the genial admiral, "and we'll have room for you."

Finally when we had overcome the problems of draft, props, and space, we heard that we couldn't be taken out "because the Travelift is too busy." Remo discovered that it was making only one lift per day and that we were getting stalled off. "Who do we pay? How much?" I said to the admiral who expressed horror at the thought of a gratuity changing hands at the club. "Not here," he sniffed. "Wait only a moment, and we will have you out of the water."

Three days later I was in the inner basic and ready to be lifted out when the Travelift broke down. "It's an electric coil," said the admiral. "We have ordered eight new coils but none have appeared yet. In the meantime we have an electrical shop rewinding a coil. Please be patient. Do not get excited. You Americans are too—shall I say—anxious. Relax a bit. Come with me and have a coffee."

All these delays were so typical of South America that I had to smile to myself. There was always a new excuse for nonperformance. Finally on April

4th we were taken out of the water, blocked up on the yacht club grounds, and we got to work cleaning the bottom. Remo, Margaret, and I plus a local laborer wet-sanded the bottom until it was smooth as glass.

Then I got out the special Awlgrip Awlstar bottom paint I had been given in Australia. Before the race in Newport I had used the Awlstar Gold Label variety. The new paint, however, was Awlstar White Label. Margaret—hawk-eyed as usual—noticed the difference and began to read the instructions.

"It says under no circumstances to use White Label over Gold Label. What are we going to do? There is no other paint available."

Remo summoned the chief painter, who had been slapping on bottom paint for forty years."

"All that stuff on the label means nothing," said the painter through Remo, who translated. "Those directions are put on by chemists and scientists, not people who do the things in the real world. What we're going to do is to try a test. A practical test. A trial that means something." The painter then carefully sanded a small test patch on the old bottom paint on the side of the keel. Next he mixed up the new paint and applied a coat to the test area. "Now we'll let that dry and have a look after lunch," he said.

That afternoon the paint appeared perfect. We tried every way to scratch and scrape off the paint, but it was as tenacious as old glue. We went ahead and painted the bottom.*

I was astonished at the amount of sail damage on the various yachts at the end of each leg. Either I was too conservative in my sailing or I had learned better sail care during my years of world cruising. In rising winds the racing fraternity apparently hung on to each sail until it began to come apart or disintegrated entirely. After each leg it was a field day for the sailmakers. Rio was no exception, and soon there were forty or fifty sails—a great mountain—ashore to be repaired. Brazil seemed to have only one sailmaker capable of dealing with large sails, a North loft in São Paulo—250 miles away—and a very capable woman sailmaker flew to Rio to deal with the business. Instead of setting up a temporary loft at the Rio Yacht Club, however, all the sails were flown to and from São Paulo in a DC-3 airplane at vast expense. I had a few seams that needed attention, and the changes that a Sydney sailmaker had made on *American Flag's* fully-battened mainsail had not worked out at all. But the sail repair estimates from the São Paulo sailmaker were so exorbitant ("You're sponsored. What the difference?") that I elected to stitch my own sails and to bend on my new spare mainsail for the passage to Newport. Unfortunately the specially-tapered top batten had gotten broken and was impossible to replace or repair. I had various spares but

---

* The paint job turned out to be excellent and worked well in spite of the directions.

somehow not the one I needed. Mark Schrader kindly gave me one of his spare battens, which fitted my new mainsail perfectly.

One person who was particularly helpful in Rio was Kathy Giblin, who was in charge of public relations for the BOC race. Kathy went out of her way to do favors for everyone and was always ready with a cheery smile and a good word no matter what the problem or how much extra effort it took. It was Kathy who had put me in touch with a source of funds in Australia when I was ready to sell *American Flag* in Sydney. Without her help I couldn't have completed the race.

So far I had had no luck getting a new spinnaker pole. I asked everyone I met and tried both industrial and sports companies. I considered a length of plastic pipe, but it was too weak. Wood was too heavy. "Certainly somewhere in this vast country is a piece of aluminum pipe," I said. I attempted to buy a used pole and looked through several storerooms in the yacht club. I was about resigned to my balancing act on the foredeck with my single pole when Remo thought of another supplier. "This fellow doesn't even have a telephone," said Remo. "I will borrow a car and go out to see him on the other side of Rio."

Sometimes Margaret, Remo, and I took a day off from *American Flag* and went out sightseeing or shopping, although we had to watch out for the extremely dangerous high-speed car and bus traffic. Since there was some risk for well-dressed tourists on city buses, and we had heard that Mike Plant had already been robbed, we locked our jewelry, watches, billfolds, and purses on the yacht, wore old clothes, and carried a little paper money in our shoes. We traveled all over Rio and twice took the little train that ran up to the mountain top at Corcovado (740 meters), where we marveled at the view and the great 700-ton statue of Christ. Another day we took an aerial tramway up to Sugarloaf (395 meters), where we had lemonades and looked down at the entrance to the bay. We ate delicious chicken on the spit in inexpensive little restaurants in Copacabana, one of the most densely populated places in the world, and walked along the great beach at Ipanema, where we visited a large art fair.

One night we were invited to the luxurious home of Henry and Mechthild Pflug, a charming, cultured German couple who belonged to the yacht club and were curious about solo sailors and their motivations. Henry ran the Brazilian subsidiary of a large German company and entertained us for hours with fascinating talk of his travels and work in Mexico and Indonesia ("It's so beautiful . . . the people love you . . . you need only learn a hundred words of their language."). Henry told us why it was that drivers didn't stop for red lights at night in Rio. ("You are likely to find a gun at your head. A neighbor

of mine stopped, felt a gun against his temple, resisted, and was shot dead.").
We learned from Henry that there was a pulsing drive and vigor and style to
life in Brazil; you couldn't resist the booming energy; all you could do was to
give it an educated nudge now and then.

By this time *American Flag* was back in the water (after all the trouble
to get hauled I was surprised how low the charges were). My efforts with the
Travelift had succeeded, and now some of the other smaller yachts were taken
out for painting. Margaret and Remo helped get fresh stores for the next leg.
I bent on the new mainsail, which fitted perfectly and had a gorgeous shape. I
had asked North to make the third reef a little deeper, and when I reeved the
reefing pendant I found that the 12 mm. Samson braid line was sixty feet long
by the time it traveled from the mast, through the boom, up to the third
cringle on the leech, and back down to the boom (which gives an idea of the
size and cost of the gear on a fifty-foot yacht).

By now I had the autopilot working. An expert from the Monitor
company checked over the wind vane gear and made a few adjustments. I
changed the Richey compass for the Southern hemisphere (which has a different dip problem) to the Northern hemisphere compass and ran a couple of
amplitudes to check the deviation, which was only one or two degrees.
Margaret helped me string a new compass light wire, and I tidied up various
other wires. Meanwhile Remo shortened one of the lifelines and did a little
joinery job in the galley.

[From my journal]. March 21st.
   0625. I spoke with John Hughes last night. He has been making wonderful
time and is already around Cape Horn and up to Burdwood bank south of the
Falklands. He was at 54°40′S. and 60°58′W. and says that he has only 187 miles
to go. What an achievement to sail his handicapped vessel around Cape Horn
from the mid-Pacific. Some 4,200 miles so far!

   John was doing 6.5 knots and heading 040°T. Since I'd been to Mare
harbor, I passed on detailed information about the approaches. I suggested that
he stay *very close*—say one tenth of a mile—to the eastern shore of East
Falkland so he would have the option of anchoring. (If he got blown east, his
situation would be fairly desperate because of his food and water).*

   John could go on the west side of a small island (Lively island) south of
Choiseul sound. In case of a foul wind he would have to anchor because *Joseph
Young* couldn't sail to windward at all. John's hardest task would be to sail
westward in Choiseul sound because the strong prevailing winds were all from
westerly quadrants. He might have to anchor and wait for suitable conditions
to sail to Mare harbor. I advised him to tackle the unlighted entrance only in
daylight.

   "Don't forget about the two-mile rule," I said. "Remember what happened to Harry Mitchell."

---

* See map 13.

John was in good form but almost out of water. "I am making only half a pot of tea at a time because I have only four cups of water left," he said. "I am certainly looking forward to a whole pot of tea."

One morning I spoke to the race chairman about the weather report problem. "Excuse me for bringing up the subject of private weather reports again, but it's become an issue for the unsponsored yachts," I said. "Why can't the weather information be given to everyone? The sponsored vessels pay big sums for private forecasts and tactical tips from shore. The unsponsored vessels get none of this and are severely handicapped."

"Nothing can be changed for this race," said Robin Knox-Johnston, "but the system should be changed for the next race. I prefer the Whitbread round-the-world race scheme, in which information made available to one must be made available to all.

"You know I believe you Americans ought to be able to get free weather information for the fourth leg from the American meteorologist Bob Rice, who is already being used by several of the contestants in the race," said Robin. "Bob Rice is a friend of Peter Dunning."

I went to see Peter Dunning, a member of the race committee who was in Rio.

"Sure," said Peter. "Bob Rice will supply whatever you want. The cost will be $3,000 a month, payable in advance."

On March 23rd the news came through that *Joseph Young* had reached Mare harbor on East Falkland island. John Hughes had not only gotten to port unassisted after being dismasted, but he had sailed his damaged vessel 4,400 miles in forty-five days and rounded Cape Horn as well. It was a remarkable achievement. John was a master mariner in the Canadian merchant service and right from the first was determined to look after himself and not to call upon others to rescue him.

While John was slowly sailing toward East Falkland island, his friends in Canada had gotten him a new mast, rigging, sails, and deck gear, which was flown to the Falklands at no cost by military aircraft on routine delivery flights. Not only did all his new gear appear, but two rigging experts flew south from Canada to help install *Joseph Young's* replacement rig.

It was a big job to deal with the new mast, boom, sails, pulpit, and deck gear. John and various helpers at Mare harbor worked at top speed and overcame one problem after another. Not only did John have to go out on sea trials to test and adjust everything, but he had to put stores and water aboard while he masterminded the whole project. John finally sailed for Rio de Janeiro on April 5th, six days before the fourth leg was to start.

Meanwhile 1,850 miles to the north in Rio, I got acquainted with

Joseph Young on her arrival at East Falkland island. Note the bipod rig made up of two eighteen-foot spinnaker poles and the storm trysail set as the mainsail. John Hughes' pluck in crossing half of the Pacific and rounding Cape Horn with this rig will be long remembered.

Darker B. de Mattos, a prominent member of the Rio yacht club. Darker spoke flawless English and was an enthusiastic sailor. He kindly presented me with a set of Brazilian pilot charts for the Atlantic and marked them up with his own observations from years of sailing up and down the coast. At the top of the April chart he wrote: "From here north, farewell and Godspeed." It was a nice gift.

Two days before the start of the fourth leg to Newport, the yachts were asked to go out sailing for photographs. A professional film maker named Julian Plowright was hard at work on a video presentation of the race. Julian chartered a fast launch and a helicopter, and we made arrangements to meet out in the ocean in the late afternoon. As five or six BOC yachts were tacking out the entrance of Rio's great bay we were suddenly overtaken by a high-speed Brazilian navy launch. Men were frantically waving and gesturing for us to turn around and go back to the yacht club. Already, however, Julian's helicopter was circling overhead, and we could see the photo launch far out at sea. From the shouted Portuguese, Remo managed to work out that the navy was having military maneuvers with live ammunition and that the port was closed. The navy cared nothing about a film. "Go back. Go back," they shouted. The crewmen on the launch were shooting at us like six-year-olds with imaginary machineguns (rat-ta-ta-ta-ta-ta) to give us the idea. . . .

We turned around and sailed back to Botafogo bay, fed up with a wasted afternoon. When we saw Julian later, he was even more disenchanted, because the yacht club had arranged the whole movie exercise.

Brazilian tourist officials would have had us believe otherwise, but the public health standards of this largest South American country were steadily declining. Mosquito-borne malaria, yellow fever, and dengue (breakbone) fever were real problems. In addition, public water supplies were suspect for other severe ailments. Most people—particularly tourists—drank bottled water. This meant that when the BOC sailors left Rio we had to fill our water tanks with bottled water since the last thing we wanted at sea was the Brazilian Revenge. We needed about 2 liters per day, and because the time for the next leg was estimated at thirty days or so, each sailor had to have 60 liters of drinking water. Most took twice this amount, or 120 liters. Since the water came in 1-liter bottles, and there were fifteen yachts, this meant 15 times 120, or 1,800 bottles. Each bottle was expensive if bought in the club store, and it didn't take much savvy to suggest that someone in the BOC office ought to arrange for a tank truck to bring in a load of spring water, both for convenience and to save the high handling charges and the inconvenience of dealing with almost 2,000 bottles of water. Somehow we couldn't get through to the BOC officials the seriousness of this small problem, which became particularly aggravating. Finally at the last minute we had to buy the individual bottles at vast expense and lug case after case out to the yachts on the launch. The drinking water episode made the captains furious.

Harvey Berger from Newport Beach, California, had been an early entrant in the BOC race in his yacht *Lightspeed,* but he didn't make it to the starting line. Harvey was keen to do something for the American contestants, so he and his wife Edda (from Iceland) flew to Rio with a bag of goodies, which he loaned to three of the yachts for the last leg. Mike Plant was handed a satnav, Mark Schrader got a lightweight reaching staysail, and I was brought a weatherfax machine to substitute for my broken one. Harvey's generosity was a nice gesture. Unfortunately, the special paper for the weatherfax machine was left behind.

On the morning of April 11th, the day the race was to start again, there was still no sign of a spinnaker pole. Margaret refused to mention the subject. I was resolved to sail without a second pole. Remo was still hopeful ("The fellow promised."). Finally at 1100, one hour before we were to be towed out to the start, a man came hurrying along the stone quay (where I was tied up taking supplies) with a beautifully wrapped cylindrical object nineteen feet long. It was the pole! The day seemed like Christmas, and I unwrapped my present at once. The end fittings were well fastened, and the pole was beautifully painted and ready for sea. Incredible. The bill was only $130.

"See!" said Remo, "You've got to have faith."

I could only shake my head in amazement.

Just then David White from *Legend* came along the seawall and handed me a roll of special paper for Harvey Berger's Furuno weatherfax machine. "I knew I had some on board somewhere," said David. "Here's a present for you!"

The sixteen competitors at the start of leg 4 in order of their standing:

CLASS I (8)

name	yacht	length	designer
Philippe Jeantot	*Credit Agricole*	60 ft.	Guy Ribadeau Dumas
Titouan Lamazou	*Ecureuil d'Aquitaine*	60 ft.	Bouvet, Petit and Ogden
Jean-Yves Terlain	*UAP*	60 ft.	Joubert and Nivelt
Guy Bernardin	*Biscuits Lu*	60 ft.	Joubert and Nivelt
John Martin	*Tuna Marine*	60 ft.	Angelo Lavranos
Bertie Reed	*Stabilo Boss*	60 ft.	Bruce Farr
Ian Kiernan	*Spirit of Sydney*	60 ft.	Ben Lexcen
David White	*Legend Securities*	56 ft.	Kelly, Gurney and Bergstrom

CLASS II (8)

name	yacht	length	designer
J. L. Van Den Heede	*Let's Go*	45 ft.	Leif Angermark
Mike Plant	*Airco Distributor*	50 ft.	Rodger Martin
Hal Roth	*American Flag*	50 ft.	Bill Lee
Harry Harkimo	*Belmont Finland*	50 ft.	Germán Frers Jr.
Richard Konkolski	*Declaration*	44 ft.	N.a.
Mark Schrader	*Lone Star*	49 ft.	Robert Perry
Pentti Salmi	*Colt by Rettig*	47 ft.	Hoken Sodergren
John Hughes	*Joseph Young*	42 ft.	Hoken Sodergren

. . . .

CHAPTER TWENTY-FIVE

Back to the Equator

*A*t noon on April 11th the fifteen BOC yachts were towed from the yacht club to the starting line out in the Atlantic off Punta do Arpoador at the east end of Rio's great Ipanema beach. The tropical sky was clear and beautiful, and a light wind blew from the southeast. A slight haze lay over the mountains to the north as the sails on the BOC boats went up one by one, and the fellows began to sail back and forth on a tranquil ocean.

A launch filled with wives and sweethearts and friends pulled alongside *American Flag.* I shook hands with Remo, kissed Margaret goodbye, and thanked them for their help. My trusty crew jumped aboard the launch, and I glided away and began to get a feel for the sailing conditions. *Biscuits Lu* was near me and slowly sailing under her mainsail alone, a new sail of shiny white Dacron with accents of brown Kevlar here and there. *Colt* was prominent in the fleet because the top of her triangular mainsail was painted bright red. The other twelve yachts milled around the committee boat. On this day there was no confusion, no press of spectator boats, no hard sailing conditions. After the frantic earlier starts with congestion and collisions and trouble, the 2 P.M. start at Rio was easy.

Since there was plenty of room, I decided to stay a bit to leeward to avoid a possible collision with the other yachts clustered around the commit-

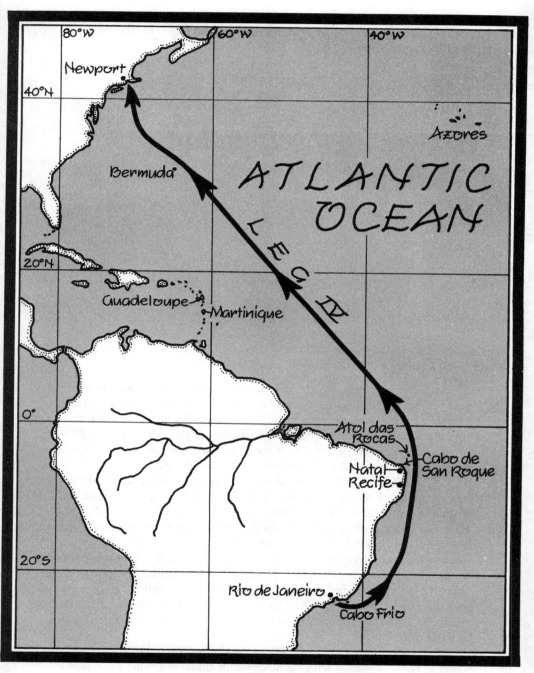

16. Rio de Janeiro to Newport

tee boat. In a month-long leg of almost five thousand miles, what was a few hundred feet at the start? I dared not risk a collision because I had absolutely no resources for repairs.

Just before the start, Jean Luc Van Den Heede in *Let's Go* approached me at high speed on port tack while I had right of way on starboard. I could see that Jean Luc's head was down while he adjusted something at the forward end of *Let's Go's* cockpit. The French captain certainly wasn't aware of me. I reached for my horn to give him a beep, but there was no time, and I swerved sharply to port to avoid the French yacht. As *American Flag* flashed by *Let's Go's* cockpit I called out to Jean Luc, who suddenly looked up wide-eyed as the yachts almost touched. The startled French captain patted his heart with embarrassment and flashed his eyes heavenward. I smiled at my friend and wished him good luck and fair winds.

At the starting gun there were a few moments of confusion and some bumps and shouts while the vessels got clear of one another. Then John Martin on *Tuna Marine* and Bertie Reed on *Stabilo Boss* emerged in the lead and were soon charging to the east. *Stabilo Boss* looked good, although the Bruce Farr design left a strangely disturbed wake behind her in the water. I had an excellent start (third I believe) and rushed after the leaders. The wind increased a little, and *Tuna Marine* must have been doing eleven knots with her water ballast, twelve-foot draft, and fifty-four-foot waterline.

The first destination on the route north was Cabo Frio, a headland east of Rio de Janeiro. At Cabo Frio the coastline of Brazil changes from an east-west direction and runs to the north-northeast for a thousand miles. The men in the race had a choice. In winds expected to come from easterly quadrants we could either tack to the north along the coast or keep going east until we were offshore far enough to tack north to clear the hump of Brazil. The coastal route was shorter, and the mountains and shoreline were intriguing to watch from the sea as you sailed along. Nevertheless, there was danger of running into the shore, coastal shipping traffic, offshore oil rigs, a south-flowing current (unless you were really close to shore), and possible calms and fluky winds generated by the daily heating and cooling of the land along the coast. The easterly route was longer, but there was a chance of steadier winds. Since I had fought the current and marginal winds along the coast on an earlier trip, my decision was easy: get offshore at once.

The next mark on the way to Newport was a point a few miles east of the Brazilian city of Recife (rah-SEE-fee) near eight degrees south latitude. Once clear of Brazil (Cabo de São Roque) and a few offshore islands, it was a straight shot to Bermuda and Newport with the likelihood of fair or reaching winds all the way except when crossing the Gulf Stream and approaching the American coast.

In tabular form my hoped-for course looked like this:

Starting line at Rio de Janeiro to Cabo Frio (23°S.; 43°11′30″W. to 23°02′S.; 42°W.)	66
Distance to an arbitrary offshore tacking point to head north (23°S.; 37°W.)	278
Recife (offshore point at 8°S.; 33°50′W.)	919
Bermuda (a little to the east: 32°10′N.; 64°W.)	2,973
Newport (Brenton tower finish line at 41°26′N.; 71°23′W.)	660
	total 4,896 miles

My first problem was to get around Cabo Frio, a small island at the end of a series of long beaches that stretched eastward from Rio for sixty-six miles. The local wisdom was to sail as close to the beach as possible to beat the west-flowing current ("just at the edges of the breaking waves"). This was good advice for a vessel with a large crew, but impossible for a singlehander. I tacked a half-mile from shore and continued sailing east with the big North genoa working to perfection in the light airs. I could see the rest of the fleet doing the same.

Late in the afternoon the wind increased to fifteen knots from the southeast. I changed down from the genoa, which was always an awkward business with the roller furling gear. As usual I gathered in the sail on the heeling foredeck with one hand while I eased the halyard with the other hand. This time the halyard slipped away from me. The big sail plummeted down on deck, and with the luff not attached to anything kept right on going over the side and instantly became a giant sea anchor. A moment before I was going along at eight knots. Now *American Flag* was dead in the water. It seemed to take ages to haul the 915 sq. ft. sopping wet sail back on board.

I then hoisted the yankee, but the luff tape got fouled. It took two tries to get the sail up properly. Finally I got going again, but I had thrown away an hour or more and a lot of energy. By now I knew for certain that it was patently unseamanlike to change sails on a furling gear at sea. With a better arrangment for handling the genoa, I would have used this important sail much more often and with a great deal less effort. It's an axiom of sailing that if something is hard or difficult, you tend to avoid it.

Later when I was reefing the mainsail a seagoing tug came close on a collision course. It was just at dusk so I rushed below and turned on my bright deck running lights to augment the masthead navigation light. By now we were close-hauled into twenty-two knots of apparent wind and going nicely at six to seven knots. I sat in the cockpit and watched the shore lights and coastal ships while I ate part of a meal that Margaret had prepared before I left.

[From the log]. April 11th.

2020. We are making long tacks, so I can nap for half an hour or so on the offshore leg. I seem to have no strength for winching and hoisting and lifting. Too much soft living in Rio! Also I burned myself twice last night. Once on the stove and once with a soldering iron while dealing with an electrical problem. I am a danger to myself! I need a few days to get sorted out and under control.

2210. A snatch block unexpectedly opened when I was tacking, and the flogging sheet gave me a good crack on the back of the neck. I saw stars for a minute. Will this day ever end?

There was a bright moon, the coast was well lighted by shoreside dwellings, and the soundings were gradual. I made good time, and soon the Cabo Frio light was winking in the distance. By midnight I was past the cape and into a northeast wind and sea. The south-setting current was charted at 0.8 knot. Two fishing boats with practically no lights came very close, and I was obliged to run off to avoid them. I was glad to be heading offshore.

At noon the next day I showed 131 miles and was banging along close-hauled in nineteen knots of wind. I spoke with Jean Luc on the radio and heard that *Ecureuil* was going to protest *Colt, Spirit of Sydney,* and *Credit Agricole* for bad starting line maneuvers. I was pleased that I had kept a little distance at the start.

At the beginning of the fourth leg of the race in Class II, Mike Plant in *Airco Distributor* had a lead of more than four days over Jean Luc in *Let's Go.* Mike was a tough, determined sailor who had built his vessel with his own hands and had sailed her well throughout the race. All Mike needed to win his class was to have a reasonable passage on the last leg. But the handsome, thirty-five-year-old American from Rhode Island had bad luck at the start. On the first night his half-inch-diameter, nineteen-strand stainless steel head-stay wire broke at the bottom of the stay.

"I had to cut everything down," said Mike on the radio. "The jib and the roller furling gear all came down on the deck in a crash and then fell overboard. It was an absolute mess."

Mike set about to make repairs. He put a Norseman wire-end fitting on the bottom of the headstay and shackled on a piece of heavy anchor chain to extend the shortened wire. In order to hold his sails to the stay, Mike attached bronze hanks along the luffs of the sails. He had forty hanks, only about half of what he needed, but he thought he could manage.

By noon on April 13th I was 208 miles east of Cabo Frio and hammering away close-hauled into fifteen knots of wind from the northeast. There was a lot of water flying around, and I had the yacht closed up to stay dry, which made it hot and airless below. I made a mental note to put in a couple of Dorade vents in the future.

That evening the wind eased to twelve knots. I immediately hoisted more sail. It was a lovely night with a clear sky. A full moon came up from ahead in the east, and the sea glittered with a thousand silver mirrors. Later the brilliant constellation of Orion rose in the sky to my left; the Southern Cross, Hadar, and Rigel Kentaurus glowed in the black sky to my right. I was eating hugely after a few skimpy days, sleeping a lot, and getting back my strength after the rigors of Rio and the trials of the start. I felt marvelous.

At midnight I reached thirty-seven degrees west and tacked to starboard. Twelve hours later I showed a noon run of only 100 miles because I'd sailed two sides of a triangle (the daily run is based on mileage made good from successive noon positions, not the distance sailed). Now at last I was headed roughly northward into a northeast wind. Where were the others?

[From the log]. April 14th.

1206. This morning there was a great crash as a galley drawer suddenly opened (I'd forgotten to turn the catch) and dumped its contents on the cabin sole. The weather is quite settled. We are hard on the wind, changing back and forth slightly as the wind shifts a little from the northeast. The Monitor vane is handling the shifts well. The Argos information from France shows that *Belmont* is ahead, but the winds are reported to be variable along the coast where all the fleet is except *Let's Go, Airco,* and *American Flag.*

I've been sewing bands of sticky-back sail-mending tape on the genoa where it got torn on the staysail hanks last Saturday. The new mainsail has marvelous shape and is performing very well, although the black draft stripes have peeled off because they were not sewn in place.

Yesterday I spilled a plate of chicken and rice (made from a freeze-dried package) in the cockpit. I thought I had cleaned it all up, but this morning I found a big lump of the stuff that had solidified into a hard, flint-like substance that gives me pause about eating any more such food. Think of digesting such a meal!

I learned that Harry Harkimo on *Belmont* was having a tough time. Although Harry had stayed in the finest hotels in Rio, he had contracted an acute case of the trots. Poor Harry's stomach inflammation was so severe (he could eat nothing at all) that a local doctor ordered him to remain in Rio until he recovered. Harry refused to stay in bed, however, and left with the fleet. He was sailing well along the coast, but it took a week before he began to eat proper meals and feel like a human being again. It was a tough business to sail by yourself when you were sick.

On the next four days I had runs of 174, 160, 180, and 175 miles—an average of 7.18 knots—in easterly winds of 15 knots or so, although the wind range went up and down as usual. I was trying to stay offshore to make a straight-line course to the north-northeast to clear Recife and the hump of Brazil without tacking. As we got farther north we began to get into the confluence of the Brazilian (southbound) and Guiana (northwest-bound) currents, which made the sea a bit agitated and gave me another reason to work offshore.

Gradually we moved closer to the equator, and the heat on the yacht got more intense each day, especially because I was hard on the wind with the portlights and the front hatch closed. From time to time big white-tailed tropicbirds fluttered past *American Flag*. How well I knew their rapid wing flaps, nervous habits, and chi–chi–chi–chi calls.

On April 16th I heard from Mark Schrader for the first time since the leg had begun. Mark had been in a severe blue funk because of various frustrations in Rio and—snapping at everyone—had vowed to stay off the radio. I missed his usual cheery voice and bubbling optimism. Now after five days of solitude, his spirits were rising. Mark said that he had been tacking along the coast and was thirty miles offshore. He had just gone on deck when he suddenly saw a man's head at the bow of *Lone Star*.

"I figured he'd bagged it," said Mark. "I must have missed the guy by six feet, but I didn't hit him, and as I went past his rowboat we both waved. The fisherman was utterly unperturbed; I was shaking like a leaf.

"When I looked around I saw rowboats all over the place," said Mark, who learned that a local mother ship towed out dozens of rowboats every morning.

Bertie Reed relayed position reports of the fleet, which showed every-one closely grouped, with *UAP* in the lead and *Declaration* far behind. Bertie mentioned that the gas regulator on his stove had packed up, which meant cold food for the next twenty days. I was a firm believer in kerosene Primus stoves and always carried a small spare stove and a few extra jugs of kerosene. I wish I could have passed the spare stove to Bertie.

I stopped using the Monitor wind vane gear to replace a worn steering line and found that the Alpha autopilot wouldn't work. I discovered that the small electric motor which ran the screwjack—the part that did the actual steering—had burned out. I had a spare so I got busy and replaced the defective motor. I had to roll up the headsail for two hours to slow the yacht while I changed the autopilot drive and soldered various small wires. It was fix fix fix all day long!

My energy level had been low since leaving Rio, and I missed Margaret and Remo. I felt hot and ill-tempered, so to boost my well-being I had an extra-thorough wash and shave. I then put on clean clothes, mixed myself a stiff bourbon and water, and cooked a hearty meal. Meanwhile I listened to *Siddhartha* by Herman Hesse, a book on tape beautifully read by Derek Jacobi. My horizons looked better.

The big sixty-foot French yacht *Credit Agricole* led the eight entrants in Class I by three and a half days. Most people thought that *Ecureuil* was faster (she had won leg 2 by more than five hours, and lost leg 3 by only four hours). On the first leg, however, Titouan Lamazou—suffering from technical problems—had arrived almost four days behind *Credit Agricole.* If Philippe Jeantot sailed a conservative, safe fourth leg, he was certain to win.

Nevertheless, the big cream and green *Credit Agricole,* with her ugly bulging topsides, was lucky to be in first place and even more fortunate not to be an abandoned, half-sunken hulk floating on her side because her lead keel had come off. As we've seen, only luck and a good engine-driven bilge pump kept the yacht afloat during leg 2. If Philippe had run out of diesel oil, or if his pump had failed to discharge *400 liters of water each hour,* the leading yacht would have been out of the race. Philippe knew this very well and was prepared to abandon his vessel, but in the meantime had pushed onward at high speed and—certainly with angels on his shoulders—had managed to get to Sydney before the keel fell off.

In Sydney—as we noted in Chapter 18—the vessel was lifted from the water and found to have five broken keel bolts. In addition, the stub keel—to which the lead ballast keel was fastened—needed major rebuilding. The shipyard bills for all this had totaled thousands of dollars. Earlier there had been the repairs in Cape Town.

Now on the fourth leg, *Credit Agricole* had a substantial lead and a chance of breaking the round-the-world course record by as much as twenty-four days. But there were new problems. Two days out of Rio, Philippe discovered that strands of wire on both his port and starboard mast shrouds were breaking and beginning to untwist. Already three strands (sixteen percent) of one wire cable had parted. Would the rest of the cable fail? In addition, his powerful main radio had stopped working, which meant that he couldn't receive private weather information or tactical advice from France.

Philippe sailed close to the Brazilian coast and used his VHF transmitter to call a shore station, which put him in contact with the French telephone network and the Credit Agricole officials. "There is a possibility I cannot finish the race because my rig is broken," he radioed across the crackling airwaves. "You must try to do the maximum, to organize a new rig in Recife, and you have just forty-eight hours."[39]

The bank people realized at once that their chance for golden publicity all over world might slip away from them just when victory was in sight. If their star sailor lost his rig and mast, their investment would be gone. Worse yet, all the publicity would go to Caisse d'Epargne Ecureuil, a competing French bank that was a principal sponsor of *Ecureuil d'Aquitaine!*

Philippe quickly outlined what he needed for the emergency repairs in northern Brazil. He reckoned that a well-organized stop should take no more than ten hours, which was trifling compared to the time he might lose if he sailed through the equatorial calms on his way north to Newport without the private weather information that he could receive only with a new radio.

His support group in France rushed into action. Rigging experts worked all night to cut and prepare new cables. Meanwhile radio specialists checked over a new single sideband set and a ham radio. The Credit Agricole people chartered a small plane, which flew around the country, collected everything, and met Philippe's assistant, who climbed on a big jet headed for Recife with all the boxes and rolls of cables. Two other French mechanics and a radio specialist were recruited in Brazil and flew north toward Recife.

Meanwhile the manager of the Credit Agricole bank branch in Brazil arranged for a powerful small tugboat in Recife and for the reception of the mechanics, their tools, and the boxes and cables on the incoming flights. In addition, the bank people fixed things with the local customs, immigration, police, and harbor officials so there would be none of the delays and wasted time so endemic in the tropics. Everything had to operate at high speed; there could be no waiting for import permits, no lost luggage, no visa problems, no difficult officials, no out-of-gas taxis—none of this—because the competition was speeding toward Newport! Damn the expenses! Would the tugboat be reliable? Charter a standby as well! The mechanics and their gear had to arrive on time and be rushed out to meet the French yacht. Could this all work? Would it all work? Nothing like this had ever been done before in a yacht race. What was banking coming to anyway?

At midnight on April 18th, *Credit Agricole* arrived outside the big port of Recife, a long U-shaped harbor with its entrance facing north. Philippe hadn't had a suitable chart for the approach, so his enterprising support crew had chartered a small airplane, which had flown out to meet the yacht some hours earlier and radio down information about dangers and where to go. All of this was allowable under the race rules.

The night was sweltering as usual at eight degrees south, and the sweet, cloying smell of tropical vegetation drifted across the water. Here and there lay anchored tankers and container ships, and in the distance a silhouetted cargo crane creaked wearily in front of a cluster of lights. Philippe wondered if he had been crazy to try such a meeting. Would the mechanics be there? Would the parts fit? Would the rig last to Newport? Where was Titouan and *Ecureuil?* The whole thing was like some sort of a spy movie. Was Humphrey Bogart watching from shore?

Suddenly—when Philippe was a little north of the harbor—a tugboat pulled alongside the big cream and green yacht. Philippe let out a great sigh of relief as Jean-Luc Bodineau, his faithful assistant, waved and climbed on board. Together the two Frenchmen furled the sails and took the towline. The tugboat quickly pulled the yacht to a large buoy near the harbor entrance, where *Credit Agricole* was made fast. Although it was night, the experts went to work at once. The electrician unpacked the new radios. The other men started on the rigging.

In order to change the shrouds, the mast spreaders had to be removed, but the threads on the root fittings had seized. The mechanics tried special lubricants, hammers, and wrenches, but they could not budge the big bolts. Faced with this new problem, Philippe decided not to replace the heavy wire shrouds, certainly a major undertaking in a thirteen-ton vessel at night in a rolly anchorage. Instead he reinforced each defective shoud by running a four-part tensioned rope tackle parallel to the entire length of the wire. Philippe was disappointed at not changing the cables; certainly the rope tackle reinforcement was a poor substitute.*

Meanwhile the electrician had repaired a short circuit in the ham radio wiring and had both of the new radios working. As dawn began to break in the east toward the open sea, Philippe announced that he was ready to go. The mechanics hoisted the mainsail for the weary captain, wished him a fast passage north, and jumped into the tugboat with their tools.

Philippe sailed northeast from Recife after a stop of only five and a half hours. It was a miracle. But it was a miracle conducted by a wealthy and powerful sponsor who wanted his entry to win. "Without such support and help, the race would have come to an end for me," said Philippe later.[40]

It's easy to say that such help is pretty tough for the unsponsored yachts to buck. There's no doubt that the statement is true. Yet the mark of a champion is to do all he can to win under the rules of a contest. Help such as *Credit Agricole* and many of the other yachts received during the race was legal under the rules. I may have been envious of such assistance, but it was permitted. If I had had access to such help and needed it, I would have used it to the maximum.

At noon on April 19th I was at 7°18'S., finally north of Recife, and sixty-three miles east of the hump of Brazil. The sea was fairly smooth, and the east wind a trifle freer. The area was a major crossing point of shipping lanes, and I had been seeing a big ship every four or five hours. While I was figuring the day's run (200 miles), I heard a thump on deck and went out to find a small silvery snake mackerel. I should have photographed the slithery fish before I heaved it over the side, but it was so horrible-looking that I was glad to see it go.

---

* It's unclear why *Credit Agricole's* spreaders had to be removed to change the shrouds. Certainly a far easier repair would have been to span the broken wires with short pieces of wire cable clamped to the existing wire above and below the damage with U-bolts or bulldog clamps, a common procedure. Or he could have cut off the damaged end, put on a new wire-end fitting (Norseman or Sta-Loc), and used shackles or a piece of chain to extend the shortened wire.

My satnav instrument spewed out a couple of faulty position fixes. The trouble came from infrequent satellite coverage near the equator, the long interval between fixes, and the high speed of the yacht. These three things combined to exceed the instrument's sixty-mile limit between fixes. I reprogrammed the satnav with my dead-reckoning position, but I was unsure of the current (I suspected one knot to the northwest). I had gotten so dependent on the device that I tended to panic when there was any problem when in truth one fix a day was sufficient. If I'd been using a sextant I would have been quite happy with two sun shots in twenty-four hours. These electronic devices were like eating salted peanuts—the more you had, the more you wanted.

After lunch the wind backed to the east-southeast. I put up a spinnaker, but the wind was unsteady, and the chute jumped around a lot and required constant tending. Late in the afternoon I dropped the spinnaker (while a ship steamed nearby) and hoisted the genoa, which I poled out to leeward. With the genoa and full main, *American Flag* made good speed with a controllable, easily adjustable rig. After six straight hours on deck in the tropical sun changing and adjusting and trimming sails, I was able to go below for a meal and a nap.

By midnight we were 73 miles east of Natal, Brazil. It was goodbye to South America as the coastline began to fall away to the northwest. I was worried about driving down on an isolated island—Atol das Rocas, 124 miles offshore—so I kept careful track of our position. The wind was up to twenty-one knots from the east-southeast, and we were tearing along with both the full main and genoa while the autopilot steered flawlessly. By 0715 the next morning I was seeing lots of terns, presumably from the island.

As we neared the equator I noticed significant changes in the Greenwich time shown on the satnav, whose time I always thought was inviolate once the machine was running. Now I began to pay attention to this detail and noticed thirty-second fluctuations. It appeared that the satnav lost one or more minutes each time it missed a satellite pass. I began to reprogram the instrument with the time from my two quartz crystal watches, which were accurate to a half a second a day.

Near the atoll we ran into one squall after another. I put a reef in the mainsail and rolled up the genoa on the furling gear as needed. We sailed past thousands of birds resting on the water: noddies, blue-footed boobies, masked boobies, and terns. I decided to cook some potatoes for lunch, but I found that my nice new potatoes had been stored in a plastic sack (instead of on an open dry rack) and had spoiled because of moisture. I dumped the potatoes over the side and stored the plastic with my other plastic junk for land disposal later.

At noon I logged 225 miles, an average of 9.4 knots. During the afternoon I had a brief radio chat with Pentti Salmi, the first since Rio. The weather continued to be squally, and as daylight fell I wound the genoa in and out.

Joseph Young arrived in Rio de Janeiro on April 20th, the same day that I passed Atol das Rocas, 1,273 miles to the north. John's total time for the Sydney-to-Rio leg was ninety-two and a half days, more than three months.

"I was very apprehensive as I approached Rio," John told me later. "I had opted for continuing the race at sea. I called again and again on various radio frequencies, but there were no answers—even three miles from the finish line. Suddenly I saw a fifty-foot launch coming toward me. In it were two Brazilians—Nora and Fillet, who had worked in the BOC office. Near the line, however, I was becalmed. Nora and Fillet took photographs of me from the launch and then went off. Finally a little wind came up, and I crossed the line off Ipanema beach.

"The launch then came alongside and passed across food, bottled water, and a new sail," said John. "I took a shower on the launch, and we had some champagne. There was a newspaper reporter from Canada aboard and a gorgeous girl with the skimpiest bikini swimming suit. I had trouble keeping my eyes away from her. Maybe I'd been at sea too long.

"I then got sailing again, crossed the line, and was off on the fourth leg for Newport," said the Canadian sailor. "In all, the restart only took about three hours, which was a quick turnaround. Unfortunately, just before I left, a couple of swells rolled the yacht against the launch and bent several of *Joseph Young's* lifeline stanchions."

I spoke with John on the radio many times and gradually heard the details of his adventures. He had had a bad time after Cape Horn.

"It was the only time I was really knocked down," said John. "It was unbelievable. All the drawers came out. Various bottles from the galley were broken, and pickle relish was flying all over the place. Every one of the floorboards came out as well. I was sleeping on the settee, and suddenly I was buried in tools and food. It took a while to get back to normal.

"However I am a great believer in luck," said John. "Everything worked out in the end."

When John approached East Falkland island he stayed close to Lively island. "All I could see was a line of breakers ahead," he said. "It was pretty frightening. I went up the east coast of Lively island about a half mile off and made long tacks and gradually crept in. A navy ship was standing by and gave me a tow.

"I was extremely lucky to get in," said John. "I was absolutely exhausted." The new mast and other things were late because the Canadian plane that took the parts to England had engine trouble and missed the twice-weekly connecting flight to the Falklands.

"I never left Mare harbor," said John. "The facilities were excellent, and the men were a great bunch of guys who couldn't do enough for me.

"We stepped the mast by moving *Joseph Young* alongside a cargo ship and using one of the ship's cranes. It was blowing fifty-five knots when the mast went in, but I couldn't wait any longer. I had to get going. Fortunately we had lots of manpower—in fact, we had men from three ships helping.

"After I made it to the Falklands there was a lot of talk in the Canadian press," said John. "Interested people in Halifax raised $20,000, and a Halifax fishing company gave me $50,000 with almost no strings. ('Our whole business is being at sea,' said the company man. 'We think what you've done was terrific, and we want to help. Just give a few talks to schoolchildren.'). After being a poor sailor for so long it was all unbelievable!"

John's new mast was donated, but he had to pay for the rigging, sails, pulpits, and other gear. The fishing company also gave him a new spinnaker.

[From the log]. April 21st.

0920. A long night of rain and squalls. My shoulders and arms are about winched out. I need to trade in my body for a new model.

1225. 185 miles today. A little earlier I spent half an hour in the lazarette checking over the autopilot and tightened the drive arm pivot bolt. A few of the parts are rusty as old nails so I oiled everything in sight.

Pentti reported that his yacht broaches every time he transmits on his single sideband radio. Apparently his Autohelm 6000 autopilot (unshielded in its plastic case) is inordinately sensitive to high frequency radio signals. I don't have this problem, perhaps because my autopilot lives inside a metal case. I must suggest that Pentti try wrapping his autopilot in aluminum cooking foil, if he has any. It might help.

The weather has cleared, and I've been looking up at masses of splendid clouds. High in the distance is a layer of wispy cirrus so thin that the clouds appear a bit bluish from the sky behind. Closer and a little lower is a solid bank of clouds tinged with yellow. Not a lot of yellow, just white brushed with the morning sun. Then nearer and not so high is a thick layer of clouds as white as bleached cotton. Finally low down and close by is a bank of stratus (in the shade of other clouds) touched with gray. I never thought about different colors of clouds before, but I have been able to see four tints at once: blue, yellow, white, and gray.

We crossed the equator today and soon should run out of the southeast trade wind, which for me has come mainly from the east. God only knows what will happen during the next two weeks. I could be first or last.

CHAPTER TWENTY-SIX

Newport

*W*hen I was a child I liked to walk along beaches looking for bottles with messages in them. I always hoped to find a scrawl from a pirate, or a frantic communication from a sinking ship. Or maybe even a dollar bill. I found lots of bottles, but they were always empty.

Now instead of a seeker I was a sender. On April 22nd I had an empty wine bottle in which I'd put a piece of paper with my name, address, the name of the ship and her position, and an offer of $5 for the return of the message. I shoved home the cork and tossed the bottle over the side. Would I ever hear from that youngster on the beach?

That noon I chalked up 194 miles in reaching winds that averaged 11 knots. I tried hard to exceed 200 miles, but it was difficult to average 8.3 knots.

I cleaned out all the lockers in the galley and found that most of the Brazilian onions had gone bad. Part of the trouble was my fault, and I resolved to always store onions in string bags, not in plastic. By a lot of judicious cutting out of bad parts and careful slicing, however, I managed to get half a pot of onions, which I put on the stove to make my favorite soup. During spare moments I read in Squire Lecky's *Wrinkles,* an obsolescent book on navigation by a famous captain who wrote marvelous stuff a century ago. Some of the material was old-fashioned, but Lecky's devotion to prudent sea-keeping was legendary, and my copy of his book was the *22nd edition,* which will give an idea of his reputation to seamen of the past.

There wasn't too much time for reading, however, because I had lots of squalls and rain. In the late afternoon the sky got quite dark with a thick bank of altocumulus. "A heavy blue to the east, a cerulean blue overhead, and a greenish tinge to the south," I noted. It looked like the end of the world was coming, but after an hour of lightning and thunder and a little rain, the weather cleared.

Jean Luc told me that he painted the bottom of *Let's Go* with a special paint (made by International) for big ships that keep moving. The paint was no good for harbors and layovers, but excellent for seagoing. The paint was red when it went on but soon became gray and very smooth.

My borrowed Furuno weatherfax machine had steadfastly refused to run since Rio, though I had tried every dodge I knew to make it work. In the middle of the night I got an idea: Could the wires that power the device be hooked up backward? The next morning I switched the polarity and clicked on the switch. Suddenly the machine awoke from its long sleep, began to chatter and talk, and to print out a weather chart on silver paper.

The Finnish boat *Belmont* was going well in the fourth leg. Harry Harkimo had recovered from his illness, and—with steady advice from Europe—was driving the heavy Swan for all she was worth. For a time *Belmont* and *Let's Go* sailed almost in sight of one another and talked back and forth on VHF radio.

Mark Schrader, John Hughes, Jean Luc, and I discussed at length the race committee's handling of Harry Mitchell in New Zealand. We believed that with advice and help, Harry could have continued in the race. We thought that the committee should have worked more *to keep people going in the race*—particularly after they had completed more than half—and not to have been so concerned about safety and danger and *taking people out of the race.*

Though the circumstances were different, John Hughes had refused to pull out after his mishap. He had calmly kept going and eventually surmounted his problem. If Harry Mitchell had done the same he would still have been in the race. Harry got a tow exceeding two miles, but since the tow was in the opposite direction and Harry was in last place, the rule clauses that gave the committee some discretion certainly could have been used. Instead of Harry being told that he could apply to the committee for relief, he was told that he had broken a rule and that was it. John, Mark, Jean Luc, and I all hoped that Harry would try the race again in the future and perhaps be better prepared, but the likelihood was slim because the costs of entering would no doubt escalate and make private entries harder and harder.

The BOC race was a dangerous enterprise with some degree of risk, and the chance of two or three fatalities always hovered in the background. Nevertheless, the entrants accepted the challenge. Each captain had ample experience, a qualifying trip behind him, and a well-equipped, inspected vessel.

Fear didn't seem to be a problem with the fellows in the race; it was the people on shore who were the scaredy cats. Once the sailors had entered the race, they accepted the various dangers and worked either to conquer a problem or to skirt it. Certainly each sailor got pleasure and satisfaction from making his complicated wind machine work. The "death or glory" attitude of the media was all wrong. The captains wanted to complete a good voyage. To win would have been wonderful, but just to finish such an undertaking was a small victory, too.

For myself I well knew that this race was the watershed event between amateur and professional sailing. By making the yachts big and costly, and rigging the sailing help and publicity in favor of sponsored superstars, the little guys were gradually being forced out. (I hoped I was wrong, but I doubted it.)

One morning I turned on the radio while I made breakfast and heard the most lilting African music from Mali. Intricate and bewitching melodies with the most appealing rhythms—delicate traces of rock, calypso, and even an occasional chord from a hymn. I could visualize fairies dancing. Stravinsky would have loved it.

[From the log]. April 23rd.
0930. It's been raining steadily for two hours. I must have caught forty-five or fifty liters of water, which I put in the starboard tank. A moment ago I was standing in the cockpit getting my breath after unrolling much of the genoa when a flying fish whizzed diagonally across the coachroof (from starboard to port), cleared everything, and made it back to the sea. The first time I've ever seen that! The fish made a slight buzzing sound as it zipped past me.
0945. The nut on the autopilot drive arm pivot bolt worked loose again. I replaced the elastic stop nut with another (perhaps newer).
1103. An exhausting morning. I got chilled in all the rain and took a small brandy (a bad sign in the morning). I was so hungry that I cooked a big meal of roast beef, mashed potatoes, and gravy. I must keep driving!
1200. 192 miles.
1753. Lots of flying fish. Sometimes a hundred or more at one time suddenly jumped from the surface of the sea. One curious tropicbird, and one brown, stubby-winged bird, a giant petrel, I think.

The next day the wind was a little more northerly, and there were more squalls, which dropped my mileage to 180. The squalls kept me busy reefing and unreefing the sails. I discovered that when I transmitted on single side-band radio the apparent wind speed on the Brookes & Gatehouse indicator jumped from sixteen to thirty-two knots.

The Class II standings on April 24th relative to *American Flag:*

Airco	+118 miles ahead
Let's Go	+55
Belmont	+51
Colt	+16
Lone Star	−45 behind
Declaration	−208
Joseph Young	−1,803

The following morning I had a good breakfast of melon, tea, cereal, two boiled eggs, and cake. At noon (196 miles) *American Flag* was at 9°21′N. The wind had settled in the northeast at seventeen knots. My course was roughly northwest, which meant that I was close-reaching. The upsetting factor was the continuing squally weather. Visibility was poor. There had been a sort of damp haze or ephemeral fog ever since we had gotten to the northeast trade wind. It was still hot. To keep the sweat from smudging my writing I had to rest my forearm on a cloth. I had been troubled with a small leak in the head plumbing for several days and had been swamping out a bucket of water every ten hours or so. It was too rough to take the plumbing to pieces, but I finally discovered a loose hose clamp on a line that I hadn't suspected earlier.

Colt was only a dozen miles away so that evening Pentti Salmi and I had a long talk on the VHF radio. The Finnish sailor had been unable to have his vessel hauled out in Rio. Since he was not only a sailor but a flier and a diver as well, he elected to put on his scuba tanks and mask and to scrub the bottom of *Colt*. "It was easy for me," he said, "a fairly routine business."

Unfortunately, the warm water of Botafogo bay was horribly polluted with sewage, and during the scrubbing Pentti cut one of his thumbs slightly on a sharp barnacle. He thought nothing about it, just a minor scratch, but now, nine days later, the trifling scratch had turned into something nasty.

"My left hand is infected," he said. "I can't use it at all. I'm going to try to get medical advice.

[From the log]. April 26th.

0415. A lot of crashing and banging as we rush along. Generator on twice in the night for a thirty-minute charge. We seem to be more heeled than ever. I move around the cabin like a robot, clutching at handholds and leaning my butt against the cabin furniture. Still 2,315 nautical miles to go to Newport. Will we ever break 2,000? We're on the same latitude as Trinidad and Tobago, which are 1,000 miles to the west.

0749. The visibility is a little better—especially overhead, where I can see a bit of blue sky and a few high clouds. Closer down, however, the murk and poor visibility persist. This sort of sailing is a bore. Same weather, same wind, same sails, same angle of heel, and the same lack of ventilation with the vessel all closed up.

1200. Wind east-northeast 20 knots. 218 miles at noon. My average for 2,668 miles from Rio is 178, or 7.4 knots. I've got to push harder.

Late in the afternoon I spoke with Pentti again. His infection sounded nasty. "I dug some of the bad stuff out of my thumb," he said. "It's bad all the way up to my armpit. I hope it will go no further." Pentti was taking antibiotics and following advice from a Coast Guard doctor in Miami. "The doctor's advice was pretty cheeky," said Pentti. " 'You'll either be better or dead in three days,' he said, 'so stop worrying.' "

I began to realize that Pentti's problem was very severe when he spoke of diverting to Bermuda (1,633 miles north-northwest from my noon position). He also mentioned a helicopter.

That evening I had a pleasant meal in the cockpit while reaching along at nine to ten knots (once twelve). Each night the Big Dipper rose higher in the sky toward the north. I looked forward to seeing the North Star again, but there were low clouds in that direction. Earlier in the day I saw that the starboard side of the rig—the African side—was covered with red dust, presumably from the Sahara desert. David White on *Legend* and Ian Kiernan on *Spirit of Sydney* also reported reddish sails. Though I tried to pay attention to sailing, I couldn't help but worry about Pentti. "What can I do to help him?" I said to myself.

[From the log]. April 26th.

2118. Since Pentti is quite ill, and my radio capability is excellent, I have been relaying information between *Colt* and Chuck Ashworth (W1BIS), a Rhode Island doctor who is a ham radio operator. Can Pentti move his fingers? (yes). Temperature? (no). Name of oral antibiotics on board (Ermysin and Tricanix). Pentti was told to elevate his arm and to wrap it in a hot, moist towel. He was to continue the oral antibiotics for seven to ten days. Between days five and seven there should be an improvement; if not, he should go to an injectable antibiotic (which he did not have on board).

Pentti reported that he had split open his thumb and drained out a lot of putrid matter. The red line of infection had gone up his arm to his armpit, but not further. Pentti suspected barnacle or diesel fuel poisoning.

Pentti's Finnish doctor is Miss Myllymaki. I gave her Helsinki telephone number to Dr. Ashworth, who wanted to call her to discuss Pentti and the antibiotics that she had packed in his medical kit. Pentti was ill last night and asked me (1) to find out what shipping (with medical doctors aboard) is in the area and (2) to notify the U.S. Coast Guard doctor in Miami that Pentti is still among the living. I was glad to see that even in adversity, Pentti's sense of humor was alive.

In the middle of the night there was a great crash on deck. When I slipped up to find the cause, I saw the main boom waving around in the night. One of the snapshackles on the Schaefer boom vang tackle had somehow worked open. It was only the work of a minute to ease the tackle, resecure it, and to crank in some tension again. I then took a careful look around, decided the wind was lighter, and unrolled more of the genoa.

After sunrise there was less murk in the air. As the latitude climbed (we were now at fourteen degrees north), the air seemed to get clearer. I saw blue sky overhead and a blue sea around the yacht. Not deep blue colors because some murk persisted, but certainly the conditions were better than a few days earlier.

While I was cooking breakfast, a squadron of fruit flies invaded the galley. I got out my fly swatter and killed a dozen or so and worked toward the source. I discovered that all my Brazilian eggs had gone bad and were alive with horrible swarming and flying insects, no doubt a breeding ground for the ultimate pestilence. The smell was terrible. Ugh! I heaved all the eggs over the side and scrubbed the containers with soap and furiously boiling water.

During the morning I relayed Pentti's condition to Dr. Ashworth and the doctor's instructions back to *Colt*. Pentti thought that he was slightly better, but he was very tired and had a slight fever. He was able to move the fingers of his injured hand except for his infected thumb and forefinger. He had some pain in his armpit, but less than the day before; the red line was still under his armpit. He was taking oral antibiotic medicine, one pill every six hours and another every eight hours. He drained more white matter from his thumb, and covered the wound with antibiotic Band-Aids.

Pentti wanted to know what his symptoms would be if his condition got worse, and the time frame, since he figured eight days to Bermuda. He asked me to call the Coast Guard doctor in Miami and tell him what was happening. Again Pentti asked for a list of cruise ships—or other large vessels with a doctor aboard—that were near him.

Dr. Ashworth said that if the infection spread to Pentti's bloodstream he would have the shakes and chills and be cold all over for about five minutes once each hour. And no appetite. The swollen lymph nodes and the red line should begin to go away or diminish in one to three days after taking the antibiotics; if not, he should begin intravenous antibiotics. Pentti was told to soak his bad fingers in peroxide, then cover with antibiotics and bandage. If no peroxide was on board, then fresh water or sea water. He should continue the hot soaks for his entire arm and elevate the limb. The doctor was not surprised that Pentti was tired.

Pentti had told me that he didn't realize the infection was gaining. "I was stupid and steered all day long and got even more tired," he said. "The yacht is going like hell. The spinnaker has been up for days, but I am too weak to take it down. I have been thinking of a plan to deal with it by cutting the halyard if the wind changes. In the meantime I am staying up with the gang and even worrying Harry Harkimo."

According to the Argos reports for 0720 GMT on April 27th, *American Flag* was seventy-five miles from *Colt,* which was twenty-seven miles south and sixty-nine miles west of my position. Pentti's speech was becoming slurred, and he was shouting over the radio, something he never did. Not only was Pentti feverish, but he was slightly irrational. Certainly he was very sick. The only thing in his favor were his puckish jokes, a sort of gallows humor.

There was a chance of death. What could I do? I had to do something!

I could sail over to *Colt* and take Pentti on board. I had various oral antibiotics in my kit but no injectable types. My nursing would be superficial and unskilled. And what would happen to *Colt?* You just don't abandon a yacht worth a quarter of a million dollars. Or do you when a man's life is involved? Could I put a towline on *Colt* and take her to Bermuda? I was unsure whether one yacht could tow another under sail. Maybe it would be better to lash them side by side (with the masts staggered) and make a sort of catamaran. Would you use the sails of one vessel or both? Imagine a single-hander sailing *two* yachts. My God, what a business to contemplate! But in my case, the yacht salvage was a side issue. The main thing was the well-being of my Finnish friend.

Dr. Ashworth talked of injectable antibiotics. But how to get them to Pentti? What were the possibilities? I made a list:

1. *Bermuda.* Excellent medical and nursing facilities. Chance of a heli-copter pick-up when within 300 (?) miles. Rescues of this sort have been done many times. Reasonable chance of getting *Colt* to port without problems. Easy to approach. Distance from *Colt's* 0720 GMT April 27th Argos position: 1,470 miles.
2. *Caribbean.* The French islands were closest and had good medical facilities. Guadeloupe was 826 miles west of *Colt;* Martinique lay 786 miles on a course of 275°T. I judged Fort de France, the capital of Martinique, to be the more suitable. To ensure control, it would be best to have the French military deal with all aspects of the rescue. There might be problems with approach charts, language, and helicopters.
3. *Big ships with doctors.* Following Pentti's request, I contacted the U.S. Coast Guard in Miami and asked for the names and positions of suitable ships within 600 miles of *Colt.* My request was technically possible, but I had some doubts about follow-up. I therefore broad-cast a series of pan messages on 2182 KC—the distress frequency—over a period of hours and requested any ships with doctors within

600 miles of Colt's position to come in. I had no replies either from
ships or the Coast Guard.*

4. *Help from the BOC fleet.* I then got the idea that injectable antibiotics
   might be available on one of the BOC yachts, since every captain
   had an extensive first aid kit. I went around the fleet and asked each
   captain to check. Maybe one of the thirteen other yachts (*Joseph
   Young* was too far to the south) spread out between 7°20'N. and
   22°33'N. had the right medicine on board.

On the fifth call I found that Jean Luc on *Let's Go* had a drug called
Orbenine for "very severe infections." It was cloxacilline sodique for intra-
muscular usage. Jean Luc also had five syringes and five needles.

[From the log]. April 27th.
    2200. An exhausting series of discussions with Pentti, Dr. Ashworth, Mark
Schrader, Jean Luc, and various hams who relayed portions of the messages.
Except for his thumb, Pentti thinks he is better, but his arm is all red, and the
red line—though down a little—is wider (formerly half an inch; now one
inch). This upset the doctor, who sent new instructions for dosage for the two
oral antibiotics on board *Colt.* When I reported that I had found an intravenous
antibiotic on *Let's Go,* the doctor said that the medicine should go to *Colt* at
once. *Let's Go* has diverted toward *Colt's* course to Bermuda. All these messages took ninety minutes and much effort.

During the night I spoke with Pentti, who sounded a little better. "My
thumb, however, is hopeless, nasty, and the cause of all the trouble." *Let's Go*
was converging on *Colt* little by little. Pentti said the red line had moved
slightly down from his armpit.

While the medical drama continued, *American Flag* hurried toward
Newport. On the 27th we logged 205 miles at noon. On the 28th we did 198.
My wind dropped to thirteen knots and blew directly from the east. A cloud
of brown dust from the Sahara flew out of the mainsail when I shook out a
reef. Instead of putting up a spinnaker I headed up ten degrees and flew both
the full mainsail and poled-out genoa. I continued to reach along—sailing
beautifully—and it seemed to me that I was logging exactly the same mileage
as I would have made with a spinnaker but with much less effort. What
would have helped would have been a jib to leeward on another headstay or a
big, lightweight booster. During the afternoon the wind dropped to nine
knots. The sea and sky were clear, blue, and absolutely gorgeous. A very large
crude carrier (VLCC) laden with oil passed headed eastbound.

After lunch I spoke with Jean Luc, who had turned around and sailed

* There are three types of emergency radio messages: mayday, pan, and securité. A pan
alert means an urgent ship's message.

south and west to meet Pentti. The rendezvous involved a tricky bit of navigation, made easier by satellite navigation, but still not simple because each vessel was on a different course at a different speed. Two tiny dots on an infinite ocean had to find one another.

"I was happy to see *Colt* this morning," said Jean Luc. "When I sighted her mainsail I was about three miles astern. Pentti came alongside on my port (leeward) side for the transfer. Fortunately the conditions were mild. Wind east at twelve knots; seas about two meters. I sailed alongside on autopilot. Meanwhile Pentti steered to within five to ten meters. "I threw Pentti a line at the end of which was a waterproof bag with the antibiotic, the syringes, and the needles," said Jean Luc. "I had radioed a medical officer in France for details of the dosage (one injection in the morning; one in the evening) and wrote the recommendation on a piece of paper which I put in the bag. There was enough medicine for ten injections."

Jean Luc did a good job. I was proud of him.

During the day I spoke with Dr. Ashworth and relayed information back and forth between *Colt* and Whitford, Rhode Island. The doctor was concerned with a welt or lump on the thumb that might need lancing and was worried about any swelling in the arm (up or down?). Had Pentti had any chills?

The doctor directed that the French drug be given intravenously if possible; otherwise intramuscularly, and not to use the drug at all if Pentti was allergic to penicillin. "Keep soaking the elevated arm, and additionally, soak the infected thumb in hot salt water," said the doctor. Pentti would be taking three drugs: two oral; one intravenously. Since the supply of Orbenine was limited, the amount should be spaced out, perhaps half a gram per dose. Finally, Dr. Ashworth advised Pentti to go to Bermuda if his thumb did not improve.

That night *Lone Star* told of a close call with an oil tanker bound for Venezuela. Converging courses, no lookout, and no radar. Mark had to change courses at the last minute. *Joseph Young* at 14°30'S. complained about poor winds. Once again I filled my four kerosene bottles from my big red jug. I burned one liter of kerosene in my Primus stove about every four days, which worked out to about two gallons a month. This seemed an ample allowance for a good deal of cooking and endless cups of tea and coffee.

[From the log]. April 28th.

2020. Pentti: "The red line has moved toward the hand and is below the elbow. The line itself seems smaller. The thumb is better but matter is still coming out. I have injected the French drug in my rear end. Two questions: (1) How long should I continue the drugs? (2) The injectable medicine capsules

make enough for two injections. Can I save the unused part for use later? I
don't want to waste it."

Dr. Ashworth: "Okay to use the drug later. The news sounds favorable. I
want matter to come out of the thumb. Continue soaks. Stop Tricanix in
forty-eight hours."

Each new day grew more beautiful. The heat got a little less, and the
cooler weather was increasingly pleasant. The sea was smooth with swells of
only two or three meters. Now at twenty degrees north I had a blanket on my
berth. The light covering felt good. I had a slight stomach ache. Maybe from
too much nervous tension the past few days. I had tea and toast and oatmeal
for breakfast.

Pentti's morning bulletin was that his left arm was very sore, but not as
bad as earlier. His thumb remained in poor condition, and matter was still
coming out. He had soaked it three times the day before. Pentti was feeling
okay, but very tired. He had no questions for the doctor. My transmission
was relayed by ham operators because my signal was cut out by a station in
Alabama.

During the morning there were some heavy-looking clouds to windward. Lots of large low cumulus and some filmy cirrus up at five miles. I
expected the worst and shortened down in a hurry, but nothing much happened. At noon (191 miles) I put up a spinnaker. After it was up, something
came loose at the head of the sail because the sock retrieval line and bronze
hook fell on deck with a clatter. On a northwest course before an easterly
wind of thirteen knots I showed only eight knots or so. After five hours I
took down the chute and poled out the genoa. On some running courses this
big sail was faster than the spinnaker and infinitely easier and safer to handle.
It wasn't that the spinnaker was poor; it was just that the big genoa fitted the
yacht so well with certain wind strengths. I repaired the spinnaker sock line
and put the chute away.

I hoped that Jean Luc's medicine would take care of Pentti's arm, but
when I spoke to him at supper time, there was an ominous development.
Pentti said that he was feeling better. Pus still drained from his left thumb, but
less of it. The red line was below his elbow, but his lower arm around the red
line had become dark and discolored. Pentti was worried about the color.

When I relayed these symptoms to Dr. Ashworth there was an eventful
pause in the conversation. I could almost feel the tumblers clicking in the
doctor's mind as he unlocked the doors on a new set of symptoms. Chuck
Ashworth thought my news was very bad indeed. He asked me to repeat my
transmission.

"The discoloration means gangrene and possible amputation," replied
Dr. Ashworth in a grim voice. This news took my breath away. I wanted to
put my hands over my ears. A decision was to be made on April 30th, the

following morning. The doctor hinted at big things, perhaps an air evacuation, but I didn't see how that would be possible unless a U.S. navy aircraft carrier or a vessel with a helicopter happened to be in the area. I felt discouraged and blue and hoped the doctor was wrong. Maybe the French medicine would do something during the night. . . .

During the early hours of April 30th near twenty-two degrees north, the light east wind began to collapse. I feared it was the end of the trade wind. Soon *American Flag* was down to three knots. By 0600 there was no wind at all, and the empty sails snapped like angry dogs as the ship rolled in the slight swell. The barometer read 1020 millibars. I was stuck in a high pressure area with low, heavy cloud cover and a few sprinkles of rainfall. Would private weather and routing information have improved my situation? A few hours later a little wind from the northeast filled the sails, and we began to move slowly.

I had been speaking with Dr. Ashworth on a ham frequency even though my novice license did not authorize such transmissions. Both Dr. Ashworth and I thought that Pentti's problems constituted a medical emergency of the gravest nature. Nevertheless there were some complaints from other hams, who were apparently unconcerned that a man's life was in jeopardy. So at 0916 on April 30th I put through an expensive priority medical call to Dr. Ashworth via commercial station WOM in Florida.

Pentti's news was all good. His arm and hand were better and almost the same color as his good right arm. The thumb swelling was down, and there was no longer a red line on the arm. He was able to move his fingers except for the thumb and forefinger. Pentti felt stronger and not so weak, and admitted that he had been much sicker than he had realized.

Dr. Ashworth asked me to inquire about any areas that were black and blue (none). Pentti was told to continue with the French antibiotic until it was gone. The doctor repeated that Pentti was to stop using Tricanix in forty-eight hours. He was to continue soaking his thumb (three times a day was not enough), and he was to continue the hot towels on his arm and to keep it elevated.

I felt that Pentti's crisis had passed and that I could stop all my radio efforts. With a great sigh of relief at Pentti's recovery I switched off the set and turned my attention to sailing.

At noon on April 30th I showed 140 miles. The next day only 136. I began to see gulfweed and in the afternoon passed a piece of large-meshed net floating in the sea. With an idea of better winds to the west I headed west-northwest. The wind varied between ten and fifteen knots from the east so I put up a spinnaker for nine hours. It was an exceptionally beautiful day and a good chance for photographs. I climbed to the top of the mast with a camera and clicked away at the yacht from all angles while the big red, white, and blue spinnaker pulled steadily. I always found it amazing to see the yacht going through the water from the masthead. I peered down and watched the tiller moving back and forth slightly as the autopilot corrected the course. From sixty feet up—as I wrote in Chapter 15—the hard dark line of the horizon was 8.9 miles away, which meant that my private sailing world encompassed 249 square miles. It was hard to believe that I could see almost 250 square miles of ocean.

While I was aloft I noticed that the headsail furling gear needed some attention at the top, so when I finished with photographs I climbed down on deck, traded the camera for a few tools, and went back up. I tied myself to the masthead with a safety line (so I could use both hands) and adjusted the plastic guard that prevented halyard wraps when using the furling gear. We were doing eight knots, and the motion was steady and easy, but afterward down on deck I found myself trembling from the exertions of the two climbs. I treated myself to a slug of excellent Brazilian brandy.

The frontrunners of the fleet were running into poorer winds and slowing down. From the Argos reports I saw that *UAP* had done only 71 miles. *Credit Agricole* 70. *Biscuits Lu* 68. *Spirit of Sydney* 115. However *Tuna Marine* did 171. I was 149 miles behind *Airco,* 47 miles behind *Let's Go,* and 43 miles

A view from aloft on *American Flag* during the fourth leg. Here we have a spinnaker up, and the captain at the top of the mast taking the photograph (note my shoe). The Monitor wind vane is correcting the course by pulling the tiller a little to windward. The black square midships is the four arco solar panels which worked to perfection.

behind *Belmont*. Amazingly, all through his medical crisis, Pentti had flown a spinnaker and kept up excellent runs. In fact, he was 43 miles ahead of me.

I learned from Ian Kiernan that Brazilian customs had wanted $22,000 to clear *Thursday's Child's* shipping container that had been following the fleet around and hauling unwanted sailing gear for some of the yachts. The matter was finally settled with a $1,000 bribe in U.S. dollars.

The next day I managed 170 miles by playing with the spinnaker and my largest sails in light east-northeast winds. I reckoned on a weather change because the upper sky was full of cirrus streaks. Sunset was a hard crimson with tall pillars of cumulonimbus outlined against the red. The sight reminded me of hollyhocks sticking up around the edge of a garden. While I was cooking supper (canned roast beef and rice and a dessert of coconut and chocolate), a medium-sized Russian container ship appeared a mile ahead. The vessel altered course and crossed in front of me about a half mile ahead and disappeared eastward. She was a handsome cargo vessel with good lines. The Japanese and Russians seemed to dominate foreign trade. I hardly ever saw an American or British vessel at sea anymore. I was now at twenty-four degrees north and pulled out a long-sleeved shirt and a sweater to wear at night.

[From the log]. May 3rd.
0712. A night of squalls and low clouds. I have the feeling that the days of using the full genoa and mainsail are about over. During one heavy squall I wound up the entire sail, but it was hard and I strained my left shoulder again. Fortunately I can crank the winches with my other arm.
1200. 173 miles. Position 27°29′N. and 58°44′W.

The winds began to be more variable closer to Bermuda, and there was a lot of sail drill. It was spinnaker up, spinnaker down, six rolls in the genoa, six rolls out, one reef in the main, one reef out, eight rolls in the genoa, and so forth. But sail handling is the sailor's life, and I was well used to *American Flag* and her gear by now.

Just after noon on May 4th (176 miles) I spoke with the 7,000-ton German ship *Koten* bound from Rotterdam to Cuba with 300 containers on board. A ten-inch flying fish landed in the cockpit and made a terrible commotion until I slipped him back into the sea. David White on *Legend*, 181 miles to the north-northwest, radioed that he expected northeast winds of thirty knots. "Gales are raging up and down the east coast of the United States," he said.

Twice on this passage I saw a large dark-brown bird with wide wings slowly flapping along like a plane on a police patrol. The bird had a blackish head, a prominent white patch underneath each wing tip, and a short, rounded tail. I worked out from the Harrison bird book that the creature was a great skua and no doubt on a mission to harass other birds and steal their food.

The morning position reports on May 5th showed everyone in the fleet about the same. *UAP,* which had been in first place a few days earlier, had slipped to ninth place. At noon (203 miles), I spoke to a German ship with the unlikely name of *Abateba Mikado* that was carrying newsprint from New-foundland to Puerto Rico.

Off and on during the day I worked on my cooking stove, whose burners had gotten increasingly feeble and finally died altogether. The stove was made by a company named Force Ten. I had bought it because I thought the design was clever. The Primus burners threaded directly on to small pipes that led to the bottom of a long horizontal cylindrical tank that had pivots on the ends for gimbals so the stove would stay level as the ship rolled. Instead of the burners being screwed down on the inside of tapped metal nipples as usual, however, the burners had been tapped *inside* and screwed on the outside of nipples soldered to the tank. During the qualifying run and the first leg I had had the greatest trouble trying to get the stove to work at all because of uneven pressure or pulsing. I recalled that years before on a Taylor's paraffin stove the company had installed a small brass plug with a tiny hole under each burner. This had solved the fuel pressure problem nicely. Fortunately I had two of the tiny plugs with me so I installed them in the stove, which then worked somewhat better, but not perfectly.

Now, even though I put a newly overhauled burner in place, there was no fuel flow at all. What could be wrong? I wondered if when I tightened down the burner, I was also tightening down on the plug I had added underneath. I quickly unscrewed one of the burners, and sure enough, there was the imprint of the brass plug inside the Primus burner passage. The burner was bottoming out against the plug, and no fuel could flow through the tiny hole in the middle of the plug.

I quickly cut a little metal away so that the plug could bottom against the burner but would leave a passage for kerosene to flow. Result? Perfection! Suddenly the burners hissed with blue, white-hot flames, something I had never seen before on the stove. It had taken nine months of frustration to make the stove work properly.

A large ship with a cream-colored superstructure and a light blue hull passed *American Flag* during the early afternoon, and at 1636 a satnav fix put us thirty-one miles east of St. David's light at the east end of Bermuda. Because of the Gulf Stream, the weather had become hot again. The yacht was running well in a light sea that was surprisingly rough. I had eighteen knots of wind from the southeast.

By 0600 the next morning, however, I had more wind from the south and—with some difficulty—gybed the rig. The sky was covered with clouds, the barometer dropped slightly, two ships passed nearby, and the sea remained lumpy. I needed to take down the genoa and put up the yankee in its place, but there was too much wind to drop the big sail. All I could do was to roll it up partway. By midmorning the wind was twenty-five knots from the south. I had never been stuck with the genoa in this situation before. However, I was going along nicely with just part of the big sail unrolled and reefs in the mainsail.

At noon I had logged 221 miles on the knotmeter and thought I had done wonders, but the distance between the noon satnav fixes for two days was only 186 miles. Apparently I was in a south-flowing eddy of the Gulf Stream. The Argos reports now showed *Let's Go* eight miles ahead of *Airco*. *Belmont* and *Colt,* the two Finnish boats, were tied for third and fourth, although *Belmont* was some distance north and east, a detail that was to assume the greatest importance. I was fifth, 51 miles farther back. During the afternoon a few light sprinkles began to fall, which increased to very heavy rain. Enormous clouds swirled around nearby, and squalls swept the ship. During a lull, I changed down from the genoa to the yankee and felt quite snug with the smaller sail. I had less than 500 miles to go to Newport.

That night the barometer dropped a little, and the wind switched to the north-northwest. I was close-hauled on a westerly course with shortened sail and figured that the Gulf Stream would push me north. The wind gradually collapsed and by the next morning was down to only four knots.

[From the log]. May 7th.
   1200. Only 129 miles in the last twenty-four hours. 400 miles to go to Newport. *Tuna Marine* was in first place and only 102 miles from Newport at 0308 this morning so she may finish today. *Let's Go* has a good wind and is way ahead in the smaller class.
   The conditions out here on the Gulf Stream don't look promising. No wind. Marvelously blue skies and seas of cobalt. Gentle swells. White-tailed tropicbirds. I am almost last, but nothing can be done. Racing, bah!

Years before on a passage north from Bermuda, Margaret and I had been similarly becalmed. Then we'd jumped into the hot water of the Gulf Stream and afterward played game after game of chess. In two days the current had swept us northward 120 miles. Would this happen again?

While I waited for wind on *American Flag,* I repaired the autopilot control linkage, fixed a rip in the genoa, added water to the batteries, and prepared new sheets for the yankee. I had a bath on deck with a few buckets of seawater. I washed my hair, shaved, and put on clean clothes. I swept out the yacht, cleaned the galley, and tidied up all the lines in the cockpit and at the foot of the mast. Still no wind came.

According to the charts printed by the weatherfax machine, I should have had light southwest winds or northeast winds of five to ten knots. The verbal weather report read by the U.S. Coast Guard from Norfolk talked of fifteen to twenty-knot westerlies north of 35°N. I was at 35°20′N. How could the two weather predictions coming from the same country be so different? In any case, I had no wind.

I listened to the evening news on the BBC, cooked a good meal and ate it slowly, and read in *The Set of the Sails,* the autobiography of Allan Villiers, until I was sleepy. When I got up from a nap and peered out, *American Flag* was as still as a coffin in a graveyard.

A bit later I heard Mark Schrader talking to Pentti Salmi on the radio. *Belmont,* with the advice of weather routing, had sailed farther east, had missed the calm belt, and was making reasonable miles. However, *Lone Star* and *Colt* were becalmed, too. Mark was really fed up, and he sounded as if he were shredding bedsheets and flinging the strips over the side to control his temper. "Relax, old dad," I said to Mark. "Calms are part of sailing. You've

Comparison of individual sailing times for the 1986–87 BOC race

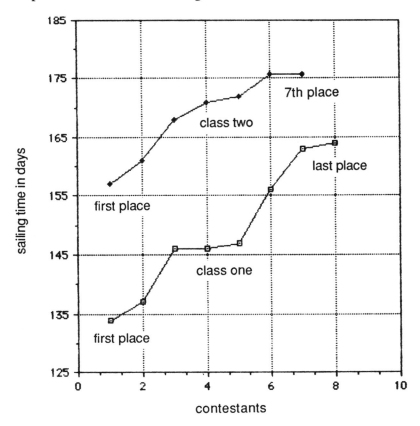

got to accept them just as you take the fair winds and squalls. Getting upset isn't going to solve a thing."

"What you say is true," said Mark, sighing heavily, "but calms when we're so close to the end aren't fair. Damn it! Where is the wind?"

Pentti, who had miraculously recovered from his brush with death, was more stoical. "Just wait till the next race. Already I am making plans. Too many mistakes this time."

On the day we were becalmed, the BOC yachts to the west and north had good winds. Six of the Class 1 vessels crossed the line within a few hours of one another. *Tuna Marine* (John Martin) was first (in twenty-six days), having slipped ahead of the others by sailing eastward into better winds as advised by weatherman Bob Rice and tactician Bill Biewenga.[41] Next came *Ecureuil d'Aquitaine* (Titouan Lamazou), then *Credit Agricole* (Philippe Jeantot), *Biscuits Lu* (Guy Bernardin), *Spirit of Sydney* (Ian Kiernan), and *Stabilo Boss* (Bertie Reed).

At dawn the next morning, May 8th, I watched Venus and Jupiter gradually fade out in the eastern sky as the new sun filled the heavens with delicate tints of pink and rose. The sea was a sheet of glass; there was still no wind. At noon I found that I had done only forty-nine miles, my poorest twenty-four-hour run of the entire race. Meanwhile Jean-Yves Terlain in *UAP* and David White in *Legend Securities* crossed the finish line to complete the list of eight Class I yachts. Jean Luc Van den Heede in *Let's Go* arrived in Newport, followed twenty hours later by Mike Plant in *Airco Distributor.*

The overall winner of the sixty-foot class was Philippe Jeantot, with a total time of 134 days, 5 hours, 23 minutes, and 56 seconds for all four legs. Mike Plant was the victor in the smaller class with 157 days, 11 hours, 44 minutes, and 44 seconds. Both sailors had done good jobs and were champions.

A little wind came up in the early afternoon, and soon *Flag* and I were sailing nicely to the north. Two hours later I changed down to the yankee, but in the evening the wind dropped, and I hoisted the genoa again. Just when I had it up and drawing well, I saw lightning in the west. Was it a cold front? By 0200 squalls were racing overhead. I had furled the genoa and was doing five to six knots on the starboard tack under a double-reefed mainsail with twenty-eight knots of wind from the north.

At noon on May 9th we showed 105 miles and were hammering along with the staysail and two reefs. The wind was twenty-four knots from the north-northwest, directly from where I wanted to go. We got some help from the Gulf Stream, but with the wind against the current the seas were large, steep, rough, warm, and very blue. "I guess the Gods want to give us a

Crossing the finish line in Newport at 0221 in the morning after the long voyage. Margaret and a helper have just climbed on board while the launch and film crews shout across the water.

little test before the end of the long voyage," I wrote in the logbook. "Can the hull and the crew take such hammering? Hang on!"

I heard that Harry Harkimo had arrived in Newport to clinch third place in Class II.

At sunset the wind began to back to the west and ease. I ran off, unfurled the genoa, dropped the big sail, stuffed it below, and put up the yankee. By midnight we were tearing along toward Newport in twenty-five knots of wind from the west. *American Flag* was clearly overloaded so I reduced sail further, and we sped through the night. By midmorning the wind had eased a little. I increased the sail area to match the wind strength. At noon we showed 170 miles. I saw a curious black-headed gull, and later a flock of small birds—phalaropes?—flitted about. I knew I was ahead of *Declaration,* and I learned that I had slipped ahead of *Colt* and *Lone Star.*

At 1800 Newport was fifty miles ahead. I knew I would be up all night so I had had several short naps (under two blankets now) and felt quite rested. For dinner I had one of the special cans of French sport food that Jacques de

Roux had given me in Cape Town and which I had saved for a special occasion. As I ate I thought of Jacques and felt sad that he wasn't speeding alongside in *Skoiern IV*. At least he had died at sea, which was an honorable way for a sailor to go.

During the evening I put up the U.S. flag and the racing pennants. I began to see the loom of shore lights and later picked up the flashing green light on the southeast corner of Block island. A number of tugs hauling barges on very long cables were headed east or west, and I had to sail with caution and dodge around the traffic. I had hoped to finish by midnight, but the wind fell light, and I was aware of some tidal action.

The finish line was at Brenton Tower near the mouth of Narragansett bay, which according to my chart had an extremely powerful twenty-five-mile navigation light. I tried hard to see the light, but I simply couldn't find it and had to triangulate from other lower-powered lights. When I was a few miles away, a BOC photo launch suddenly appeared and began to take strobe pictures. Each flash was blinding, and I couldn't see a thing for a few seconds afterward. The photographer on the launch reassured me about my position. He said the powerful light on the Brenton light tower had been shut off.

I began to get excited when the light tower finally hove into position ahead of me in the night sky. The wind was light. *American Flag* slowly slipped through the water. A long motion picture film of the race ran through my mind's eye as I thought about the fun, the adventure, the meeting with people, the excitement of the great oceans, and the challenge of trying my skills against all the things that people said were impossible. "You'll never find the money," they said. "You'll never get ready in time." "It's too dangerous." "You're too old." "It's a stupid race." "Why do it at all?"

I knew all these doubters and skeptics were dead wrong because none of them had their eyes on the distant mountain, the far valley, the place beyond. "What kind of a man would live where there is no daring?" wrote Charles Lindbergh after his great flight across the Atlantic in 1927.[42]

I thought of all the wonderful people who had helped me get *American Flag* ready for the race. I felt a small touch of pride that I had upheld their faith. I hadn't caught the rainbow, but I chased it, and my heart and imagination sang with gladness.

I thought of the day I left Newport. I remembered the start at Cape Town. The shocking weather in Bass strait. The church service for Jacques de Roux in Sydney. Cook strait in New Zealand. Cape Horn. The terrible storm south of Isla de los Estados when I got dipped in the sea. The stop in the Falklands. The sojourn in Rio. The long trip back.

I reached over and gave *American Flag* a little pat. She hadn't won. She had only come in fourth. But the slim yacht had sailed honorably and was in better condition at the end of the race than at the beginning. I had learned a lot about sailing large yachts and looking after myself. I suppose what she probably needed was a better captain. Yet the race had been a great enterprise, and in spite of various frustrations and shortcomings, I was glad I had made the effort to push on. I had a badge that couldn't be lost.

American Flag slipped over the finish line to the sounds of horns and a gun at 02:21:39 on May 11th. She had taken a little over 171 days to sail 27,597 miles around the world. The race was over.

Notes

The epigraph is from the introductory chapter of the 1922 (Oxford) edition of *Seven Pillars To Wisdom*.

1. For accounts of the 1982–83 BOC race, see Barry Pickthall, *The Ultimate Challenge* (London: Orbis, 1983); and George Day and Herb McCormick, *Out There* (Newport: Seven Seas Press, 1983). The Pickthall book is generally more accurate; the Day book is a bit overwritten, in my view.

2. M. F. Maury, *Explanations and Sailing Directions to Accompany Wind and Current Charts*, vol. 2 (Washington, D.C.: Cornelius Wendell, 1859), pp. 588, 594. Ocean sailors of today will find this fascinating stuff. Also see Maury, *The Physical Geography of the Sea* (New York: Harper, 1860), p. 336. For a biography of Maury, see Francis Leigh Williams, *Matthew Fontaine Maury, Scientist of the Sea* (New Brunswick, N.J.: Rutgers University Press, 1963).

3. Yves Le Scal, *The Great Days of the Cape Horners* (New York: New American Library, 1966), p. 48. A marvelous book based on the experiences of the French Captain Henri Briend that gives a graphic picture of the Cape Horn trade and its background. Wonderful photographs.

4. W.H.S. Jones, *The Cape Horn Breed* (London: Jarrolds, 1956), p. 320. I note that these figures don't quite add up to the overall total.

5. For many details of this region, see Hal Roth, *Two Against Cape Horn* (New York: Norton, 1978).

6. Alec Rose, *My Lively Lady* (Lymington: Nautical, 1968), p. 3.

7. For an account of this trip, see Hal Roth, *Always a Distant Anchorage* (New York: Norton, 1988).

8. See Jean Yeager and Dick Rutan, *Voyager* (New York: Knopf, 1987), pp. 54–60, for a bittersweet parallel to my fund-raising efforts. *Voyager* was a special round-the-world

nonstop airplane built by private people who also encountered incredible funding problems.

9. *New York Times,* September 1, 1986 (Barbara Lloyd).

10. This account is based on an interview with Dick Cross—who now works as a land surveyor in San Diego—on January 1, 1988. Also see Tod Cheney, "In the Wake of a High," *Wooden Boat* (March/April 1987): 22–27; *The Ellsworth American* (Maine), October 2, 1986, sec. 3, p. 8 (Arthur Layton Jr.); *Bangor Daily News* (Maine), September 5, 1986, p. 1 (Jon Johansen); *Boston Globe,* September 5, 1986 (Tony Chamberlain). The navy report was detailed in a letter to me from Lt. H. S. Hamby, U.S.N., Maintenance officer, Air operations, NAS Bermuda, and dated February 19, 1988.

11. *Weekend Argus* (Cape Town), November 1, 1986, p. 21 (Vivien Horler).

12. Skip Novak, *One Watch at a Time* (New York: Norton, 1988), p. 14. A gutsy account of the 1985–86 Whitbread race.

13. Mac Smith wrote in *Practical Sailor* (November 1, 1988): 3, as follows: "When *Quailo* pitchpoled in the South Atlantic, the only rod failures occurred several hours later as a result of the toggles. Four toggles had been pulled through the mast wall, causing the shrouds to be levered against the mast wall with no toggling action."

14. Philippe Jeantot, *Vaincre autour du monde* (Paris: Arthaud, 1987), pp. 76–79.

15. A cassette tape of the committee hearing is in my possession. Although I was a biased participant, I have tried to be scrupulously correct in the presentation of this difficult affair.

16. Interview with Dr. Larry Kneisley, February 26, 1988.

17. David Dellenbaugh, *Learning the Racing Rules* (New Haven, Conn.: Sea-TV, 1988). Quoted from the introduction to part one of a two-part video series.

18. Miles Smeeton, *Once Is Enough* (London: Rupert Hart-Davis, 1960). One of the sailing classics—well-written, understated, clear, and totally honest. My friends Miles and Beryl Smeeton and John Guzzwell were the valiant crew that brought *Tzu Hang* to safety.

19. *Ocean Passages for the World* (London: Hydrographic Department, 1950). The three quotations are from p. 239.

20. For a look at the operation of such a weatherman, see Barbara Lloyd, "Sailing's Weather Guru," *Nautical Quarterly* (Spring 1988): 108–117.

21. The best book that I know of for pelagic birds is the wonderful recent volume by Peter Harrison, *Seabirds: An Identification Guide* (Boston: Houghton Mifflin, 1983). Not only does this big book have lots of drawings and text, but at the back are 312 tiny distribution maps that give good clues to bird locations. Well worth a place in a voyager's library. The old faithful guide to seabirds is by W. B. Alexander, *Birds of the Ocean* (New York: Putnam, 1963). First published in 1928, but still in print and helpful (also small and easy to stick in a jacket pocket).

22. Jeantot, *Vaincre autour du monde,* p. 99.

23. My wind speed was a steady 36–40 knots (Force eight) plus squalls. I was traveling at about 8.5 knots. The time between crests (as I timed them while sailing forward) was ten to eleven seconds. According to Bowditch (*American Practical Navigator,* 1958 ed., p. 729), the length of the waves was about 625 feet (table 3303b). Table 3303 says the wave height should have been 27.5 feet or 8.38 meters (perhaps a bit more since I was at the upper limit of Force 8 or may have underestimated the wind strength). John Hughes' report of 10-meter waves was certainly within reason. In thinking about this I wonder if I could have perhaps carried more headsail area and have gone faster. There is an excellent chapter on this subject by Cornelis Van Rietschoten and Barry Pickthall in *Blue Water Racing* (New York: Dodd, Mead, 1985), pp. 223–247.

24. The information from Bill Biewenga and Courtney Hazelton is based on the offical police reports made in Eden, New South Wales, on December 20, 1986.

25. *Skoiern's* collision analysis is from Mr. John Majewski, the present owner of the yacht, who kindly sent me the results of his detailed inspection of the hull during the time it was repaired. I also have the comments of Mr. Barry Steel of Birkenhead Marina. I am indebted to Mr. Gil Forrester, who assisted in this matter.

26. John Hughes, *The Sailing Spirit* (Toronto: Seal Books, 1988), pp. 88–92.

27. Jeantot, *Vaincre autour du monde,* pp. 121–122.

28. *Soundings* (May 1987): A-34 (Jane Eagleson).

29. Jack Grout, *En course autour du monde* (Paris: Librairie Hachette, 1974), pp. 122–123.

30. John and Marie Christine Ridgway, *Round the World with Ridgway* (New York; Holt, Rinehart and Winston, 1978), pp. 140–152, 208–216.

31. Robin Knox-Johnston, *Last but Not Least* (Brighton, England: Angus & Robertson, 1978), pp. 98–99, 137.

32. Clare Francis, *Come Wind or Weather* (London: Pelham, 1978), p. 162.

33. Bob Fisher, *The Official Story* (London: Robertsbridge, 1986), p. 89.

34. Quoted from the 1987 *Biscuits Lu* videotape *20,000 Leagues Over the Sea* (New Haven, Conn.: Sea-TV, 1988). It's ironic that this careful captain lost his vessel on March 3, 1988, during an attempt to break the eighty-nine-day New York-to-San Francisco record of the *Flying Cloud* set in 1854. Guy set out from New York in January and rounded Cape Horn in forty-two days, ahead of schedule. Shortly afterward, while heading north in the Pacific, the yacht was dismasted and holed in heavy weather. Despite watertight compartments and several very large air bags (for buoyancy), the yacht sank quickly. Guy took to his liferaft and was rescued eighteen hours later by a Chilean navy vessel, which was sent out in response to an Argos distress signal. Except for some frostbitten fingers, Guy was picked up in good health.

35. Details of the committee role are from a taped interview (in the possession of the author) with Robin Knox-Johnston, May 30, 1987.

36. Philippe Jeantot, "From Kangeroos to Carnival," *Cruising World* (June 1987), p. 87.

37. Quoted from the transcriptions of the live video interviews conducted by Julian Plowright at the end of the race. A set of the tapes is in the author's possession.

38. Margaret's fund-raising efforts in the United States raised $3,335 during legs 3 and 4. In all the funds raised totaled $40,977 (minus $2,010 in expenses) from forty donors, who gave amounts from $25 to $16,000. The actual expenses during the race were $9,444. The big items were $2,800 for food, $2,135 for the new furling gear in Cape Town, $1,085 for three haulouts, and $891 for special clothing. The net cash outlay for *American Flag* was $177,890, which came from the cost ($207,413), plus expenses ($9,444), minus funds raised ($38,967). This did not include Roth labor, nor that of volunteers.

39. Quoted from Barbara Lloyd, "Assessing the Finish," *Sail* (August 1987): 54.

40. The Recife stop is detailed in Jeantot *Vaincre autour du monde,* pp. 164–172.

41. Bill Biewenga worked as John Martin's tactician after the withdrawal of Warren Luhrs and *Thursday's Child* in Australia.

42. Quoted from Yeager and Rutan, *Voyager,* p. 174.

Photograph Credits